Trekking in Peru

50 Best Walks and Hikes

The Bradt Trekking Guide

Hilary Bradt

*Updated by Kathy Jarvis
and Mark Smith*

www.bradtguides.com

Bradt Travel Guides Ltd, UK
The Globe Pequot Press Inc, USA

40th
anniversary
edition

Hilary backpacking in the Cordillera Huayhuash in 1985 as the early morning mist evaporates in the hot sun. 'This remains the most exhilaratingly beautiful of all the treks I have done in Peru. It is also, perhaps, the toughest, but the remoteness and staggering mountain scenery makes the effort well worthwhile.'

above　The market in Caraz, Cordillera Blanca. Produce markets like this are found in every town and are the best places for tasty cheap eats as well as photo opportunities. (AH)

below left　The festival of Pentecost in Ollantaytambo. Any religious festival is an excuse for elaborate costumes and dancing. (AF/A) page 46

below right　The festival of Inti Raymi takes place around 24 June, the winter solstice, and re-enacts the ceremony of sun worship traditionally performed by the supreme Inca at the time of year that the sun threatened to disappear. (GT/PP)

above &
right Cusco claims to be the oldest continuously inhabited city in
the Americas. Although Spanish architecture now dominates,
several Inca walls remain in the city. (Above: S/AR; right: JP)
page 233

below left The Baroque façade of San Agustín Church in Arequipa (SS) page 346

below right The statue of _conquistador_ Francisco Pizarro dominates the
Plaza de Armes in Lima, the city he founded. (SS)

above left & right　Several species of orchid, such as these from the *Epidendrum* genus, are found along the Inca Trail (AH & AZ/PP) page 23

far left　The kantu (*Cantua buxifolia*) is the national flower of Peru and often represented in weaving designs (S/ZA) page 23

left　Peru's most beautiful mountain orchid, *Masdevallia veitchiana*, is sometimes seen around Machu Picchu and Choquequirao (HB) page 319

below left　The *Puya raimondii*, the tallest flower spike in the world, is most easily seen in the cordilleras Blanca and Negra (S/JV) page 20

below right　Plants at very high altitudes need to conserve moisture and avoid freezing. Thus succulents growing close to the ground, such as this yareta cushion plant, are found near the snowline. (GD/MP/FLPA)

above left   Most rural families keep free-range guinea pigs which run happily around the kitchen, awaiting the next feast day (JP) page 31

above right   Viscachas are often seen — and heard — in the Cordillera Vilcanota (S/JGZ) page 31

right   The cock-of-the-rock, one of Peru's most flamboyant cloud forest species, may be seen in the Chachapoyas region (H/DT) page 147

below   Llamas can be differentiated from alpacas by their long ears and the jaunty angle of the tail (JLB/FLPA) page 33

AUTHORS

Hilary Bradt wrote *Backpacking along Ancient Ways in Peru and Bolivia* with her then-husband George in 1974, thus accidentally founding Bradt Travel Guides. Between 1979 and 1992 she spent two or three months each summer leading treks and natural history tours of South America for the American company Wilderness Travel, clocking up some 25 visits to Machu Picchu in the process.

Although retired from the day-to-day running of the company, she remains a director and a keen traveller when she can be lured away from her Devon home.

Kathy Jarvis has been a regular visitor to Peru since 1994, when she led her first adventure trekking tour. She contributed to the seventh edition of this guide, and updated the eighth edition, as well as writing *Ecuador, Peru and Bolivia: The Backpacker's Manual*. She also writes and photographs for other publications and presents slide shows and lectures on

various aspects of the Andes. She is the director of the Edinburgh-based adventure travel company, Andean Trails, which specialises in trekking, mountaineering, mountain biking and cultural tours to the Andes.

CONTRIBUTING AUTHORS

Mark Smith led treks all over the world for many years before settling in Cusco in 2004. Always keen to explore new trails, his route notes and stories of treks around the Cusco region can be found at www.trektheandes.com.

Dr Jane Wilson-Howarth (*www.wilson-howarth.com*) first visited Peru in 1982 when she led an expedition to research mountain sickness and catalogue the animals that inhabited caves in the Andes and Amazon. She has done innumerable treks to high altitude with her family.

PUBLISHER'S FOREWORD

Adrian Phillips, Publishing Director

In the 40th year of the founding of Bradt Travel Guides, here is a revised edition of the book that kickstarted it all. I'll leave Hilary to describe the roundabout way in which the original came to be (see opposite), but it's worth reflecting upon just how pioneering it was at the time. This book literally put the Inca Trail on the map for trekking tourists. But it wasn't only the first guide to the Inca Trail – it, and its successors, were some of the first guidebooks full-stop, at least in the form we know them today. Four decades on, Bradt has evolved considerably, but it remains shaped by the pioneering spirit that compelled Hilary to explore and write in 1974. And that spirit isn't just about publishing guides to places other publishers can't reach – it's also about viewing guidebooks as colourful things to be 'read' as well as 'used'. With its fascinating stories about Hilary's experiences blazing the trail, I know you'll find *Trekking in Peru* as entertaining as it is informative.

First edition published February 2014
Bradt Travel Guides Ltd
IDC House, The Vale, Chalfont St Peter, Bucks SL9 9RZ, England
www.bradtguides.com
Print edition published in the USA by The Globe Pequot Press Inc,
PO Box 480, Guilford, Connecticut 06437-0480

Text copyright © 2014 Hilary Bradt
Maps copyright © 2014 Bradt Travel Guides Ltd
Photographs and illustrations copyright © 2014 Individual photographers and illustrator
(see page 374)
Cover research and design: Pepi Bluck, Perfect Picture

ISBN: 978 1 84162 492 1 (print)
e-ISBN: 978 1 84162 790 8 (e-pub)
e-ISBN: 978 1 84162 691 8 (mobi)
British Library Cataloguing in Publication Data
A catalogue record for this book is available from the British Library

Photographs and illustrations See page 374
Maps David McCutcheon FBCart.S & Daniella Levin; maps include data © OpenStreetMap contributors (under Open Database Licence)

Typeset from the authors' disc by Wakewing, High Wycombe; design by Chris Lane, Artinfusion
Production managed by Jellyfish Print Solutions; printed in India
Digital conversion by the Firsty Group

How did it happen? How and why was my life completely changed by one evening in London? I know exactly.

In 1964 I went to the newly opened National Theatre at the Old Vic to see a performance of an Ibsen play, *The Master Builder*. It was only when I bought a programme that I realised that I'd got the date wrong and had tickets for a preview of a new play called *The Royal Hunt of the Sun* by Peter Shaffer. It was about the conquest of the Incas, and it was stunning. Magnificent. And profoundly moving. Until that point I had not heard of the Atahualpa and Pizarro and had only a hazy idea of where Peru was but the play set in motion a chain of events that resulted in the founding of Bradt Travel Guides.

I was determined to go to Peru and see the remnants of the Inca Empire for myself. I got a job in Boston to earn enough money, and made my first visit to Peru in 1969 (page 288). In 1973 I took my new husband George to Peru and we made our first trek through the Cordillera Blanca, relying on local information to help us find the route over the mountains (page 178). There were no guidebooks for backpackers and no maps. We did another walk along a newly discovered route known as The Inca Way to Machu Picchu, which was just starting to be popular with backpackers. Then, in Bolivia, we found a pre-Inca route over the mountains and into the jungle. Apart from the Inca Way these paths were used exclusively by the local farmers. When we hiked past a settlement, women would sometimes scream, grab their children and flee inside their huts.

During a three-day river journey in Bolivia we wrote a description of the three treks and added a couple of day walks along with a few notes to help other travellers get around. 'The Little Yellow Book' was published in 1974 and cost US$1.95. So 2014 is not only the 40th anniversary of the founding of Bradt Travel Guides – from that stapled booklet we now have nearly 200 rather smarter-looking guides on our list, as well as a clutch of awards – but it's the 50th anniversary of that muddled trip to the theatre. I knew there must be advantages to being absent minded!

BACKPACKING ALONG ANCIENT WAYS
IN PERU AND BOLIVIA

HILARY AND GEORGE BRADT

Acknowledgements

Special thanks from Kathy to the following contributors who provided updates and additional material for this edition: Constantino Aucca Chutas (*Natural History*), Alberto Caferrata, Fiona Cameron, Paul Cripps, Kat Dougal, Rob Dover, Alberto Brou Figari, Lucho Hurtado, Rodolfo Oropeza, Emma Redfoot, Tullio Sanchez,Tom Shearman, South America Explorers Club in Cusco: Alex Lemeshkov and Lina Basedina; Alain Schneider, Dougie Stewart, Ariana Svenson, Carol Thomas, Hugh Thomson, Nick Ward, and Michael Woodman. The following people updated their contributions from previous editions: Dr Chris Fenn, John Forrest, Ann Kendall, and John Pilkington.

Hilary would like to thank Charles Motley for his contribution to the Chachapoyas section and Joyce West for her entertaining Inca Trail story. Additional appreciation too, to Mark Smith who stepped in at a late stage to help with the Cusco area, and also 'Roland', an otherwise anonymous trekker who contributed some valuable information but whose full name and contact details are missing or lost.

Huge thanks to Managing Editor Anna Moores, who has literally worked day and night on this book for months, assisted by Laura Pidgley.

Finally, George Bradt deserves an accolade for coming up with the idea, 40 years ago, of a guide to trekking in the Andes!

Contents

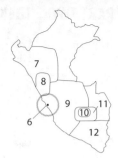

FOLLOW BRADT

For the latest news, special offers and competitions, follow Bradt on:

🅕 www.facebook.com/BradtTravelGuides
🐦 @BradtGuides
🅥 @bradtguides
🅟 pinterest.com/bradtguides

FEEDBACK REQUEST AND UPDATES WEBSITE

I have compared the process of writing new editions of popular guides to nurturing my compost bin. 'Layer is added to layer, the original material gets compressed but its goodness remains, and new matter is incorporated… it is never finished; there is always more to add.' And it is my readers who provide the rich new material that helps to keep these guides up to date. I love receiving letters and emails from travellers, it brings back the joy of walking in Peru. But it is the descriptions of new routes, or changes in established ones, or corrections if we've got our facts wrong which are the most welcome. Also if you've found a particularly friendly or comfortable hotel or *hostal*, or a special restaurant, do give us the details (with address, phone number and website, please). Now this guide has made its reappearance after a decade of hibernation I intend, with your help, to keep publishing new editions. You are invited to share your feedback via this book's companion website: www.bradtupdates.com/perutrekking.

Alternatively you can add a review of the book to www. bradtguides.com.

LIST OF MAPS

KEY TO MAP SYMBOLS

----------	Featured trek	🍽	Café
----------	Footpath	⚲	Bar
🏃	Start of trek	ℓ	Telephone
✈	International/regional airport	℮	Internet
🚌	Bus station	†	Church/cathedral
🅸	Tourist information	⇘	Beach
🏛	Museum/gallery	☀	Viewpoint
🏢	Historic/important building	⦀	Waterfall
👤	Statue/monument	⸪	Ancient site
$	Bank	○	Hot spring
✉	Post office	‿	Mountain pass
✚	Hospital	▲	Summit (height in metres)
✚	Clinic	●	Other place of interest
⌂	Hotel		Urban market
Å	Camping		Park/national park/reserve
✕	Restaurant		Glacier

Introduction

I am in the process of trying to persuade a friend that if she wants to see magnificent snow mountains, she should go to the Andes not the Himalayas. I have trekked in both, and to me the accessibility of the Peruvian *sierra*, combined with the jaw-dropping scale and sheer beauty of its great mountains, is unique. Where else can you find the combination of dense cloudforest sheltering one of the highest number of bird species on earth, and corniced glaciers where virtually all life is frozen out? Where else can you drive almost to the snowline, and yet within hours feel that you have time-travelled back a couple of centuries? Where else are the local people unchanged in custom and costume from pre-colonial times? And – perhaps above all – where else can you explore the remains of one of the greatest cultures the world has ever known, while enjoying a beautiful trek in the mountains?

Thirty three years ago, Dervla Murphy wrote in her foreword of the third edition of this book: 'Truly to experience a country on a personal level one must walk, ride or cycle. Day after day one is moved by the kindness of the locals, one curses or rejoices at the texture or gradient of the path, one is elated by the beauty of deep valleys between grotesque peaks, at the splendour of the night sky at 4,000 metres, by the sound of the wind on the Puna.' And this year Kate Humble, who spent weeks filming in the Peruvian Andes, writes: 'Being in the Andes makes you breathless – literally and metaphorically. Historically rich, with tangible and visible links to Peru's turbulent past, they also offer the more intrepid traveller an unforgettable insight into the lives of the people who live in this most challenging of environments.' So it's not just me who's smitten.

THE TOOTH OF TIME   *George Bradt (1978)*

Each time we return to South America and start hiking again, something goes 'click' as we relax with a sigh of relief into the realities of the Third World. We see the rich tapestry of *campesino* life all around us, so low, so simple and so permanent. Tomorrow will be much like today. It's this sense of inevitability that's so wonderful in South America.

Instead of watches and clocks with their eager faces swept by busy hands, these people rely on the sun, moon and the seasons to order their lives. So today and tomorrow are constant, reliable and predictable.

Although, with the ever-widening influence of transistor radios, these people are slowly becoming aware of the rest of the world, and its mode of time, they're bound to the land, and tomorrow, whatever it brings. The land is the centre of their universe. Watch them construct their lives: cutting wheat, winnowing beans, milking their cows. Or herding animals, spinning wool, weaving cloth, making bricks. Not only are these sights exotic to us, but even the smells and sounds are.

It's easy to talk to these people living such simple lives. We ask the same questions of each other: Where are you going? Where have you come from? What are you doing here? Where do you live? How many children do you have?

It is wonderful to have all the time in the world for listening and talking, to have a drink with the local men or make the market women laugh.

Part One

GENERAL INFORMATION

Location Western South America, bordered by Ecuador and Colombia to the north, Brazil and Bolivia to the east/southeast, Chile to the south, and the south Pacific Ocean to the west

Area 1,285,216km^2 (20th-largest country in the world)

Status Republic

Population 30.5 million (2013 estimate)

Life expectancy 72 years (male), 77 years (female)

Capital Lima, population 8.5 million (2011 estimate)

Other large towns Lima, Arequipa, Trujillo, Chiclayo, Piura, Iquitos, Cusco, Chimbote, Huancayo, Pucallpa

Economy Copper, zinc, gold and lead are found in the coastal and mountainous regions, whilst the coastal waters are rich fishing grounds. Coffee, sugar and cotton are also exported.

GDP US$301 billion (2011 estimate); per capita US$11,148 (2013 estimate)

Languages Spanish and Quechua are official languages; Aymara and Ashaninka, as well as a number of other native languages, are also spoken

Religion 81% Roman Catholic, 12% Evangelical and the remainder follow various smaller or traditional beliefs

Currency Nuevo sol

Rate of exchange US$1= 2.8 soles, £1= 4.5 soles, €1= 3.8 soles (Nov 2013)

Head of State Ollanta Humala

Prime Minister Oscar Valdés

National airline/airport LAN Perú/Aeropuerto Internacional Jorge Chávez

International dialling code +51

Time GMT −5

Electrical voltage 220V; 60Hz. Standard outlets accept round prongs some have dual-voltage outlets and accept flat prongs.

Weights and measures Metric, except for petrol (gas), which is measured in US gallons

Flag Three equal, vertical bands of red, white and red symbolising the blood spilt in the pursuit of independence and peace. In the central, white column there is a coat of arms comprising a shield bearing a vicuña, cinchona tree and yellow cornucopia spilling out coins.

Public holidays 1 January, 1 May, 24 June, 29 June, 28–29 July, 30 August, 8 October, 1 November, 8 December, 25 December; also Holy Thursday, Good Friday, Easter Monday

1

Background Information

HISTORY

PRE-CONQUEST The earliest cultures of any significance emerged around 900BC: Chavín de Huántar in the area now known as the Cordillera Blanca, and Sechín Alto, inland from Casma on the north coast. During the 700 years of their prominence they achieved some remarkable works of architecture, ceramics, textiles and metalwork, including gold, silver and copper. Around 500BC their powers declined and the **Nazca** culture emerged in southern Peru, lasting until about AD500. The textiles excavated from the tombs of Paracas, preserved by the dry desert, are arguably the finest ever found, and the Nazca ceramics are their equals in intricate and imaginative design. The famous Nazca Lines – vast 'line drawings' cut into the desert and easily visible only from the air – add weight to the awesome achievements of this culture, though little is known of the Nazca beliefs and way of life.

The **Moche**, on the other hand, left us a perfect record of their day-to-day concerns in the form of their wonderfully realistic pottery vessels depicting scenes from everyday life (including sexual activities). Their desert kingdom stretched from Piura to Casma, with Chan Chan, later a Chimú city, their capital. Many Moche achievements were echoed some 500 years later by the Incas: including roads and other engineering feats, and irrigation canals.

Around AD600 the power shifted from the north coast to the Andes and the Huari–Tiwanaku cultures. The **Huari** dominated the central highlands and the **Tiwanaku** had their religious centre around Lake Titicaca, but there was apparently friendly communication between the two. What we now think of as Inca achievements were further developed by these cultures with road-building, land terracing and irrigation being perfected, along with efficient administration and a labour tax.

3

When these civilisations collapsed, the **Incas** stepped in and completed what is widely considered the model of successful socialist government. Inca dominance was short compared with that of its predecessors: about 300 years, from around the year 1200 to the Spanish conquest in 1533. During this period they developed from a small tribe in Cusco to the largest empire ever known in the Americas, stretching from the present-day Ecuadorian–Colombian border to the Río Maule in central Chile, and east to the Amazon. The story of the empire's decline through civil war and its destruction by the Spanish conqueror **Pizarro** is told in the *Cajamarca* and *Cusco* chapters of this book.

The impression is often given that Pizarro's conquest was the end of the Incas, but in fact they struggled to regain power through uprisings, with the last reigning Inca, Tupac Amaru, killed in 1572, and the last Inca noble, Tupac Amaru II, meeting his death in 1780.

POST-CONQUEST The Spanish also had to defeat groups that had largely resisted Inca domination. These included the Chimú in the north, whose capital, Chan-Chan, had fallen to the Incas a century earlier, and the Chachapoyas culture, with their main fortress at Kuelap (pages 140–2).

A sea-going nation like Spain needed a port as its New World capital and Francisco Pizarro founded **Lima** in 1535. For the next 200 years the viceroys ruled throughout the Andean countries, retaining much of the old Inca system with Indian chiefs controlling large groups of natives. Quarrels among the conquistadores led to Pizarro's assassination in 1541, and constant uprisings by the Incas and later the Peru-born Spaniards made government of this valuable acquisition an unrewarding task. It took a foreign-born liberator, **José de San Martín**, to lead Peru's struggle for independence. San Martín was born in Argentina and educated in Spain. He returned to his home country in 1812, playing a leading part in gaining independence for Argentina before crossing the Andes to Chile with his army to help liberate that country. From there he sailed to Lima, and in 1821 proclaimed Peru's independence, even though the country was still in the hands of the viceroys.

The great Venezuelan liberator **Simon Bolívar** came to San Martín's assistance three years later, and the decisive Battle of Ayacucho in 1824 led to full independence in 1826. However, independent Peru was as turbulent as in the colonial era. In the 1830s Peru and Bolivia briefly united in a confederation, and in 1883 the two countries went to war with Chile; as a result Bolivia lost its coast and Peru lost much of its southern territory. Peru was under military rule from 1968 until 1980, but, most unusually, the junta in power in the early part of that era was socialist and instigated the agrarian reforms and redistribution of wealth that the country so sorely needed on moral grounds. Economically the reforms were a disaster, however, and the subsequent military rulers were right wing. Peru was one of the first South American countries to move away from military rule towards **democracy**, and in 1980 presidential and congressional elections were held and Fernando Belaunde Terry was voted in as president. His successor was **Alán García**, who was elected with enormous enthusiasm in 1985 and rejected with equal enthusiasm in 1990 having failed dismally to deal with the rising economic problems and increasing terrorism from the **Sendero Luminoso** (Shining Path) organisation. The Sendero Luminoso was a Maoist group aiming to impose what they considered the purist form of communism on Peru, and their activities blighted the lives of rural Peruvians for many years, and virtually halted tourism. It was only when their leader, Abimael Guzman, was captured in 1992 that their activities diminished. The next president, **Alberto Fujimori**, enjoyed early successes in dealing with the plague of inflation inherited from Alán García. In 1992, Fujimori interrupted democratic rule with his controversial *autogolpe* (or self-inflicted coup) during which congress was shut down and the constitution suspended. The country drifted towards authoritarian rule, though elections were still held on a regular basis and there remained considerable freedom of the press.

THE LAST 20 YEARS In 1995, on the back of notable success with the economy and the fight against terrorism, Fujimori was re-elected in a landslide victory. But by the middle of his second term, his government was losing prestige both at home and abroad as evidence emerged of human rights abuses, government control within the judiciary, widespread corruption and excessive media controls. The Fujimori juggernaut finally juddered to a halt in 2000, with dramatic and irrefutable video evidence of major corruption at the highest levels. Fujimori tendered his resignation and called for elections in early 2001.

Fujimori's subsequent flight to Japan to escape corruption charges fed long-held suspicions that he'd been born in Japan and was not Peruvian after all; and ex-president Alán García, exiled since fleeing Peru following his election defeat, returned in 1990 to contest the 2000 elections. He was narrowly defeated in 2001 by **Alejandro Toledo**, whose rise from rural poverty to become Peru's first ethnic president is the stuff of legend. His government initially led to economic growth but was soon being accused of incompetence and of failing to fulfil its promises to end corruption, reduce poverty, decentralise government and reduce unemployment.

Alán García waited in the wings and in June 2006 was elected president once again. García claimed that he had learned from mistakes made in his first presidential term, and returned with many promises to improve social conditions, seeking to balance social spending with economic stability. Peru prospered under his leadership, with foreign investment increasing, public debt decreasing and the economy improving generally. However, Garcia was accused of permitting too much foreign control of natural resources, and there was still a high rate of poverty in certain parts of the country.

In 2011 **Ollanta Humala**, a former army officer, was elected Peru's 94th president after narrowly defeating the daughter of former president Fujimori. He stood on a leftist platform but has since changed many of his staff and adopted a more centralist approach. He has promised to reduce poverty by raising wages, improving both health care and education, introducing a non-contributory pension and paying for this by sharing the wealth from Peru's natural resources through taxing the mining industry. Since 2005, Peru has seen an average economic growth of 7% a year. Foreign investment has increased and money has been pumped into mining, hydrocarbons and large infrastructure projects, often fossil fuel extraction. Export income brings tax revenue and the domestic consumer market is growing fast, both helping economic growth. However, although the economy continues to grow strongly, there is concern about the exchange rate, as the sol strengthens against the dollar, and the credit and housing boom. The political system is fragile, without strong political parties, and the unchanging gulf between rich and poor is likely to lead to instability if economic conditions worsen.

PEOPLE: PAST AND PRESENT

Most sources believe that the South American 'Indian' crossed the Bering Strait from Asia to North America and gradually migrated south over thousands of years. (Note: the native Peruvians are rarely called Indians these days since it is considered derogatory as well as being geographically inaccurate. For convenience and brevity, however, we have kept this term and hope that it causes no offence.) Myths, however, are more interesting than facts, and the beliefs of the origin of Man are central to the spiritual life of the **Quechua** people, who are by far the largest linguistic group in the Andes, being descendants of the Incas.

Quechua-speaking people are found throughout the old Inca Empire, from the Colombian border with Ecuador to southern Bolivia and beyond. This wide dispersal of the language is due to the Inca custom of subduing newly conquered tribes by establishing Quechua settlements within their territory. **Inca** mythology has Lake Titicaca as the birthplace of Man, with the son of the sun and the daughter of the moon arising from two eponymous islands on the lake. Whatever the truth about their origin, the visible monuments of the Incas arguably surpass all others in the Americas. Yet it is the unseen achievements that are so awe-inspiring: their empire still stands as one of the most perfect examples of organisation and administration in the history of Man.

INCA ROADS AND COMMUNICATIONS One of the most exciting aspects of hiking in Peru is that the ancient trails linking village to village and mountain to valley were once the means whereby an empire was conquered and controlled. The Inca Empire was criss-crossed by roads forming a complex administrative, transport and communications system. Roads radiated out from the centre ('navel') of the empire, Cusco, to the farthest point of its four quarters. Since horses and the wheel were unknown, relays of runners provided the speed and efficiency required. Roads were engineered to give the shortest and easiest route between two points. Steps were quicker to negotiate than a short steep slope, so steps were cut into the rock or laid as paving. Less precipitous slopes were made manageable by zigzag paths, and tunnels were cut through the outcrops of rock obstructing the direct route.

From sea level to 5,000m, and down again to the Amazon, the roads looped and curved over a distance of thousands of kilometres (estimates vary from 5,000km to 40,000) In particularly mountainous areas the footways were steep flights of steps no more than half a metre wide, but across flat open spaces the surface was often 6m wide with a fan arrangement of shallow steps going round corners.

The Inca runners, *chasqui*, relayed verbal and numeric messages to all parts of the empire from the Sun King in Cusco. The Incas had no written language, only one of several reasons we know so little about their culture, oo the numeric messages consisted of knotted llama wool strings, *quipus*. With strings of different colours and thicknesses the Incas were able to keep detailed records. A *quipucamaya*, a record- or account-keeper, could look at a quipu and learn a great deal. Gold, for example, was represented by a golden string, while the amount of gold was recorded by a series of knots along the cord. Silver was represented by white threads, and a series of red cords detailed the fighting strength of an army unit. Once the size, length and colour of a cord had been standardised throughout the empire, it was relatively easy to keep records.

The chasqui, sons of civil servants, were youths of great pride and physical strength. In order to fulfil their labour tax they had to run messages for two weeks every month for about a year. Each runner was equipped with a conch-shell to blow as he approached the next *tambo* or *tampu* (resthouse), where he would pass his message to the next man. In this manner the runners could do about 9km an hour, even at altitudes close to 5,000m. No point in the empire was more than five days' run from Cusco. From Cusco to Lima, 672km, took 72 hours. The Inca was known to send down to Acari, on the coast, for seafood and in less than two days he was eating fresh fish.

Tampus or tambos were built at intervals of about 20km along the roads. These also functioned as storehouses, stocked with provisions from the surrounding countryside. Some also had corrals for llamas, because not only chasquis made use of these roads; they were also crowded with traders, tax collectors, farmers, priests, soldiers, gangs of labourers and perhaps a royal delegation off to foreign parts.

For the Andean Indian the earth is his entire world – he exists as another plant in it and life apart from the land is inconceivable. The earth is called *Pachamama* (Mother Earth). She is alive, and during most of the year is passive and receptive, feeling nothing and leaving man free to cultivate her. There are days, however, when she is actively happy or sad, giving rewards or punishment, and it is prohibited to touch her. There is also a period of time (Holy Week) when she dies.

She is mother of all things, including men and women. This is meant literally, biologically. Thus offerings are made to her. At certain times there are large offerings (usually involving alcohol), and these you are more likely to witness or participate in. They are fairly simple but extremely important:

T'inka Before drinking alcohol, you allow several drops to fall from the glass on to the soil. Thus Pachamama is served first. This is done whether outside or inside the house.

Ch'ura Similar to the *t'inka* except the alcohol is scattered with the fingers. Often it is sprinkled this way on a house, animal or other object to be blessed.

Ch'alla From a small glass the alcohol is thrown to the major *apus* (spirits or gods – usually the snowpeaks) of the area. The *ch'alla* is done standing up, and the person doing it completes a full circle.

Each community was responsible for the maintenance of the road in its area, and for the construction of bridges over major rivers. These were made from twisted *manguey* fibre, and had to be re-made every other year. The most famous bridge of this type, over the Apurímac River, a few kilometres downstream from Cconoc on the Cusco to Lima Inca highway, was immortalised by Thornton Wilder in *The Bridge of San Luis Rey*. Nowadays only the supports can be seen.

Modern travellers rather glibly refer to any stone-paved trail as 'Inca' but we know that many of the civilisations conquered by the Incas had achieved a high standard of stonemasonry and it is likely that these pre-Inca people also had an interest in well-built roads to help the transport of tropical produce from the low valleys to the highlands and vice versa.

Little is left of the Inca and pre-Inca roads. However, some wonderful stretches do remain, most famously on the Inca Trail, giving us glimpses of the past as impressive and tantalising as the ruins of temples.

These rituals may vary from place to place, but they are omnipresent in the Andes. They only begin to indicate a value system of extreme complexity and richness. From these basics, however, we should be able to glimpse the Indians' humility before, and respect for, the environment.

The Andean Indian, before first digging his *chaquitaclla* (foot plough) into the soil, asks pardon and permission of Pachamama. This is an attitude that we should attempt to adopt and be constantly aware of as we walk through the Andes. The earth is alive, and we are a very small organic part of her. We should therefore approach her and the people who live with her with a profound sense of respect and humility.

We have much to learn from the Indians. Although it is impossible to generalise about so many different tribes, the people are usually honest, warm and friendly. They have not lost the sacred connection with their environment and are aware of the spirits of the mountains, springs and rivers. If one reason we are walking through these mountains is not to re-establish some such connection, then we probably have no business here in the first place.

Robert Randall died of rabies (following a bite from a puppy) in 1990 but is still talked about in his hometown of Ollantaytambo, near Cusco. During the 15 years he lived there he did more to support the local community and their culture than any foreigner before him. At Randall's funeral in Ollanta a village elder said: 'Most who have come to our valley have come to take. This good man … came and gave back to us. He reminded us of who we are, of the value of our heritage and tradition.'

VILLAGE LIFE TODAY Since the Spanish conquest, the Indians of Peru have developed various protective mechanisms to help them cope with present-day exploitation and discrimination. They are remote not only geographically but culturally as well, and often seem indifferent to the modern world. Communication is not only difficult between Indians and whites (be they Peruvian or European) but also between Lima and the highlands, and neither side seems anxious to change the status quo. The difference between the two worlds will be obvious to the trekker who spends a few days in Lima before journeying up to the Andes.

In highland villages the way of life is based on structure and rituals, and visiting backpackers and trekkers will have much more empathy with the locals if they understand some of these. They are a hybrid of Spanish and Inca, but the Spanish influence is – at least outwardly – dominant.

Village land is generally owned collectively, although private ownership still prevails in some places. Each village has its headman, who may be the governor (*gobernador*), mayor (*alcalde* or *warayo*), or council chief (*agente municipal*). He carries a ceremonial stick (*personero*) as a symbol of his position. The headman holds office for one year, and during this time is expected to sponsor traditional fiestas, paying for the musicians and supplying food and drink for these occasions. Most headmen are therefore wealthy when they first take office, and as poor as the other villagers when they leave it.

Rural Indians live virtually outside the cash economy, and day-to-day life is organised on the basis of reciprocity or mutual help. Any big job, such as harvesting, threshing and house-building, is done with the help of neighbours who receive aid in return when required. Finishing a house is an occasion for great celebration. *Safacasa*, putting the roof on, is done by a godmother or godfather who goes up on the unfinished roof, lays the last tiles or thatch, and puts a ceramic figure or pot, or a cross, on the ridge for good luck. Ceramic bulls, to ensure fertility, are popular, as are little vessels of *aguadiente* ('firewater' brewed from sugarcane). The godparent then throws gifts of sweets, cigarettes and so on down to the family and neighbours who have helped build the house.

BECOMING A GODMOTHER   *Kathy Jarvis*

After two years of visiting the island of Taquile on a regular basis, and having spent many happy hours playing with the local children, I was asked to become a godmother. This meant being the person responsible for performing the elaborate pagan/Catholic ritual of the first haircut, known as *rutuchiy*. Practised all over Peru when a child reaches the age of two and is beginning to learn to talk, this rite signifies the child becoming a part of the community. Its unbrushed hair has been left to grow untended until then, in the belief that the greater the number of knots and tangles, the luckier the child will be in the future.

My godchild-to-be was called Cristian, the two-year-old son of Dolores and Benigno in whose house I often had the good fortune to stay on my visits to the island. Cristian was beautifully dressed for the occasion in his best white *almilla* (shirt), a clean white *phantila* (a kind of wraparound skirt), an *incaj chullu* (knitted woollen cap with fringe) and *wawa chumpi* (a narrow woven belt). Although these clothes are worn every day on Taquile, many months are spent weaving or knitting new items for important occasions such as this.

A large woven cloth was laid on the ground and the family members, parents and grandparents, gathered round. From a small heap of coca leaves each family member took three leaves and, holding them over

LANGUAGE

SPANISH AND QUECHUA Spanish is not a difficult language and backpackers should make every effort to learn the essentials: a few greetings and a basic backpacker's vocabulary, even if you don't aspire to discussing politics and philosophy. Trekkers travelling in a group have less need of the local language, but it adds to the enjoyment to know a few words.

For independent travellers, both a dictionary and a phrasebook are essential. The dictionary should have a Latin-American bias; avoid buying one based on the language of Spain – too many words are different.

Language courses An excellent way to become fluent in Spanish and at the same time learn about Andean cultures is to sign up for a language course in Latin America. Many of the language schools listed overleaf offer courses in Spanish and Quechua, as well as in various arts and crafts. I love the idea of using both sides of my brain and emerging from a beautiful and fascinating part of Peru not only speaking Quechua but able to weave, cook or play the traditional stringed instrument, the *charango*!

the child, made a blessing: three wishes for his future. These leaves were then placed in a separate bowl. Next I made my wishes that he grow up to be healthy, happy and prosperous, and placed my coca leaves in the bowl, too. Dolores then explained how I should sprinkle grains of quinoa on Cristian's head in the form of a cross. Then came the hair cutting, each chunk being added to the bowl of used coca leaves. I say chunk because of the extremely large pair of blunt scissors I was given to cut the hair with. Several people who were with me also rather nervously had a go. They thus became hair-mothers or hair-fathers too, and are always welcome back to stay with the family. After the hair had been cut and put in the bowl with the coca leaves and quinoa, it was all buried as an offering to Pachamama, Mother Earth. Throughout this rather strange ritual Cristian looked on somewhat bewildered, but returned to his usual, admittedly now short-haired, joyful self as we celebrated with large platefuls of fresh lake fish, rice and eggs, washed down with beer and soft drinks. As we enjoyed this gift from the family we presented a photo album, some toys and money for Cristian's future to his mother. I have been fortunate in having many opportunities to return to Taquile to watch this child grow up to fulfil the wishes made for him.

UK and US organisations The following UK- and US-based companies are among those who organise such courses.

AmeriSpan Unlimited USA; ✆ 800 531 7917; worldwide: 215 531 7917; e info@ amerispan.com; www.amerispan.com. Spanish-language programmes in Cusco.

Andean Trails 33 Sandport St, Edinburgh EH6 6EP, Scotland; ✆ 0131 467 7086; e info@andeantrails.co.uk; www.

andeantrails.co.uk. Volunteer work & Spanish-language classes in Cusco. Also trekking, climbing & adventure tours. See advert, colour page 3.

Language Courses Abroad UK; ✆ 01509 211612; www.languagesabroad.co.uk. A worldwide resource for language courses.

Local organisations There are several companies offering language courses that are based in popular tourist towns such as Cusco, Huaraz and Huancayo.

Amauta Calle Suecia 480, Cusco; ✆ 084 262345; e info@amautaspanish.com; www. amautaspanish.com

Amigos Spanish School Zaguan del Cielo B-23, Cusco; ✆ 084 242292; e amigos@ spanishcusco.com; www.spanishcusco.com

THE TRADITIONAL ROLE OF COCA

For the Andean people the chewing of coca leaves heightens the significance of almost all social or ritual activities. Both Quechua and Aymara Indians view the leaves as a sacred gift from Pachamama (Mother Earth). The name coca comes from the Aymara language and means 'food for travellers and workers' because the narcotic effect of chewing the leaves dulls the pangs of hunger and relieves fatigue. The practice has been going on for at least 2,000 years: pre-Inca Mochican ceramics show the telltale ball of coca leaves in one cheek. Under the Inca Empire, coca was probably a privilege reserved for the royal family and priests (although historians disagree about this) and specific communities were given the job of growing it. The leaves were carried in a finely woven shoulder bag, the *chuspa* or *k'intu*.

Contrary to popular belief, the highland Indians do not use cocaine (which is extracted from the leaves through a complicated process) but the leaves themselves are used for many purposes:

CHACCHAR/CHACCHEO Quechua words for chewing coca leaves. To extract the narcotic juice the leaves are chewed until they are soft, then formed into a ball with some *llipta*, a mixture of lime (the mineral not the fruit) and potash. The ball of coca and llipta is held in the cheek and chewed from time to time.

Cusco Spanish School Urbanizacion el Ovalo de Pachacuteq, Avda La Paz A-5, Wanchaq, Cusco; 084 226928; e info@tripsinperu.com. Spanish lessons, all levels, 1-to-1 or small groups. Flexible schedules, salsa classes, hiking, homestays & volunteer programmes.

Excel Language Centre Cruz Verde 336, Cusco; 084 235298; e info@excelinspanish.com; www.excel-spanishlanguageprograms-peru.org

Incas del Peru Avda Giraldez 652, Huancayo; 064 223303; e incasdelperu@gmail.com, travelinfo@incasdelperu.org; www.incasdelperu.com. See advert, page 16.

Teach Huaraz 043 425303; www.teachHuarazperu.org/spanishlessons. In addition to Spanish-language classes, they organise volunteer work teaching at a school in Huaraz.

QUECHUA Spanish is still the second language for many people in Peru and Quechua remains widely spoken. Place names in the sierra are usually Quechua, which explains the variety of spellings: the Spanish transcribed the names as best they could.

The following list of Quechua names is designed to help you understand the Inca culture, interpret place names, and ease your travels through non-Spanish-speaking communities. Some basic vocabulary is

SOCIAL Sharing coca leaves with a stranger is the equivalent of our shaking hands.

OFFERINGS Before entering a valley or climbing a mountain, campesinos will offer coca leaves to Pachamama asking the *apus* of this region permission to tread on their slopes and for protection during the journey. Three nice coca leaves are put under a rock or in a ditch.

MEDICAL Traditional healers put great value on the use of coca leaves for many curative processes (and not just as a medicine – see pages 34–5).

READING OF THE LEAVES The leaves are 'read' for advice on a variety of problems and for predictions. Some Quechua elders interpret the leaves by examining the form, shape and colour.

PROTECTION The leaves are believed to protect the person carrying them.

DEATH When a person dies, coca leaves are given to the mourners as a sign of affection and sympathy. After three days these coca leaves and the clothes of the deceased are burned. The belief is that his/her soul goes to heaven with the smoke.

given in *Appendix 1*, pages 362–3. In addition, you will find a Quechua phrasebook a great help.

Inca words

amanta	royal Inca's advisers
apu	mountain spirit or deity
ayllu	the basic community, or clan, of the empire
capac	lord or chief (literally, magnificent)
Capac Raimi	December fiesta in honour of the sun
Condorachi	the annual killing of a condor to ensure good crops or banish evil spirits from a town
coya	star; wife of the ruling Inca, often his sister
huatana	to tie, eg: Inti Huatana, the hitching post of the sun
inti	sun
Inti Raymi	summer solstice fiesta
Tahuantinsuyo	the land of the four quarters; the Inca Empire
tambo	warehouses or resting places along the roads
wasi	house or home

Origins of place names

bamba	place of	*paca*	valley fork
caja	pass	*pampa*	meadow

cota	lagoon	*pata*	summit, hillside
cucho	corner	*paucar*	flowery
jirca	mountain	*raju*	glacier, snowpeak
huanca	rock	*rucu*	old
huaru	ford	*rumi*	stone
huaylla	meadow	*tambo*	roadside resthouse
lacta	land	*tingo*	junction of two
llacta	village		rivers
machay	crevice	*urcu*	mountain
marca	city	*yurac*	white

A QUECHUAN PRAYER

Pachi Pachamama,
Imaraycuchus ricusayku caipicainiykita,
P'achallisqa p'isqomanta,
sut'iyaimanta Urq'manta.
Pachi asirihuasqaykurayku
chay ashka chaupi t'ika ukhumanta.
Pachi, imaraycuchus ch'inkayniykiwan
supu chisiyaspa yachachiwaiku:
'Wajchakayqa, nan winay Janajpachaman'
Pachi kay k'acha kutimanta.

Thank you, Pachamama,
because we feel
your presence, dressed as a bird,
a mountain or a dawn;
thank you for smiling at us
through flowers of many colours;
thank you because, in silence,
you show us each nightfall.
'Humility is the way to eternity'.
Thank you for this wonderful opportunity.
(Free translation)

Reproduced from *The Gate of Paradise* by Luis Espinoza Chamulú,
published by Gateway Books

16

2

Natural History and Conservation

Updated by Tino Aucca of Asociacion Ecosistemas Andinos – ECOAN (www. ecoanperu.org), with contributions from Dr James Luytens of New York Botanical Gardens and Brian Hamilton, trustee for the charity Eye on the Wild

The Quechua word *puna* is still used in the Andean countries to describe the windswept grasslands between the trees and snowline on the high plateau. The puna area can best be defined as above the limits of agriculture, generally between 3,800m and 4,800m. It is characterised by expanses of coarse Andean grassland with low vegetation and a large variety of cushion plants adapted to survive the strong daytime sun and freezing nights. Typical in the puna are lakes, marshy areas and remnants of forests of *Polylepis*, *Escallonia* and *Buddleja*. The fauna is equally well adapted to the environment.

This is the landscape most familiar to trekkers and the only biological zone which can feasibly be described here. It is also the region covered by Bradt's *Peruvian Wildlife* (see page iv). The lower regions are so rich in flora and fauna that specialist books or information are needed.

GEOLOGY

The central Andes are the dominant feature of Peru, their glaciated peaks rising to over 6,000m. These are young mountains formed during the late Secondary and early Tertiary periods, at about the same time as the Alps. On the geological time-scale 'young' is a relative term; before the Andes were born some 50 to 60 million years ago, the South American continent was a going concern with the Amazon flowing into the Pacific!

Continental drift, resisted by the earth's crust beneath the Pacific, created intense compression and crumpled the land's surface, releasing igneous rocks which form most of the high peaks, and folding the original strata into grotesque shapes. You will see evidence of this in many of the high valleys.

The effects of glaciation, volcanic action and water erosion have completed this process and helped form the deep gorges and sheer mountainsides that we see today.

Glaciers are still shaping the Andes. As the ice moves down a mountain, its snout forms a cutting edge and glacial debris piles up on each side, forming lateral moraines. The maximum extent of the ice is marked by a terminal moraine. This glacial footprint remains long after the glacier retreats, and can be seen far below the treeline on the eastern slopes of the Andes of Peru. Those flat, rock-strewn, grassy areas so commonly found at the base of mountains were once lakes, dammed by boulders or ice, into which the rocks and silt carried down from the mountains were deposited. Gradually the lakes dried up and meadows were created.

GEOGRAPHY

A cross-section of the country, from west to east, would reveal the following picture. First there is the Pacific Ocean, teeming with fish and their predators, and bringing the cold Humboldt Current close to shore. The strong sun and the influence of the cold water create a mist, *garúa*, which blankets the entire 2,500km coastal strip for part of the year. This strip is desert, some of the world's driest land, which depends on meltwater from Andean glaciers for irrigation, drinking water and life itself. The width of this desert strip varies from 40 to 200km, across which over 50 rivers carry water to the Pacific Ocean. Cotton, fruit and sugar crops are grown in irrigated valleys, and most of the nation's industrial sector is located along the coast, including Lima, the capital.

Crops don't really begin to grow without irrigation until a height of about 2,000m is reached on the western slope of the Andes. Corn, potatoes and

EL NIÑO

El Niño is a warm ocean current which periodically flows south through the Pacific Ocean. Ocean temperatures heat up and storms ravage Peru's coast. Since it tends to arrive at Christmas, fishermen call it the Christ-child, although its effects are anything but beneficial. The warm water displaces the cold, nutrient-rich water of the Humboldt Current, driving the anchovy and other fish that fishermen and seabirds depend on to deeper, cooler waters, and the numerous species further up the food chain starve to death. The whole balance of nature is upset, with land animal species profiting from the burst of lush vegetation caused by the excessive rains, while the ocean shores are littered with the corpses of marine creatures.

sun-loving vegetables flourish up to about 4,000m, then cattle and general livestock take over, with mining and some grazing the only activities in the very high altitudes around 5,000m. There are 20 distinct mountain ranges in Peru, extending from central-northern Peru to its southern borders. They include two major glacial systems, the Cordillera Blanca north of Lima and the Cordillera Vilcanota in the southeast.

Crossing the continental divide, with peaks ranging from 2,500m to 6,768m, the descent begins to the Amazon Basin. The change is noticeable immediately. Warm, moist air rising up from the jungle makes these slopes greener and wetter. At a height of about 3,000m dense rainforests begin, and continue uninterrupted to the Atlantic Ocean.

CLIMATE

With three distinct geographical regions you have three distinct climates.

THE COASTAL DESERT (*LA COSTA*) The Austral winter runs from April until November during which time the coastal region is mostly cloudy, with daytime temperatures around 10–18°C, and a cold wind sweeps over the desert. It rarely rains but *garúa* hangs over the region from time to time, with Lima suffering this fine drizzle throughout the winter.

Summer is from December to April. It's very hot, with temperatures between 20°C and 36°C – sometimes higher – and a warm breeze.

THE MOUNTAIN REGION (*LA SIERRA*) In the Andean highlands there is a dry season and a rainy season. In contrast to the coast, it is dry and sunny from April to the end of September or beginning of October. At 3,500m or over it is very cold (around or below freezing) at night and in the early morning and evening. It is cool on cloudy days – even the dry season is no guarantee of sunshine. Daytime temperatures range from 10° to 18°C.

The rainy season runs from October/November to late April/early May (when it is sunny on the coast). The mornings are mostly clear, but it usually starts raining in the afternoons and sometimes continues during the nights. It is a little warmer than in the dry season, though snow is possible at high altitudes. Night-time temperatures are around 5–8°C (at 3,500m).

Peru has been one of the early victims of climate change. Its glaciers have retreated by over 20% since 1975, according to a recent World Bank report, and warmer temperatures are expected to erase them entirely by 2030. The report warned that the disappearance of the Andean ice sheets would threaten hydro-electric power and the water supplies of nearly 80 million people.

THE RAINFOREST (*LA SELVA*) The weather pattern is the same as the highlands. In the dry season it gets very hot in the rainforest (23–32°C during the day), and is not much cooler at night. There is an exception, however. During June, July and August a cold front, *el friaje*, may pass through from the south, pushing temperatures down to 8–10°C, which can come as a nasty shock to the unprepared traveller. However, it only lasts for a few days.

As you would expect, the rainy season in the rainforest is very wet indeed. The rivers rise – some are not navigable during this season – and road connections with the sierra can be closed by mud slides. Temperatures only drop about 5°C, but it feels chilly in the constant rain. During the fine spells it is very humid with lots of mosquitoes.

FLORA

Although descriptions in English of the flora of the Andes are hard to find, much research has been done in this field, mostly by local biologists and university students. The descriptions below are not intended to be a complete guide but will help you identify and appreciate the more common flora you come across. The local name is given in parentheses.

FAMILY COMPOSITAE (ASTERACEAE) This is the well-known daisy family, most of which are short-stemmed. ***Werneria dactylophylla*** (margarita andina) is also known as the *Boton Boton*. It has crinkly leaves and a small white daisy flower growing in felty clumps. A common and attractive Andean daisy, ***Werneria nubigena*** (margarita andina) has large white flowers, often tinged with pink, and blue-green strap-like leaves. This daisy seems to grow directly out of the ground, which it hugs

PUYA RAIMONDII

The monster of the Andes, this puya is the tallest flower spike in the world, sometimes topping 10m. It is said to live 100 years and flower once before it dies. And how it flowers! An estimated 8,000 greenish-white blossoms grow on one stalk between October and December, and attract the hummingbirds and moths which pollinate it. Other birds nest among the spiky leaves and some stab themselves to death on their doorstep. The sharp spikes are also a danger to livestock. *Puya raimondii* are found only in Peru and Bolivia where they are protected in Andean national parks. In the north, the local name is Llacuash and in the south, Titanca. There is an easily accessible group in Parque Nacional Huascarán, in the Cordillera Blanca (page 155).

closely from its long tap roots. ***Bidens andicola*** grows at altitudes up to 4,000m and has a tendency to use other plants as a support. They grow to the size of a small, twiggy bush. The ***Espeletia*** (frailejon) genus is typical of the puna and the *paramo*. It has a giant species which is more often seen in the *paramos* of the northern Andes, where it is known as *Frailejon*, or 'tall friar'. In Peru's puna a smaller variety is seen at high altitudes where the downy hairs on the grey-green leaves and stems prevent it from freezing at night. The flowers are yellow.

FAMILY BERBERIDACEAE Berberis, some of which grace our gardens, exhibit spiny bluish-green evergreen leaves like miniature holly, orange and blue flowers, and blue waxy-looking fruit. Berberis is quick to grow after deforestation or fire. ***Berberis lutea*** (checche) is a shrub which fruits from April to June. They make very effective hedges to enclose farmland. The locals also use the saffron-yellow wood for dyeing wool.

FAMILY CACTACEAE ***Opuntia floccosa*** (huaracco) is a spiny, hairy cactus with white flowers, typical of the cushion forming plants of the puna. The hairs act as insulation in the freezing nights. ***Opuntia subulata*** (cholla or p'atakiska) is a columnar cactus which is also known as a harpoon cactus since its thorns are shaped like harpoons, and are therefore difficult – and painful – to remove from the skin. Known as the Peruvian Torch cactus, ***Trichocereus cuzcoensis*** (j'ahuaccollay) is a fast-growing large branched cactus that reaches a height of 8m. It has creamy white flowers very popular with hummingbirds. This is a very important plant due to the high concentration of latex it contains, which was used in construction and more recently the reconstruction of Inca buildings. ***Opuntia ficus indica*** (tuna) is the familiar prickly pear cactus, introduced from Mexico. The fruits are eaten by many of the Indians (hence their popular name 'Indian fig'), and the large pads provide fodder for cattle. Sometimes a white powder-like substance is found on the leaves. This is excreted by the bright red cochineal beetle, which – crushed – is used as a red dye or paint base.

FAMILY CAPRIFOLIACEAE *Sambucus peruviana* (sauco). This shrub is a relative of the familiar European or North American elder, *Sambucus nigra*; it fruits from March to May and the berries are used to make jams and drinks.

FAMILY FABACEAE (LEGUMINOSAE SPP PALILIONACEAE) The lupin family is familiar to most people. The seeds have traditionally been used as food, but the long preparation needed to get rid of the bitter chemicals has caused them largely to be replaced by broad beans (known to the Americans as Lima beans). *Lupinus weberbaueri* (q'uera or tarwi) is a giant species of the lupin family, which grows to nearly 2m. *Lupinus mutabilis* (q'uera or tarwi) is the species most often used for its seeds, which must be leached in running water to remove the poison. The water is then used as a fish poison (the poisoned fish float to the surface and are easily caught).

FAMILY GENTIANACEAE The majority of this family cultivated in British gardens is from Europe or Asia; the gentians of South America are rarely seen in cultivation yet are the most spectacular, ranging from the common blue to vivid red or yellow. The flowers vary in shape, too, being crocus- or cup-shaped, rather than the more familiar trumpet shape. The plants range from tiny plants to upright stems of 1 to 2m, clothed in gorgeous pendulous bells. *Gentiana sedifolia* (phallcha) are the tiny, blue star-shaped flowers seen on open puna especially near moist areas.

FAMILY LOASACEAE All members of this family have hairy leaves with a powerful sting. Beware! *Cajophora horrida* (helechos or Otis colorada) has large orange-red scrotum-like flowers and – as its name implies – is unpleasant to touch. It stings.

FAMILY MALVACEAE This family includes the mallow genus, commonly grown in British gardens. They are compact rosettes of tiny grey-green leaves, often covered in hairs or fine wool, with proportionately large flowers which may be bright yellow, white, rose or magenta, all exhibiting stamens with a prominent globose head protruding from the centre of the flower.

FAMILY MELASTOMATACEAE *Brachyotum rostratum* (Macha macha). It occurs more on the eastern side of the Andes, in the *queñoa* or *queuña* forests between the puna and the cloudforest. The shrub has pairs of oval, deeply parallel-veined, dark-green leaves and purple or greenish flowers with pendulous furled petals. Their fruits look like little red apples and are enjoyed by many fruit-eating birds, and the flowers by many hummingbirds.

FAMILY ONAGRACEAE This is the fuchsia family. Most of the hundred or so species come from South America. They vary from scarlet tubular flowers, almost bush-like, to peach-coloured downy flowers struggling

to gain a foothold between ancient stone walling. The name comes from a 16th-century German herbalist, Leonhart Fuchs.

FAMILY ORCHIDACEAE Of the several species of terrestrial orchid found in the Andes, the purple and orange *Epidendrum* genus is the most familiar. In Peru the purple species is known as *wiñay wayna*, which means 'forever young'; the ruins near Machu Picchu bear the same name.

FAMILY POLEMONIACEAE *Cantua buxifolia* (Kantu or Q'antu). The national flower of Peru. The red, bell-like flowers hang from bushes near rivers, and are loved by hummingbirds. The *kantu* is a popular motif in ancient weaving designs, and is still used in some religious ceremonies and fiestas. This is also the one species of the genus cultivated in British gardens, usually against south-facing walls.

FAMILY RANUNCULACEAE Ranunculus is the botanical name for buttercup, a very primitive family with many species in the Andes, some of which look more like anemones than buttercups.

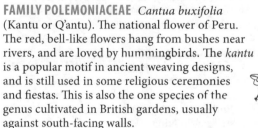

Ranunculus guzmanii (rima rima) is a beautiful flower and quite common in the Cordillera Blanca. It has large, red flowers and the whole plant is covered in dense golden hairs. *Rima* means 'speak' in Quechua (as in the river Apurímac – 'The Great Speaker') and the popular name for the flower indicates its use in folk medicine: it is given to children who are slow to learn to speak. It is also known as 'the rose of the Andes'. Resembling a Turk's head or turban, ***Ranunculus weberbauerii*** (chapu chapu) has a fist-sized, bulging yellow-orange flower.

FAMILY ROSACEAE There are about 27 different *Polylepis* species; these Andean endemics grow at altitudes between 3,000m and 5,200m, just below the treeless puna. They have a characteristic peeling, papery, red bark, with small dark-green leaves. The most common species are

Polylepis incana, *Polylepis lanata* (racemosa), and *Polylepis besseri* (all known as queñoa, queñua and quinual).

FAMILY CRASSULANACEAE Escallonia are common garden shrubs in Britain with a profusion of pink blossom in the summer months. *Escallonia resinosa* (chachacomo) – as the name implies, the resin content makes this tree suitable for kindling.

FAMILY SCROPHULARIACEA The butter-yellow ladies' slipper (or slipperwort) *Calceolaria engleriana* (ayac zapatilla) is one of the most attractive and recognisable trailside flowers.

FAMILY AGAVACEAE The fleshy, thorn-tipped agaves known as *Agave americana* (pacpa) were introduced from Mexico and are characteristic of high farming land where they are used as (very effective) hedges.

FAMILY BRASSICACEAE (CRUCIFERAE) The cabbage family has several representatives in the Andes. *Eudema nubigena* is a striking-looking 'cushion plant' with a rosette of shiny dark-green leaves, and yellow or cream-coloured flowers. It grows on the puna or above.

FAMILY ALSTROEMERIACEAE *Bomarea* spp are beautiful flowers found in many mountain valleys. Some are cane-forming from 30cm to 2m. Others are twining climbers, straggling over bushes and displaying different vivid colours of tubular flowers in a terminal cluster. All flowers grow from little white tubers.

FAMILY AMARYLLIDACEAE *Stenomesson miniatum* (michi michi) and *Zephyranthes parvula* (again known as michi michi) have dark-green leaves that stay on the ground, while the flower grows on a long stem. It is a small crocus-like yellow flower, its reverse streaked with violet. In Britain it is grown as a pot plant and commonly called rainlily or windflower.

FAMILY BROMELIACEAE This family includes the pineapple and Spanish moss among its 2,000 or more species, but its most spectacular member in Peru is the **Puya raimondii** (page 20). Other species that are more often encountered include the smaller and more common *Puya herrerae* (Achupalla) and **Guzmania morreniana** which grows in trees as an epiphyte at 1,500–2,500m (so is not a puna species).

FAMILY LABIATEAE This family includes the *Salvia* genus, of which the familiar sage (used in cooking) is one species. Salvias are popular with British gardeners, and include many flowering shrubs. The **Minthostachys glabrescens** (muña) species smells like mint but the leaves are smaller, growing on little bushes in the higher altitudes. When made into a tea this is a popular natural remedy for high-altitude sickness. Children on Taquile Island offer small bunches to newly arrived tourists. The Incas used this herb to cover their potato harvest, preventing it from sprouting, and repelling insects. Potatoes stored this way were said to keep for up to a year.

FAMILY LILIACEAE The **Nothoscordum andicola** (chullcus) lily is often found in the ruins of Sacsayhuamán. It resembles an onion flower, but is delicately scented and coloured a white-tinted mauve.

FAMILY POACEAE (GRAMINEAE) **Stipa spp** (ichu) is the spiky, tough grass commonly found in the puna, and the cause of many a resting trekker rising hastily. It is used for thatching houses.

FAUNA

BIRDS Given the scarcity of large mammals in the high Andes, birds are, for most hikers, the most interesting fauna. They are also easy to see and quite easy to identify. Peru has over 1,800 species – the second-highest number of any country (after Colombia) – with over 120 endemics. And new species are still being found on a regular basis.

The *Polylepis* forest holds 57% of Peru's endemic birds, and 65% of those are classified as endangered. Deforestation is a major problem in the Andes, and this habitat destruction is threatening the survival of many species. Trekkers have a particular responsibility not to disturb the fauna, particularly nesting birds.

Attention wildlife enthusiasts: For more on wildlife in Peru why not check out Bradt's *Peruvian Wildlife*. Go to www.bradtguides.com and key in PERU40 at the checkout for your 40% discount (while stocks last).

The list below covers all the species you are most likely to see while hiking in the mountains, classified by size (largest first). The local name – when known – is in parentheses (the original inhabitants of the sierra understandably only named birds and mammals that were good to eat or had a cultural significance, like the condor).

Caracaras, hawks, eagles, vultures and falcons Being the largest, these are at least easy to see, although telling them all apart takes some practice. The **Andean condor** (*Vultur gryphus*; Quechua: kuntur; Spanish: cóndor Andino) is the largest and heaviest flying bird in the world. A male can weigh 12kg and has a wingspan of 3m. He differs from the female by his crinkly comb. You may be fortunate enough to see an Andean condor circling below you as you rest at the top of a high pass or on the rim of the Colca Canyon. From this vantage point they are unmistakable, with broad white bands on the top of their wings, and you'll probably pick out the neck ring of fluffy white feathers. Seen high above you, against a bright sky, they are harder to identify, but the 'fingering' on the end of the wings is a distinctive feature. Despite their name, Andean condors are more often seen on the coast of Peru scavenging the sea lion colonies; carrion is harder to find in the high places. A condor's feet are not designed for grasping prey, so the occasional stories you hear about them carrying off babies are untrue. Their legs often hang down as these birds glide on air thermals, rarely flapping their wings.

In the air the **black-chested buzzard eagle** (*Geranoaetus melanoleucus*; Quechua: ank'a; Spanish: aguilucho de pecho negro) look like flying triangles, with tail and wings as one. They are usually seen alone. The plumage is grey and white, with a conspicuous dark-grey breast, white belly and black tail.

The **puna** (or **variable**) **hawk** (*Buteo poecilochrous*; Quechua: hat'um huamancha; Spanish: aguilucho variable) is white, grey and brown and is seen at high altitudes: 3,000–5,000m. The altitude and the white tail with a black bar aid identification.

Very similar to the puna hawk, the **red-backed hawk** (*Buteo polyosoma*; Quechua: h'uchuy huamancha; Spanish: aguilucho común) is smaller and has a larger tail relative to its size. Found below 3,500m.

Mountain caracara (*Phalcoboenus megalopterus*; Quechua: lkamari, Acchi; Spanish: China linda, Caracara Cordillerano) have a wingspan of 1m and are very common throughout the Andes – there's no mistaking them with their black-and-white plumage, bare red faces and orange legs. Caracaras find road kill a particularly good source of food and often follow vehicles. You will see them solo or in groups of two or three.

The **aplomado falcon** (*Falco femoralis*; Quechua: huamán; Spanish: halcón aplomado) is an elegant bird with long wings and tail, easily seen and recognised by its light eyebrow, thin but distinct moustache, and dark 'vest'.

The **American kestrel** (*Falco sparverius*; Quechua: quillichu; Spanish: cernícalo Americano) is a small ruddy-coloured raptor often seen hovering. It has a characteristic pattern on its head of two vertical black stripes, and a rufous-coloured tail tipped with black. It's widespread.

Waterfowl (grebes, ducks, geese and others) Puna lakes are excellent places for birdwatching, especially the shallow reedy ones that support a large number of waterfowl. The ones you are most likely to see are listed below.

The **silvery grebe** (*Podiceps occipitalis*; Spanish: zambullidor plateado) is recognisable by its grey back and grey plumes behind the eyes. The back of neck is black.

A large, handsome bird, the **crested duck** (*Lophonetta specularoides*; Spanish: pato creston) has a blue bill and brown crest and back: the largest of the ducks likely to be found on a mountain lake.

The **Andean duck** or **ruddy duck** (*Oxyura jamaicensis*; Spanish: pato rana) can be recognised by the blue bill and black head and tail of the male; it may be mistaken for the much smaller Puna teal.

A small duck, the **puna teal** (*Anas puna*; Spanish: pato de la puna) has a conspicuous blue bill, which is yellow at the base, creamy-white sides of head and throat and a black cap.

The **speckled teal** (*Anas flavirostris*; Spanish: pato barcino) is recognisable by its yellow bill and speckled black-and-brown head and neck.

Torrent duck (*Merganetta armata*; Spanish: pato de los torrentes) are fascinating little creatures found not in lakes but on boulders in the middle of fast-flowing rivers. They dive into the torrent in search of larvae and insects and can swim against almost any current using their very large, powerful feet for propulsion and long, stiff tail as a rudder. They are found in pairs up to an altitude of about 4,000m. The male is very conspicuous with a black-and-white patterned head and bright red bill. The female is a more subdued reddish brown.

Andean goose (*Chloephaga melanoptera*; Quechua: huallata; Spanish: cauquen huallata) are handsome and very common birds that feed in pairs or in large groups on marshy ground near lakes or on the open puna in boggy areas. Their white head and body and black wings are instantly recognisable.

Andean lapwing (*Vanellus resplendens*; Quechua: lek'echo; Spanish: avefria Andina) is another very common bird, which is found on the puna even in quite dry areas, as well as around lakes. Its black-and-white V-shaped markings, visible as it flies off with a noisy alarm call, make it unmistakable.

The **Andean gull** (*Chroicocephalus serranus*; Spanish: gaviota Andina) is a species of the familiar black-headed gull of the Old World but it spends the summer (and some of the winter) in the high puna. In the winter its black head turns white.

Puna ibis (*Plegadis ridgwayi*; Spanish: ibis de la puna) is a handsome bird with a greeny-blue sheen to its black feathers while the **Andean ibis** (*Theristicus branickii*; Spanish: bandurria Andina) is another bird found in flocks on marshy ground, with grey wings and a fawn-coloured neck.

Identifying the **giant coot** (*Fulica gigantean*; Spanish: gallareta gigante) is easy: it is a goose-sized coot with a dark-red bill tipped with white, yellow frontal shield, and enormous feet. It builds a huge floating nest of weeds, nearly 2m in diameter.

The **slate-coloured** (**Andean**) **coot** (*Fulica ardesiaca*; Spanish: gallareta Andina) and **common gallinule** (*Gallinula chloropus*; Spanish: polla de agua comun) are familiar water birds similar to their North American and European counterparts, with a black body and white (coot) or red (gallinule/moorhen) 'shield' above the bill.

Tinamous
These chunky birds look a bit like a small chicken and hide in the long grass, to fly off with a great commotion when nearly stepped on. It scares the hell out of most hikers! The locals call them *los perdizes de los Andes*, or Andean partridges, a misnomer although superficially they do look and behave like partridges. Their speckled colouring offers perfect camouflage. There are many species; all are ground-nesting, laying olive-green or purple eggs which have a beautiful porcelain-like sheen.

The **ornate tinamou** (*Nothoprocta ornate*; Quechua: llut'u; Spanish: perdiz cordillerana) is a speckled greyish ochre, with a grey breast and a whitish head spotted with black.

Also look out for **Andean tinamou** (*Notoprocta pentlandii*; Spanish: perdiz Andina) and the largest one at puna altitudes, the **Puna tinamou** (*Tinamotis pentlandii*; Spanish: perdiz de la puna).

Swifts and swallows
The **Andean swift** (*Aeronautes andecolus*; Spanish: vencejo andino) has a white collar, rump and underparts, including vent. The **brown-bellied swallow** (*Orochelidon murina*; Spanish: golondrina de vientre pardo) is dark smoky-grey below and is found between 2,100m and 4,300m, mostly in humid and semi-humid regions.

A chunky bird, the **Andean swallow** (*Orochelidon andecola*; Spanish: golondrina andina) has triangular wings and only a slightly forked tail. The throat is grey-brown, and the belly whitish. It is found between 2,500m and 4,600m in open arid country.

Woodpeckers
Those found in the puna have hardly seen a tree in their lives. They live in holes in rocky areas and are extremely well camouflaged. The **Andean flicker** (*Colaptes rupicol*; Quechua: jac'acho; Spanish: carpintero Andino) is an attractive bird with a speckled brownish back, yellowbuff breast, and a tell-tale yellow rump which shows when it flies away whistling its loud alarm call.

Sparrows, finches and siskins
The **rufous-collared sparrow** (*Zonotrichia capensis*; Quechua: pichitanka; Spanish: gorrion de collar rufo) has a distinct rufous half-collar and blackish spot on the sides of its

HUMMINGBIRDS

These little birds, widespread throughout the Americas, elicit many superlatives: the smallest, the most brightly coloured ... and the most interesting of the birds found in the Andes. The local name for these tiny nectar-feeders is *picaflor* and the Quechua name is Q'entes. Surprisingly, many species of hummingbird live on the chilly slopes of the Andes, and they show a remarkable adaptation to their habitat and food source. About half of the flowering plants of the puna are pollinated by hummingbirds, and have evolved trumpet-shaped flowers so that the nectar can only be reached by the hummingbird's long bill and even longer tongue, and long stamens which dust the bird's forehead with pollen. An example of this mutual dependency is the white, trumpet-shaped datura flower, which is pollinated by the swordbill hummingbird whose bill is actually longer than its body. Such flowers generally have little scent because hummingbirds have no keen sense of smell. Cross pollination is ensured by providing the birds with just enough nectar to reach the next plant. Hummingbirds need to feed every 12 minutes or so; they use energy faster than any other animal. Their wings beat 70 times a second (one-third of their body weight is wing muscle), and in flight their heartbeat may reach 1,200 per minute!

The Andean hillstar, a hummingbird that lives just below the snowline, shows a special adaptation which allows it to survive the freezing nights. It saves energy by perching on, rather than hovering over, the flowers (usually the *chuquiagua*), and at night goes into a state of torpor. Its body temperature may drop to 15°C (from its normal daytime 39.5°C) and its heart slows down to 36 beats per minute. Thus the bird is able to conserve energy. The large, well-insulated nests of the Andean hillstar are usually built on the eastern face of rocky cliffs to catch the morning sun.

breast. A very common bird. Equally common, the **ash-breasted sierra finch** (*Phrygilus plebejus*; Quechua: pichingo; Spanish: fringilo de pecho cenizo) lives in large groups, feeding in the open fields or on farmland. They are greyish with a white belly and a large bill.

Hooded siskin (*Carduelis magellanica*; Quechua: chayña; Spanish: jilguero encapuchado) is another common Andean bird with several similar species. Like the finches, they feed in large groups in open fields. They are identified by their black and yellow colouring.

Thrushes **Chiguanco thrush** (*Turdus chiguanco*; Quechua: chihuaco; Spanish: zorzal chuguanco) are woodland birds but are common in open areas, feeding on a large variety of seeds and fruits. Recognised by their brown colour with a yellow bill and legs and a great variety of calls: this bird is said to produce 14 different sounds.

Hummingbirds General information on the Trochilidae family is given in the box on page 29; the following species are most likely to be seen by hikers. The **giant hummingbird** (*Patagona gigas*; Quechua: huáscar q'ente; Spanish: colibri gigante) is, as the name suggests, a very large hummingbird, the size of a small dove, with a whitish rump and cinnamon below. It flies with erratic wing beats interspersed with gliding, and does not hover over the flower like other hummingbirds.

Another very large hummingbird, the **great sapphirewing** (*Pterophanes cyanopterus*; Quechua: sihuar q'ente, sihuar q'ente; Spanish: ala-zafiro grande) has dark-green with blue wings, with a thinner and straighter bill than the giant hummingbird, and with a more typical hummingbird flight pattern, though it still has some erratic wing beats and glides.

The **green-tailed trainbearer** (*Lesbia nuna*; Spanish: colibri de cola larga verde) has a deeply forked tail, about the length of the bird's body, and the tips of feathers are a glittering emerald green. The bill is generally small and straight. Common.

Quite large, the **sparkling violetear** (*Colibri coruscans*; Spanish: oreja-violeta de vientre azul) is a shining-green hummingbird with a dark, subterminal bar on its tail. The blue of its ear-plumes continues as a chinstrap.

MAMMALS In post-conquest Peru the wildlife suffered the same depredations as gold and silver artefacts: it was squandered for immediate gain. Whereas during Inca times hunting was controlled and restricted, now it was available to anyone and the Spaniards' superior weapons must have decimated the edible mammals. As always, however, destruction of habitat played, and still plays, a more serious role in the extinction of species. The widespread cutting down of forests, particularly the slow-growing native woodlands of the sierra, has resulted in wildlife being scarce and timid.

That said, however, an alert hiker will see quite a few animals in the puna, especially in remote areas where they inhabit small groves of trees or seek protection among rocks.

Peru has over 400 species of mammal of which about 70 are endemic and over 60 are threatened or endangered. These include spectacular species like the jaguar and spectacled bear and rare endemic species like the yellow-tailed woolly monkey.

Peru has about 35 species of marine mammal, in which we include whales, dolphins, porpoises, sea lions, seals and sea otters. There are 21 species of small cetaceans including two, the bottlenose dolphin (*Tursiops truncatus*) and the Burmeister's porpoise (*Phocaena spinnipinis*), that live in inshore waters.

Carnivores Puma (*Felis concolor*; Spanish: puma) was the symbol of power in Inca and pre-Inca cultures in Peru. This elegant tawny cat is now an endangered species, having been hunted as an enemy of farmers. The name is Quechuan (one of the few Quechua words to join the English language). **Colpeo fox** (*Dusicyon culpaeus*; Quechua: at'oc; Spanish: zorro colorado) is a grey fox seen throughout the Andes and regarded as a predator of livestock, so killed whenever possible. It is also a useful scavenger.

The **Andes skunk** (*Conepatus rex*; Spanish: zorillo) is rarely seen, but often smelled! An attractive black-and-white animal. Meanwhile, the **Andean weasel** (*Mustela frenata*; Spanish: comadreja) is a common animal in the puna but seldom seen; it lives in rocky crevasses. They are about 50cm long.

Herbivores Spectacled bear (*Tremarctos ornatus*; Quechua: ukuku; Spanish: oso de anteojos) – the only bear in South America – is an endangered species most commonly found in cloudforest. Lucky hikers have occasionally seen them in Parque Huascarán, in the Vilcabamba range and even along the Inca Trail.

Despite being heavily hunted, the **white-tailed deer** (*Odocoileus virginianus*; Quechua: luychu; Spanish: venado de cola blanca) is still common in the more remote areas. Very adaptable, it occurs from the coastal plain to 4,000m, and on the humid eastern slopes of the Andes. An endangered species, the **Andean huemal** (*Hippocamelus antisensis*; Spanish and Quechua: taruka) is less adaptable than the white-tailed deer so more affected by loss of its favourite habitat, small isolated patches of woodland at high altitudes. It is recognised by its location (just under the snowline), its greyish brown colour and having no white tail.

The wild mammal you are most likely to see is a **mountain viscacha** (*Lagidium peruvianum inca*; Spanish and Quechua: viscacha), a member of the chinchilla family. It looks like a cross between a squirrel and a rabbit, and whistles when alarmed. Groups of viscachas live at the foot of scree slopes where they can take refuge among the rocks. If you see one you'll see 20, bounding from rock to rock, or standing upright to see you better. At rest they are hard to spot, their yellow-grey colouring providing perfect camouflage.

Domesticated animals
Guinea pig Cavia cobayo (Quechua and Spanish: cuy) The South American guinea pig has been domesticated in Peru for thousands of

years. Archaeologists investigating Culebras, in the north of the country, found the remains of hundreds of the animals. Those ruins date from 2500BC, and cuy housing was already part of the architecture. The Paracas culture, too, evidently raised guinea pigs, and by Inca times they were well established: excavations in Pisac have revealed cuy 'cages' beneath the classical niches of Inca buildings. Indians in the sierra still raise guinea pigs in much the same way, and they are one of the main sources of meat in the central Andes.

One explanation for their continuing popularity is that they are so easy to raise. Even city dwellers keep them, and every rural house has a horde of squeaking cuyes – the name is onomatopoeic, since the animals seem to chirrup 'cuy cuy cuy' – scuttling around in the kitchen. Sometimes they are confined in cages or boxes, but they usually run free, making full use of the thoughtfully provided holes in adobe 'furniture'. I once visited a house in a remote part of the Cordillera Blanca and questioned the householder about a row of tortoise shells arranged neatly by the wall. She lifted one up and out popped a guinea pig. A fiesta was starting the next day …

Guinea pigs eat household scraps, with an occasional supplement of alfalfa or green barley, and are remarkably clean, producing small dry droppings that are easily swept up. Like all rodents, the animals are prolific breeders: litters of three or four are born every three months. Adults usually weigh about 1kg – not much meat considering the time taken to prepare them. Various research projects in Peru have produced super-cuyes weighing in at about 2kg, but the benefit of higher meat production is counterbalanced by the extra work involved in selected rather than haphazard breeding, and in keeping the animals separated in cages.

Guinea pigs are usually raised for home consumption or sold within the village. You may sometimes come across a cuy transaction taking place in the market: a squeaking sack on the ground and the potential buyer expertly testing the animals for plumpness.

CUY ROULETTE

One of the charms of travelling to out-of-the-way places in South America is the homemade entertainments devised by the locals. At a small fiesta I once watched a most effective form of roulette.

A circle was made of up-ended cardboard boxes with holes cut in the sides and numbers chalked on the tops. Onlookers bought numbered tickets and a guinea pig was released into the centre of the circle. It scurried into one of the boxes, and the holder of the corresponding ticket won a prize. Simple and fun!

The cameloid family: llamas, alpacas, guanacos and vicuñas

Llamas and their relatives were the only large animals domesticated by the Incas, and have been associated with man for at least 7,000 years. They were described appreciatively by Augustín de Zarate, a Spaniard, in 1544:

> These sheep of Peru are large enough to serve as beasts of burden … their wool is very good and fine … and they can go for four or five days without water. Their flesh is as good as that of the fat sheep of Castile.

De Zarate also noted that the Spanish used to ride the llamas – something unknown to the Indians past and present. Not surprisingly a tired llama 'turns his head around and discharges his saliva, which has an unpleasant odour, into the rider's face'. Llamas and their relatives do spit (the contents of their stomach, not saliva!) but rarely at humans. They prefer to get the message across to other llamas.

These are the New World camels, as perfectly suited to the harsh environment of the *altiplano* as the humped camel is adapted to the deserts of the Old World. These cameloids show a special adaptation to the altitude. They have more red cells in their blood than lowland mammals, thus increasing the amount of oxygen-carrying haemoglobin available, and a higher respiratory rate. Special water cells in the stomach rumen enable them to survive long periods without drinking.

There are two wild cameloids, the guanaco (which is common in the southern part of South America but seldom seen in Peru) and the vicuña. Their two domesticated descendants (almost certainly the result of a vicuña/guanaco cross) are llamas and alpacas.

Llamas *Lama glama* (Quechua and Spanish: Llama) Bred as beasts of burden and for meat, llamas are willing to carry only about 25kg of cargo, so large herds are necessary for efficiency. Llamas can be distinguished from alpacas by their long ears (curved like parentheses), long legs and necks, and the cocky angle of their tails. The height of a full-grown, full-size llama is 1.7 to 1.8m at the top of the head, and can weigh between 130kg and 200kg. They can live for 30 years.

Alpacas *Vicugna pacos* (Quechua and Spanish: Alpaca) These are bred for their wool (and their meat), and consequently have a much heavier fleece than llamas, with a characteristic 'apron' of wool bushing out from their chests. Their noses, legs and ears are shorter and more sheep-like than those of llamas. Ideally, alpacas should be sheared every three years, but if their owner needs money this may be done more often. Just as frequently, however, the animals are not sheared at all but slaughtered with a full coat of wool, which is sold with the hide.

Guinea pigs, *cuyes*, have always played an important part in Indian rituals as they are thought to ensure health and good fortune. Recent findings suggest that the animals were sacrificed in Inca times, and no doubt the *jubeo* ceremony, still practised by *curanderas* (native healers), goes back thousands of years. If a person falls seriously ill in Peru, his or her family is as likely to call in a curandera or, more specifically, a *jubeadora* as a doctor, even though the former may be more expensive.

To diagnose and cure the patient, a black guinea pig is required, and these animals cost three times as much as those of other less potent colours. The jubeadora must also be paid and, since her powers are increased by good food, she is feasted as well. Her job is considered a risky one – there's a chance she may catch the patient's disease or, more obliquely, her 'destiny may change', and because of this she can command a high price.

The relatives of the patient ensure that this money is well spent by scrupulous attention to the details of jubeo. The ceremony should take place on a Tuesday or Friday (although in an emergency any day of the week will do). A black guinea pig of the same sex and equivalent age to the patient is selected, and a candle burns by the sick person, along with aromatic herbs.

Owners of llamas and alpacas will often put colourful tassels in the animals' ears during fiesta time. Large herds of llamas and alpacas are easily driven over the mountains since each group has a leader, so the herdsmen only need to control one animal.

Vicuña *Vicugna vicugna* (Quechua and Spanish: Vicuña) Reputed to have the finest wool of any animal, the vicuña was reserved for the Inca emperor himself. The animals were captured, shorn and then released. But after the conquest, vicuñas were killed for their wool, and their numbers declined to near-extinction. The wool is extremely fine and highly prized as they can only be shorn every three years.

After careful protection the species has recovered and vicuñas are not uncommon in southern Peru, usually above 3,200m. Poaching and habitat loss still pose a threat to this singularly beautiful little animal, slim and graceful with a golden coat and white underparts. It stands from 75cm to 85cm at the shoulder and weighs from 35kg to 65kg.

Guanaco *Lama guanicoe* (Quechua: Wanaku'; Spanish: Guanaco) Not often seen in Peru but unmistakable since it looks like a llama but has an

The jubeo begins at midnight, but preparations involving coca chewing and the consumption of aguadiente (a regional alcoholic beverage) begin well before that hour. At midnight the jubeadora picks up the guinea pig and, filling her mouth with aguadiente, blows the alcohol over the animal's belly, face, nose and ears. After a prayer and the sign of the cross, the guinea pig is held firmly by its fore and back legs, belly well exposed, and systematically passed over all parts of the patient's body, beginning with the chest. As the animal takes on the symptoms of the sick person, it struggles violently and – so they say – dies. (If it doesn't die the patient's illness is considered not to be serious.) Relieved of his symptoms the patient is well on the road to recovery, but diagnosis is still necessary before herbal remedies can complete the cure.

The dead cuy is carried into the next room wrapped in a black cloth; and after further coca chewing, helped along with shots of aguadiente, it is opened up and its organs examined. An enlarged heart shows that the patient was suffering from a cardiac problem, an inflamed liver points to hepatitis, and so on. The animal may even be skinned so that the muscles and joints can be examined. Mission accomplished, the jubeadora is further fortified with food and drink, collects her fee, and goes on her way.

orangey-brown coat shading to white on the underbelly. Between 107cm and 122cm at the shoulder, they weigh about 90kg and have grey faces and small straight ears.

PROTECTED AREAS OF PERU

Peru is one of the most biologically rich countries in the world, ranking second in bird diversity, third for mammals and fifth for plants. Of the world's 114 life zones, 83 are found within Peru's borders.

Conservation of this unique natural heritage was officially begun in 1961 when Peru's first national park was established: Cutervo, in the department of Cajamarca. Approximately 17% of the country is now officially protected – over 21 million hectares in 71 protected areas. Conservation is under the control of the Servicio Nacional de Areas Naturales Protegidos de Flora y Fauna Silvestre, part of the Ministerio del Ambiente. Contact them through their website for further information: www.sernanp.gob.pe/sernanp/.

There are seven categories of protected area, the most significant of which are the following:

PARQUES NACIONALES (NATIONAL PARKS) These are areas with complete protection and preservation of fauna, flora and ecosystems. Entry permits are required for visitors. There are 13 national parks in Peru, listed here in the order in which they were established. They now cover an area of over eight million hectares.

Name	Department	Date established
Cutervo (2,500ha)	Cajamarca	1961
Tingo María (18,000ha)	Huánuco	1965
Manu (1,532,806ha)	Madre de Dios	1973
Huascarán (340,000ha)	Ancash	1975
Cerros de Amotape (91,300ha)	Tumbes	1975
Río Abiseo (274,520ha)	San Martín	1983
Yanachaga-Chemillén (122,000ha)	Pasco	1986
Bahuaja-Sonene (1,091,416ha)	Madre de Dios and Puno	2000
Cordillera Azul (1,353,190ha)	San Martín, Loreto, Ucayali, Huánuco	2001
Otishi (306,000ha)	Junín and Cusco	2003
Alto Puras (2,510,694ha)	Ucayali	2004
Ichigkat Muja – Cordillera del Condor (88,480ha)	Amazonas	2007
Güeppi-Sekime (203,628ha)	Loreto	2012

RESERVAS NACIONALES (NATIONAL RESERVES) These areas are set aside for wildlife protection, but government-controlled culling is allowed, and the local people have the right to use the resources except for forestry.

Pampas Galeras (6,500ha)	Ayacucho	1967
Junín (53,000ha)	Junín and Cerro de Pasco	1974
Paracas (335,000ha)	Ica	1975
Lachay de Lomas (5,070ha)	Lima	1977
Titicaca (36,180ha)	Puno	1978
Salinas y Aguada Blanca (366,936ha)	Moquegua	1979
Calipuy (64,000ha)	La Libertad	1981
Pacayá Samiria (2,080,000ha)	Loreto	1982
Tambopata-Candamo (1,500,000ha)	Madre de Dios	1990
Allpahuayo Mishana (58,070ha)	Loreto	2004
Pucacuro (637,919ha)	Loreto	2005
Tumbes (75,100ha)	Tumbes	2006
Matsés (420,635ha)	Loreto	2009
Sistema de Islas, Islotes y Puntas Guaneras (140,833ha) (islands and guano sites)	Ancash, Lima, Ica	2009
San Fernando (154,716ha)	Ica	2011

SANTUARIOS NACIONALES (NATIONAL SANCTUARIES) Here there is complete protection of fauna, flora and nature. Special entry permits are required and no-one is allowed to use the resources.

Name	Department	Date established
Huayllay (6,815ha)	Cerro de Pasco	1974
Calipuy (4,500ha)	La Libertad	1981
Lagunas de Mejía (69,060ha)	Arequipa	1984
Ampay (3,635ha)	Apurímac	1987
Manglares de Tumbes (2,972ha)	Tumbes	1988
Tabaconas-Namballe (29,500ha)	Cajamarca	1988
Megantoni (215,868ha)	Cusco	2004
Pampa Hermosa (11,543ha)	Junín	2009
Cordillera de Colán (39,215ha)	Amazonas	2009

SANTUARIOS HISTÓRICOS (HISTORICAL SANCTUARIES) These areas of historical or archaeological importance receive complete protection, including the fauna and flora. No use of resources is permitted. Tourism, recreation, research and education are permitted.

Chacamarca (2,500ha)	Junín	1974
Pampa de Ayacucho (300ha)	Ayacucho	1980
Machu Picchu (32,592ha)	Cusco	1981
Bosque de Pomac (5,887ha)	Lambayeque	2001

These are the best-known protected areas; also important are the **Bosques Nacionales** (national forests) and **Zonas Reservadas** (reserve zones). There are many national forests, but they receive very little protection. Reserve zones are protected areas awaiting further scientific study.

ZONAS RESERVADAS (RESERVE ZONES)

Chancaybaños	Cajamarca	1996
Santiago – Comaina	Amazonas, Loreto	1999
Cordillera Huayhuash	Ancash	2002
Sierra del Divisor	Loreto, Ucayali	2006
Humedales de Puerto Viejo	Lima	2008
Illescas	Piura	2010
Bosque de Zárate	Lima	2010
Lomas de Ancón	Lima	2010
Río Nieva	Amazonas	2010
Yaguas	Loreto	2011
Ancón	Lima	2011
Reserva Paisajística Cerro Khapia	Puno	2011
Laguna de Huacachina	Ica	2012

ENVIRONMENTAL CONSERVATION IN THE 21ST CENTURY

John Forrest

In February 1992, President Fujimori gave the annual environmental lecture at Kew Gardens. He highlighted poverty levels within Peru and argued that the government could only prioritise environmental issues once the basic standard of living of most people had improved. Subsequent presidents have adopted a similar approach towards the environment, including viewing the Andes and Amazon regions as vast reserves of resources to be exploited to benefit the urban poor.

In the last 20 years Peru has experienced significant economic growth. This, principally, results from many large new projects in the fossil fuel extraction and mining sectors. These activities have been further stimulated by the signing of free trade agreements with the USA, China and the EU, which have opened up opportunities for transnational companies. The resulting wealth has not trickled down in to environmental conservation. Instead, it has led to severe environmental degradation as Peru's environmental laws are bypassed and strip mines alter the landscape as at the huge Yanacocha mine, near Cajamarca; and informal gold-mining clears large areas of forest as in Madre de Dios. The affected areas in the Amazon are peripheral regions but they are also the most environmentally valuable and fragile, with huge biodiversity.

In a rare example of environmental concerns winning the day, permission to prospect for oil within the Pacaya-Samiria National Reserve, near Iquitos, was withdrawn after local and international protests in 1992. A few years later a similar campaign in the Tambopata region, in southeast Peru, discouraged oil and gas explorations and led, firstly, to the expansion and then the retention of the Bahauja-Sonene National Park. However, there have been few such 'victories' in recent years.

Instead, the 21st century has brought many new potential environmental concerns, including the manner in which the vast Camisea gas reserves in the central Amazon region will be exploited, given that they impinge on the territories of uncontacted native peoples living in voluntary isolation.

Nearby, the impact of the recently constructed Interoceanic Highway cutting through the rainforest of southeast Peru to Brazil has been immediate facilitating the sudden arrival of thousands of informal gold-miners and widespread clearance of the forest.

In 1992, Fujimori also promoted the concept of international co-operation through environmental projects. This was partially realised along Peru's border with Ecuador in 1995 as part of a package to resolve the 40-year-old border dispute as both countries established new national parks in the Cordillera del Condor overlapping the border zone.

The Amboro–Vilcabamba conservation corridor links a series of conservation units running from central Peru, including Manu National Park and the Bahauaja-Sonene National Park, into northern Bolivia, including the Madidi National Park. There is scope for greater joint conservation management along this corridor to handle the threats posed by the Interoceanic Highway, gold mining and oil/natural gas exploitation.

In 2008 Peru appointed its first Environment Minister, as responsibility for environmental matters was removed from the Ministry of Agriculture where there was an obvious conflict of interest. A clear structure now exists with SERNANP (Servicio Nacional de Areas Naturales Protegidas) responsible for protected areas at a national level, working alongside a number of other specialist institutions. However, the Ministry has one of the lowest profiles in the cabinet.

Almost all protected areas in Peru are severely underfunded and are reliant on international aid to enable them to carry out at least part of their mandates. Even so, it took many years for Manu National Park, arguably the best-known protected area in Peru, to finalise a management plan despite receiving significant international funding. A national management plan for all protected areas exists but is not necessarily followed.

There is still much to be done to integrate local peoples into the planning and administration of protected areas and to demonstrate that protected areas can bring benefits to local communities. Overall, attitudes towards the environment are changing as more Peruvians are able to travel, and throughout the country more concrete conservation actions are being carried out both by individuals and some excellent local grassroots organisations. However, there have been large-scale, violent protests in Cajamarca, Madre de Dios and Puno pitching the interests of those concerned about the environment and impacts of the free trade agreements against those supported by the mining sector.

Along the northern coast increasing numbers of washed-up whales, dolphins, etc have been linked to increased discharge of pollutants, and over-fishing remains a concern along many coastal stretches, including around the Paracas Peninsula.

The ever-less predictable threat from El Niño (page 18), which brings rain and strong winds to the northern coastal desert and quickly wipes out any benefits gained from years of economic growth, remains although the last major event was in 1998. Conversely, the La Niña phenomena which brings severe cold to the southern Peruvian Andes, has increased in frequency and intensity.

CONSERVATION ORGANISATIONS
In Peru
Asociación Peruana de Turismo de Aventura y Ecoturismo (APTAE) Calle San Fernando 270–No 1, Miraflores, Lima; 01 4441853; e secretaria@aptae.org.pe; www.aptae.org. The Peruvian Association of Adventure & Ecotourism is made up of tour operators & individuals working towards sustainable ecotourism. If you are interested in taking a proactive role in supporting ecotourism in Peru, contact them for more information.

Asociación Peruana para la Conservación de la Naturaleza (APECO) Parque José de Acosta 187, Magdalena del Mar, Lima 17; 01 2645804; e comunicapeco@apeco.org. pe; www.apeco.org.pe. This organisation is actively involved in environmental education & protection in many regions of Peru. Their main conservation efforts are concentrated on the Peruvian Amazon Basin & cloudforest in northeast Peru. APECO runs penguin conservation projects on coastal & marine areas of Peru & they are also active in the buffer zone of Manu Biosphere Reserve where they are working with communities in environmental education.

ECOAN www.ecoanperu.org. Started by Constantino Aucco, a naturalist guide & keen birdwatcher who was worried that the deforestation of the high slopes of the Andes was threatening the survival of indigenous bird species. Among other projects, they work with communities in the Lares

---

ℹ ECOLOGY AND EVOLUTION ON TROPICAL MOUNTAINS

Jonathan Hughes

In travelling from the base of a tropical mountain to its peak, you undertake a journey similar, in ecological terms, to a much longer trip from the Equator to the poles. At the foot of the mountain, if rainfall is sufficient, there is tropical forest. As you climb, the temperature drops, and the palms and evergreens give way to deciduous and then coniferous trees – a displacement that occurs gradually over entire continents as the distance from the Equator increases. Above about 3,000m, regular night frosts occur and trees cannot survive, hence the upper limit of forest or treeline. The severity of night frosts continues to increase with altitude until, at about 5,000m, the temperature drops below freezing every night and a permanent snowline exists, bordering the arctic environment of the highest peaks.

Between the tree and snowlines there is a cool, treeless habitat, similar to the tundra found in Siberia, Canada and Patagonia, and often referred to as alpine, after the European mountain range. To survive at these altitudes a species must be frost resistant, a characteristic not normally demanded within the tropics. Hence alpine communities are composed of atypical species, and in the tropics are subject to peculiar evolutionary rules.

watershed near Cusco, planting or restoring native indigenous forests.

Fundación Pro Naturaleza   For more information, contact Martín Alcande Pineda (Executive Director), Pro Naturaleza, Calle Doña Juana No 137, Urb Los Rosales, Surco, 271-3662, Lima; 01 2712662; e malcalde@pronaturaleza.org; www. pronaturaleza.org. Formerly known as the Fundación Peruana para la Conservación de la Naturaleza (FPCN), this organisation works closely with many foreign agencies such as the Nature Conservancy of the USA, IUCN, WWF & CI to protect viable, representative examples of each natural community or ecosystem in Peru & the biological diversity it contains. This is being achieved through the establishment & management of protected areas, by promoting the sustainable use of natural resources & by building environmental awareness.

Peru Verde   No J-1, Urb Santa Mónica, Cusco; 084 226392; e postmaster@ peruverde.org; www.peruverde.org. This organisation is involved in several conservation & environmental education projects in the rainforest. Together with its partner group Selva Sur, it operates ecotourism lodges in partnership with local people.

Sociedad Peruana de Derecho Ambiental (SPDA)   Prolongacion Arenales, 437, San Isidro, Lima; 01 6124700; www.spda.org.pe – email via website. This organisation investigates the rights of indigenous peoples with respect to conservation initiatives.

Darwin was famously inspired to contemplate evolution after witnessing the unusual species found on the Galapagos Islands. He surmised that these species had immigrated from the South American mainland and then adapted to the various environments by natural selection – survival of the fittest. This created a wealth of new and unusual species in a process known as adaptive radiation.

Any isolated habitat is subject to this 'island effect'. Tropical mountain tops can be viewed as islands in the sky, isolated by a low-altitude 'sea'. The animals and plants inhabiting these originally arrived, by long-distance dispersal, from more typical tundra environments in higher latitudes. Once isolated, they adapted to the individual patterns of season, landform and precipitation that they encountered, eventually becoming new species, significantly different from their ancestors.

Where a mountain range exists there is an archipelago of sky islands. The alpine species island-hop along the chain, adapting each time to the local environments. Species that are less mobile, such as plants, or reproduce more quickly, such as insects, tend to undergo a more dynamic adaptive radiation as they migrate. The end result is a string of new species along the range, in some cases each mountain having its own unique flora and fauna. This evolutionary history, although fascinating, makes tropical alpine communities particularly vulnerable to extinction.

UK-based

Survival International 6 Charterhouse Bldgs, London EC1M 7ET; ☎ 0207 687 8700; e info@survival-international. org; www.survival-international.org. A worldwide organisation working for tribal peoples' rights in 3 complementary ways: campaigns, education & funding. Survival International works closely with local indigenous organisations & focuses on tribal peoples who have the most to lose, usually those most recently in contact with the outside world.

US-based

International Society for the Preservation of the Tropical Rainforest Los Angeles office: Roxanne Kremer, 3302 Burton Av, Rosemead CA 91770, USA; ☎ 626 572 0233; e pard_ expeditions@yahoo.com; www.isptr-pard. org. Works hands-on with native villages & provides a free medical clinic, animal orphanage & education/conservation trips particularly in the Amazon area. Volunteer opportunities.

FIELD GUIDES

FLORA Sadly, there are no widely available field guides to Andean flora but this one (in Spanish) is available locally in the Huaraz area.

Flores silvestres de la Cordillera Blanca (Wild flowers of the Cordillera Blanca) (Institutode Montaña) by Helen Kolff.

GENERAL WILDLIFE

Peru (Travellers' Wildlife Guides) by David L Pearson, Les D Beletsky and Priscilla Barrett. This book contains colour illustrations of more than 500 of Peru's most common insects, amphibians, reptiles, birds and mammals from Machu Picchu to Lake Titicaca in the south, Iquitos in the northeast. Information on the identification and location of the most frequently seen animals, the ecology, behaviour and conservation of the animals, information on Peru's habitats and on the most common plants encountered, and brief descriptions of Peru's most frequently visited parks and reserves.

Peruvian Wildlife: A Visitor's Guide to the High Andes (Bradt Wildlife Guides) by tour leaders Gerard Cheshire, Barry Walker and Huw Lloyd. This useful wildlife guide is slim enough to carry around and makes excellent background reading while also providing colour photographs and drawings to aid identification of all animals over 3,000m and most of the common plants. As well as information on the region's most interesting fauna and flora, there are suggested wildlife itineraries, practical information on when to go and what to take, and photography tips. Hot spots covered include some of the mountain areas included in this trekking guide: Machu Picchu, Cusco, Sacred Valley of the Incas, Inca Trail, Lake Titicaca. The book also covers geography and geology. Not least, it makes an excellent souvenir too. Pick up your discounted copy by keying in PERU40 at the checkout on www. bradtguides.com.

BIRDS

A Field Guide to the Birds of Peru (Pemberly) by James F Clements and Noam Shany. This is the classic book and standard reference.

A Photographic Guide to Birds of Peru (New Holland) by Clive Byers. This concise and easy-to-use guide features 252 of Peru's most interesting and spectacular birds, with each illustrated in full colour and with key information on identification, habitat and distribution.

Birds of Peru (Helm Field Guides) by Douglas F Stotz, Thomas S Schulenberg, John P O'Neill, Theodore A Parker III, Dale Dyer, Daniel F Lane, John Schmitt and Larry B McQueen. Published in 2007 (and updated 2010) this is a comprehensive and fully illustrated field guide to the birds of Peru. The text is arranged opposite the plates, in conventional field guide manner.

Birds of the High Andes (Apollo Books, Lundbyvej 36, DK-5700 Svendborg, Denmark) by Jon Fjeldså and Niels Krabbe. Of the world's 9,000 bird species, nearly 900 are found in this region, and are all described and illustrated here. The book covers the temperate and alpine zones of the Andean region, from Venezuela and Colombia in the north, through Ecuador, Peru, Bolivia and Argentina, to the southernmost point on the coast of Chile. For each species, there is a full description, including plumage, habits, voices, breeding, habitat selection and range, plus detailed distribution maps. The colour plates depict over 2,000 separate plumages in nearly 1,000 species and subspecies. In addition there are numerous line drawings showing differential details, postures and nests. It is priced at around £90.

South American Birds (Harrowood Books, USA) by John Dunning. Very useful and has some good colour photos.

The Birds of Machu Picchu and the Cusco Region (Nuevas Imagenes) by B Walker. Available secondhand on Amazon Marketplace.

There are several specialist books, DVDs and CDs of birdsong listed in the extensive catalogue of the Natural History Book Service (*www.nhbs.com*) including a number of laminated guides: *Peru Forest Bird Guide* and *Peru Raptors Bird Guide* by Robert Dean and Mark Wainwright, *Birds of Peru MP3 Sound Collection* by Peter Boesman, and *Birding Southern Peru DVD* by Malcolm Rymer.

! **Updates website:** For the latest updates go to www.bradtupdates. com/perutrekking. You can also post your feedback here – corrections, changes or even new hikes. Your information will be put on our website for the benefit of other travellers.

MAMMALS

Mammals of the Neotropics (Vol 3): The Central Neotropics: Ecuador, Peru, Bolivia, Brazil by John F Eisenberg and Kent H Redford

44

3

Practical Information

WHEN TO VISIT

Most people, if given the choice, will prefer to trek in the dry season: April to October (the southern hemisphere winter). The most popular

> ### 📖 TAKE A BREAK!
>
> No-one will go to Peru purely for the walking; you are bound to want to visit some of the sights and pleasures of the country in between hikes. Here is a selection of places and ideas not described in the hiking chapters to get you started.
>
> **COLONIAL ARCHITECTURE** Lima has some very fine buildings – and terrific museums – but the architectural gem is Trujillo in the north.
>
> **PRE-INCA RUINS** Visit Chan Chan and Sechin (northern Peru). Chan Chan is a huge city complex of adobe buildings. Sechín is smaller and more intimate, and has some wonderfully gruesome depictions of the horrors of war.
>
> **BEACHES** Huanchaco in the north is noted for the traditional reed boats used to ride the surf. Puerto Chicama is where the surfers go. Máncora is usually sunny with a great sandy beach and good surfing.
>
> **WILDLIFE** The Paracas Peninsula and the Ballestas Islands are teeming with marine mammals and birds. Manu National Park or Tambopata, on its edge, are the places to go for rainforest species.
>
> **FOOD** Lima is *the* place for really fine-dining, though Cusco is fast catching up.

months are June to September, since the rains can finish late or start early in the season. However, don't rule out hiking in the rainy season. There are three main advantages: cheaper airfares, fewer trekkers and a lush greenness to the countryside that you miss in the long, dry winter months. It is also slightly less cold. In the rainy season, generally speaking, the mornings will start fine but clouds will build up during the day and rain is likely in the afternoon. You can be lucky, however, and have days of unbroken sunshine. Or unlucky and have days of

FIESTAS

The rich traditions of history and religion come together in local festivals. In the larger towns and cities these are often little more than an opportunity to close banks and businesses and take off for a long weekend, but in the mountain regions the people grab this chance to escape the rhythm of their daily lives and explode into an orgy of colour, music, dance and drinking.

Most fiestas are similar in atmosphere, but are different in detail. They are common all year round throughout the Andes so you can hardly avoid being caught up in the action.

If you are a lone woman be cautious about participating in fiestas: the combination of alcohol and dancing liberates the male spirit. Your apparent availability could lead to rape. Attend in the company of a man, either local or gringo. If you feel you can handle it on your own you should expect some sexual harassment and be prepared to laugh it off or leave. Do not get angry or upset.

Never participate in a local festival unless you are invited. If you are invited, be prepared to enjoy yourself. Western inhibitions have no place here. For the locals, gringos are part of the fun.

To give a flavour of the fiesta experience, I am including the descriptions of two fiestas that George and I attended in the 1970s. These three towns now see plenty of tourists so the attitude to gringo participants may have changed, but not the fiestas themselves.

CHACAS This village in the Cordillera Blanca is proud of its Spanish heritage, and the principal events in its week-long fiesta have a Spanish flavour. We arrived for the *carrera de caballos* (horse race). The morning was occupied by a religious procession, with the plaza full of expectant villagers as the Virgin of Chacas was carried from the church, elaborately attired for the occasion. The procession was led by the village elite, with a banner-carrying horseman representing the *caballeros*. Then came the dancers, gloriously dressed and masked, some with large head-dresses of peacock feathers, and dancing to music from pipes, a

continual rain – or snow – which bring discomfort and the unpleasant experience of white-outs or of being surrounded by clouds with very poor visibility. Make sure you have good quality kit with you if you are thinking of trekking during the rainy season and keep in mind that guides and muleteers may not be available in the Andean summer. Also be aware that some trails may disappear under landslides, and independent hiking becomes risky when cloud covers the landmarks. The Inca Trail closes in February.

fiddle and an enormous harp. After the procession had wound its way round the square and the Virgin was returned to the church, the plaza started filling up with horsemen riding magnificent Peruvian 'walking horses' (*caballos de paso*). The riders' wealth was represented by the beautiful animals they rode. We'd been expecting horse races, but in fact the afternoon contest measured the skills of the riders rather than the speed of their animals. Between two posts hung a row of sashes with a ring sewn on to the lower end. The riders had to spear this ring with a short wooden pick as they galloped between the posts. The prize for the most successful was the leadership of next year's contest. There were, perhaps, more desirable prizes; the village maidens had written their names on the sashes.

PAUCARTAMBO This is one of the finest of all Peruvian fiestas, and deservedly popular. The dancing is continuous for three days, and performed with a tribal intensity by the Indians involved. The costumes are varied and incredible: one group reminded us of agitated birds' nests, others of animated sacks. The dancers were fantastically masked and dressed. There were monsters and African gringos, symbolic figures that had played a part in the Indians' history or mythology.

The procession of the Virgin of Carmen was the climax of the last day. She swayed towards us, resembling a stiff white cone of lace and jewels, smothered in flowers and with her doll's face almost hidden under an elaborate crown. Preceding her came a pure white llama, beautifully decorated. On the rooftops of the houses lining her route were dancing devils, demons and winged creatures, but before the Virgin could come under their evil influence, a flight of angels conquered them, beating them out of view. Later, at night, we heard music. Peeping in through a doorway we saw a large room with tables laden with food, and the victors and vanquished dancing together in the middle. A friendly shout went up; we were pulled into the room, filled with food and drink, and danced with until we had to beg for mercy.

PUBLIC HOLIDAYS At least once a month a saint has his or her birthday, which is lots of fun for the saint who gets to leave the church for a parade around town. It's an excuse for a fiesta (see below) and a national holiday. If the day falls in the middle of the week, it is automatically moved to the next Monday to make a long weekend. Remember that banks, shops and offices are closed on these days.

The national school holidays run from the end of December until the end of February. As at home – but worse – everyone wants to get out of town for Christmas so prices of hotels and transport double and all tickets on all means of transport are sold out days before. Avoid travelling at this time.

The same problem occurs around Independence Day (28 July), bang in the middle of the tourist season, when school holidays start one or two weeks before the holiday and continue until mid-August.

Fiestas Below are the main festivals in Peru. Check dates with the tourist office in the nearest large town before you go. Cusco and the Sacred Valley are particularly well endowed with fiestas; see pages 248–9.

1 January	Año Nuevo: throughout Peru
1–6 January	Fiesta del Año Nuevo: Apurímac, Huancayo
6 January	Día de los Reyes Magos: Cusco, Puno
6 January	Niño Occe: Huancavelica
12 January	Fiesta de Negritos: Huancavelica
20 January	San Sebastián and San Fabián: Huancayo, Cusco
February (one week)	Carnival: throughout South America
2 February	Virgen de la Candelaria: Huancayo, Ayacucho, Cusco, Puno
8 March	San Juan de Dios: Puno
March or April	Semana Santa: throughout Peru
25 April	San Marcos: throughout the Andes
May (first week)	Feria de las Alasitas: Puno
1 May	Labour Day: throughout Peru
3 May	La Invención de la Santa Cruz: throughout the Andes
15 May	Fiesta de San Isidro Labrador: Moche (La Libertad), Huaraz
Early June	Qoyllur Rit'i: Cordillera Vilcanota, Cusco
Mid-June (Thursday)	Corpus Christi: throughout Peru after Trinity Sunday
15 June	Virgen de las Mercedes: Huancayo
24 June	Inti Raymi (Festival of the Sun): Cusco and San Juan Bautista. Día del Indio: Lima.

28 June	San Pedro and San Pablo: throughout Peru
End of June	Semana del Andinismo: Cordillera Blanca
June	Fiesta de Torre-Torre: Huancavelica
6–8 July	Santa Isabel: Callejón de Huaylas
16 July	Virgen del Carmen: throughout Peru but notably Paucartambo (see box, page 47)
24–28 July	Fiesta de Santiago: throughout the Andes
26 July	Santa Ana: Puno
28 July	Independence Day
4 August	Santo Domingo: throughout the Andes
15 August	Fiesta de Asunción: throughout the Andes
30 August	Santa Rosa de Lima: Lima
8 September	Virgen de la Natividad: Cajamarca, Huancayo, Cusco
14 September	Fiesta de las Lucas: Huaraz and some other mountain villages
23–24 September	Virgen de las Mercedes: throughout the Andes
30 September	San Jerónimo: throughout the Andes
4 October	San Francisco de Asís: throughout the Andes
7 October	La Virgen del Rosario and Uma Raymi (Festival of the Water): most Andean villages
18 October	El Señor de los Milagros: Lima and San Lucas, Huancayo and some other mountain villages
1–2 November	Fiesta de Todos los Santos and Día de los Muertos: cemeteries throughout Peru
4–5 November	Festival of Manco Capac: Lake Titicaca, Puno
3–13 December	Virgen de Guadalupe: Huancayo
8 December	Fiesta de la Immaculada Concepción: throughout the Andes
25 December	Danza de las Tijeras: Huancavelica
28 December	Fiesta de los Santos Inocentes (similar to April Fools' Day): throughout Peru

BACKPACKING OR ORGANISED TREKKING?

At an early stage of planning your trip, you'll need to decide whether you want to explore the Andes as a self-sufficient backpacker or join an organised trek where all the arrangements are made for you and your gear is carried by porters or pack animals.

If you speak good Spanish, you have the option of compromising by travelling independently but hiring a muleteer (arriero) and his animal to carry your pack at the trailhead. These options are described in more detail in *Chapter 4*.

TOUR OPERATORS

Chapter 4 (pages 81–2) lists tour operators specialising in trekking; the following companies run trekking tours in Peru along with cultural or natural history tours:

UK-BASED

Abercrombie & Kent e info@ abercrombiekent.co.uk; www. abercrombiekent.co.uk

Bailey Robinson e travel@ baileyrobinson.com; www.baileyrobinson. com. Occasional treks plus horseriding in Peru.

Discover Adventure e info@ discoveradventure.com; www. discoveradventure.com. Charity treks on the Inca Trail.

Dragoman Overland Journeys e bradt@ dragoman.co.uk; www.dragoman.com

Far Frontiers e info@farfrontiers.com; www.farfrontiers.com

Footloose Adventure Travel e info@footlooseadventure.co.uk; www. footlooseadventure.co.uk

Footprint Adventures e sales@ footprint-adventures.co.uk; www.footprint-adventures.co.uk

Gane and Marshall · e holidays@ GaneandMarshall.co.uk; www. GaneandMarshall.co.uk. Wildlife holidays.

KE Adventure Travel e info@ keadventure.co.uk; www.keadventure.com. See advert, page 210.

Last Frontiers e info@lastfrontiers.com; www.lastfrontiers.com

Naturetrek e info@naturetrek.co.uk; www.naturetrek.co.uk

Oasis Overland e travel@oasisoverland. com; www.oasisoverland.com

Original Travel www.timbesttravel.com

Rainbow Tours e info@rainbowtours. co.uk; www.rainbowtours.co.uk. See advert, colour page 20.

Reef and Rainforest Tours e mail@reefandrainforest.co.uk; www. reefandrainforest.co.uk

Sunvil Traveller e latinamerica@sunvil. co.uk; www.sunvil.co.uk

Tribes Travel e info@tribes.co.uk; www. tribes.co.uk. See advert, colour page 8.

VentureCo e mail@ventureco-worldwide. com; www.ventureco-worldwide.com. Gap Year programmes.

Walks Worldwide e info@ walksworldwide.com; www. walksworldwide.com

World Expeditions e enquiries@ worldexpeditions.co.uk; www. worldexpeditions.co.uk. See advert, page 114.

World Wide Adventures Abroad e info@adventures-abroad.com; www. adventures-abroad.com

US-BASED

Breakaway Adventures e info@ breakaway-adventures.com; www. breakaway-adventures.com. Offer a week's walking with the comfort of a hotel each night.

Mountain Travel Sobek www.mtsobek. com. Long-established trekking operator with a selection of walking holidays in Peru.

SouthAmerican.travel e TravelTeam@ SouthAmerican.travel; www.SouthAmerica. travel. See advert, colour page 24.

Wildland Adventures e info@wildland. com; www.wildland.com

PERU-BASED

Aracari e info@aracari.com; www.aracari.com. Award-winning tour operator based in Lima & serving the luxury end of the market. Their regular newsletter about different aspects of Peru is exceptionally interesting.

Trekking Peru e info@trekkingperu.net; www.trekkingperu.net. Custom-built tours from local experts, includes hotel-based day walks to multi-day treks. See advert, colour page 28.

TOURIST INFORMATION

iPerú is Peru's tourist information and tourist protection organisation. It has a network of tourist information offices throughout Peru, with a 24-hour phone service (01 5748000; e iperu@promperu.gob.pe; www.peru.travel/en/, www.promperu.gob.pe). Check out www.editoraperu.com for the latest news and political information.

SOUTH AMERICAN EXPLORERS (SAE) The South American Explorers Club (now shortened to South American Explorers) was founded in 1977 with the aim of providing unbiased information and honest advice for independent travellers in South America. It is a simply marvellous organisation and anyone travelling for a few weeks in Peru should join so they can make use of the extensive facilities in the club houses in Lima and Cusco. Here they can swap stories with other travellers over a cup of tea, get answers to those tricky questions about off-the-beaten track travel, or study trip reports, buy a wide range of maps including the best trekking maps, store luggage, access the internet, or settle down to read in the extensive library. There is also a book exchange, a comprehensive database of volunteer positions in Peru, and discounts on travel services throughout South America. Remember, to get all these benefits you need to be a member. The hard-pressed volunteers who work here do not have time to answer enquiries from non-members. See www.saexplorers.org for membership details (*single membership US$60, double US$45pp, triple US$40pp & 4 people+ US$35pp*).

Club houses

Lima Enrique Palacios 956, Miraflores; 01 4442150; postal address: Casilla 3714, Lima 100; e limaclub@saexplorers.org; www.saexplorers.org/clubhouse/lima-clubhouse

Cusco Atoqsaycuchi 670, San Blas; (084) 245484; www.saexplorers.org/clubhouse/cusco-clubhouse

MAPS The maps in this book will give you an adequate idea of the hikes described and are fine for organised treks with a guide, but for independent hiking you should take a detailed map. Many of the maps recommended in this book are available from the specialist map shop

Stanfords (*shops in London & Bristol; www.stanfords.co.uk*). Once in Peru, SAE has some good detailed maps of the popular hikes, and for serious exploring the government-run Geographic Institute (Instituto Geografico Nacional – IGN) publishes maps which are available in Lima (page 128).

MINISTRY OF CULTURE This is the public body responsible for protecting, restoring and publicising all things cultural in Peru. Its website has information on the sites under its protection, organised events, museums and more. If you are taking replicas of pre-Hispanic artefacts out of the country you may need a certificate from them. Check their website: www.mcultura.gob.pe, or visit their office (*Ministerio de Cultura, Avda Javier Prado Este 2465, San Borja, Lima 41;* 01 6189393).

RED TAPE

Visas are at present not required by western Europeans or North Americans, but rules may change so check www.discover-peru.org to be on the safe side. All nationalities are given a **tourist card** by the immigration authorities on arrival in Peru: a stamp and a little white slip of paper. Don't lose it, as you need it when leaving the country, and you may be asked to show it to prove you are in the country legally. All nationalities are automatically given a 183-day stay (but often only stamped for 90 days, so ask if you need longer), and once inside Peru you cannot extend this – you have to cross a border and then return. You'll be fined if you overstay your visa. Legally, you need to show a ticket out of the country when you enter, although this is not always strictly adhered to.

GETTING THERE AND AWAY

Several airlines fly in to Lima from all parts of the world, and there are always some special prices available, though usually only in the low season. Airfares are more expensive in the high season: from April until September and around Christmas time.

Your best bet is to use one of the specialist agencies for South America who offer low prices and informed advice. Check online at the usual websites such as www.cheapflights.co.uk (or, in the US www.cheapflights.com), www.skyscanner.net, www.travelsupermarket.com, www.flighthub.com, www.travelocity.com, www.orbitz.com and www.expedia.com. Also worth checking is Matrix Airfare Search. Popular US-based airline sites are www.farecompare.com and www.kayak.com.

FROM EUROPE At the time of writing there is no direct flight to Lima from the UK. Several airlines fly from mainland Europe to Lima:

Air France, Alitalia, Iberia, Air Europa, LAN, Lufthansa, and KLM. Alternatively, you can choose to fly via the USA. Delta, Continental, United and American Airlines fly this route.

It is possible to avoid overnighting in Lima and to connect straight through to Cusco or Arequipa if you can get an overnight flight to Lima arriving there early in the morning.

Sometimes companies specialising in flights to South America, such as Journey Latin America (℡ 020 8747 3108; e flights@journeylatinamerica.co.uk; www.journeylatinamerica.co.uk) can save you time and effort when researching flights. A sample low-season fare at the time of writing is with Iberia: £700 with tax direct from Madrid to Lima. High season would be about £180 more.

FROM THE USA Several airlines serve the route Miami–Lima: United, Continental and American Airlines. The last operates flights from the USA to Lima and directly on to Cusco (with a change of planes). All have direct connections with New York. Direct flights from Los Angeles to Lima are served by Aerolíneas Argentinas and Varig, but these direct flights tend to be more expensive than flying via Miami.

FROM AUSTRALIA The worldwide operator STA Travel (www.statravel.com.au) has branches in the major cities in Australia – so does Flight Centre (www.flightcentre.com.au). Links are through a South American operator such as LAN Chile or Aerolíneas Argentinas, or through the United States.

LUGGAGE ALLOWANCE When you choose your airline ask about the baggage allowance both to and from Peru. Some airlines allow two bags of 30kg each going out but only 25kg coming back. Others allow two bags (unlimited weight) each way or only 25kg in total. Airlines vary enormously in what they allow and trekkers arriving on US airlines generally have a much more generous allowance.

WHAT TO TAKE

What to bring depends on whether you are on an organised trekking trip where your camping equipment will be supplied and your luggage carried by porters or pack animals, or whether you will be a self-sufficient backpacker. Either way, try to keep your luggage as light as possible; you will enjoy your trip much more and it is easier to look after your stuff during bus and train rides. However, good kit is difficult to find and expensive to buy in Peru and the quality is variable. Renting

i **First-aid kit:** see page 106 for a suggested medical kit.

is increasingly becoming an option, especially in Huaraz but this is not ideal if you are planning several treks.

CLOTHING Remember the old travellers' maxim: 'Bring twice as much money and half as many clothes as you think you'll need.' All of your clothes should be chosen for comfort, but select one outfit which will render you respectable for that blow-out in a good restaurant, or an invitation to visit an upper-class Peruvian home.

A popular saying describes a day in the Andes as including all the seasons of the year: nights are as cold as winter, mornings are spring-like, the afternoon heat can be as fierce as summer, and evenings have an autumn crispness. So you need to be prepared for extreme temperature changes. In the mountains, cold is the biggest enemy (temperatures drop to well below freezing at night). There is plenty of high-tech outdoor clothing around nowadays to suit all activities and tastes. It is expensive though, so think carefully about what you need and how much on-going use you will get out of it before splashing out. If you choose one expensive item of clothing, make it a good fleece or down jacket.

The best way of keeping warm and comfortable is by wearing layers of clothes. Since you'll warm up rapidly in the sun and through exercise, you can peel off successive layers of clothing during the day. The best clothing combines light weight with warmth, windproofing and breathability to give versatile layers that cope with all but wet weather. Cotton holds moisture next to the skin, which means you will get cold as soon as you stop moving, so is not recommended. Better by far to go for the Merino wool products on the market or for synthetic fibres that wick the moisture away. Thermal underwear is very useful for these freezing nights, being light but very warm. A down parka (duvet jacket) is warm, lightweight and perfect for high altitudes. It also doubles as a pillow. But down is useless when wet.

> **Note:** It is inadvisable to wear military-style clothing in Peru. The army is not viewed with much affection by rural people.

You'll also need gloves and a woollen scarf/muffler. At lower altitudes a fleece or wool sweater and wind and waterproof top are adequate. Peruvian alpaca woollens are warm, cheap and a good way to support the local economy. Don't forget a good warm hat.

It is likely to rain, even in the dry season, and a waterproof jacket and trousers are essential. A big rain poncho which covers your backpack is also very useful and can double as a groundsheet. Waterproof jackets come in an astonishing range of materials, designs and prices. You will definitely want a breathable fabric for trekking and, in addition, look for useful features such as sealed seams and zips that stop water getting in, ventilation zips, pockets in the right places, and a hood that, ideally, moves with your head.

Quick-dry walking trousers (pants) over long underwear, or fleece trousers are the best options. Fleece trousers are lightweight, quick to dry, can be used as pyjamas at night or leisure wear in hotels, and worn under other clothing give an extra warm layer. Lightweight polyester trousers that unzip above the knee are increasingly popular, providing a two-in-one, trousers-and-shorts option, but they are not that good for warmth once the sun goes down. Jeans are not suitable for hiking because denim is heavy and takes ages to dry. Shorts are fine for hiking though they may give offence in some towns. Give some thought to pockets; all trousers should have deep pockets, secured with a button or zip. Sunburn is a danger at these altitudes. Bring a quick-dry long-sleeved shirt for protection against sun (and insects) and remember that T-shirts leave the base of your neck vulnerable. A broad-brimmed hat is better protection than a simple baseball cap and a bandana or neckerchief protects the base of the neck from sunburn. It's also handy as a mouth and nose protection in dusty conditions.

ELECTRICITY Voltage 220V, 60Hz. Most outlets are for two round prongs, but some have dual-voltage outlets for US-style flat prongs.

BACKPACKING AND TREKKING EQUIPMENT AND PROVISIONS
Experienced backpackers probably already own all the equipment necessary for a South American trip but newcomers should get expert advice. Good outdoor equipment shops should be able to advise you (see page 59) and climbing/hiking magazines always have good, independent information.

The requirements of backpackers differ from those of trekkers who need not be quite so careful about weight or bulk (the long-suffering mules or porters will be carrying their stuff) so comfort becomes the primary objective.

Backpack Be willing to spend some money on this – it will be your most important 'companion'. Spend time trying on different makes and models and only settle for the best one for you: size, weight and capacity. Some manufacturers make packs especially for women. Choose one that can be adjusted to your back and avoid buying online. This is a case of getting advice from knowledgeable store staff. Hikers on an organised trek need **daypacks**, with strong hip belts, to carry all their daily needs, from cameras to waterproof clothing, as they will not have access to their main luggage during the day. A **backpack cover** is recommended even if your pack is waterproof. Trekkers will find a waterproof cover very handy for their daypack (you'd be lucky to have no rain at all on your trek) and backpackers need a thief-proof cover to keep their stuff secure on planes and public transport, as well as one which protects it from the elements.

Boots Footwear is the most important item for an enjoyable trek. It is also a very personal choice. Where once the universal advice was for sturdy supportive boots, there has been a recent change to lighter footwear by many people. Although some still prefer the ankle support provided by boots, many now swear by lighter trail running shoes and are able to backpack and hike long distances in these. The theory of this lighter footwear is that with practice your ankles and feet become stronger than if they were in more supportive footwear precisely because they are required to work more. Once strengthened, they are freer to react and recover from a stumble or slip, which is much harder if they are encased in the solid structure of a boot. Remember: you pick up your feet thousands of times throughout the day, so the less your shoe weighs, the easier it is to pick up, which can add up over a day.

Advocates of boots would say it affords more protection to your foot on the often rough ground and helps support you when carrying a heavy pack.

The choice is yours, but the most important thing is to make sure to practise and get comfortable with your footwear long before you come to Peru. Half way along your trek is not the time to discover you do not like your chosen footwear you have.

For information on avoiding and dealing with **blisters**, see page 100.

Tent Although my (Hilary's) first year of backpacking in the Andes was spent under a shower-curtain, I concede that a good tent is necessary. It not only protects you from the elements but also keeps your gear from the acquisitive eyes of the locals when you are camping close to villages. Good tents are expensive so, again, explore the option of buying secondhand. If you buy a cheap or used tent, be sure to bring some sealant to block those dripping seams. It is also useful to bring a tent-repair kit for broken poles or rips in the fabric.

Sleeping bag There are some very effective synthetic fillers on the market now, but you still can't beat goose-down, which is the lightest and warmest insulation available. It is virtually essential for backpackers – synthetic bags take up too much space. Backpacking or trekking in the Andes poses a problem, however, in that in the valleys nights can be quite warm and you may be too hot in a bag that is just right for 4,000m. Your best bet is to have a sleeping-bag cover or liner, which gives you the versatility for moderate and freezing temperatures. A sheet sleeping bag not only keeps your down bag clean, but is perfect for jungle hiking and for use in cheap hotels with dubious sheets. Silk is warmer and lighter than cotton. A pillow can be made from a T-shirt stuffed with a sweater or duvet (down) jacket.

Mattress/sleeping pad It is essential to have some sort of insulation from the cold ground, as well as padding. Closed-cell foam is cheap and adequate, but the best mat of all is the Therm-a-Rest, a combination of air mattress and foam pad. It's lightweight and compact, but expensive. However, if you can't afford a full-length Therm-a-Rest, there's a cheaper (and lighter) three-quarter length one. Some trekkers recommend carrying both lengths for extra comfort. Be careful not to put your mattress out on the grass – some grasses have little spines which could puncture it.

Stove Since it is illegal to make a wood fire in national parks, a good stove is one of the most important items on a backpacker's list and worth spending some money on. The most practical are the multi-fuel stoves (widely available from good outlets) which run on any fuel – but note that spare parts are not available in Peru. You can buy white gas/stove alcohol/benzene (*benceina*) at pharmacies (*farmacias, boticas*) or hardware shops (*fereterias*). Gas cartridges are readily available in Cusco and Huaraz and are a good alternative to the multi-fuel stoves (except on longer hikes). Kerosene/paraffin (*kerosina*) is available at most petrol stations or in small stores. *Alcohol potable* (drinking alcohol) is readily available and works as a fuel for some stoves.

For emergencies, it's sensible to bring a tiny 'hot pot' – an aluminium cup and stand that burns tablets of solid fuel (you can buy these in Peru). Bring waterproof matches.

Torch A small but powerful torch (flashlight) should be on your list and kept handy for hotels, which are subject to power cuts, and for exploring ruins, as well as for camping. Trekkers need a LED headtorch. These cost anything from US$15 to US$60, but it is worth investing in a good one, particularly if you are backpacking in the mountains independently. It is essential that you can see properly at night.

Pots and pans If you don't already own a lightweight aluminium saucepan, buy it in Peru. Make sure it has a well-fitting lid as this makes cooking more efficient – a process already hindered in the highlands by the reduced oxygen in the atmosphere. Pots are cheap and available everywhere. Plastic plates and mugs keep food and drink hot and are great for warming hands as well. Most backpackers make do with just a spoon.

Food There is a good choice of suitable pack food available in Peru and Bolivia, so you don't need to bring it from home. You can shop in the local markets or at supermarkets in the bigger towns.

Packet soups, noodles, purée potato, sugar, oatmeal, dried sausage and dried milk all provide a good basis for your hot meals. Ginger, chillies, onions, garlic, salt and pepper and stock cubes add flavour. For lunches, cheese, fresh bread and dried fruits are excellent. Powdered fruit drinks make treated water more palatable.

Dried fruit and vegetables (sliced carrots, cabbage, onions and apples) make excellent backpacking food, and are easy to do yourself in the strong sun of the mountains.

What to bring from home? Maybe your favourite special treat (for me, marmite!), and a packet or two of dehydrated food for emergencies.

Miscellaneous useful items for backpackers Below is a checklist of items we have found to be indispensable: toilet paper, small trowel for digging toilet hole, rubbish bags, a travel alarm clock, good quality penknife, sewing kit, safety pins, large needles and strong thread (or dental floss) for tent or other repairs, scissors, heavy-duty sticky tape, felt-tipped pens, pencils and ballpoint pens, a small notebook, plastic zip-lock bags, large plastic bags for keeping your clothes dry, universal plug for baths and sinks, elastic clothes-line or cord and clothes pegs, small scrubbing brush, biodegradable liquid soap, shampoo, travel towel, toothpaste, wet wipes for washing when water is scarce, disinfectant hand gel, earplugs, insect repellent, sunscreen, handcream, lipsalve, money belt and sunglasses.

If you have a digital camera, MP3, tablet or mobile phone, remember a solar device for charging or plenty of extra batteries. Batteries run down more quickly in cold temperatures; lithium batteries last much longer. It is a good idea to keep any electrical items in waterproof bags and in your daypack, where they are less likely to get broken or stolen. Remember a plug adapter for electrical devices. If you wear glasses or contact lenses, bring a spare pair. Women should bring tampons (which may not be

---

i MAKING DO

If you arrived in South America planning to relax but are seduced by the mountains and inspired by the tales of other trekkers, don't feel that your lack of equipment is a barrier. Back in 1973 George and I were in the same position when much of our equipment was stolen: we used a shower-curtain as a tent (rigged between trees with a cord) and a poncho as a sleeping bag (until we found a fellow traveller in need of funds).

Renting equipment is no problem in the major towns of the hiking areas, like Huaraz, Arequipa and Cusco. At the South American Explorers in Lima (page 61) you can find some used kit for sale, and at the popular backpackers' hostels you can put up a notice requesting equipment. When it is your turn to go home, consider selling your gear to help out other backpackers and make more space for all those alpaca sweaters.

available in smaller towns) and panty-liners which not only are very handy for their official purpose but make excellent coverings for wounds as well. There is a suggested medicine kit on page 106.

You'll probably need compact binoculars and camera, a couple of paperback books, a phrasebook and Spanish/Quechua dictionary, a pack of cards or other small pocket games, water bottle and one two-litre container, water-purifying tablets, compass and/or GPS unit, waterproofing for boots, and a survival (space) blanket. An inflatable neck pillow is useful for long bus journeys.

Consider bringing an anti-dog device and, in case you do get bitten, keep a scrubbing brush and soap handy for cleaning the wound.

If you are accustomed to using hiking poles, these are a must (but may not be allowed on the Inca Trail unless the sharp tip is protected).

RECOMMENDED COMPANIES SELLING OUTDOOR EQUIPMENT
UK-based
Backpacking Light www.backpackinglight.co.uk. A great personalised service with next-day delivery. Offers a well thought-out range of lighter-weight products, ideal if you are carrying your own pack.

Compass Point www.compasspoint-online.co.uk Call themselves the 'orienteers' choice' so Particularly good for those heading into the wild unknown.

Cotswold Outdoor www.cotswoldoutdoor.com. A highly respected company with a wide range of products.

Ellis Brigham Mountain Sports www.ellis-brigham.com. Wide range of outdoor gear.

Field and Trek e cs@fieldandtrek.com; www.fieldandtrek.com. They deliver to over 60 countries worldwide. Have a comprehensive selection of outdoor gear at discounted prices & an excellent website.

GoOutdoors www.gooutdoors.co.uk. The UK's biggest outdoor stores.

Hawkshead www.hawkshead.com. Family outdoor outfitter.

Nomad Travel www.nomadtravel.co.uk. Experts in travel health & tropical camping equipment.

Rohan www.rohan.co.uk. Offer a range of camping accessories, as well as clothing. See advert, colour page 25.

SafariQuip www.safariquip.co.uk. Wide range of travel & adventure gear. See advert, page 44.

Snow and Rock www.snowandrock.com. Ski clothing & climbing equipment.

Summits Outdoor Gears www.summits.co.uk. Extensive range of outdoor gear.

Ultralight Outdoor Gear www.ultralightoutdoorgear.co.uk. See advert, colour page 27.

US-based
EMS (Eastern Mountain Sports) www.ems.com. Outdoor gear.

REI www.rei.com. Outdoor gear & supports conservation efforts nationwide.

MONEY AND BUDGETING

The currency in Peru is called the *sol* (plural *soles*) or *nuevo sol* but has changed a few times over the years. In former days of high inflation the government would, from time to time, lop off a few zeros and change the name. It went from the (old) *sol* to the *inti* in 1986 and to the *nuevo sol* again in 1991. The annual rate of inflation has been brought down from its high in 1990 of 3,000% to a very respectable 2.31% in 2013. In November 2013 US$1 = 2.8 soles.

FOREIGN EXCHANGE AND ATMS Very few people use **travellers' cheques** these days, although a few banks do still accept them in large towns; Banco de Crédito is probably the best bank. Far easier are **debit and credit cards** and enough carefully hidden cash for emergencies.

The most easily exchanged currency is **US dollars** – trying to change other currencies can be time consuming and frustrating. Make sure that dollar bills are not damaged or they may not be accepted. Forged dollar bills are common so be wary about buying dollars in South America.

If you are changing cash dollars it is best (and safest) to do it in a *casa de cambio*. Unfortunately, you'll only see them in the bigger towns; in the smaller places you may have to trust the street money-changers. Sometimes it's hard (or impossible) to change dollars, so plan ahead when heading off into the more remote areas of the mountains and take enough soles. Try to get small denominations of soles: no-one ever has change.

Cashpoints or **ATMs** are common in major cities and are a convenient source of local currency for holders of Cirrus, MasterCard and Visa cards. The limit per day is normally 700 soles (but sometimes 1,400 soles, depending on the card and machine). You can also get cash from major banks with an American Express card and other credit cards (but a commission is charged), and most upper-range hotels, restaurants and shops accept credit cards.

! **Note:** Because of inflation, prices are often published in dollars in the upper-range hotels, restaurants and shops. Most of these places will accept credit cards, or you can pay with local currency using the exchange rate of the day, which is sometimes slightly lower than that offered by the *casas de cambio* and banks.

Whether you are backpacking or trekking, keep all your valuables in a moneybelt under your clothing, while travelling, and if possible leave them in a hotel safe against a receipt when in town. It is a good idea to make sure you know what bank telephone numbers to call should you lose your cards or if they are stolen, and make photocopies of all your documents (keep them separate from your money) and email copies of all important numbers, contact addresses and so on to yourself.

BUDGETING Peru is inexpensive by the standards of the developed world, but you will still need to assume an expenditure of around US$25–35 per day although probably you will spend less. As a guide, a bed in a clean backpacker hostel will cost no more than US$10 and a simple meal will be around US$2.

Whilst you will spend virtually nothing when hiking the trails (assuming you are backpacking, not hiring muleteers or guides) it's a rare backpacker who can resist the lure of a bit of luxury on hitting the cities. Keep costs down by buying food in the markets and staying in *hostales* and backpacker places. And bear in mind that prices in this book may have risen by the time you travel. Be sure to take adequate funds. If you do hire pack animals, the daily cost will jump a further US$20 per day.

Given that a meal in a good tourist restaurant will set you back around US$30 and that an indulgence hotel could be US$50 or more – and you'll want to do some shopping – a daily budget of US$100 is sensible for those looking for a good holiday rather than stretching the pennies for a trip of several months. Those on a more upmarket tour will also need to add **tips** to their budget (see page 95).

See also *Guides, porters and pack animals* (page 90), for an idea of the costs associated with hiring local help.

GETTING AROUND

In terms of availability, public transport is excellent in Peru. Specifics of travel are dealt with in each relevant section, but in general any village served by some sort of road will have some sort of vehicle running there on some sort of schedule. On major routes the quality improves dramatically so it's up to you whether you go for comfort or for cheapness.

BY BUS These come in various shapes and sizes, from luxury vehicles speeding along the intercity routes to ramshackle affairs serving the rural villages, and combis, or minibuses. Luxury buses travel mostly along the coast and on paved roads into the mountains, with video, toilet and reclining seats (*semi-cama*). They charge about 30% more than the normal price. When taking a bus, make sure you buy a ticket with a well-known company where the buses mostly leave on time, stick with the route and don't stop at every corner. The smaller bus companies seldom leave on time or cancel the scheduled departure altogether if there are not enough passengers.

Recommended bus companies are included in *Part Two* of the guide where appropriate. A good website for researching bus routes is http://theonlyperuguide.com – it offers clear, up-to-date information.

Try to travel during the day for more comfort, safety and scenery. Also avoid long bus rides; break your journey. You'll enjoy the trip much more, avoid problems with theft (most of which happens when you are tired), and arrive in better shape. Most buses stop for meals (except the luxury

3

buses, which feed you on board), but not necessarily at mealtimes. Make sure you understand how long you will be stopping for, or the bus will leave without you. Better still, have your meal within sight of the driver. Sometimes snacks are available from local vendors who will offer them through the bus window. Remember to fill your water bottle before you leave although soft drinks are usually available from vendors.

Your luggage will be lashed to the roof or stowed away in the luggage compartment. Checked luggage is usually safe: most bus companies have an effective security system to prevent someone else claiming your luggage. Either way, it will be inaccessible, so bring warm clothes and something to use as a pillow during night trips (those crescent-shaped inflatable neck pillows are ideal. You'll also need a music system or a book for entertainment during unexpected delays or breakdowns. Keep your passport on you for police checks. Watch your luggage like a hawk, especially when boarding and leaving the bus. Strap small items to the luggage rack or seat. Robbery is common on buses, but by professional criminals, not your fellow bus passengers. Some bus companies impose a luggage weight limit of 20kg per person.

BY COLECTIVO These are minibuses (combis) or cars that follow the same routes as buses but generally cost more because they are faster. There are two types: the ones that operate within towns will generally be old and overfilled, but on many inter-town routes, especially in the Cusco area, more modern minibuses are now slowly taking over from the belching, slow diesel buses. They cost slightly more but are newer, quicker and generally only take enough passengers as there are seats.

BY TRUCK Lorries/trucks used to form the backbone of public transport in Peru. This is no longer the case, with buses now serving all but the most remote villages. However, if you are heading way off the beaten track you may find your only transport option is the back of a truck. If you do find this is the case, keep all your warm clothes (including gloves, hat and even your sleeping bag) handy, and carry your foam pad to cushion those bare boards; also bring protection from rain and snow. Protect your pack from the effluent of furred or feathered passengers by putting it in a strong bag such as a flour or rice sack (which can be purchased at any market). Bring something to eat and drink during long trips, although long-distance trucks, like buses, stop for meals.

HITCHHIKING This doesn't really exist as a way of getting around as most drivers charge for the ride. There are exceptions, of course, but it is courteous to offer payment unless you are quite sure this would be offensive. However, hitchhiking can come into its own when you've finished a trek and the twice-weekly bus service left a couple of hours previously.

BY TAXI There is no shortage of taxis in Peru. If you can join up with other travellers to share the cost, and strike a good bargain with the driver, a taxi need cost little more than conventional transport and will save you a lot of time and effort – for example when you need to get to the trailhead and are carrying a heavy backpack. Save your energy for the hike.

Always settle the price beforehand and make sure the taxi is reasonably likely to make the journey without breaking down. Make sure, too, that the driver knows where you want to go (in the hiking areas most know the popular trailheads) but don't expect him to know how to read a map.

BY TRAIN Although slower than buses, trains are a pleasant alternative – and the views are better. Recent changes in regulations, however, mean that tourists generally have to travel on designated tourist train services. You will have to buy a ticket in advance (except in low season) as all the trains get very busy. This is easy to do online through the PeruRail website or through a travel agency.

The famous train from Lima to Huancayo via La Oroya is currently operating on an irregular basis (page 213) but there is a daily train between Huancayo and Huancavelica. From Cusco there is a line via Ollantaytambo and Aguas Calientes (the nearest station to Machu Picchu) to the hydro-electric station just below Machu Picchu. Train schedules may be reduced or cancelled in the rainy season.

Most of Peru's trains are run by **PeruRail**; their easy-to-use website is in English (*www.perurail.com*).

BY AIR Distances in the Andes are big and Andean roads are often in poor condition so a taking a domestic flight can be the best option, even though such flights are not cheap. There are, however, sometimes good bargains in the low season. The tourist peak season is from June until September, with July the busiest month, and from December until February, when Peru enjoys its main holiday season. Be prepared for overbooked and delayed flights, and cancellations – especially during the rainy season (December, January and February). For security always make sure that your checked luggage is locked and, if possible, put backpacks in another strong, protective bag or tape the straps so they can't get caught up on the carousel. Most domestic airlines are pretty generous with extra luggage and don't charge for excess.

Details of the relevant domestic airlines are included in *Part Two* of this guide.

ACCOMMODATION

There is always a wide variety of hotels to choose from in Peru, from a little dark cell with a too-small bed that feels more like a hammock,

Note: Laundries in posh hotels are very expensive, but the public *lavanderías* charge by the kilo: about US$3–4. You bring your laundry to the laundromat in the morning and it is ready in the evening or the following day.

to boutique hotels which are the equal of any in the developing world. Budget hotels are generally called **hostal** or **residencial**. Expect to pay US$5–20 per person for a cheap hostal, around US$30–70 for a mid-range hotel, and US$70–250 for most of the top-class hotels. Prices vary according to the size and tourist interest of the town, high or low season, and for groups. Sales tax (IGV) at 19% is applied to the room price for Peruvians but foreigners are exempt from paying this. A photocopy of your passport and tourist entry visa is required by the hotel in order to process this, so all hotels require those documents. The hotel feature of abiding interest to budget travellers, most of whom have diarrhoea or are expecting to have diarrhoea, is the toilet. In the cheapest hotels this will be communal and probably occupied when you most need it. You may prefer to go for the middle range to ensure that your room has its own bathroom. Plumbing systems in Peru tend to be rather half-hearted, so in the cheaper places don't try to flush your toilet paper (yes, you may have to supply your own) down the lavatory, but put it in the basket or box in the corner. No, it's not nice, but a clogged toilet is nastier. Cheap hotels are often lit by 40-watt bulbs. If you are really keen, get your own 100-watt bulb to allow you to read at night.

All towns of interest have their backpacker hangouts; we list some of the recommended ones. It is worth deciding beforehand where you will stay and taking a taxi there to avoid being hassled by hotel touts in the airport or bus station of larger towns. On the other hand, finding your own, unlisted, hotel ensures lower prices and fellow guests who are not all foreigners. The cheapest hotels are almost always clustered around bus and train stations. In villages that have no obvious hotel, there is always a *señora* with a room to rent for the night, so just ask around.

Your possessions can be at risk in any hotel. The better places have safe-boxes in your room or at reception (where you should take the precaution of putting them in a sealed envelope, and get a receipt). Don't leave enticing valuables on show in your room – even an honest chambermaid can succumb to temptation. Keep your valuables in a locked case or at the bottom of your backpack in a bag that you can recognise by touch. If something goes missing, do report it to the hotel owner and if this has no effect go to the police.

Make sure you know the hotel rules and eccentricities: checkout times, discounts, electricity or water cuts, hot water availability and whether there is an extra charge for this, and if the price includes taxes (especially in middle- and upper-range hotels), special services, and so on.

Only mid-range or upmarket hotels take credit cards. It's always safest to assume that only local currency is accepted and carry enough – dollars may be accepted if you're stuck, but the proprietor may not know the exchange rate.

CAMPING It is generally perfectly safe to camp well off the beaten track and usually all right in or near smaller villages, although in remote areas you may infringe the rules of rural etiquette if you refuse offers of accommodation and then pitch a tent. In some places there may be a nominal charge for camping. Avoid leaving your campsite unattended and always keep all your valuables inside the tent. Never camp in, or close to, towns or cities; a hotel is much safer.

EATING AND DRINKING

Eating in Peru is enjoyable. For up-market travellers it has developed into a foodie centre, but for those on a budget there are all sorts of tasty snacks sold on street corners and in cafés, and even the cheapest restaurant food is usually good, although starchy. Peru is a meat, fish, potato and rice country and vegetables are rarely served in restaurants catering to locals, although people eat a lot of them at home and markets are full of superb produce. Vegetarianism is becoming increasingly recognised in tourist hot spots, but not off the beaten track. If you don't fancy what is on the menu, most restaurants will serve eggs, potatoes and rice on request.

Part of the fun of being in Peru is experimenting with the local food. Bring your dictionary to the restaurant and don't be embarrassed to wander round looking at other people's choices. Sometimes that's the easiest way to select a meal – simply point to someone else's.

All the cheaper restaurants serve set meals at lunchtime, listed as *menú*, or *almuerzo* (the menu, in the English sense, is *la carta*). Some restaurants offer a fixed meal for each day of the week, the *menu del día*. In a set menu you'll get soup of the day, *sopa del día*, a main dish, *la segunda*, and a dessert, *postre* or/and a cup of herb tea, *mate*. The helpings will be substantial and the price low at around US$2–5. Everywhere in Peru you'll find a Chinese restaurant, a *chifa*. Food here is invariably good and cheap, with vegetarian options.

In the mid- and upper-range hotels and restaurants a meal will cost between US$5 and US$40. Sales tax (IGV) is 18% and service tax is 10%. Always check whether they have been included in the menu price – sometimes they are added at the end. Check your bill carefully, and count your change.

Don't get so carried away with the joys of eating that you consume risky food. Cold buffets served at upmarket hotels can be particularly dangerous because they may have been sitting around for a while breeding a nice variety of bacteria. Be particularly careful to avoid mayonnaise and salad, and cold meat. You'll be safer eating freshly cooked food in the market.

Do-it-yourself meals bought at markets provide a welcome change and the chance to eat fresh vegetables and fruit. It is still better not to risk salad.

In tourist areas restaurants have learned to cater to gringo tastes and provide yummy chocolate cake and pizzas and so on. They also provide menu translations which can leave you more confused than ever. What, for instance, is 'Bifstek with pickpocket sauce' or 'a small locust'?

Tipping is not customary in the cheaper local restaurants, but waiters in mid-range and international restaurants will expect a tip, usually 5 to 10% of the meal value. For more on tipping, see box page 95.

Credit cards are accepted in upmarket restaurants.

LOCAL DISHES The classic Andean dish, guinea pig (cuy), is rarely served in restaurants other than in touristy spots, but you will find it at street stalls during fiestas, since the locals eat it on special occasions. Once a pet-owning gringo sees the little roasted animal lying whole on the plate and grinning, they tend to lose their appetite. It's worth a try though and the spicy sauce and potatoes that usually accompany the cuy are delicious.

CUY

In Cusco Cathedral (and in the cathedral of Ayacucho) there is a 17th-century painting of the Last Supper. The scene is traditional, but the main dish is startlingly different: as befits a meal of importance in Peru, Christ and his disciples are about to dine on guinea pig.

The domestication of the native guinea pig as a source of meat for special occasions would have been noted by the priests and Spanish artists who set out to save the souls of the Inca heathens by using images they could relate to. To this day the animals, known as cuy in Spanish and Quechua, are kept by the Indians of the high Andes.

Cuy takes hours to prepare for the table. After the neck is broken (no blood must be shed, since this is an important ingredient in cooking), the animal is plunged into boiling water to loosen the fur, which is plucked and finally shaved with a razor blade. All organs are carefully preserved, including the intestines, from which tiny sausages, *pepián de cuy*, are made. These contain minced innards and blood.

The method of cooking cuy varies by region. Generally, they are grilled whole over charcoal after the skin has been rubbed with herbs and garlic (an important step, since the skin is the tastiest part). In

The classic coastal dish in Peru is *ceviche*, raw fish or shellfish marinated in lemon juice with onions and chillies. The following are the items most commonly found on the menu:

Starters

Palta rellena	Avocado filled with chicken salad
Palta reina	Avocado filled with mixed salad and mayonnaise
Papa a la huancaina	Cold potatoes with a rich egg-and-cheese sauce
Rocoto relleno	Stuffed green peppers (often very hot)
Tamales or *humitas*	Ground maize steamed in banana leaves, filled with meat or cheese; sometimes they are served sweet, with sugar instead of meat
Sopa criolla	A creamy spiced soup with noodles and a little chopped meat
Chupe de mariscos	A very rich and creamy shellfish soup
Causa	A dish made from yellow potatoes, peppers, hard-boiled eggs and other ingredients

Main dishes
Meat dishes

Churrasco or *lomo*	Fillet or rump steak
Apanado	Breaded meat cutlet

Arequipa fried cuy (*chactado*) is popular: deep oil is used and the cuy covered by a smooth river stone to flatten it during cooking so that it resembles Peking duck. Sometimes *cuy al horno* (baked guinea pig) is offered in the Cusco area, and in other mountain villages it may be casseroled in green (herb) or red (chilli and peanut) sauce.

While gringos fastidiously nibble at the scant meat on slender bones, locals crunch their way happily through head, brains and paws. One bone is carefully preserved, however: the *zorro*, a tiny bone from the middle ear said to resemble a fox. This is used for gambling. Wagers may be placed on the number of zorros collected in a given time, or the bone is placed in a glass of beer and the drinker challenged to swallow it with the beer (surprisingly difficult, because it tends to stick to the bottom of the glass).

Foreigners more used to seeing guinea pigs as cherished pets than culinary ingredients will be relieved to hear that the former role is not completely denied them in the Andes. A Peruvian friend told me his younger brothers and sisters refused to allow their pet cuyes to be dished up to an uncle in honour of his visit. It was three years before the uncle would speak to his family after this insult!

| *Chorrillana* | Meat smothered in fried onions |
| *Adobo* | An Arequipan speciality; chopped, marinated pork in a richly seasoned gravy, served only in the mornings |

CACAO AND CHOCOLATE IN PERU

Alain Schneider (owner of ChocoMuseo)

It is said that cacao originated somewhere in the Amazon between Peru, Ecuador and Brazil and then was brought to Central America where the Mayans turned the cacao seeds into a sacred beverage (the ancestor of our hot chocolate). So this would mean that there are still a lot of wild varieties of cacao tree in Peru, and recently there has been a trend among Peruvian scientists to try to discover them. Examples include the *porcelana* cacao in Piura, the *nacional* cacao in Cajamarca and the *chuncho* cacao in Cusco.

For a long time, Peruvian people only knew chocolate as a drink. In Cusco, for instance, where the weather is quite cold, people often drink hot chocolate which is prepared by melting pure cacao paste into water with some spices and plenty of sugar. The cacao paste is obtained from cacao beans from Quillabamba six hours from Cusco. These are roasted, shelled and ground into a paste. Peruvians visiting Cusco often bring back pure cacao paste as a gift for their family. Chocolate is mainly consumed at Christmas with a slice of panettone.

Over the last three years, Peruvian cacao has become well known on the international stage, with some of the best chocolates being made from it. The country has the largest variety of cacao types (genetically speaking) with six varieties out of the total of ten. Peru is also the second exporter of organic cacao (after the Dominican Republic) and 100% of the cacao produced here is considered as 'fine aroma' cacao.

I now source my cacao from the region of San Martín where there has been an effort to remove the coca plants and plant cacao trees instead. I also buy cacao from Quillabamba (*chuncho*) and from Piura (*porcelana*) in the north of the country. From the cacao we make a cacao paste and then we refine it and use this chocolate for moulding our bars, and preparing our delicious hot chocolates or chocolate truffles. We run two-hour chocolate workshops where we teach people about the process, from the cacao tree to the chocolate bar.

ChocoMuseo, workshops in Lima and Cusco: www.chocomuseo.com

Piqueo	A very spicy stew with meat, onions and potatoes
Sancochado	Meat, vegetables and garlic
Lomo saltado	Chopped meat in a sauce containing onions, tomatoes and potatoes
Picante de ...	Meat or fish with a hot, spicy sauce
Aji de gallina	Chicken (or other meat) in a slightly spicy nutty sauce
Parrillada	Barbecued beef, pork, sausage and viscera
Chicharrones	Chunks of pork fat, deep fried
Chaufa	Chinese-style fried rice
Cabro or *cabrito*	Goat meat
Antichuchos	Baby beef-heart shish kebab
Pollo con papas	The ubiquitous chicken and chips
Pachamanca	Typical in the highlands, this is a delicious mixture of meat and vegetables cooked underground on hot stones

Fish dishes
Corvina	Pacific sea bass
Pejerrey	Freshwater fish
A lo macho	The main fish dish comes with a spicy shellfish sauce
Trucha	Trout

Vegetarians
| *Tortilla verduras* | Vegetable omelette |

Desserts
Mazamorra morada	Pudding made from purple maize and various fruits
Flan	Crème caramel
Picarones	Delicious rings of fried batter served with syrup or honey
Keke or *torte*	Cake

Drinks
| *Pisco* | Grape brandy, very popular in the form of *Pisco sour* with lemon, sugar and egg white |
| *Chicha* | Maize beer. This is an integral part of any celebration or communal work project in rural areas. In Andean villages look out for houses with flowers or coloured plastic tied to a pole above the door: this indicates that the householder sells *chicha*. |

Chicha morada	Unlike *chicha* not alcoholic, but a soft drink made from purple maize.
Cerveza	Lager-type beer, which is very popular. There are several regional brands such as *Cusqueña* and *Arequipeña*.
Vino	Local Peruvian wines, which are worth tasting although very sweet by gringo standards. Tacama and Ocucaje are the best choices. *Tinto* is red wine.
Agua mineral	Mineral water, which is mainly drunk by foreigners so not usually available in rural areas. You will need to specify *con gas* (carbonated) or *sin gas* (non-carbonated).
Mate	Herbal tea, which has become very popular. The best known is *mate de coca*, which is served to tourists on arrival in Cusco or La Paz to ward off symptoms of altitude sickness. Many other herbal teas such as *manzanilla* (camomile), *yerba luisa* (lemon grass), *yerba buena* (mint), and *inojo* (dill) are available. *Mate* is usually served after lunch.
Jugo	Fruit juice. Markets always have a fresh juice stand. Yummy!
Jugo con leche	Fruit juice with milk. A meal in itself.

HANDICRAFTS

Peru has a wide variety of beautiful handicrafts and the artisans are proud of their work and its origin in their *tierra* (hometown): handwoven alpaca products from Huancavelica and Puno, ceramics from Cajamarca, Ayacucho and Cusco, carved gourds, silverware and weavings from Huancayo, tapestries from Ayacucho, wooden articles from Piura, and so on.

Lima is the main outlet for the sale and export of handicrafts, and it's also the refuge for many artisans of the sierra escaping poverty. So the range and quality is likely to be better in Lima than in the place of origin.

The biggest and best craft market in Lima is situated along Avenida La Marina (from the 9th until the 12th block) in the suburb of Pueblo Libre. Spend some time looking around and examining the items on display, and feel free to bargain. For top-quality goods it is better to go to a shop that only buys the best, which usually means somewhere in Miraflores or San Isidro. Of course you will pay more, but it will be money well spent. If Lima has the selection and quality, the tourist centres such as Cusco, Puno and Huancayo have the fun. Shopping for handmade items is one of the ways that travellers can make a positive contribution to the local economy and wellbeing of the people and their culture. It encourages the continuation of traditional crafts and the development of new ones, and it helps prevent the drift to the cities. For this reason try to rethink the cliché that it is somehow shameful for a traveller to pay a little too much for an article. If it's not too much for you it certainly won't be too much for the vendor!

PHOTOGRAPHY

CAMERA AND LENSES You have to make a considered decision here: do you expect to take professional-quality photos on your trip or do you just want to have some memories afterwards? Serious photographers need to take more care over the safety of their equipment, give themselves time during the hikes for photography, and even organise a pack animal to carry the camera equipment. Others will be happy with a small, automatic camera, preferably with a built-in zoom. The comfort of carrying less weight and the security of looking less like a rich tourist are ample compensation for the poorer-quality photos at the end.

When travelling, every spare bit of space you can make in your luggage can really help. Cameras have changed a lot since the digital revolution. You can get some pretty good results from some very compact systems like the Micro-Four-Thirds (MFT) platform offered by Olympus, Sony and Panasonic. Light and durable, MFT systems give results close to those achievable by an APS-C sensor system from Canon or Nikon, but are much more compact and easy to travel with. But maybe you don't need to stretch to a new camera system. Most modern mobile phones like the Android phones and those produced by Apple give excellent results, and may be just what you're looking for, and they are more discreet than larger cameras, too. If you are more seriously minded though, and wish to take a decent SLR system with you on your travels, the adage less-is-more stands. If you are using a full-frame system then a standard 24–70mm zoom lens would be used a great deal, while if you opt for an APS-C camera system, a zoom lens of 17–55mm would be a good option to start with.

CAMERA ETIQUETTE Peru is wonderfully photogenic, and few visitors can resist capturing as much as possible on camera. However, you must bear in mind that, for people living in the remote mountain areas, this can be a highly intrusive practice. The rural people are reserved but very courteous and their initial contact with strangers has a ritualised pattern. By photographing them without establishing some sort of human contact you are being rude and insensitive. Once you have established contact you should ask permission to take a photo. If you are refused, or the person is uneasy, put your camera away. For more on village etiquette, see pages 91–3.

It is a different matter for people living in the popular tourist areas. Here they can make a nice living posing for photos. This is a business and should be respected as such: if you don't want to pay, don't take a photo. Try to find out the proper price beforehand – there is something obscene in paying a child posing with a llama the same fee that her father may earn working all day in the fields. If money is not demanded, don't offer it. Many people love to have their photos taken, particularly those who do not look 'ethnic'. You can get some delightful portraits of these grinning kids. These days they are camera savvy and love to see the results on your camera. If you are able to get their address and send them a print, that present will be treasured forever. But this is only possible in villages or towns; there are no postmen in rural communities.

Never take photos of any military objects. If in doubt, ask someone in authority.

MEDIA AND COMMUNICATIONS

TELEPHONES The **country code** for Peru is 51.

Peru's telephone company is called Telefónica and operates all over the country, even in small villages. Almost all public telephones on the streets accept either coins or phonecards, which you can buy from vendors on the street or from Telefónica offices. Many internet cabins offer cheap long-distance calls. You can also buy phonecards such as '147' either from newsstands on the street or from local grocery shops which can be used from public phone booths to phone home. You simply scratch off the code on the back, mark the number depending on the card, dial the scratch code when asked, then dial the phone number you want to reach.

Useful numbers
Directory assistance 108
Emergency (police) 105
Operator 100

MOBILE PHONES Mobile (cell) phone numbers generally start with a 9. Movistar/Telefónica and Claro are the two main providers of mobile phone services. Check which network is most used in the area you are heading to, then buy yourself a SIM card. Local calls are not expensive if it is the same network, but are pricey if not; lots of locals have two phones, one on each network.

INTERNET Internet services are available in nearly all towns and there are literally dozens of internet offices in Lima, Cusco and Huaraz. Expect to pay around US$1 per hour. Wi-Fi is widely available.

POST

Receiving These days most visitors will use the internet, but you may still want mail to be sent to you at the post office. Letters should be addressed to you (last name in capitals) at *Lista de Correo* or *Poste Restante*, followed by the town. Letters are held for up to two or three months, and a small collection fee is charged. Never risk having any money or valuables sent by mail unless they are registered.

Letters sent from the USA or Europe to Peru can take anywhere from eight days to a couple of months to arrive and sometimes not at all.

Tell your nearest and dearest not to send you a parcel. Getting it through customs is an unbelievable hassle (at least a day is needed) and extortionate taxes are charged.

! Note: In a Peruvian address, *Casilla* or *Apartado Postal* are not street names, they are the equivalent of 'PO Box'.

For this reason you will be doing no great service to your Peruvian friends if you send them a parcelled gift once you get home.

Sending Surprisingly, most letters sent from Peru do reach their destination, taking between five days and three weeks. Be warned, postage is very expensive. Some post offices (eg: Huancayo) are very efficient, providing you with a box and a tracking system. Others are less co-operative, so allow plenty of time for all the form filling. Some shops will mail purchases for you. If you are desperate to get a parcel home you could use a courier such as UPS or DHL.

Air freight This is a good alternative to the post office or couriers, particularly if you have more than 30kg of stuff to send home, but involves a day at the airport. It's reliable and they will deliver to your home address (though it's cheaper to have it picked up at the airport). Receiving an air freight parcel is a different matter – it involves as much hassle, time and bureaucracy as receiving a mailed parcel. If this is unavoidable, for instance for a large expedition, set aside several days and expect to hire a 'fixer' at the airport.

NEWSPAPERS AND MAGAZINES

The Peruvian Times www.peruviantimes.com. Well worth reading as it provides lots of insider information on what's going on in Peru.

Peru Guide A tourist guide, available from many hotels & tourist offices (mostly in Lima). Very useful for listings of what's happening, restaurants, etc.

Caretas www.caretas.com.pe. The best

Spanish-language current affairs magazine (weekly).

Rumbos www.rumbosperu.com. An excellent monthly online geographical magazine with good photos.

El Comercio www.elcomercioperu.com.pe. One of 2 main daily papers; see also below.

La Republica www.larepublica.com.pe. Another main daily paper worth reading.

BUSINESS

Siesta is rigidly observed in some areas of Peru throughout the year, except in Lima. You might as well join them since everything is closed from 13.00 until 16.00 (although some tourist shops remain open). Outside Lima, business and bank hours run from 10.00 to 13.00 and 16.00 until 19.00. Shops are open from 09.30 to 13.00 and 16.00 until 20.00.

Lima has the normal business hours of 09.00 to 17.00, but places are closed for one hour at lunchtime. Government-run offices are mostly only open in the mornings. Banks in Lima are usually open from 09.30 to 18.00 and on Saturday morning.

VOLUNTEERING AND GIVING SOMETHING BACK

Many travellers to Peru would like to repay their enjoyment of the country by getting more involved. There are many locally run organisations in Peru who welcome volunteers as well as donations. Some of the language schools in Peru also offer volunteer opportunities (page 12).

CHARITIES IN LIMA

Centro Ann Sullivan Calle Petronila Alvarez 180, Urb Pando 5a Etapa, San Miguel, Lima 32; ☎ 01 5147103; www. annsullivanperu.org An educational charity for children with Down's Syndrome, autism & other learning difficulties.

Posadita del Buen Pastor Jr Tacna No 340 – Magdalena del Mar; ☎ 01 2634481; e posaditabp@gmail.com; www.pamsweb. org/lima.html. A residential home for children & mothers with AIDS, supported by the Peruvian American Medical Society. They welcome medical supplies, donations & volunteer workers.

CHARITIES IN THE CUSCO AREA

Amantani ☎ +44 (0)1865 201477; e chris@amantani.org.uk, fred@amantani. org.uk; www.amantani.org.uk. Amantani helps to bridge the gap between home & school for children living in Ccorca, a handful of Quechua communities nestled high in the Andes of southern Peru. Amantani provide boarding houses & a relevant education,

which means that the children don't lose touch with their families & communities. Volunteers are always needed in the boarding houses.

CAITH – Centro Yanapanakusun Urb Ucchullo Alto, Pasaje Sto Toribio N-4 (just off Avda Argentina), Cusco; ☎ 084 233595; e reservascaith@gmail.com; www.caith. org. This project has been set up to help homeless or abused girls in the Cusco area. The girls are given a home, health care, education & are taught the skills necessary to help them find work. It also includes a travel agency for sustainable tourism & tourist accommodation in Cusco – with plans to extend to Yucay & Puno. They welcome volunteers.

Cusichaca Trust e aacusichaca@terra. com.pe; www.cusichaca.org. Founded by archaeologist Dr Ann Kendall in 1968, this organisation has been active in restoring Inca canals & pre-Hispanic agricultural terraces to improve the agricultural practices of the descendants of the Incas, & other past civilisations such as the

VOLUNTEERING: QUESTIONS TO ASK

Emma Redfoot (research student)

In order to make sure that the organisation is making a positive contribution as well as providing the type of volunteer experience that will meet your personal preferences and abilities, it is important that you question what you need and what you want to support.

QUESTIONS YOU NEED TO ASK YOURSELF AS A VOLUNTEER:

How comfortable to you want to be? For example, are you willing to share a room? Live without heat or air conditioning? Take a cold shower?

Do you prefer to work in a rural or urban setting?

How much of your time can you commit to work as opposed to wanting to explore the area?

How much management and structure do you need in order to complete your project? Do you prefer to work in groups with other volunteers or by yourself?

Are there specific activities you'd like to take responsibility for?

QUESTIONS YOU NEED TO ASK THE VOLUNTEER CO-ORDINATOR OR THE PROJECT FOUNDER:

Do they get results consistent with their objectives?

Are they willing to be transparent about how the money is distributed? (Be especially aware of this if you are paying to participate in the programme.)

Has the organisation consulted the local community to decide what services they will provide?

Does the project have plans for growth? Would you support those plans?

Does the project allow volunteers to provide feedback? Does the project have adequate resources to support the volunteer's plan for the project?

3

Chankas & Wari living in the Cusichaca & Patacancha valleys in the Cusco region, & the Chicha Soras & Sondondo valleys in the Apurímac & Ayacucho regions. Its offshoot NGO, the Asociación Andina Cusichaca, continues to implement projects relating to traditional water management & climate change in the southern highlands.

The importance of terracing maintenance for food production is critical. Money donations to continue this work will always be needed.
Huchuy Yachaq Association ☏ +44 (0)131 467 7086 ; e info@huchuyyachaq. org, huchuy_yachaq@yahoo.es; www. huchuyachaq.org. This project has been set

up by a volunteer social worker & teachers to provide social & educational support to the children & families of the neighbourhood of Los Hermanos Ayer, on the outskirts of Cusco. There are high poverty levels & little in the way of guaranteed income. You can help by volunteering or making donations of equipment.

Living Heart www.livingheartperu.org. A registered Peruvian charity & official UK charity supporting remote, impoverished highland communities above the Sacred Valley in Peru.

Manos Unidos Urb San Luis D-5, Distrito de San Sebastian; m 984455888; e manosunidasintl@gmail.com; www.manosunidasperu.net. The 1st & only private/not-for-profit school for Special Education in Cusco founded in 2008 as the Centro de Educacion Basica Especial Particular.

CHARITIES IN OTHER AREAS

Asociacion Benefica Prisma Calle Carlos Gonzales 251 Urb Maranga, Lima 32; \ 01 6165500; e prisma@prisma.org.pe; www.prisma.org.pe. Work in health & nutrition nationwide.

CARE Peru Avda General Santa Cruz No 659, Jesús María \ 01 4171100; e postmaster@care.org.pe; www.care.org.

pe. Run assorted projects in various areas of Peru including Huaraz & Ayacucho.

Dental Project Peru www.dentalprojectperu.org. Emergency dental care & education to the most impoverished & rural areas of Peru. Opportunities for volunteers & donations.

Remar Prolg La Mar No 799, La Victoria, Lima; \ 01 3247666; e pan@remar.org; www.remar.org. A Spanish organisation that run homes & day care centres for street children in Lima, Tacna, Arequipa, & Trujillo. Visits should be arranged through their Lima office.

The Mountain Institute Lima office: Instituto de Montaña, Avda República de Panamá 6539, Surco, Lima 33; \ 01 7192570; Huaraz office: Instituto de Montaña, Pasaje Ricardo Palma, No 100, Pedregal Alto; e southamerica@mountain.org (Huaraz), summit@mountain.org (USA); www.mountain.org/andes. An America-based charity working in the Appalachians & Himalayas as well as Peru, aiming to conserve the delicate ecology of the mountain areas around Huaraz. They work with local communities on a variety of projects to promote : sustainable development. There are volunteer opportunities for biologists, & research assistants are sometimes needed.

FINALLY ... If you are travelling to Peru with any space in your luggage, check out www.packforapurpose.org or www.stuffyourrucksack.com. Both organisations put you in touch with schools, children's homes or other organisations that are in desperate need of easy-to-pack items that you can deliver. A simple and excellent way of making a contribution before you start trekking.

> **!** **Updates website:** For the latest updates go to www.bradtupdates.com/perutrekking. You can also post your feedback here – corrections, changes or even new hikes. Your information will be put on our website for the benefit of other travellers.

4

Backpacking and Trekking: Deciding What's Best for You

WHERE TO GO: AN OVERVIEW

Although some readers will be familiar with South America and can plan their itinerary from an informed position, the majority will have no idea what to expect and where to go. This summary, along with the photo section, will help you select areas that suit individual interests and physical capabilities.

THE CORDILLERAS BLANCA AND HUAYHUASH (pages 151–210) This region in the north has attracted mountain climbers for over a hundred years, and organised trekking since the late 1970s – it was one of the first places in South America to compete with the popular Himalayan routes. The appeal is the magnificent scenery with tightly clustered *nevados* or snowpeaks, many over 6,000m, numerous turquoise-blue glacial lakes and a large choice of trails. Distances to the trailheads from the main town of Huaraz are not great, and the variety of lowland scenery is an added bonus, with green, flower-filled valleys grazed by cattle providing contrast to the high, cold passes. There are always stunning close-up views of the snowpeaks.

This area, however, is less traditional than the southern Inca heartland of Cusco. The local people are *mestizo* (mixed blood) rather than pure Indian so you do not see the colourful costumes and hats of the Cusco area, nor do you see many llamas and alpacas, nor much in the way of Inca remains, though there are some.

The cordilleras Blanca and Huayhuash, therefore, are primarily for lovers of mountain scenery. The advantage of the Blanca is that it can be enjoyed by walkers of any age or level of ability (page 83); several roads lead over the cordillera providing access to vehicles. At present the area is equally suitable for backpacking or organised trekking. Do note, however, that there is a rumour that it may become mandatory to hire a guide within Huascarán National Park. The Cordillera Huayhuash, by contrast, is one of the most remote and challenging ranges in this book, and suitable only for fit, experienced hikers.

THE CORDILLERAS VILCABAMBA AND VILCANOTA The two mountain ranges near Cusco provide, between them, a bit of everything: Inca ruins, Inca roads, colourful local people tending llamas and alpacas, thermal springs, snowpeaks and subtropical jungle – and plenty of other hikers.

The Cordillera Vilcabamba (pages 283–320) The world-famous **Inca Trail** runs through this range, but there are several other choices, many of which descend into densely forested valleys and along river gorges to ruins almost as impressive as Machu Picchu – and without the crowds, for example Choquequirao. Because the countryside is less open, there are not many opportunities to get off the beaten track and find your own route. This area is unsuitable for llamas and alpacas, so once you are hiking you are unlikely to see these animals. The chief attraction is the

---

CAPAQ ÑAN

The Incas built a **road system** that networked their empire, allowing their administrators access to their entire realm (pages 6–8). Many of these beautifully constructed roads remain, some buried in the jungle, some cleared and restored (such as the famous Inca Trail) and some which have survived, untouched except by the feet of local campesinos, for hundreds of years.

Capaq Ñan (also spelt Qhapac Ñan) is the Quechua name for Inca road. It can be roughly translated as **'road of our ancestors'** and usually refers to the main Inca highway which ran down the spine of the Andes (though often, erroneously, attributed to the short stretch to Machu Picchu). It is also the name of an international project by Ecuador, Peru, Bolivia and Chile to rebuild the two primary Inca roads through the former empire, along with shorter routes leading to important Inca ruins. It is hoped that this project will eventually become part of UNESCO's World Heritage List, but this is a long way off.

Trekkers, however, have no reason to wait. Several parts of Capaq Ñan are described in this book: Castillo via Huánuco Viejo to Yanahuanca (pages 224–30), the Salkantay Trek (pages 298–306), Cusco or Sacsayhuamán to Lamay via Huchuy Qosqo (pages 304–6), Patabamba to Huchuy Qosqo and Lamay (pages 265–6) and Cachora to Huancacalle via Choquequirao (page 313). You don't have to hike the Inca Trail to see this remarkable Inca engineering.

> ## ℹ THE INCA TRAIL
>
> Everyone has heard of the Inca Trail to Machu Picchu and it will feature in many people's trekking plans. If you are thinking of doing this trek you need to be aware that it cannot be done independently but must be booked with a licensed tour operator in Cusco (or organised through an operator in your own country – see listing on pages 81–2). Numbers on the trail are limited and in the dry season – May to September – it is booked up months in advance. So plan early. You will have a better chance of getting a place in the off-season, but bear in mind that the trail is closed in February.

greenness of the scenery contrasting with the rugged snowpeaks, and the marvellous, and often quite remote, Inca remains that form the focus for many of the routes.

The Cordillera Vilcanota (pages 320–4) This is an austere, challenging area of high, cold altiplano with low rainfall, sparse vegetation and mountain passes that test the fittest walker. Here the lives of the Quechua people can have changed little since the days of the Incas as they scratch a living from land that no-one else wants. Brightly coloured, hand-woven garments are worn by the women and some of the men, and in each community the women sport a different-style hat. The people can be remote and seemingly unfriendly – the consequence of isolation. The grass is nibbled to its roots by large herds of llamas and alpacas. The Vilcanota is the 'real' Peru, and worth the effort for the stunning mountain views. You cannot drive to these views, as in the Cordillera Blanca and, to a lesser extent, the Vilcabamba. You must walk there. This is one of the best areas for finding your own route.

OTHER MOUNTAINOUS AREAS IN PERU The cordilleras mentioned above are the best known and the most popular for trekking and climbing, but that is not to say there aren't other mountainous areas good for trekking. The northern highlands, in particular the areas around **Chachapoyas** and **Cajamarca** (pages 129–48), have many trekking routes, and a rich pre-Inca and Inca history to be rediscovered. The newly opened-up routes to some of the world's highest waterfalls (pages 146–8) are particularly exciting thanks to the wealth of subtropical wildlife on view and the refreshing lack of other tourists. The **Cordillera Central** (pages 217–30), easily accessible from Huancayo, is an extensive glaciated range of mountains that is relatively unexplored so perfect for backpacking, rather than organised trekking.

Further north there is the longest accessible stretch of Capaq Ñan, 160km of Inca road (pages 224–30). Then there are the snow-capped **volcanoes** of southern Peru around Arequipa (pages 350–4) and the **Colca Canyon** (pages 354–61), which offer beautiful routes through remote landscapes, relatively free of other trekkers and red tape, and with a drier climate than the cordilleras so suitable for off-season hiking when prices are often lower.

BACKPACKING OR TREKKING?

Broadly speaking, trekking differs from backpacking in that your gear is carried by pack animals (or, in the case of the Inca Trail, porters) and that a ground operator is involved in supplying tents, food, transport, etc. In effect, a trek is a package tour that leaves you free to enjoy the mountains without worrying about any of the logistics.

Trekking has many advantages over backpacking, not least that all the hassle and anxiety of travel in rural Peru is taken out of your hands. For most trekkers there is no choice: for those with only three weeks' holiday a year, or who are disinclined to heave a 20kg pack around, or to cope with the uncertainties of arranging their own porters or pack animals, the only way to set foot in the Andes is with an organised group. Furthermore, it is only with pack animals that really long distances can be covered: most backpackers find a week's supply of food is all they can carry. Finally, with transport laid on, an organised trek can reach areas that are inaccessible to backpackers using public transport. Besides, it's often more fun (if you are with a compatible group) than doing it on your own.

In spite of this, the ultimate hiking experience for many people will be with one or two chosen companions, and all the effort and hassle of **backpacking**. For this is what exploring the wilderness is all about. Whatever the brochures say, with an organised group you are not exploring; on your own, even with this guidebook, you are. You are open to serendipitous events, can interact with the local people, stop when you are tired, go as far as you want, and choose the route that most appeals to you. And it will cost much less.

A **compromise** between trekking and backpacking may be to use the services of the Lima-based Trekking and Backpacking Club (page 82).

There are some routes, notably the Inca Trail, which you can only do as an organised package; independent walking is forbidden. The Cordillera Blanca may be heading that way as well.

ORGANISED TREKKING: CHOOSING THE RIGHT COMPANY

Trekking companies advertise in all the usual places: travel sections of daily or Sunday newspapers, travel magazines, walking and climbing magazines – and of course on the internet. Care must be taken when selecting a tour operator. Read between the lines of the brochure to be sure that you can cope physically and mentally with the trek. Check the altitude gain each day, and find out the height of the highest passes and the number of rest days. Do not be beguiled by talk of 'verdant rainforests and glistening peaks'; the former will be hot and wet, the latter cold and exhausting. You can only enjoy the beauty if you can cope with the terrain. Check whether there are horses that can be ridden in an emergency. A good tour operator will happily put you in touch with someone who has done the trip, so you can get an unbiased account of what it's like. Remember that costs usually reflect the quality of the tour operator and the comforts lavished on you, so, unless you are very tough and adventurous, be wary of just going for the cheapest.

If you want to join a trekking group then you will need to select a tour operator who does fixed-departure treks. The advantage of arranging a tailor-made trek through a company based in your home country is that they will be covered by ABTA which protects your rights should something go wrong, and will sell you the complete package including flights.

If you are planning to put together your own group, however, and are not worried about the risks inherent in non-ABTA companies (and want to bring more money to the local community) you can just as easily organise the trek through a tour operator based in the various trekking centres. These are listed in the relevant chapters.

As before, remember that the cheapest operators may be cutting corners or paying their support teams less than the minimum wage. The best Peruvian companies have joined up to form the Asociación Peruana de Turismo de Aventura y Ecoturismo (APTAE) which, theoretically at least, promotes protection of the environment and works towards improving working conditions for its staff.

Always make sure you have a written agreement for the services you are expecting and a receipt.

TOUR OPERATORS SPECIALISING IN TREKKING
More general tour operators are listed in *Chapter 3*, page 50; the following companies specialise in trekking:

UK-based
Andean Trails e info@andeantrails. co.uk; www.andeantrails.co.uk. Specialise in trekking. See advert, colour page 31.
Andes e john@andes.org.uk; www.andes. org.uk. Climbing & skiing expeditions in the Andes.

Exodus Travels e sales@exodus.co.uk; www.exodus.co.uk. Small group tours. Inca Trail, cordilleras Blanca & Huayhuash.
Explore! e info@exploreworldwide. com; www.explore.co.uk. Small group tours & treks in Peru. See advert, colour page 29.

High Places   e treks@highplaces.co.uk;
www.highplaces.co.uk. See advert, colour
page 27.
Journey Latin America   e adventure@
journeylatinamerica.co.uk; www.
journeylatinamerica.co.uk. Flights, culture,
adventure, small group & tailor-made tours.
Western & Oriental   e enquiries@
westernoriental.com; www.wandotravel.
com. Flights & tailor-made tours to Latin
America.
Steppes Latin America   e info@
steppeslatinamerica.co.uk; www.
steppeslatinamerica.co.uk. All aspects of
travel in Peru.

US-based
Wilderness Travel   e info@
wildernesstravel.com; www.wildernesstravel.
com. They introduced me (Hilary) to
organised trekking (indeed, to tour leading),
for which I shall be forever grateful. See
advert, colour page 21.

Peruvian
Trekking and Backpacking Club   Jr Huascar
1152, Jesus Maria; www.angelfire.com/mi2/
tebac. Provides a compromise between fully
organised trekking & doing it yourself. Using
local transport & backpacker hotels, they will
organise the trek for you & provide a guide, but
at the lowest possible cost.

TREKKING: THE EXPERIENCE

The pampering normally starts shortly after you sign up, with pre-departure information giving you a good idea of what your particular company provides. Most likely they will deal with your flights, send you an equipment and reading list, and generally prepare you for what is in store.

In Peru you will be met by your trip leader (or he/she may travel out with you) or local guide and will not have to think for yourself until you pass through passport control on your way out of the country! It's a wonderful chance for high-powered people to regress into complete dependency, and the happiest trekkers are often those who do just that.

All well-organised treks will have a built-in period of acclimatisation. In Peru, this is usually a few days' sightseeing in the Cusco area, or perhaps some gentle hiking around Huaraz. You will probably be agreeably surprised at how comfortable and well fed you are during this period. When you arrive at the trailhead you will be surprised by how many pack animals are needed – an average of one donkey per person. And you may likewise be surprised by the number of people taking care of your needs. A typical camp crew is led by a local guide and organiser. It is usually he who hires the arrieros (muleteers) or porters, organises the food, supplies the tents, decides where each night will be spent (pasture for the animals being the deciding factor) and deals with any crisis.

If you have a tour leader as well, it is his/her role to keep you happy, healthy and well informed. There may be a trip doctor who takes care of the healthy part, although his/her job is almost always limited to treating colds and diarrhoea (in the score or so treks I (Hilary) led in the 1980s and 90s, there were no cases of serious illness or injury; the same with Kathy's more recent experience). All treks provide an impressive medical kit. Subordinate to the guide are the cook (plus helper) and the arrieros or porters. The cook generally works exclusively for that particular operator, whilst the arrieros are contracted locally, near the trailhead.

A typical day begins at dawn (about 06.00) with a wake-up call, although those sleeping near the camp crew (something you learn not to do) will have been woken long before by sounds of chattering and laughter as breakfast is prepared (the cook gets up at about 04.30 to start this chore). The concept of 'I'm not a morning person' seems to be exclusively Western: all Peruvians are morning people! Most operators wake the sleeping trekker gently with hot water and a cup of tea.

With outside temperatures below freezing it's a question of putting on even more clothes, packing your bag ready for the arrieros and staggering out to the tea tent. This is one of the joys of trekking. It's big enough to stand and walk around in, and with 15 tightly packed bodies can become quite cosy. Breakfast is a substantial meal. You will usually get porridge, eggs and bread, and sometimes even pancakes. The quality of food on a trek often comes as an unexpected pleasure.

While you are eating breakfast, the arrieros are rounding up the animals and starting to dismantle the tents. This is a long procedure, and

GERIATREKKING

Many years ago, when I (Hilary) decided to introduce my 77-year-old parents to the Andes I chose the Cordillera Blanca. For a couple who had been avid walkers all their lives but now looked for an adequate level of comfort and only a few miles of walking per day, this was an excellent choice. Huaraz has some good hotels and enough reliable tour operators to ensure that a driver and sturdy vehicle could be hired. Then it was just a question of selecting the most scenic of the new roads leading into the Cordillera.

Each day our driver took us high into the mountains, then drove back down the road to wait for us at a pre-selected place. We would walk downhill for a couple of miles, eat our picnic in meadows full of wild flowers and surrounded by the mighty peaks of the Cordillera Blanca, then continue walking down to the car. Thus were we able to see some of the finest scenery described in Chapter 8.

The same tactics would work fine these days. In fact, with more roads being built into the mountains, it is if anything easier. No-one needs to be deprived of a mountain experience through age or mild physical impairment.

you will get a head start, leaving camp at about 08.00 for the day's walk. In your daypack you will carry your picnic lunch, camera, sweater, raingear (however bright the day looks) and any other goodies you need. Your main luggage will not be accessible during the day.

Lunches tend to be rather dreary – there's not much that can be done with week-old bread – and most trekkers bring their own trail snacks. The group will possibly spread out on the trail but assemble at lunchtime, at a pre-arranged spot. The day ends around 15.30 when the first walkers march into camp. There is a distinct advantage in not walking too fast. If you arrive before the pack animals and camp crew, you will have a chilly wait. If you struggle in at dusk, at least someone will have put up your tent and tea will be almost ready. And tea is the most welcome 'meal'

---

i TREKKING NUTRITION · *Dr Chris Fenn*

Fluid is easily lost at high altitude via your lungs and as a result of sweating. Breathing cold, dry mountain air can result in a loss of two litres of water each day at moderate altitudes. You need to make a conscious effort to replace this fluid loss. Thirst is not a good indication of your need to drink – it's too late by then; dehydration has already set in. Aim to drink at least three litres of water a day, more if you sweat a lot. Hot drinks made from boiled water are the safest way of drinking fluid. If you prefer plain water, make sure that you filter and sterilise it thoroughly.

THE NEED FOR SALT It is logical to think that you need to take extra salt to replace that lost in sweat. However, taking salt without adequate water can be dangerous. Sweat is a very dilute solution of salts and proportionally more water is lost from the body, causing the concentration of salts in the body to rise. Taking extra salt without adequate water will disrupt the salt and water balance in the body even more. Salt tablets are then not useful, but if you find you develop an increased taste for salt, you could be a little depleted. Remedy it by adding extra salt to your food.

TREK FOOD During strenuous exercise the body uses carbohydrates as the main fuel to provide energy. Several research studies have shown that a diet based on carbohydrates can also help reduce the symptoms of acute mountain sickness. At high altitudes the body is more able to metabolise carbohydrate foods than fatty foods, and generally speaking you will find that carbohydrates are more appealing at altitude than fatty food. All carbohydrate foods will help keep your energy levels high, but for energy and health it is best to eat more of the starchy

of the day; a chance to take your boots off and ease your aching limbs, and warm your hands round a mug of hot liquid while discussing your experiences. Supper comes at around 18.30 to 19.00. Meanwhile there is desultory or lively conversation, cards, Scrabble, jokes, boozing, reading, complaining … depending on the disposition of the group. The evening meal is usually ample: three courses, often with fresh meat (chickens ride on donkeys, along with the luggage, and sometimes sheep join the trek – for a while), although vegetarians are also catered for. Most people are in their sleeping bags by 20.00.

THE PRACTICAL SIDE Most trek operators provide **horses** that can be ridden in emergencies (other than on the Inca Trail where no animals

carbohydrate foods. This is because the starchy ones also provide valuable nutrients such as vitamins, minerals, fibre and proteins. So aim to eat at least half of your daily calories in the form of carbohydrates. Sugary foods should not form a regular part of your eating pattern as too much sugar leads to a rapid rise and subsequent rapid fall in blood sugar. Foods with natural sugars are a much more healthy option than chocolate, biscuits and cakes.

* Food containing starchy carbohydrates: Bread, pasta, rice, noodles, potatoes, sweetcorn, peas, beans, lentils, cereals, oats.
* Sugary food containing simple carbohydrates: Sugar, jams, biscuits, cakes, tinned fruit.
* Food with natural sugar: Fresh fruit, dried fruit, honey.

SNACK FOOD FOR THE TREK Whether you enjoy the trekking food or not, it is a good idea to take an extra supply of your favourite snacks. These should be foods that supply a lot of carbohydrates for energy. Regular nibbling on carbohydrate snacks will help to prevent mental and physical fatigue during strenuous trekking days.

Dried fruits such as ready-to-eat apricots, prunes, figs, raisins, etc are widely sold in Peru; muesli bars can be found locally or brought from home; energy bars, although nutritious, may not be to your taste, so try them at home before buying; liquorice is a good source of iron, which helps in the making of red blood cells during acclimatisation; marzipan keeps well and is a good source of energy; chocolate bars contain a lot of fat, and some carbohydrate; powdered drinks are good to disguise the taste of water purifiers, and isotonic drinks and oral rehydration solutions help the body absorb water.

are allowed), and these are often in use for ill or tired trekkers. There is generally a rest day built into the itinerary which can be used as a sick day. Professional evacuation by helicopter in Peru is very rarely possible. The most popular trails now have permanent toilets, but on less-used areas outfitters will supply **toilet tents**, which allow pit latrines to be dug, thus dealing with one of the major environmental problems caused by trekkers. These days a bowl of hot water is usually supplied in the morning for **washing**. On some trails there are welcoming dips in a river or hot springs which allow trekkers to have a more thorough wash when the sun is hot.

BACKPACKING: THE EXPERIENCE

Backpackers from North America, where areas of wilderness are set aside for recreation, are often surprised at the lack of solitude in the Andes. They tend to forget that the indigenous people cultivate fields and tend their animals in remote areas and at extraordinarily high altitudes, and some live just below the snowline. The trails here are footpaths, made and maintained by the campesinos who use them, and there is a constant traffic of people and their pack animals moving along them. Only in very remote areas will you be alone in the mountains.

The reception you receive in small villages depends a lot on how popular the trail is with gringos and of course your own demeanour. Mostly the locals will be friendly and curious, and your chance to observe their way of life and make temporary friends without being obtrusive is one of the highlights of walking in the Andes.

THE PRACTICAL SIDE Where to **camp** is governed by water supplies. The most idyllic camping places are near lakes or at the upper end of a *quebrada* (ravine, or narrow valley) where the water is unpolluted and

 BITING INSECTS

Although not much of a problem at higher altitudes (above 4,500m), in the low valleys small biting midges or blackflies can be a real pest (they are particularly bad around Machu Picchu and other parts of the Cordillera Vilcabamba). They tend to be near streams, damp green meadows and around cattle. Keep your tent closed and always carry insect repellent. At least they are not mosquitoes so are unlikely to carry diseases, but the bites itch like crazy. There are also horseflies (sometimes called deerflies), which bite painfully. Some solace comes with the fact that they are slow and easily killed.

the views exceptional. Often, however, you will need to set up camp near a village or small community, since houses are also built near available water (see *Village etiquette* on page 91 for advice on appropriate behaviour). The route descriptions in this book generally indicate water supplies, but towards the end of the dry season some may dry up so it is wise always to carry water. Always treat the water you use, whether with iodine, filter, tablets or boiling – this is, unfortunately, essential.

Even in remote areas try not to leave your campsite unattended, nor possessions outside your tent. Theft is common near villages on popular trails. If you can lock your tent it will help protect your belongings from being pilfered.

All the valleys are used as **grazing land**, mostly for cattle and horses. You will find them as high as 4,500m. The **cattle**, even virile-looking bulls, are almost never aggressive and usually flee as people approach. Be wary, however, of approaching cows with newborn calves.

If you encounter cattle being driven along a trail, stand well back, preferably on the down side of the track so if the animals spook they will run uphill (slowly), not down. However, if you meet pack animals stand on the upside of the trail to avoid being knocked over the edge by the projecting load.

It's a great treat for hikers to encounter a herd of ear-tasselled and laden **llamas** coming towards them on the trail. Everyone reaches for a camera and waits for the animals to get within photographic range. And the llamas stop dead or scatter. For the sake of their campesino herder move well off the trail so the herd can pass uninterrupted on their way.

Most families in the Andes have at least one **dog** for guarding the property or livestock. See page 112 for advice on dealing with vicious dogs.

FINDING YOUR OWN ROUTE This is the most exciting sort of trekking, and one which I hope all independent backpackers with sufficient time will adopt. Apart from the thrill of stepping into the unknown with only your map, compass, GPS and passing campesinos to guide you, finding your own trails will help prevent over-use of the popular ones – and be cheaper as entry fees and red tape increase. There are thousands upon thousands of footpaths in the Andes, well used and passing through beautiful scenery, and only a very few of them have been trodden by gringos.

As well as the anticipation generated by not knowing what is over the next hill, you have the wonderful bonus of never being lost, because you never know where you are anyway.

The methods George and I used to find the trails described in our first books published in the 1970s can easily be adopted by other fit and adventurous people. First we selected an area known for its natural beauty, or perhaps somewhere recommended by the local people and with a population large enough to maintain trails between the villages.

BROTHER CAN YOU SPARE SOME RICE?   *George Bradt (1977)*

I went to Cajamarca for a vacation, Hilary went to do some hiking. I slumped around eating and sleeping while Hilary scurried about organising a trek. After two days of frantic activity, Hilary broke the news: 'George, you won't believe the hike I've plotted out for us. Out of bed and let's go.'

'Isn't it too late to start walking this afternoon?' I suggested hopefully.

'Isn't it too late still to be in bed?' she countered.

'OK. Where are we going, and how long is this gem of a walk?'

'Well, I asked a nice man if we could walk from Cumbe Mayo to San Pablo and he said it would only take a few hours.'

We reached the outskirts of town and I admired Hilary's new hiking style: she was walking on her heels like a penguin.

'What's this, the new Bradt Ergonomic Propulsion Technique?'

'No, it's athlete's foot, and I don't want to hear any jokes about it.'

Before we could pursue the subject further we heard the welcome sound of a vehicle climbing the hill behind us. A lift to Cumbe Mayo! We had plenty of time to look around the site with the archaeologist driver before finding a camping place and eating a lavish supper. I asked about food for the rest of the trip.

'There's quite a big village on the way so we can stock up with more food there.'

The next day in the village of Chetilla we met the mayor sitting outside a house. We told him about our walk and asked if we'd reach San Pablo that evening. He wasn't encouraging. Hilary nervously asked directions to the village shops.

'There is only one, and it's closed.' As we continued through the village Hilary kept nipping off down side streets and asking for eggs or bread. No-one had any, and this was the only village along our route. We ate our lunch in some fields. I was just reaching for a third roll when Hilary said 'George, two are plenty, why not save the rest for tomorrow?'

'OK, fill me in on your supper plans to give me something to look forward to.' Just as I was beginning to suspect, there would be no supper. In icy silence we walked down to the river valley. On the way, Hilary's search for local food became more vigorous. Braving hysterically barking dogs, she asked at every hut we passed to no avail. We crossed the river at the bottom of the valley and had started up the other side when we met a man milking cows. We asked to buy a litre, and to our relief he agreed readily. After he'd filled our water bottle with warm frothy milk he refused payment. We continued in better spirits, but after four hours of climbing our legs felt like jelly.

We climbed, slower and slower, until just before sunset. 'After all, there's nothing to cook, so there's no point in stopping early,' said Hilary philosophically. We found a campsite, set up the tent and tucked into 'supper'. Hilary swapped four peanuts for my share of milk.

'If you're still hungry, George, you could walk over that rise and see if there's a village. I think I saw a soccer field up there from across the valley.'

'Me? Hungry? After a roll and four peanuts? I'm full to bursting!'

'I'd go myself, but I don't think I can walk.' She'd taken off her boots and socks to reveal ten swollen, oozing toes with raw areas where the skin had come off. I sped up the hill, hoping to see a road. But there was no village to be seen, not even a house.

It was rather depressing to wake up to no breakfast, and to climb uphill all morning and find how our energy drained. Our food-finding efforts continued unsuccessfully. Hilary was now hobbling along like an old crone. Eventually we came across a woman weaving, with lots of hens scratching about in the dust.

'Have you any eggs?' we asked, casually waving a large bank note. 'Yes, I've got two,' she said, weaving all the harder. Better check. Yes, we'd heard correctly, but she wasn't interested in getting them.

'You know, we're very hungry.' More weaving. 'We haven't eaten anything for three days.' She was completely unmoved. A day or two without food means nothing to these people. Then she saw a youth hurrying towards us, and unhitched her backstrap loom immediately. She lifted a sitting hen, gave us the eggs, and took the money. The young man said, 'Why don't I cook those for you, and give you some rice as well?' We couldn't think of any particular reason why not, so followed him to a nearby hut. Soon we were ploughing through two bowls of rice topped with a fried egg.

After watching us satisfy our initial hunger, he asked where we'd come from and where we were going. Then he asked the obvious question: 'Why didn't you bring any food with you?' We told him and he laughed long and loud. He kindly suggested we take extra rice with us in case we didn't reach San Pablo until the next day. But he assured us that even walking slowly, 'like fat ladies', we'd reach the town before sundown.

We were so full of rice we could hardly get up, let alone carry our backpacks. But we liked the stuffed feeling better than the empty feeling. And we liked our arrival in San Pablo better than the journey.

This piece first appeared in the 1980 edition of this guide. As a reminder of what can happen to unfit, unprepared hikers it is worth reprinting.

No problem in the Andes. Then we tried to find a topographical map covering the area, preferably 1:100,000 or 1:50,000 scale. Again, usually no problem with the geographical institute in Peru. Even with only a basic road map you can pick a likely looking area above the treeline, between two small towns, and be fairly confident that there will be a trail. Then we packed enough food to last the estimated number of days, plus two more, and additional emergency rations. And that was it …

Here are a few dos and don'ts for Andean explorers:

- **Do** carry a compass and GPS unit and know how to use it.
- **Do** carry and know how to read a topographical map.
- **Do** turn back if the route becomes dangerous. Use your GPS's backtrack function.
- **Do** ask the locals (as many as possible) for advice and directions.
- **Do** carry extra food.
- **Don't** underestimate time, distance, or weather conditions.

GUIDES, PORTERS AND PACK ANIMALS For independent travellers the reverse of finding your own route is to use local expertise to ensure a trouble-free trek. Guides, cooks, porters, arrieros and their pack animals – either donkeys (*burros*), mules (*mulas*) or horses (*caballos*) – are often hired by hikers to take the donkey work out of backpacking. You will not be allowed to hire the animal without its owner. Llamas are not usually available.

Arrieros and porters can be hired in the majority of towns and villages next to the trailhead of popular routes, for US$12 a day for the man and US$8–12 for his donkey. These charges have only gone up a couple of dollars

PORTER WELFARE

Spearheaded by the British organisation Tourism Concern, the welfare of porters has become an important issue worldwide, and in Peru on the Inca Trail where pack animals are not used.

Since 2002, the law states that porters must receive a minimum wage of 60 soles a day (around US$15) and on the Inca Trail must not carry more than 20kg. These regulations are strictly enforced but there are other aspects in which you can play your part. Make sure that your porters have enough to eat, share some of your sweets or snacks with them, and don't linger in the dining tent if that's where they sleep.

Away from the Inca Trail, the law is much more lax so it is up to you to treat your arrieros fairly. If the fee isn't fixed, then pay a fair price and resist the temptation to bargain fiercely.

in the last few years, but they do vary a little, region to region. Remember you must pay for the arriero and his animals to return to the starting point. If he has done a good job a 10% tip can be added to the fee (see box, page 95). A porter (*portador*) charges US$10–35 a day (necessary on certain routes, such as the Inca Trail, where pack animals are not permitted, or on high passes and peaks where pack animals can't go).

In most well-known trekking areas, the arrieros have formed an association, and control the prices and conditions. This has done much to avoid exploitation by unscrupulous tour operators or individual hikers. Always go through the association, if there is one, not only to provide local employment and to encourage the maintenance of standards, but also to iron out any misunderstandings or problems that may arise.

Most arrieros are trustworthy, but you need to make your requirements clear, and to keep your valuables with you. When choosing an arriero try to get a recommendation from another traveller. Discuss the price (only pay half up front, and the rest at the end of the trip), the duration of the trip, side trips, whether cooking is part of the deal, and whether you need to provide his food and/or sleeping equipment as well. Arrieros will have their own idea of how long a trip will take and it is almost impossible to shift them. Part of this seeming obstinacy is the necessity of camping where there is good pasture for the donkeys. Part of it is about making money, so you may end up paying for more days than you need. So ask them how many days it will be, and agree on a total price for that time period.

Despite what may appear to us as occasional cruelty to animals, campesinos are very solicitous over their general welfare: they need fit, healthy animals.

Hiring local people is an important way for tourists to help the rural areas and bridge the cultural gap. However, for many hikers the freedom of walking alone outweighs the moral and practical advantages of using arrieros. A compromise is to hire someone for the first day to take your packs to the top of the first pass, and then continue on your own.

VILLAGE ETIQUETTE FOR INDEPENDENT BACKPACKERS

The villages you pass through on the hikes described in this book are mostly well accustomed to backpackers and no special behaviour is needed apart from greeting people in a friendly manner, and avoiding potentially offensive behaviour or dress (men should not go shirtless, for instance).

If you explore on your own you should always remember that because you are there in the village and on their land, you will be treated as either guest or intruder. The former is much more common. The indigenous people, still popularly known as Indians, have a strong tradition of extending hospitality to strangers. It is not rude to politely refuse such hospitality if you want to move on; however, it is considered rude to reject offers of accommodation and then put your tent up just outside the village and cook your own meal. Be sensitive to this: either accept the hospitality and stay with the family or move on and camp some way beyond the village.

If you are well off the beaten track, in a very remote area, the people – the women and children, at least – may flee in terror from this alien. Don't further intimidate them by approaching their house. Move on quietly, unless you want to make contact, in which case let them come to you.

On popular trails (most of the trails in this guide) you can be more relaxed. Even so, you should always ask permission to camp, both as a courtesy and for security. Don't feel you have to overdo the friendliness, and especially do not hand out sweets or other *regales* (presents) – your entertaining presence will be reward enough! You'll probably be surrounded by curious kids – and adults – who are fascinated by your state-of-the-art camping gear. Chat to them as you set up, explain what everything is, where you came from and where you are going to. Try to use a few words of Quechua. But be formal and polite. If the attention becomes tiresome withdraw into your tent for a while, having bid a firm goodbye.

If you accept a meal and accommodation in a remote area, make sure you share some of your food with your hosts; that is what is generally expected, not money or presents. On popular routes, however, an offer of accommodation is most likely made on a commercial basis, so offer to pay.

Indians are usually both friendly and shy, polite and curious. However, there are always exceptions. If you realise that you are not welcome, or if the locals ask you to leave, then do so without fuss. It is their land and there will be a good reason for them feeling hostile, whether through fear or – more likely – because they have had a bad experience with other gringos.

Keep your distance from drunkards. As in all societies they may be aggressive or lecherous. Excessive drinking is common; indeed it is part of the culture, especially during fiestas.

Respecting a culture, warts and all, is one of the great challenges confronting travellers. It does not just mean enjoying their music, their weavings and their *chicha*; it means accepting inefficiency and poor hygiene, and even turning a blind eye to cruelty to animals (unless it seems the latter is done to impress or please you, in which case explain calmly how you feel). It means trying to answer yourself the question that keeps springing to mind: 'Why don't they …?'

Many travellers feel awkward answering the constant questions about how much they earn and how much their gear or clothing cost. Assuming you speak reasonable Spanish, try to put your enormous wealth into perspective. Tell them how much a house costs in your country, or a kilo of oranges or a horse. Something they can relate to. Explain also about unemployment in the West. Sharing stories about your respective ways of life is an excellent way of getting to know each other, providing it does not lead to envy on their side. I vividly remember my first visit to Chinchero near Cusco in 1973, when South America was part of the Hippie Trail. An American, who had chosen to live in that community as part of the process of dropping out, was deeply upset by the materialism of the villagers, who in turn were puzzled by his praise of the quality of their lives. Few of the world's unavoidably poor people view their position as enviable. Most envy our affluence. Few, come to that, share our admiration (especially if we are taking photographs) for their heavy, earthenware pots and banana-leaf wrappers. They would much prefer plastic pots and plastic bags, and would see no reason to dispose of them in an environmentally responsible manner.

If you are hiking into really remote areas, try to find out about the people and their customs before you go. A local guide will do much to prevent misunderstandings as well as showing you the way.

MINIMUM IMPACT

Now that trekking and hiking is as popular in Peru as in the Himalayas hikers need to be aware of their effect on the environment. Even the problems besetting the national parks in developed countries, such as erosion caused by over-use, are now seen here. Inca ruins that have withstood hundreds of years of the forces of nature have been damaged by the campfires of tourists, and flights of Inca stairs built for the light tread of bare feet have been worn down by the heavy tramp of hiking boots. The Inca Trail has banned the use of metal-tipped hiking poles to protect the trails (although rubber-tipped walking sticks are still allowed). On popular trekking routes the hoofs of pack animals have worn the trails down to rock and dust.

Environmental abuse, however, takes on a wider meaning since the foreign hiker is making his mark not just on the landscape, but on the local people. Ironically, of the two major problems, litter and begging, one is caused by imitating local customs and the other by ignoring them.

LITTER We should be truthful about litter. With the exception of plastic, most rubbish offends the eye (and sometimes the nose) but does little permanent harm to the environment. However, it is so easy to put right, and so unpleasant when left, that we should do everything in our power to ease the problem. The quantity of litter and rubbish left on the popular hiking trails in Peru used to be horrifying and has only improved a little in recent years. In the countryside it's worse. Waste matter of all sorts: paper, fruit peel, plastic, and so on, is thrown from bus windows or dropped on the highways and byways, rivers and creeks. Local people are the worst offenders, and you the visitor are not going to change that. However, tourists – both gringo and South American – are responsible for most of the litter on trails. The culprits are unlikely to be readers of this book so it is a waste of space to preach about it. All I can say is try to clear up other people's litter as well as your own, unpleasant though it may be. And remember that orange peel is just as unsightly as toilet paper, even though it is biodegradable.

Tell your porters or arrieros that you will pay them extra if they carry all the rubbish back to the main town, and help you clear up littered areas. This is a case where interfering with their culture is a good thing!

The preservation of the beauty of Peruvian hiking trails is up to you. Here are a few recommendations:

- Leave the trail and campsite cleaner than you found them. If you can't carry out other people's tin cans, bury them away from the trail.
- Defecate well away from the trail and water supply; carry a trowel and dig a hole approximately 15cm deep, or cover your faeces with a rock, and pack out or burn the paper carefully.
- Don't contaminate streams. Pans and dishes can be cleaned quite adequately without soap or detergent, or use a biodegradable liquid soap. Use a bowl or pan to take water away from the stream for washing in so you are not putting any waste into the water.

CAMPFIRES Making fires is strictly forbidden in national parks and reserves because of the damage caused by their careless use. In former days, the National Reserve of Machu Picchu lost many hectares of endemic forest through hikers' carelessness, and much of the ancient Inca stonework was damaged. Even the most careful siting of fires still requires dead wood which cannot then play its part in regenerating the soil. So, cheery and warming though a campfire may be, please resist the temptation except in remote areas where firewood is plentiful, and do not allow your local guide to make a fire unless you are outside a protected area and well away from mountain villages who need the scarce fuel more than you do.

GIFTS AND BEGGING Another indication that a trail is a popular gringo route is that children rush up to you and demand sweets or money. Before you offer a child such presents, reflect on the consequences of your action. You are promoting tooth decay in an area with no dentists, or you are teaching a child that begging is rewarding and that something can be got for nothing. Increasingly insistent demands irritate future trekkers and help widen the gap between gringo and campesino. Adults, too, have been taught to beg. They usually ask for cigarettes or money and attempts at conversation or normal social interaction are thwarted.

This cultural erosion is reversible. If all trekkers and hikers stopped handing out unearned presents the begging would cease in a few years, and the campesinos would return to their traditional system of

ℹ TIPPING

There is considerable variation between what the locals tip and what visitors feel is appropriate. It is not customary to tip taxi drivers, for instance, and restaurants usually add a service charge to the bill. Locals may tip extra if the service is exceptional. If service hasn't been added, 10% is the norm provided food and service are acceptable. Hotel porters expect a dollar.

Trekkers will want to know the appropriate tip for guides, porters or arrieros. If trekking with a tour operator in your own country, they will give guidance on this (which will be on the high side since it is in their interest to keep the ground-operators sweet), but if you are a backpacker hiring guides and arrieros locally, you will be expected to tip approximately US$10 pp per day to be shared amongst the crew (more if you are solo or a small group). For the Inca Trail the total is usually US$45pp but many trekkers tip more. The driver of a tour bus will expect around 5 soles pp per day. At the end of a trek, rather than tip individually, it is best to collect the tips from the whole group, divide them up as you see fit, and then hand them out to each of the crew.

reciprocity, where presents and labour are exchanged, not given. So give a smile and a greeting instead.

There may, of course, be times when a carefully chosen present is appropriate; when accepting hospitality in a remote region, for instance. But in general aim to reward your hosts with stories, songs, games and drawings. Rural poverty is not synonymous with unhappiness, and if you examine your motives for wanting to give presents it may be that you feel good bringing smiles to children's faces, whereas with a bit more effort you could bring the same smile by playing a game. If you still feel guilty remember that your very presence is vastly entertaining and simply tolerating the stares as you go about your daily business is reward enough. If you take a photo of the locals, rather than offering to pay, show them the picture on your camera screen.

Experiencing rural Peru on foot has a profound effect on many travellers. They would like to know of ways to benefit the places and people that have given them so much. By far the best way is to support one of the small local charities listed on pages 74–6, either as a volunteer or through a donation. This ensures that your money or time is properly allocated to the people who most need it. Many of these organisations will gladly take unwanted clothing or medical supplies, and all would welcome your leftover soles or a more regular donation.

5

Health and Safety

HEALTH *Co-written with Dr Jane Wilson-Howarth*

BEFORE YOU GO

Insurance Be sure to get both medical and luggage insurance. Medical is the most important and you should get cover for two million pounds. Check that you are covered for mountain sports (ie: trekking) and check you are allowed to go to the altitude you plan to aim for. Ensure cover for anything else you plan to do and declare any medical conditions before travel.

Immunisations and malaria prophylaxis

South America is not the hotbed of disease you may imagine, but the following inoculations are recommended:

- **Diphtheria**, **polio** and **tetanus** need boosting every ten years.
- **Yellow fever** (not effective until ten days after receiving the vaccine). Until very recently boosting was advised every ten years, but whilst it's now thought that one dose gives life-long protection, at the time of writing border authorities hadn't updated their regulations to reflect this new research.
- **Anti-malarial protection** (if going on a jungle trip; not needed for high-altitude treks). The malaria risk is variable in Peru and it is best to check the current advice at www.fitfortravel.nhs.uk. Generally there is no risk and no need for tablets above 2,000m and the risk is low or absent west of the Andes but there are exceptions so check. It is also wise to avoid insect bites by using a good repellent, wearing long and loose clothes.
- **Hepatitis A** vaccine is available from British general practitioners (GPs) free of charge and the course of two injections protects for life.
- **Typhoid** vaccine is recommended although it does not provide total protection and being careful about what you eat and drink is your best defence. Immunisation may be by injection when two shots

are given, four weeks apart, and this lasts for three years. Typhoid capsules are also available and these give some protection against paratyphoid as well as typhoid.

- Pre-travel **rabies** immunisation. Hikers are at risk from rural dogs, many of which carry rabies, and immunisation is advised for anyone who may be more than a week away from medical care, as well as anyone planning on entering caves.

Women should note that high-altitude destinations are not great for anyone who is pregnant. Take specialist advice and be aware that miscarriage is common up until the 12th week.

Fitness Being in good physical condition is an essential requirement for all hikers; lack of fitness is dangerous and will mar your enjoyment of the mountains. However, independent backpackers planning a long trip have very different fitness requirements from those of trekkers or others on a short holiday where daily objectives must be achieved. The former will gradually get into shape on the trail, but the latter must make considerable efforts to get fit before they go.

Backpackers have the enviable advantage of being able to camp where they choose, and fatigue in the early stages of a long trip is almost an advantage since it encourages a very slow ascent, thus minimising the danger of altitude sickness. On the other hand, the weight of your pack at the start of the trail anyway ensures that you go slowly and there's no point in letting lack of fitness add to your suffering!

Ideally, people signing up for an organised trek or expedition must start to get fit at least a couple of months before they leave. This preparation should as closely as possible resemble what they will actually be doing: hiking in the mountains. Therefore it is much better to walk briskly in hilly country than to run along level roads. Not all potential trekkers, of course, live close to suitable countryside, but everyone has access to flights of stairs and walking, then running, up an increasing number of stairs is an excellent means of getting fit for the Andes. Cycling is also a good way of preparing for trekking, since it involves most of the same muscles. Stepping up and down on a low chair (leading 50 times with one leg then 50 times with another) is a daily exercise possible almost anywhere. This will strengthen the thigh muscles, which in turn protect the knees.

COMMON MEDICAL PROBLEMS This list of the most common health problems and their treatment assumes that you are not in easy reach of a local doctor. Even if the medical set-up isn't quite what you're accustomed to, remember that doctors in Peru are well versed in diagnosing and treating local diseases. If you are unwilling or unable to see a doctor, pharmacists treat the local population for minor complaints, but check the expiry date on any medicines they prescribe. Many drugs, available only on prescription in the USA or Europe, may be bought – expensively – over the counter in South America.

'Filth-to-mouth' diseases and how to prevent them Travellers' diarrhoea is common in Peru; it, and a host of other diseases, are caught by getting other people's faeces into your mouth. Contrary to popular belief, most of the diarrhoea-causing bugs get into you by way of contaminated food rather than via dirty water. Lettuce is often a culprit, so never eat salad, even in expensive hotels, and try to avoid all uncooked foods including ceviche (marinated raw seafood) and ice cream and farmers' cheeses. PEEL IT, BOIL IT, COOK IT, OR FORGET IT.

Take the precaution of sterilising all water by boiling it (the best method bacteriologically), or treating it with iodine or chlorine or silver-based sterilising tablets. The last are least effective but have the advantage of being tasteless. Iodine is the best chemical water steriliser; adding vitamin C after the period of sterilisation and before drinking improves the taste. Note that camping shops in the UK no longer sell iodine for water sterilisation because of EU regulations, but it is still available in the US. Whilst it is not toxic, no clinical trials have been properly carried out so it's not licensed for drinking, although it is still good for cleaning wounds, etc. Many people prefer water filters to sterilising tablets, for example the Aqua-pure Traveller which is lightweight and effective.

Be careful to wash your hands after using the toilet (this is to wash off other people's germs; your own won't harm you). Soap and water is more effective than any of the various hand gels that are on the market, but some like them for trekking since they do not need to be rinsed off. Generally where there is a toilet, there will also be a tap.

Diarrhoea Travellers' diarrhoea is caused by enterotoxigenic forms of the bacteria that everyone has in their bowel: *Escherichia coli*. The trouble is that each geographical area has its own strains of *E. coli*, and these alien strains cause diarrhoea. Everyone has his or her favourite remedy, and it is the subject of many a gringo conversation, but replacing lost fluids is the most important part of any treatment. The most sensible way to treat the problem depends on whether you are a backpacker on a leisurely trip lasting several weeks or months, or a trekker on a brief holiday. The latter needs to feel better in a hurry, and he/she could bring a supply of the antibiotic xifaxanta. Take one pill twice a day for three days; this medication must be taken in conjunction with lots of fluids – aim for several litres per day if there is profuse watery diarrhoea. Ask your GP for it before you leave.

If you are a backpacker and can rest up for a few days it is best to let your body expel the toxins and take no medication. 'Blockers', such as Lomotil or Imodium, will stop the diarrhoea by paralysing the gut, but leave you feeling ill. Drink plenty of fluids and eat bananas, papaya, crackers, mashed potatoes and/or boiled rice. If you don't feel like eating, don't eat. The body's ability to absorb fluids and salts is greatly improved by taking sugar at the same time, so, to counteract dehydration and loss of vital minerals, sip a solution of salt (½ level teaspoon) and glucose, sugar or dextrose (four heaped teaspoons) dissolved in one pint (half a litre) of water which can be made anywhere. These rehydration solutions should taste no more salty than tears. Adding a squirt of lime or citrus will improve the taste and also add potassium which is lost during diarrhoea. If you are travelling by public transport or are in other places where a dash to the lavatory is impracticable, consider taking a day off and resting until the initial out-pouring has slowed. Otherwise some sort of chemical cork may be required. Codeine phosphate (this is available on prescription, but it is addictive so carry a letter confirming what you are using it for; your GP may prescribe it before you leave) is a useful stopper as well as being a powerful painkiller; otherwise many people favour Lomotil, but if you are so sick that you need these powerful drugs you should also take them in combination with the antibiotic you are carrying. Fluid replacement is the most important part of all the diarrhoea treatments: being dehydrated will make you feel a lot worse, with a headache, dizziness and weakness, and slows recovery.

Diarrhoea accompanied by a fever should probably be treated with antibiotics. Long-term and seasoned travellers will find they gradually build up a nice collection of South American E. coli in their intestines and will seldom suffer diarrhoea attacks. This does not mean, however, that they should be casual over hygiene and run the risk of getting other more serious filth-to-mouth diseases such as typhoid, dysentery and hepatitis E.

Dysentery If, in addition to diarrhoea, you have severe stomach cramps, pass blood or mucus with your faeces and/or run a fever, then you probably have dysentery. A doctor or a clinical laboratory (*análisis clínico*) can confirm the diagnosis before you take medication. Flagyl (metronidazole) is effective for amoebic dysentery, as is tinidazole. An antibiotic should cure bacterial dysentery. Generally, while both kinds of dysentery cause blood to be passed, bacterial dysentery causes a fever and explosive diarrhoea while with amoebic dysentery there is no fever and the onset of the illness is more gradual.

Fever If you develop a fever for any reason you should rest and take ibuprofen or paracetamol. Consult a doctor if you don't start to feel better after 24 to 36 hours.

Avoiding them:

- Use well walked-in footwear
- Use quality cushioning socks
- Consider thin socks under thick
- Change your socks often and whenever they get wet
- Keep toenails cut short
- Check your feet at the end of each day.

If you get a blister:

- Use Compeed or moleskin dressings
- Try to leave the blister alone if possible
- Soaking the feet in a solution containing potassium permanganate will control infection.

Sores and skin infections

A significant infection is serious (spreading redness, increasing pain, pus discharge or even fever) and needs antibiotic treatment: flucloxicillin or erythromycin for seven days. A slow-healing sore can be speeded on its way by applications of honey or papaya. Any skin sore that still hasn't healed over after a month needs a medical assessment; it could be leishmania or skin cancer, or just in need of proper medical attention. Athlete's foot can be a problem. Treat it before it cripples you. Tinactin or other antifungals in powder form are effective in the early stages (shake it into your socks each morning).

Colds and coughs Respiratory infections are very common in the Andes. Perhaps the dramatic temperature changes are largely to blame: people go sightseeing in Cusco wearing only a T-shirt, and return blue with cold when clouds or the sudden dusk puts an end to the hot sun. Colds easily turn into coughs and even bronchitis in these conditions, so bring sore-throat lozenges. A soothing cough medicine can be made from equal parts of lemon or lime juice, honey and (optional) Pisco or other spirit in plenty of hot water. Ascending to extreme altitude when you have a cold probably increases the risk of mountain sickness.

Motion sickness The local people are not the only ones to suffer from travel sickness on the rough roads in the Andes. Stugeron (cinnarizine 30mg) is recommended at least three hours before travel (or the night before then eight-hourly); it should not make you drowsy. Remember that a full stomach is more likely to empty itself than a partially full one!

AVOIDABLE (BUT POTENTIALLY SERIOUS) MEDICAL PROBLEMS

Rabies Rabies is a viral encephalitis acquired from a bite or a lick (if the skin is broken) by an infected mammal. It is invariably fatal. In resource-poor countries vaccination of domestic animals for rabies is almost non-existent so the risk of contracting rabies from dogs and other animals is high. If you have not had the rabies vaccine before you leave home but are subsequently bitten by a suspect animal take the following course of action and forget the conventional advice about capturing the animal and keeping it for ten days to see if it dies of rabies – this is simply not practicable in an Andean village:

1) Immediately apply soap and *scrub* the bite for five (timed!) minutes under running water, followed by disinfection with iodine or with local spirits such as aguardiente or Pisco. Experiments have shown that this alone reduces the risk of contracting rabies by 90%.

2) Get anti-rabies injections as soon as possible. The infection travels along the nerves to the brain over a period of days, weeks or even months. When symptoms start, the disease is incurable, but before this point, the rabies vaccine (with rabies immune globulin, RIG) is usually effective. Make your way to a clinic in a major town as soon as you can, and don't wait until you get home. Pre-travel immunisation precludes the need for RIG which can be hard to access in South America. Don't believe anyone who tells you that it is all right to wait for symptoms to start then get treatment.

Cholera Cholera is spread through poor hygiene and contaminated foods. It is not a threat to normal travellers – the disease mostly attacks the poor and malnourished. Cholera vaccine is not needed for normal travel, although there is now an oral vaccine, Dukoral.

EMERGENCY MEDICAL TREATMENT AND BLOOD TRANSFUSIONS HIV which causes AIDS exists in Peru, and so does the hepatitis B virus which is spread in the same way but is much more infectious. Although transfusing unscreened blood is a well-understood route of transferring these infections, not everywhere has the resources to do this screening. It is possible to arrange insurance that covers sending safe, screened blood by courier. In case of an accident, ask local advice (your embassy should be helpful here) on the safest hospitals.

MOUNTAIN HEALTH Paradoxically, backpacking in the Andes is both the healthiest and the most dangerous mode of travel. Fortunately the main killers (apart from accidents) – hypothermia, pulmonary oedema and cerebral oedema – can be avoided so read the section below carefully.

Injury Most of the hikes described in this book take you well away from civilisation, but are on good and well-frequented trails. Be careful and sensible. Remember that a badly injured person cannot easily be evacuated from the Andes, and that you may or may not be able to persuade local people to assist you. All backpackers should be conversant in first aid (preferably by going on a course), and should carry an appropriate first-aid guide. There are some excellent ones specifically for mountain medicine.

Your medical kit should run the gamut from dealing with minor problems to coping with major situations like large wounds that would normally need suturing. Steristrips or butterfly closures are suitable for these. Zinc-oxide tape is useful for holding a dressing in place (non-stick Melolin dressings are good) and has many other uses as well. If you don't mind some funny looks bring panty liners as multi-purpose dressings: they are ideal, being sterile and water- (blood-) proof and the adhesive backing sticks to the bandage so they don't slip.

When compiling your medical kit (page 106) bear in mind that medical supplies in the mountain villages are very poor or non-existent.

Sunburn
The combination of equatorial sun and high altitude makes sunburn a real danger to hikers in the Andes. Protect yourself with long, loose clothing and a really good suncream made for skiers or mountaineers. Lipsalve prevents cracked lips and should contain sunscreen, and remember how vulnerable your nose is. Wear a broad-brimmed hat and a long-sleeved shirt with a collar, at least until you have built up a protective tan and, if wearing a T-shirt, protect the back of your neck with a bandana or neckerchief.

Hypothermia
Simply put, this means that the body loses heat faster than it can produce heat. The combination of wind and wet clothing can be lethal, even if the air temperature is well above freezing. Trekkers and those on day hikes are more likely to have problems with hypothermia than backpackers, who, by definition, carry their requirements with them. So if you are only carrying a daypack, make sure you include a sweater or fleece, a windbreaker, and a waterproof jacket or poncho, however settled the weather looks when you set out. If you can include a survival bag or space blanket that's even better. Always carry some high-energy snacks, too. Your porters or pack animals may easily be delayed and you can get thoroughly chilled while waiting for them. Also, should you stray away from the group and become lost, the main danger to your life is taken care of. Backpackers should concentrate on keeping their warm clothes and sleeping bag dry (everything should be kept in plastic bags).

There are various ways of keeping warm without relying on heavy or expensive clothing. Wear a wool ski hat, or *chullo*, to prevent heat loss from your head (although the oft-quoted statement that 40% of body heat is lost through the head is misleading since it includes heat loss through breathing!). Make sure heat can't escape from your body through the collar of your windbreaker; use a silk or wool scarf or a roll-neck sweater. Eat plenty of high-calorie trail snacks (pages 84–5). Hot drinks have a marvellously warming effect. Have one just before going to sleep. Fill your water bottle with boiling water, put it in a sock and treat yourself to a 'hotty' at night (which also gives you sterilised, ice-free water in the morning). Always change out of damp, sweaty clothes if you get wet and at the end of the day.

If a member of your party shows symptoms of hypothermia – uncontrolled shivering followed by drowsiness, confusion or stumbling – he/she must be warmed up immediately. Exercise is exhausting and eventually results in worse hypothermia. Conserve energy, raise the blood sugar with food, give hot drinks, and put the person in a warmed, dry sleeping bag under cover. If the condition is serious, climb (naked!) into the sleeping bag with him/her and use your own body heat as a radiator. And be prepared for your friend's astonishment when he/she regains consciousness.

Acclimatisation Acclimatisation is the process of adjusting to the reduced oxygen in the atmosphere at high altitude. This process differs for everyone and there are no rules as to who will suffer the effects of high altitude. Being in excellent physical condition does not aid in acclimatisation, nor does it make you less prone to altitude sickness; indeed, young fit men are often the most susceptible. If you have suffered from altitude sickness in the past you are likely to suffer again, but there can be a first time for everyone, sometimes after several trouble-free trips to high places. For most people it takes a week or two to become completely acclimatised, but there are some who never get there. So never compare yourself with another person, especially if travelling in a group, but respect the differing time needed for each person to be ready to proceed into the mountains.

On flying from sea level to Huaraz or Cusco, everyone feels the effects of altitude to a certain degree. The symptoms are headaches, breathlessness, dizziness or light-headedness, insomnia, and loss of appetite. You can help alleviate it by drinking lots of water (or – better – coca tea), avoiding alcohol and heavy and hard-to-digest food, and above all by resting. Spend at least three days at an altitude of no more than 3,500m, then start doing some easy day hikes. Allow at least five days to get used to the altitude before starting your backpacking trip (reputable trekking companies build a period of acclimatisation into their itinerary). Acclimatisation is achieved when the heartbeat is normal at rest, you can eat and sleep well and have no headache. If you experience any of the symptoms of altitude sickness while backpacking, try to rest for a couple of days. Then, if you don't feel better, turn back. Remember, too, that even a short visit to the coast will lose you your hard-won acclimatisation.

High-altitude sickness This can be divided into three categories: acute mountain sickness (AMS), cerebral oedema and pulmonary oedema. All three are brought on by a too-hasty ascent to altitudes exceeding about 3,000m. The potentially fatal pulmonary and cerebral oedemas can be prevented by acclimatising properly before the ascent and by climbing slowly; aim to ascend no more than 300m daily when over 3,000m. Go even slower if a member of the hiking party shows any signs of AMS.

Many symptoms of mountain illnesses resemble those of other diseases but, if you are at an altitude of more than 3,000m and someone is clearly deteriorating, *descend*. If the symptoms are due to altitude their condition will improve and you will have saved a life even though evacuating an unco-operative victim in the dark is no fun. Do not wait overnight to see if they are better in the morning.

Mountain sickness Known locally as *soroche*, the first symptoms of mountain sickness commonly develop six to 12 hours after arriving at altitude; these are severe headache, nausea and sleeplessness. If the victim slows down, ascends no higher, drinks plenty of liquids (two or three litres a day, if possible) and rests for a day or two, these symptoms should moderate. Diamox can be used to treat the headache and nausea. Periodic breathing (Cheyne-Stokes respiration) during sleep affects many people

---

i HIGH-ALTITUDE NUTRITION

Dr Chris Fenn (e eat4success@chrisfenn.com; www.chrisfenn.com)
Whilst eating good-quality foods for general health is important, there are several key nutrients associated with high-altitude acclimatisation. As the pressure of oxygen in the air decreases, the body produces more red blood cells. The nutrients associated with red blood cell production are protein, vitamins E, B12 and B6 plus folic acid and iron. Red meats such as beef, pork and lamb are plentiful in the high Andes, and these provide B vitamins and the most readily available form of iron. Iron found in plant foods is more difficult to absorb, but absorption can be improved by eating foods which contain vitamin C in the same meal. Most green vegetables and fruits will provide some vitamin C. Potatoes are not particularly rich in vitamin C, but are eaten at almost every meal in villages around Peru and so can contribute a significant amount. There are over 200 varieties of potato – look out for the unusual purple and blue ones. Another nutritious staple is quinoa (pronounce 'keen-wah'). This is a seed rather than a true cereal, like wheat, oats or barley. Unlike these cereals it is a protein powerhouse, as well as providing the all-important iron, calcium, magnesium and potassium – which help with muscle function on trek. Provided that you drink enough water, these minerals can also help to prevent muscle cramp. Quinoa has a long history in Peru and

at high altitude. This is when the sleeper takes shallower and shallower breaths until he stops altogether; then comes a gasping deep breath and the cycle begins again. It is harmless, but disturbing both to the sleeper (who may dream of being suffocated) and a tent-mate.

The prescription medicine Diamox (acetazolamide) is an effective prophylaxis for AMS. One or two 250mg pills are taken each morning for three days prior to the ascent (ie: when still at sea level or thereabouts) and continued for two more days at altitude. Since Diamox increases urine production somewhat, take the pills in the morning to avoid sleep disturbance because of the increased need to pee. Another side effect can be tingling of the hands and feet. Spacing the doses so you take them over more days will solve this problem. Diamox can also be used as treatment for AMS: take 750mg (three tablets) for small adults or 1,000mg (four tablets) for big people, then 500mg per day for up to four more days.

Cerebral oedema This is a more dangerous type of altitude sickness. Fluid accumulates in the brain, and can cause irritability, drowsiness, coma then death. The symptoms include intense headache or neckache,

over 120 varieties are known but the yellow, red or black seeds are the most common. Vitamin E is found in the germ of the seed and since that makes up about 60% of quinoa, it has plenty of vitamin E. Wheat grain, by comparison, has only 3% germ. With its high ratio of protein to carbohydrate, quinoa is a fabulous food to take with you. As a dry seed, it is easy to carry and easy to cook. Simply boil, like rice, in plenty of water until the grains are swollen and soft. Add plenty of leafy vegetables for a perfect meal. Quinoa flour and flakes are common and there is a huge range of products, including breakfast cereals and drinks, made from quinoa.

Another crop native to Peru is amaranth. Like quinoa, it is a seed rather than a true cereal and it is also high in protein, iron, magnesium and calcium. Surprisingly it also contains some vitamin C – which will aid iron absorption. Amaranth is sold on the streets of Peru, often popped like corn. It is also a traditional ingredient for porridge and the flour is used in bread, muffins and pancakes. Both quinoa and amaranth are naturally gluten-free. Some people find that they feel better if they avoid gluten. If you based your eating habits on local foods such as potatoes, quinoa, amaranth and fruits rather than gluten-containing cereals, you may find that you return from your travels feeling better than before!

nausea, staggering gait, confusion, disorientation and hallucinations. Anyone showing signs of cerebral oedema should be taken down to a lower altitude – at least 500m lower – immediately. One of the symptoms may be denial – sometimes aggressive – of the problem, so a firm hand is often needed to persuade the person to descend.

Pulmonary oedema More common than cerebral oedema but equally dangerous, fluid collects in the lungs, literally drowning the person. The symptoms are shortness of breath when at rest, coughing, frothy, sometimes bloodstained sputum, and a crackling sound in the chest. Take the victim to a lower altitude immediately. Each year climbers die in the Andes from pulmonary oedema because they have not taken the time to acclimatise and do not recognise the symptoms in time.

Western medicine and local people One of the by-products of well-equipped trekkers permeating every mountain stronghold is that local people will beg medicines above any other consumable. Even the most culturally sensitive trekker or backpacker feels that to deny them this easing of the harshness of their lives would be cruel, yet there are good reasons to say no.

---

i MEDICAL KIT

- Water purifiers
- Antiseptic (dilute iodine or potassium permanganate crystals)
- Vaseline (for cracked heels or lips)
- Moleskin and adhesive-backed foam rubber or Compeed (for blisters and sore feet)
- Steristrips or butterfly closures, panty liners
- Crêpe/ace bandage
- Fabric Elastoplast/Bandaids (a dressing strip is good)
- Zinc-oxide tape is useful for holding a dressing in place
- Non-stick Melolin dressings
- Flight socks
- Xifaxanta antibiotic and rehydration sachets
- Ibuprofen or paracetamol/tylenol
- Stugeron (cinnarizine 30mg)
- Diamox (optional)
- Thermometer (with a low-reading range). Mercury may not be carried on planes.
- Cough and throat lozenges
- Antifungal cream and powder

Apart from the risks to them of inappropriate dosage, it adds to the belief that Western medicine is good and traditional remedies are bad despite the advantages of the latter in availability and cost. In short, do not dabble in other people's health beyond perhaps offering a couple of paracetamol or some antiseptic for a nasty wound. Vitamin pills or iron tablets will do no harm.

TRAVEL CLINICS AND HEALTH INFORMATION A full list of current travel clinic websites worldwide is available on www.istm.org. For other journey preparation information, consult www.nathnac.org/ds/map_world.aspx (UK) or http://wwwnc.cdc.gov/travel/ (US). Information about various medications may be found on www.netdoctor.co.uk/travel. Other useful sites include the **NHS website** www.fitfortravel.nhs.uk (which provides country-by-country advice on immunisation and malaria, plus details of recent developments, and a list of relevant health organisations), ftp://ftp.shoreland.com/pub/shorecg.rtf and www.tripprep.com.

In the US, **Centers for Disease Control** (*www.cdc.gov/travel*) are the central source of travel information in the USA. Each summer they publish the invaluable *Health Information for International Travel*, available from the Division of Quarantine at the above address.

All advice found online should be used in conjunction with expert advice received prior to or during travel.

Further reading on travel and mountain health Consult www.medex.org.uk/ for an excellent free guide to mountain illnesses available to download.

Wilson-Howarth, Jane *The Essential Guide to Travel Health: don't let bugs bites & bowels spoil your trip* Cadogan Guides, London and Globe Pequot, Ct; 5th edition. 2009. Contains a chapter on altitude and keeping healthy in the mountains.

Wilson-Howarth, Jane and Ellis, Matthew *Your Child's Health Abroad: A Manual for Travelling Parents* Bradt and Globe Pequot, Ct; 2005. Written while the authors were living in Kathmandu and soon to be re-issued as an eBook – see www.bradtguides.com for the latest information.

SAFETY

Peru can be a dangerous country for the unwary and backpackers should pay particular attention to this section, though trekkers on an organised trip will have little to worry about when with the group. Much of the advice below comes from the South American Explorers, who are excellently placed to know the security situation.

PERUVIAN POLICE In Peru there are four types of policemen:

- Police
- Traffic police
- The private police (PIP), mostly plain clothes, who work with crime and terrorism
- Tourist police.

Of these, the traffic police are the most corrupt, but this rarely involves tourists. The private police are usually honest and can be very tough. They are mainly concerned that tourists are legally in the country (ie: that visa requirements are adhered to) and that they do not deal in drugs. The tourist police are most helpful and we recommend you to contact them when you need help.

In the rare event that you should have a problem with the police, it helps to put yourself on the same level and avoid giving them the feeling that they have any power over you. Courtesy and a firm handshake helps establish an equal footing. There have been instances of criminals dressing as policemen; if stopped (and assuming you've done nothing wrong), make sure you take a careful look at their ID and never get into an unmarked 'police car'.

DRUGS Using drugs is illegal in Peru and at the time of writing there has been much publicity over the penalties of trying to smuggle cocaine out of the country.

No-one in their right mind wants to spend time in a South American jail and we are assuming our readers are sane so will say no more about voluntary drug use. There are, however, cases where drugs have been planted on tourists, especially backpackers who fit the image of 'drug addicts'. Be suspicious of over-friendly locals and do not give the police an opportunity to plant drugs. If you feel as though you are being set up, just walk away.

Coca leaves Someone once described coca leaves as having the same relation to cocaine as ivory has to elephants. The drug is derived from the leaves of the coca plant, which is widely grown in Peru, but that is all. Chewing coca leaves is perfectly legal and has been part of the Indian culture for thousands of years. Steady and prolonged chewing has a narcotic effect but few gringos have the perseverance to achieve this. Most use it to make a pleasant herb tea which seems to help alleviate altitude sickness.

It is illegal to take coca leaves out of the country, but coca tea bags are usually not questioned by your customs authorities.

THEFT Theft can be a problem for travellers in Peru. Most theft is by deception, with the thieves working in groups. One thief gets your attention, the second grabs your belongings and throws them to a third, who escapes with them. Thieves are quick and clever, and most of the time you don't even realise what is happening. If you know the most popular tricks, however, you can stay ahead of the game. The most dangerous areas for being robbed are crowded places such as markets, and bus and train stations. Basically theft falls into the three categories listed below.

Unguarded possessions In risky situations (and that's any place where there are lots of people around) your belongings should be either attached to your person or under lock and key. In a restaurant, never hang a bag over the back of your chair, or put it on the floor without wrapping a strap around a chair leg or your foot. One minute's inattention and it's gone. Other places to be particularly careful are in the waiting areas of bus and train stations, or in the trains and buses themselves although checked luggage is secure. Backpacks are a great temptation to young or casual thieves who have a brief encounter with your unattended luggage on public transport. There are several effective backpack protectors on the market.

Thefts from the person Handbag snatching, slashing and pickpocketing are very common. Don't carry a handbag or a daypack in cities, unless you carry it in front of your body. If you can't bear to be without a handbag, make sure it is made from tough, hard-to-cut material. Never wear jewellery and don't keep a wallet in your pocket. Watches are sometimes snatched from the wrist; wear a cheap one. When wandering around cities and towns, try to carry as little as possible with you. Most people tend to carry more than they really need. When you arrive in a new place leave your camera in the hotel and take it out the next day when you have got your bearings. Keep your money and passport in a money belt, neck or leg pouch. Do not put all your money in one place.

Never carry more than you can physically handle, especially if travelling alone, and always take taxis if you have too much to carry.

If you think you are being followed, turn around, stop and walk behind the person. If someone tries to rob you and you catch them at it, shout 'ladrón!' (thief!); passers-by are likely to come to your rescue.

The best protection is not to bring belongings that are dear to you, or that are expensive.

Theft by deception One of the most popular thefts by deception is the 'mustard on your clothes' trick. When you are walking in the street a well-dressed couple will approach you and point out that you have something nasty on your clothing or shoes. One of them helpfully produces a handkerchief to assist you in wiping it off. Meanwhile his/her accomplice is skilfully going through your pockets or handbag.

These thieves are extraordinarily accomplished at their chosen trade, and generally you will not realise your wallet is missing until you get back to the hotel. Once you know about this practice you will recognise the set-up and can briskly walk away.

Also it is best not to accept any sweets or drinks from strangers, especially in bars or nightclubs; spiked drinks are not unknown.

Armed or violent robbery Armed robbery is rare but it does happen. If a robber threatens you with a knife, gun or other weapon there is little you can do but hand him what he wants, just as in any other place in the world. Avoid the same sort of places in Peru as you would at home: impoverished slums and poorly lit streets after dark. Tourist spots are more dangerous than areas that see few foreigners – thieves need a regular supply of victims. Generally speaking, your money and valuables are safer deep in your luggage in a locked hotel room than on your person.

 LONG-HAUL FLIGHTS, CLOTS AND DVT

Dr Jane Wilson-Howarth
Long-haul air travel increases the risk of deep-vein thrombosis. Flights of over 5½ hours carry a significant risk, and people whose risk is greater than average are:

* Those who have had a clot before (or have a close blood relative who has)
* People over 80 years of age (the risk starts rising from 40)
* Anyone who has recently undergone a major operation or surgery for varicose veins
* Someone who has had a hip or knee replacement in the last three months
* Cancer sufferers
* Those who have ever had a stroke
* People with heart disease
* Women who are pregnant or have had a baby in the last couple of weeks
* People taking female hormones or other oestrogen therapy
* Heavy smokers
* Those who have very severe varicose veins
* The very obese
* People who are very tall (over 6ft/1.8m) or short (under 5ft/1.5m)

A deep-vein thrombosis (DVT) is a blood clot that forms in the deep leg veins. This is very different from irritating but harmless superficial

Ways to protect your valuables

- Take a taxi if you have a lot of luggage, at night, or in risky parts of the city. Ask your hotel to phone for a registered taxi.
- Use a money belt, neck or leg pouch or inside pocket for cash and passports. Or, better, all three so your valuables are not all in one place.
- Carry a photocopy of your passport with you. This will help you replace your passport quickly should it be lost or stolen.
- Before you leave home, take photos or scans of all important documents including your passport information page, insurance certificate, credit cards and any other vital information and email them to yourself. Then even if you lose everything you can retrieve the information. If you have credit card insurance, be sure to bring the helpline number with you.
- The safest place for valuables is in a hotel. Keep them in the room safe, or in cheaper hotels put them deep in your luggage and lock it before going out.

phlebitis. DVT causes swelling and redness of one leg, usually with heat and pain typically three to ten days after a long flight. A DVT is only dangerous if a clot breaks away and travels to the lungs (pulmonary embolus). Symptoms of a pulmonary embolus (PE) include chest pain that is worse on breathing in deeply, shortness of breath, and sometimes coughing up small amounts of blood. Anyone who thinks that they might have a DVT or PE needs to see a doctor immediately who will arrange a scan.

PREVENTION OF DVT

- Exercise before and after the flight
- Keep mobile during the flight; move around every couple of hours
- During the flight drink plenty of water or juices
- Avoid taking sleeping pills and excessive tea, coffee and alcohol
- Perform exercises that mimic walking and tense the calf muscles
- Consider wearing flight socks or support stockings (see *www.legshealth.com*)
- Taking a meal of oily fish (mackerel, trout, salmon, sardines, etc) in the 24 hours before departure reduces blood clotability and thus DVT risk
- A single aspirin before flying may be protective

If you think you are at increased risk of a clot, ask your doctor if it is safe to travel.

- At most hotels you can store your unneeded luggage while you hike. Make sure it is locked, and that you are given a receipt.
- Emergency money in the form of a US$100 bill is completely safe hidden under the insole of your boot. Or think up your own secret hiding place.

Remember, the point of all the above is not to make you paranoid, but to allow you to relax and enjoy the company of some of the millions of Peruvians who wouldn't dream of robbing you.

SAFETY ON THE TRAIL Mostly you will be safe on the trail, but unfortunately the number of 'rich' gringos trekking through the mountain villages has given the campesinos a new consumer awareness but only very few of the popular trails suffer from this problem. As a general rule it is safest to camp out of sight, or to stay with a family (or camp in their yard) thus gaining their protection. Keep valuables – and most of your money – at the bottom of your pack when hiking: even armed robbers are not going to rummage through your pack looking for them.

More dangerous than the people are their **dogs**. Most rural villages keep several underfed dogs that bark hysterically when they see a stranger, especially a strange-shaped one (with a backpack). Mostly it is just bravado, but, in a continent where rabies is common, don't take the risk of being bitten. If you are planning on doing a great deal of hiking, or are cycling, it would be worth investigating one of the anti-dog sprays on the market. Usually if you ignore a barking dog and keep walking it will give up, but if you feel that you are in danger of being bitten, carry a handful of stones. Most dogs will turn tail and flee at the very sight of you stooping to pick up a stone (if there are no real ones an imaginary one works) and actually throwing the missile – accurately – is highly effective. You can also carry a stick but dogs tend to jump at a stick, making the encounter more frightening.

Read up the section on rabies (pages 100–1) *before* you start hiking and carry the appropriate first-aid items (soap, scrubbing brush, etc) where you can easily get to them. And don't worry: although the bite of these animals is certainly worse than their bark, an attack is relatively rare.

Take care to avoid accidents. Stop walking when you are very tired, don't venture off the trail without a compass and survival equipment, avoid hypothermia and mountain sickness, and have access to basic first-aid supplies at all times.

! **Updates website:** For the latest updates go to www.bradtupdates. com/perutrekking. You can also post your feedback here – corrections, changes or even new hikes. Your information will be put on our website for the benefit of other travellers.

Part Two

TREKKING AND BACKPACKING GUIDE

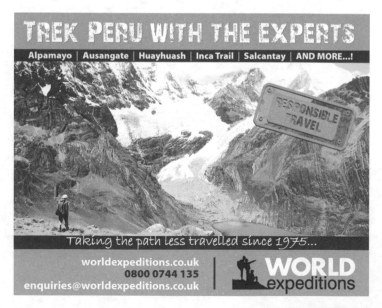

6

Lima

Telephone code: 01

Most people arrive in Lima by air. The drive from the airport to the suburbs provides their first glimpse of the city and they must wonder why on earth they came. Brown adobe slums on brown rubbish-strewn earth, and the occasional stiff body of a dead dog, line this scenic drive. Add to this the chaotic traffic which, with horns blaring, only marginally slows down for red lights. And all shrouded in the grey pall of Lima's winter garúa.

Actually it's really not that bad. If you stay in one of the suburbs such as Miraflores, and indulge in some seafood eating, shopping and museums, you will not regret your time there. Each district has its own character: the centre with its Spanish-colonial buildings; Miraflores, the affluent commercial centre; Barranco with a Colonial Spanish flavour, party atmosphere and attractive bars and restaurants; and the fishing 'village' of Chorillos.

HISTORY

The Incas, not a seafaring culture, had no use for a city in the coastal desert but after the Spanish conquest Francisco Pizarro established his capital on the banks of the Rimac River in 1535. The city's position made it beneficial for trade but vulnerable to attack, and during the next three centuries it suffered assaults from pirates and its aggressive neighbour Chile as well as by devastating earthquakes. In the 20th century economic migrants from the highlands settled in the outskirts of the city and unemployment and urban poverty remain a problem to this day. However, in 1991 the historic centre was declared a UNESCO World Heritage Site and much progress has since been made in cleaning up and greening the city.

GETTING THERE AND AWAY

BY AIR For newcomers to the developing world, arriving in Peru can be a daunting experience. You emerge from the relative haven of the customs area (where you press a button to see if your baggage is to be examined: green means walk through, red means stop for a check) to a mayhem of 'porters', taxi touts, hotel touts, and other *Limeños* intent on getting an early look in on your dollars.

You are advised to change money at the airport for the taxi ride to the town centre. You can withdraw money before you exit customs – the

◉ TEN THINGS TO DO IN LIMA

1 Plaza de Armas, Iglesia San Francisco and the catacombs The centre of Lima has been done up in the last few years and really warrants a visit. Take a stroll around the main square to see the Palacio de Gobierno, the cathedral and the Archbishop's Palace. The San Francisco Church a couple of blocks from the main square dates from the 16th century and has a series of underground crypts that served as Lima's main cemetery for many years. It is believed that 25,000 people are buried here.

2 Circuito Magico del Agua This is a large water park, with 13 fountains, excellent for both adults and children – bring spare clothes and a jacket; you'll inevitably get a soaking. It's open in the evenings, too. Take a taxi and wander at leisure; the fountains are all lit up and some have a colourful laser lightshow complete with music and projected images of dances and moving landscapes. (Wednesday to Sunday.)

3 Castillo del Real Felipe in Callao This is the most important example of colonial military architecture in Spanish America. It was built to defend the capital from pirates during the times of the Manso de Velasco, the Viceroy Count of Superunda (1745 to 1761). Callao is Lima's busy port.

4 Visit to Barranco at night This coastal bohemian neighbourhood, adjoining Miraflores, is buzzing with nightlife. See (and join in) how Peruvians really party, until the small hours. And by day take a gentle stroll through the wide avenues admiring the colonial houses and gardens as well as some small quirky art galleries.

5 Asociación Mario Testino exhibition The Peruvian photographer Mario Testino has recently opened a permanent exhibition of his work and established 'MATE', the Asociación Mario Testino, a not-for-profit cultural organisation in the district of Barranco.

safest place to do it before entering the main hall. Otherwise there are banks and ATMs in the International Departures Hall.

The contact details for **Lima International Airport** are: ☎ 5116055, 5173100; www.lap.com.pe.

For a list of airline offices, see *Useful addresses*, page 125.

6 Shopping or people watching at Larcomar Lima has several large modern shopping centres – I am not usually a shopper but enjoy a visit to Larcomar because it is easily accessible, lying right in the heart of Miraflores and it overlooks the Pacific. It has a number of cinemas, cafés (with decent coffee), restaurants and a few interesting shops so is a pleasant place for people watching well away from the chaos and traffic of the busy streets and markets.

7 Eat Peruvian food Peruvian cuisine, as yet fairly little known in the English-speaking world, is justly famous throughout Latin America. Whilst in Lima take the opportunity to taste food prepared by internationally renowned chefs like Gastón Acurio, Javier Wong, Mitsuharu Tsumura and Rafael Osterling. There are other less well-known chefs such as Pedro Miguel Schiaffino who has a restaurant in San Isidro. For listings, see pages 122–3.

Lima's fresh produce markets (there are many; Mercado de Surquillo in Miraflores is the largest and has been recently renovated) are worth wandering around to see some of the vast array of produce from this wonderfully biodiverse country.

8 Cycle tours of Lima Take a bike tour of the city or off road – from Cieneguilla to Pachacamac. This 40km ride takes you through agricultural land, giving a good insight to the local way of life. Rent bikes for city use from www.biketoursoflima.com – they also offer excellent organised bike tours. For longer, more varied routes, go to www.perucycling.com.

9 Nightlife in Lima The 'in' places to go for nightlife of course change frequently but the classics that are always popular include **Peña La Candelaria** (*Bolognesi 292 Barranco; www.lacandelariaperu.com*) and **Brisas del Titicaca** (*www.brisasdeltiticaca.com*) in the centre of Lima.

10 Paragliding in Lima Either from the Parque del Amor in the heart of Miraflores or from Pachacamac – both are popular. We haven't done it but it looks amazing!

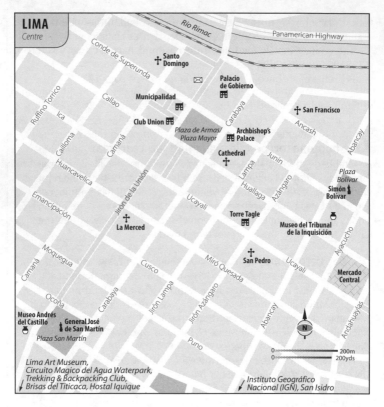

LIMA
Centre

Rio Rimac

Panamerican Highway

Conde de Superunda

✝ Santo
Domingo

Ruffino Torrico

Ica

Callao

✉

Palacio
de Gobierno

Municipalidad

Caraboya

✝ San Francisco

Ancash

Camaná

Club Union

Plaza de Armas/
Plaza Mayor

Archbishop's
Palace

Abancay

Huancavelica

Cailloma

Cathedral
✝

Lampa

Junín

Plaza
Bolívar

Simón
Bolívar

Emancipación

Jirón de la Unión

Ucayali

Azángaro

Huallaga

Torre Tagle

Museo del Tribunal
de la Inquisición

Ayacucho

Camaná

Moquegua

La Merced
✝

Cusco

Miró Quesada

San Pedro
✝

Ucayali

Mercado
Central

Ocoña

Carabaya

Jirón Lampa

Jirón Azángaro

Abancay

Andahuaylas

Museo Andrés
del Castillo

General José
de San Martín

Plaza San Martín

Puno

N

0 ———— 200m
0 ———— 200yds

Lima Art Museum,
Circuito Magico del Agua Waterpark,
Trekking & Backpacking Club,
Brisas del Titicaca, Hostal Iquique

Instituto Geográfico
Nacional (IGN), San Isidro

Transport from/to Lima airport There is no longer an airport bus. Public transport is restricted to the dozens of colectivos going to all parts of Lima from outside the airport. However, we would not recommend this form of transport until you know the city and never with luggage. Colectivos are always extremely cramped and there is no extra space for bulky gringo rucksacks. You will probably have to resign yourself to taking a **taxi**. Knowing this, it is a good idea to join up with other travellers while still in the airport for a shared ride.

The easiest and most secure option is to order one of the official airport taxis at the desk as you come out of the customs area, though it will be more expensive (about 55 soles) than taking your chance with those waiting outside the Arrivals Hall with whom you can bargain. Generally speaking, the nearer the taxi is to the door of the airport, the more expensive it will be.

The best hotels provide their own **private buses** so look out for the drivers holding up a sign with the name of the hotel. Many travellers choose to stay in an upmarket hotel for the first night for this ease of arrival. Check before travelling whether you will be met at the airport.

To get to the airport from the city (without luggage) take a colectivo from Miraflores to the entrance to the airport on the main road.

BY BUS If you arrive in Lima by long-distance bus, you should know that there is no central bus terminal in the city; your bus will deposit you at their depot. From there it is best to take a taxi to wherever you are staying and avoid hanging around; bus depots are renowned for thieves.

There are dozens of long-distance bus companies in Lima, but recommended companies are: **Cruz del Sur** (✆ *3115050; www.cruzdelsur. com.pe*), **Oltursa** (✆ *7085000; www.oltursa.pe*), **Móvil** (✆ *7168000; www. moviltours.com.pe/portal*) and **Ormeno** (✆ *4725000; www.grupo-ormeno. com.pe*). Check which terminal you depart/arrive from/to.

GETTING AROUND

Distances in Lima are huge so it is a relief that the city has an extensive bus, **colectivo** and taxi service – and now a metro as well. They run even on public holidays.

BY METRO Lima has a new Metro (*www.lineauno.pe/index.php*) and although currently only one line, it is being extended. Line one goes from Villa El Salvador to Avenida Grau, via Surco, San Borja, San Luis and La Victoria. You need to buy a rechargeable card at one of the Metro or bus stations for 5 soles, and then each ride (on the Metro or Metropolitan (see below) costs 1.5 soles.

BY BUS There is a new bus system, Metropolitano, aimed at speeding up commutes across the city, with designated bus lanes (*www.metropolitano. com.pe*). It starts in the northern suburb of Los Olivos, passes through the centre of Lima and then continues via La Via Expressa, through Lince, San Isidro, Miraflores, Barranco and ends in Chorrillos. Buses list the main streets on their route on the front window. At rush hour driving from Miraflores to the centre of Lima could take one hour, but this fast bus will get you there in 15 minutes. Apart from the Metropolitano, there are two types of buses: private ones painted in different colours according to their route and either in very good or very bad condition, and the yellow or grey government-run buses which are mostly new and connect with the Metropolitano ones. Buses run between 06.00 and midnight daily, and on some routes throughout the night. Fares cost an extra 20% after midnight.

BY COLECTIVO These are private cars or minibuses running the same routes as the buses and with routes also listed on the front window.

6

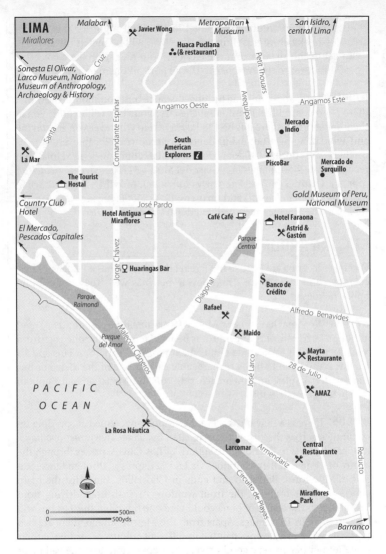

As a further aid the helper/money-collector will scream the main destination out of the window. Colectivos stop wherever the passenger wants to get off, or when they are hailed, so are more convenient than buses, and only a little more expensive. They run between 06.00 and 01.00 daily, and on some routes throughout the night, fares cost an extra 20% after midnight.

BY TAXI Taxis are ubiquitous. Settle on the price before you get in as they rarely have meters. You should pay about 11–17 soles for most trips around the city. All taxis carry a taxi sign, but they do not need any legal documents to operate, and anybody can be a taxi driver. Be extremely wary late at night. Radio cars can be ordered by phone and are punctual and secure, but double the price of the normal 'street' taxis. It is always better to ask at your hotel for a reliable taxi, especially if a lone woman or when travelling at night or with luggage. There is an open-topped **tour bus**, from US$25 for a three-hour, hop-on, hop-off tour. Tickets are available from the Tourist Booth in Parque Kennedy in Miraflores (*www. mirabusperu.com/tours.htm*).

⌂ WHERE TO STAY

The list below gives you the recommended backpackers' places, a few mid-range hotels and a couple of luxury places for a splurge (prices up to US$350 per night). **Budget hotels** offer basic rooms, mostly without private bathrooms, or dormitory-style accommodation. Prices range between 15 and 45 soles per person (*about US$6 to US$18pp*) for dorms. More for a room.

Some backpackers stay in the centre of Lima because it has the cheapest accommodation and bus stations are close. Others prefer Miraflores, which is cleaner, safer and quieter, or Barranco, which has a wild, bohemian reputation. **Mid-range** options include a large choice of rooms with en-suite bathrooms, TV, phone, left-luggage facility and laundry; prices (from US$30 per person) usually include buffet or continental breakfast. Lima has a fair range of **four- and five-star hotels**, attracting a mix of tourist and business clients. These cost around US$60 per person.

BUDGET

⌂ **The Tourist Hostal** Jr Cesareo Chacaltana 130, House B, Miraflores; ✆ 4478691; e thetouristhostel@hotmail.com; www.thetouristhostel.com. 14 beds in 3 clean but small dorms, with hot water, Wi-Fi & lockers. A bargain at 15 soles & books up fast.

⌂ **Hostal Iquique** Jr Iquique 758, Breña; ✆ 4334724; e iquique@hostaliquique. com; www.hostal-iquique-lima.com. Roof terrace, Wi-Fi. 28 soles per room upwards.

⌂ **One Hostel** Avda Grau 717, Barranco; ✆ 2477989; e one@operu.com; www.operu. com. Nice hostal with rustic/homey feel,

close to the action in Barranco. Dorms & private rooms with Wi-Fi, b/fast & towels inc. From 40 soles.

MID-RANGE

⌂ **3B** Jr Centenario 130, Barranco; ✆ 2476915; e reservas@3bhostal.com; www.3bhostal.com. Up-&-coming hostal/ hotel in up-&-coming area, mixing art with modern architecture. Optional airport transfer for an additional cost. Prices from US$40 pp.

⌂ **Hotel Antigua Miraflores** Avda Grau 350, Miraflores; ✆ 2012060;

e reservas@antiguamiraflores.com; www. antiguamiraflores.com. Spanish, colonial-style mansion with character & style. From US$50 pp.

🏠 **Hotel Faraona** Calle Manuel Bonilla 185 Miraflores; ☎ 4469414; **e** reservas@ faraonagrandhotel.com; www. faraonagrandhotel.com. The Egyptian theme may not be to all tastes, but it's clean, central & great for a 1-night stay. Airport transfer available for an additional cost. From US$50 pp.

AS A TREAT

🏠 **Miraflores Park Hotel** Avda Malecón de la Reserva 1035, Miraflores;

☎ 6104000; **e** perures.fits@orient-express. com; www.miraflorespark.com. Next to the sea, lovely ocean views & open-air pool. From US$150 pp.

🏠 **Country Club Hotel** Los Eucaliptos 590, San Isidro; ☎ 6119000; **e** reservas@ hotelcountry.com; www.hotelcountry.com. Colonial manor-style rooms, golf course nearby, & settled among the embassies of San Isidro. From US$200 pp.

🏠 **Sonesta El Olivar** Pancho Fierro 194, San Isidro; ☎ 7126000; **e** reservasolivar@ sonestaperu.com; www.sonesta.com/lima. Nice position next to a park full of olive trees & birds. Marble bathrooms. From US$200 pp.

✖ WHERE TO EAT AND DRINK

There are some excellent restaurants in Lima, which has a burgeoning gastronomic reputation; seafood is particularly recommended. Look out for the Summum guide (*www.facebook.com/summumperu*) which lists the best restaurants. Be warned that an 18% government tax and a 10% service charge will be added to the bill in posh restaurants. Service can be very slow. For that final-day splurge the following are recommended:

RESTAURANTS **La Caravana** has five sites across the city, the best chicken and chips (very popular in Peru) if you want something quick and tasty.

Miraflores

✖ **AMAZ** Calle La Paz 1079; ☎ 2219393. Amazon orientated. Owned by chef Pedro Miguel Schiaffino. See also *Malabar*, page 124.

✖ **Astrid & Gastón** Casa Hacienda Moreyra; ☎ 2425387; www.astridygaston. com. Restaurant of Paris-trained chef & TV personality Gastón Acurio, & probably the best in town. A modern take on traditional dishes. Haute cuisine & Peruvian mix – Peking guinea pig is one of the latest additions to the menu. Voted best restaurant in the World's Best Restaurants 2013 so book weeks in advance.

✖ **Central Restaurante** Calle Santa Isabel 376; ☎ 2428515; www. centralrestaurante.com.pe. One of Lima's trendiest restaurants & voted best restaurant in the Summum guide 2012 & 2013. Chef Virgilio Martinez also has a restaurant in London (*www.limalondon. com*). Ceviches, beef, fish, duck, goat – a modern take using traditional produce.

✖ **La Mar** Avda La Mar 770; ☎ 4213365; **e** lamar@lamarcebicheria.com.pe. Top lunchtime spot for ceviche & seafood owned by chef Gastón Acurio.

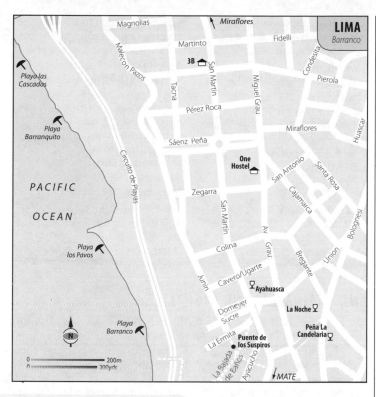

Outside Lima The influence of the great chefs is spreading – if you visit Pachacamac (page 128) try the Andean food at **Gloria del Campo** (*www.lagloriadelcampo.com*) or a variety of Peruvian specialities at **La Casa de Don Cucho** set amid beautiful colonial gardens (*Hacienda Casa Blanca, Pachacamac;* 2311415; *www.cuchosazonperuana.com/la_ casa_d_edoncucho.htm*).

✕ **La Rosa Náutica** At the end of the pier at Miraflores; 4470057; www.larosanautica.com. One of the most expensive – & one of the best – restaurants in town. Very popular with

groups, fantastic positioning, dining to the sounds of the Pacific. Possibly best known for its happy-hour Pisco sours. Delicious!

✕ **Maido** Calle San Martin 399 (cnr of Calle Colón); 4442568; www.maido.pe. This is the restaurant of chef Mitsuharu Tsumura. It serves Japanese Peruvian food, with a focus on seafood.

✕ **Pescados Capitales** Avda La Mar 1337; www.pescadoscapitales.com. Excellent seafood restaurant – second restaurant at Avda Primavera 1067, San Borja.

✕ **Rafael** San Martin 300; 2424149; www.rafaelosterling.com. The restaurant of Peruvian chef Rafael Osterling, serves Peruvian fusion food, excellent seafood. He also has **El Mercado** (*Hipólita Unanue 203, Miraflores;* 2211322).

Peruvian food, including dishes like *lomo saltado, aji de gallina* & *ceviches.*

San Isidro

✗ **Malabar** Camino Real 101; 4405200, 4405300; www.malabar.com.pe. The minimalist restaurant of Peruvian chef Pedro Miguel Schiaffino. He is a specialist in produce from the Amazon – exotic fruit & river fish. He also has another restaurant; AMAZ in Miraflores.

Huaca Pucllana

✗ **La Huaca Pucllana** General Borgoño cdra 8, Huaca Pucllana; 4454042. Good food in an unbeatable venue – Lima's adobe temple ruins, dating from AD500 & beautifully lit up at night. Tasty, hearty

La Victoria

✗ **Javier Wong** Enrique Leon Garcia 114 Santa Catalina; 4706217; ☺ lunchtime. Javier cooks & serves in his own house & doesn't have a menu. There is no choice & prices are high. Must be booked in advance. Seafood at its freshest & finest.

CAFÉS

▭ **Café Café** There are several in the city offering excellent coffee & sandwiches. Larco Mar has one & there are a couple more in central Miraflores.

▭ **Mango's** In Larcomar shopping centre. Good coffee, café snacks & treats.

ENTERTAINMENT AND NIGHTLIFE

The best sources of information for **local events** (if you read Spanish) are newspapers *El Comercio* or *La República*. Look under the cultural section, and you will find a list of cinemas (English-language films are usually subtitled, not dubbed), music, and so on. See also, *Tourist information*, below.

Peña is typical Peruvian entertainment: a restaurant with live folk music and dance shows in traditional costumes – not to be missed.

For additional suggestions, see the *Ten things to do in Lima* box, pages 116–17.

♀ **Ayahuasca** Avda El Libertador San Martin 130

♀ **Capitán Meléndez** Calle Alcanfores 199, Tda 5, Miraflores; 4470089; m 981323514; www.actiweb.es/capitan-melendez. Offers a wide range of classic & creative Peruvian cocktails using a Pisco base.

♀ **Huaringas Bar** Óvalo Bolognesi 460, Miraflores; 2222147; www.huaringas. com. Serving up a contemporary take on the traditional Peruvian cocktail & many times the winner of Summum 'Best Pisco Sour in

Peru', this bar also serves chilcanos, tunches & huaringas shots. They are soon to open a second bar in Cusco.

♀ **La Noche** Avda Bolognesi 307, Barranco. A classic lively night spot, in the heart of Barranco that hosts live bands & attracts a slightly older crowd than many of the bars in Barranco.

♀ **Mayta Restaurante** 28 de Julio 1290, Miraflores; 2430121, 4465430; www. maytarestaurante.com. Contemporary Pisco bar & restaurant. As well as classic Piscos, typical cocktails include aguaymanto, camu camu, lemongrass, maracumango & uvachado chilcanos.

🍷 **PiscoBar** Av Petit Thouars 5390 (cnr Gonzales Prada), Miraflores; ☎2411944; www.piscobar.pe. Pisco bar & restaurant serving Pisco cocktails such as chilcano, Pisco tonic, maracuyá fresh, capitán, bloody Pisco & Pisco puro of various grape varieties.

USEFUL ADDRESSES

AIRLINE OFFICES

✈ **Lan Perú** www.lanperu.com. Has 8 offices throughout Lima. Try Centro Comercial Real Plaza, Avda Garcilazo de la Vega (ex Avda Wilson) 1337, Tda 1001; ⏱ 10.00–22.00 daily, or in Miraflores try Avda José Pardo 513; ☎2138200; ⏱ 08.30–19.00 Mon–Fri. They fly all over Peru & South America.

✈ **LC Peru** Avda Pablo Carriquirry 857, San Isidro; ☎2041313; e reservas@lcperu.pe; www.lcperu.pe. Fly to Huaraz daily.

✈ **Peruvian Airlines** Several offices; try the Centro Comercial Real Plaza or Centro Civico 2 do Nivel; ☎7156343; e counter. realplaza@peruvian.pe; www.peruvian. pe; ⏱ 10.00–22.00 daily. Domestic flights including Cusco & Arequipa.

Internet access: Access to the internet is booming throughout Peru, and Lima is no exception – there are dozens and dozens of places to email from, some of which are open 24 hours a day. Many cafés, pubs, hotels and restaurants also offer Wi-Fi, so it's very easy to remain connected. There are also free Wi-Fi spots in parks.

✈ **Star Peru** ☎7059000; www.starperu. com. Several offices in Lima, the main office is in Avda Comandante Espinar 331, Miraflores (☎ 2138813; e counterespinar@ starperu.com; ⏱ 09.00–18.45 Mon–Fri, 09.00–13.00 Sat). Domestic flights including Cusco.

✈ **Taca** Avda José Pardo 811, Miraflores; www.taca.com; ⏱ 08.30–19.00 Mon–Fri, 09.00–14.00 Sat. Domestic routes within Peru.

BANKS AND FOREIGN EXCHANGE

$ **Banco de Crédito** Jr Lampa 499, central Lima; also the cnr of Avda Larco & Shell, Miraflores; ⏱ 09.00–16.00 Mon–Fri. The best bank for changing travellers' cheques & getting cash from credit cards.

$ **Banco Wiese** Diagonal 1176, Miraflores. Interbank: Jr de la Unión a 600; Miraflores branch at Larco 215.

CHARITIES AND VOLUNTEERING

If you have any leftover medical supplies or are interested in making a donation (perhaps of your leftover soles at the end of a trip) there are 2 children's charities in Lima. There may also be volunteer opportunities here. See page 74.

COMMUNICATIONS

✉ **Post office** Next to the Plaza de Armas. The main one for Lista de Correos.

EMERGENCIES

Tourist police Jr Moore 268, Magdalena del Mar; ☎4601060, 4600965, 4604525

HEALTH

✚ **Clínica Anglo-American** Calle Alfredo Salazar 314 (3rd block), San Isidro; ☎2213656

✚ **Clinica Javier Prado** Avda Javier Prado Este 499; ☎2114141

✚ **Clínica San Borja** Avda Guardia Civil 337, San Borja; ☎2000300

IMMIGRATION

Dirección General de Migraciones
España 730 (cnr of Huaraz), Breña;
📞2001000 (*08.00–18.00*); ⏰ 08.00–13.00
Mon–Fri; www.digemin.gob.pe

SHOPPING FOR PROVISIONS

In the past few years many large supermarkets have sprung up throughout Lima. The biggest & most well known are usually open from 08.00 until 22.00, &

👁 MUSEUMS

MUSEO NACIONAL DE ANTROPOLOGÍA, ARQUEOLOGÍA E HISTORIA (National Museum of Anthropology, Archaeology & History; *Plaza Bolívar s/n, Pueblo Libre;* 📞 *4635070;* ⏰ *09.00–17.30 Mon–Sat, 09.00–16.30 Sun & holidays; entry fee 10 soles*) Well worth a visit for an overview of Peruvian history. Guides available in English and Spanish.

MUSEO LARCO (formerly the Museo Rafael Larco Herrera) (*Avda Bolívar 1515, Pueblo Libre;* 📞 *4611312; www.museolarco.org;* ⏰ *09.00–22.00 daily; entry fee 30 soles*) Guides in English and Spanish on request. An utterly wonderful museum depicting the cultural history of Peru, from pre-Inca times through Spanish rule. Its collection of 'erotic' pots from the pre-Inca Moche period is world-famous. There is an excellent gourmet restaurant in the grounds.

MUSEO DE LA NACIÓN (National Museum; *Avda Javier Prado Este 2465, San Borja;* 📞 *6189393; www.mcultura.gob.pe;* ⏰ *09.00–17.00 Tue–Sun; free entry*) Guides in English, French and Spanish, and a café, bookshop and souvenir shop. Focuses mainly on archaeology and art.

MUSEO ORO DEL PERÚ (Gold Museum of Peru; *Avda Alonso de Molina 1100, La Molina;* 📞 *3451292; www.museoroperu.com.pe;* ⏰ *10.30–18.00 daily; entry fee 33 soles*) Guides in Spanish and English. A few years ago this Gold Museum was discredited when it was found that the majority of its exhibits were fakes. The administration claims that these have now been removed and all exhibits are authentic.

MUSEO METROPOLITANO DE LIMA (Metropolitan Museum; *Exposition Park, between Avdas July 28 & Garcilaso de la Vega (Wilson);* 📞*4337122;* ⏰ *09.00–17.00 Tue–Sun; entry fee 4 soles*) This newly opened museum is all about the history of Lima and is an excellent one to visit with children (over age 12). The history of the city is depicted from prehistoric times until the present day through a series of exhibits that feature holographs, 3- and 4-D movies, and photographs. Visitors enter in a small group with a guide. The visit takes nearly two hours. If you have to wait, you can grab a fruit juice or coffee in the garden.

many have free Wi-Fi & small restaurants. They are:

Plaza Vea www.plazavea.com.pe/
Metro Shell 250, Miraflores & another at Benavides 620
Vivanda www.vivanda.com.pe
Wong www.wong.com.pe/

Local markets: Local food markets are a fun way to shop for provisions, so are worth seeking out. Each neighbourhood has one. Here you will find the best of the local produce, an amazing array of fresh fish, meat, fruit, vegetables and grains from all over Peru. For handicrafts, see page 70.

TOUR OPERATORS

There are numerous good tour operators in Lima. The following are listed because they are personally recommended by the authors:

Aracari Schell 237, Miraflores; 6512424; e info@aracari.com; www.aracari.com. Tailor-made & luxury tours with a cultural emphasis.
Ayllu Viajes Calle Elias Aguirre 126, Oficina 905, Miraflores; 4459639; m 999787060; e info@ayllutours.com; www.ayllutours.com. A very helpful English-speaking travel agency; can organise flights, tours, hotel reservations & pretty much all other services in Peru.
Caral Tours Nicolás de Piérola 194, Barranco; 2473769; m 987745402; www.caraltours.com. Offer a variety of day tours in the Lima area, including Pachacamac (page 128).

TOURIST INFORMATION

Tourist information is available at the **iPerú** offices throughout the city (see page 51), and there is plenty of in-depth information from the South American Explorers (see overleaf).

There are some useful publications, too. A free booklet, *Peru Guide*, is available from many hotels and the tourist office and contains much useful information on Lima and other tourist cities in Peru as well as a listing of entertainments and local events. The online *Peruvian Times* (*www.peruviantimes.com*) will give you a very good insight into the political and economic situation in Peru. Also online is *Rumbos* magazine (*www.rumbosonline.com*) with articles on all aspects of Peru.

TOURIST INFORMATION AND OTHER USEFUL ORGANISATIONS

Municipalidad de Lima Pasaje Santa Rosa 134, Plaza Mayor; www.munlima.gob. pe. Useful information point.
Peruvian Touring and Automobile Club 6119999; www.touringperu.com. pe
PromPeru (main source of tourist information) 574 8000; e iperu@ promperu.gob.pe; www.peru.travel/en. It

you have a complaint or problem to do with hotels, restaurants, tour agencies, airlines or theft – this English-speaking, helpful tourist hotline functions day & night. There is a 24hr office at the airport, or contact Jorge Basadre 610, San Isidro (08.30–18.00 Mon–Fri) or Larcomar Entertainment Center in Miraflores (*Module 14, Plaza Gourmet;* 11.00–13.00 & 14.00–20.00 Mon–Sat).

⊙ PACHACAMAC

If you are in Lima for a few days and feel like getting out of the city I'd recommend Pachacamac, just 31km south of the city.

This is an impressive, largely adobe, pre-Inca site on the coast. It was once a temple, important first for a pre-Inca civilisation and then for the Incas. The views over the ocean are beautiful and a tour will offer a glimpse into the history of the pre-Hispanic Peruvian cultures. There is a research project at the site, and its informative official website is worth a look: www.pachacamac.net.

A taxi costs 42 soles from the southern side of Lima, and takes 30 to 60 minutes, depending on traffic. The entry fee is 6 soles. The site itself is huge, over 5km², so hard work to walk around; it's also rather difficult to understand without a guide, so I'd recommend an organised tour as a good alternative. The local tour company Caral Tours (*www.caraltours.com*) organises tours out of Lima, including to Pachacamac.

ℹ South American Explorers Enrique Palacios 956, Miraflores; ☏ 4442150; www.saexplorers.org; ⊕ 09.30–17.00 Mon, Tue, Thu & Fri, 09.30–20.00 Wed, 09.30–13.00 Sat. See page 51.

MAPS

While in Lima take the opportunity to purchase all the hiking maps you need (although if your time is short and you are trekking in the Cusco area, there is a very good supply of maps there too). The government-run **Instituto Geográfico Nacional** (IGN), is on Avenida Aramburu 1190–98, in the suburb of Surquillo (☏ 4759960; *www.ign.gob.pe*; ⊕ 08.30–17.00 Mon–Fri). Take your passport with you for the security guys. The IGN 1:100,000 topographical maps cover most of the country. Eventually the IGN plans to map the whole country, but they've been saying that for over 30 years.

The IGN also publishes a good road map of Peru, departmental maps, satellite maps and satellite photos, a political map, a geographical map and others. It's worth a visit but check at the South American Explorers first. They sell some IGN maps and can tell you – in English – what's available at the IGN.

! Updates website: For the latest updates go to www.bradtupdates.com/perutrekking. You can also post your feedback here – corrections, changes or even new hikes. Your information will be put on our website for the benefit of other travellers.

Cajamarca and Chachapoyas Regions

CAJAMARCA TOWN AND REGION   *Telephone code: 076*

Situated at only 2,750m in the northern highlands of Peru, Cajamarca nestles in a quiet, green valley surrounded by low mountain peaks. Considering its attractions it sees relatively few tourists.

The town has a colonial charm with lovely churches, and to this day the Indians have kept their traditions, fiestas and to a large extent their traditional costumes. It has a relaxing atmosphere, with open hospitality and excellent Andean food, and the surrounding green countryside is steeped in history.

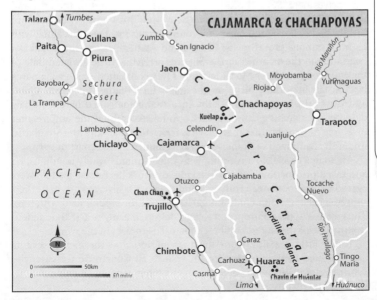

CAJAMARCA & CHACHAPOYAS

Talara
Tumbes
Sullana
Paita
Piura
Zumba
San Ignacio
Jaen
Bayobar
Sechura Desert
La Trampa
Moyobamba
Riojao
Yurimaguas
Chachapoyas
Kuelap
Tarapoto
Lambayeque
Celendín
Juanjui
Chiclayo
Cajamarca
PACIFIC
OCEAN
Otuzco
Cajabamba
Tocache Nuevo
Chan Chan
Trujillo
Caraz
Chimbote
Carhuaz
Huaraz
Casma
Cordillera Blanca
Chavín de Huántar
Río Huallaga
Tingo María
Lima
Huánuco
Cordillera Central
Río Marañón
0   50km
0   50 miles

One attraction is the **Baños del Inca**, 6km outside the town. Thermal springs are channelled into a pool and private baths. A real treat, especially after a few days' hiking.

HISTORY Cajamarca was important long before the Incas established themselves here. Several pre-Inca sites have been found in the area and archaeologists are still making new discoveries. But a pivotal point in Inca history makes the name Cajamarca resonate with most visitors, along with its most famous protagonists: Pizarro and Atahualpa. The Incas had not been long in the area before the Spanish arrived – the estimated date of the Inca conquest of the local tribes is 1460, soon after which Cajamarca became an important place on the main Inca highway between Quito and Cusco. In November 1532 the Inca Atahualpa rested here for a few days before marching down to Cusco to take control of the empire after defeating his half-brother in the civil war. At the same time, the Spaniards, under the command of Francisco Pizarro, landed on the coast of Peru.

Atahualpa agreed to a meeting with the Spaniards, and was ambushed and taken prisoner by Pizarro. In trying to secure his release his followers agreed to fill a room once with gold and twice with silver; to no avail. Their supreme ruler, the Sun God, was garrotted and the empire died with him. Thus were 179 tired Europeans able to defeat an army of 6,000 or so and destroy one of the largest and best-organised empires in the world.

Today little remains from the Inca period and these grim events are best held in the imagination. A visit to **El Cuarto de Rescate** (the Ransom Room) in town, is worse than uninspiring; it cancels out your own mental picture.

GETTING THERE AND AWAY It is 856km from **Lima** via Trujillo to Cajamarca. Most bus travellers will choose to break the journey in Trujillo but there are **daily non-stop buses** which take 14 hours (*56 soles*). Cruz del Sur (*www.cruzdelsur.com.pe; bus station in Lima: Avda Javier Prado 1109, La Victoria*), Ormeno (*www.grupo-ormeno.com.pe; Avda Javier Prado Este 1059*) and Transmar (*www.transmar.com.pe; Avda 28 de julio 1511*) are just three of the several companies that make the journey. Alternatively, it's approximately two hours travelling **by air**; LAN (*www.lanperu.com*) and LC Peru (*www.lcperu.pe*) are currently the only airlines offering this service (*US$285 & US$110 respectively*).

The distance from **Tumbes via Chiclayo** to Cajamarca is 812km. Travelling by bus between Tumbes and Chiclayo takes ten hours (*42 soles*). The onward service from Chiclayo takes seven hours (*28 soles*).

GETTING AROUND Cajamarca is not a large town so hikers can easily walk to most places of interest. Yellow taxis (without meters) are plentiful and minibuses (combis) run from the centre to the outskirts of town.

🏠 **WHERE TO STAY** At the **budget** end of the spectrum are cheap backpackers' hotels, mostly with communal bathroom and cold water. Average prices are from 28 soles to 42 soles per person (*US$10 15pp*). **Mid-range** hotels offer private bath and hot water, with a price range of US$20–50 per person.

Budget

🏠 **Hostal Plaza** Amalia Puga 669, Plaza de Armas; ✆822058. A rambling old building, with good atmosphere & restaurant. Some rooms en suite. 20–30 soles pp.

🏠 **Hostal Sucre** Amalia Puga 811, Plaza de Armas; ✆822596. Central & basic. About 40 soles pp.

Mid-range

🏠 **Hostal Jusovi** Amazonas 637; ✆362920. Clean & convenient. Approximately US$25.

🏠 **El Cabildo Hostal** Jr Junín 1062. Near the Plaza de Armas, modern, characterful, nice courtyard. Approximately US$35 pp.

🏠 **Hotel Casa Blanca** 2 de Mayo 446; ✆362141. Right on the Plaza de Armas, & recently refurbished. Approximately US$60.

🏠 **Hotel Cajamarca** Calle Dos de Mayo 311; ✆362532; hotelcajamarca.com.pe. Close to the Plaza de Armas, with rooms round a central courtyard. Approximately US$70.

As a treat

🏠 **Costa del Sol** Jr Cruz de Piedra 707, ✆362472; www.costadelsolperu.com. A smart, modern hotel in the centre of town. Around US$100 pp.

🏠 **Hotel Laguna Seca** Next to the Baños del Inca, 6km outside town; ✆584300. A luxurious, country-resort-style. Approximately US$120/150 pp.

✗ **WHERE TO EAT AND DRINK**

🖥 **Café Van Gogh** Prolongacion Amalia Puga 126; ✆369657. Said to have the best coffee in town & particularly good for b/fast. Live music Fri nights.

✖ El Batan   Jr del Batan 369; ☎ 366025; Varied menu with Peruvian dishes including guinea pig.

✖ El Zarco   Jr del Batan 170; ☎ 363421. Reasonably priced Peruvian food. Popular with locals.

SHOPPING FOR PROVISIONS Try the market on Calle Amazonas for fresh bread, fruit and vegetables. At the many Tiendas de productos lacteos (dairy stores) you can buy the famous Cajamarca cheese, also *manjar blanca* (sweet caramel spread) and *galletas de maíz* (puffed corn biscuits).

FESTIVAL If you happen to be in this area around February (therefore in the wrong season for hiking) you will be able to take part in **Carnival**, one of the most colourful celebrations in Peru. In Cajamarca there is a marvellous display of costumes, music and dancing. The downside is that throwing water – and worse – at passers-by is a traditional carnival activity. Watch out for buckets containing the 'and worse' part.

HIKING AND TREKKING OVERVIEW There is very little organised trekking around Cajamarca – that is one of its pleasures. With the appropriate IGN map *Cajamarca* (15-f) you can devise any variety of walks and treks.

SHORT WALKS AROUND CAJAMARCA
Half-day walks
To Ayllambo (*3.5km; 1½hrs*) A pleasant walk to the pottery village of Ayllambo. Leave from Avenida Independencia and walk south. Along the way you'll pass several craft shops selling the typical ceramics of Cajamarca. In Ayllambo there is a workshop, Escuela Taller, where pottery is taught.

To Cerro Santa Apollonia (*about 2hrs round trip*) This walk is to the hill overlooking Cajamarca that has a statue of Atahualpa on top and the chapel of the Virgen de Fátima *en route*. Leave from Calle Dos de Mayo, up the endless steps to the top.

A day trek through the countryside Take a bus or walk 7km to **Ventanillas de Otuzco** from Avenida Arequipa. Visit this interesting pre-Inca cemetery, which consists of hundreds of funerary niches. From here you can walk 6km to the **Baños del Inca**. Ask the locals to show you the path that runs south to the river. It can be very muddy in the rainy season. Cross the river and follow the riverbank to your right. The local people are very friendly and often stop for a chat.

Once at the Baños enjoy yourself! There is a small admission charge, then a selection of baths, saunas, massage, etc, ranging in price from 6 to

◉ CUMBE MAYO

This is an extraordinary site, so even if you do not want to do the hike. it is well worth taking a tour here (check around for the best rates) not just for the pre-Inca remains, but for the 'forest of rocks' covering the bare hilltops. There are tall, thin rocks, cut deep into the limestone by erosion, and isolated goblets. There is a cave decorated with **petroglyphs** showing the influence of the Chavín culture, and a remarkable **aqueduct** channelling water down to Cajamarca, carved into the rock with geometric precision. There are many perfect right angles, and dead-straight stretches, as well as tunnels. It serves as a reminder that the Incas didn't invent the art of stone cutting. No-one knows the exact purpose of this aqueduct, but it certainly wasn't purely for agricultural purposes. It doesn't carry enough water and there are plenty of streams watering the valley anyway. Most likely it – and the cave with petroglyphs – featured in some sort of water ritual.

20 soles. Bring a towel. Clean and relaxed, continue your walk 7km along a dirt road to Llacanora, a typical country village, with an old colonial church on its little plaza. Continue to **La Collpa**, about 7km. A dirt road connects these two places, running through flat farmland, but there are short cuts. Corn, wheat and barley are grown. La Collpa itself is a co-operative for cattle farming, and you can visit the Centro Ganadero and purchase cheese and manjar blanca.

From La Collpa it's a 2½-hour walk (11km) back to Cajamarca.

CUMBE MAYO TO SAN PABLO

This three- or four-day trek takes you through some lovely scenery and rural villages, beginning at one of the area's most important pre-Inca sites.

GETTING TO THE TRAILHEAD You may not want to walk all the way up to Cumbe Mayo. It may be worth getting a taxi, or signing up for a tour for the advantage of the lift up there and guidance round Cumbe Mayo (explain that you will not be coming back and check that they don't mind taking your luggage). It takes one hour by car.

ROUTE DESCRIPTION Starting from the **Plaza de Armas** in **Cajamarca**, pass Cerro Santa Apolonia to your right. There is a short cut, a path well used by the locals, that goes straight up, from time to time crossing the road which curves its way up to Cumbe Mayo. It takes about three to

Distance	About 85km
Altitude	2,750–3,900m, descending to 2,365m
Rating	A comparatively easy walk, but with some steep ascents and descents
Timing	4 days; 1 day less if you get transport up to Cumbe Mayo
In reverse	Possible, but a long ascent
Start of trail	Plaza de Armas in Cajamarca or Cumbe Mayo
Transport at the end	From San Pablo to Chilete (30min); pick-ups, buses and trucks, mostly in the morning. From Chilete to Cajamarca (3hrs); buses and trucks.
Maps	IGN sheet Cajamarca (15-f)

four hours to get to the **Cumbe Mayo** pass (3,500m) where there are a few houses. The main footpath continues down into the valley, but you continue along the dirt road to your right, which works its way up the valley side to the second pass. After about an hour's hike (3km), you see a road going down into the valley to your left, with steep, rock-crowned slopes and a river below. Descend into the valley. The **aqueduct** lies in front of you at the foot of the narrow valley. It's still in a very good state, and is followed by a stone path that runs into the valley for about 500m.

The area is beautiful, with steep green hillsides, incredible rock formations and deep valleys. The locals who graze their sheep here are friendly, curious and anxious to have a chat with you. There are some

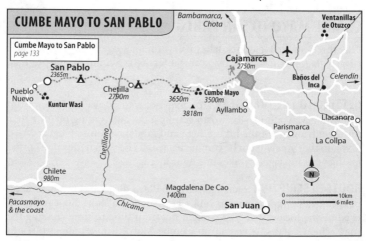

great camping spots, but it gets cold and windy as soon as the sun disappears, so put your tent up in good time.

The easiest way to Chetilla, the next community, is to follow the dirt road up to the pass (3,900m). You can take a short cut by following the path up the mountain range to your left (ask a local to direct you as the path is not very clear). At the pass you get a great view over the valley.

Follow the dirt road for about two hours, descending into the valley, passing a few hilltops with crosses and the little *casario* of **Jancate** to your left. On the third hilltop (with three crosses), which you can reach via short cuts, you'll enjoy a good view into the valley in front of you. Descend into this steep valley, following the road for about an hour until you see a well-used stone path to your right. This leads to **Chetilla** at 2,790m (which the road bypasses). The walk takes about three hours through beautiful countryside.

Continuing to San Pablo, the trail descends steeply down to the river. Cross the bridge and climb the steep hill on the other side until you reach green pastures with a few houses and a school, about three hours from the river. Sometimes the path fades away in the pasture but look ahead and you'll see the continuation; also ask the locals.

The path contours along the right slope of the valley, giving great views, and past subtropical vegetation splashed with little waterfalls. Then the path finally climbs up the mountainside, through pastures with a few houses, to the pass which is about seven hours from the school. Enjoy the view, it's the last one before you drop down to San Pablo.

From the pass, the path follows the mountainside, descending slowly, passing through the *casario* of **Tamincha**. From here it goes uphill, then descends to the river. Cross the bridge and take the steep short cut up the hill on your right. From here you can see the little picturesque village of San Pablo surrounded by green pampa. It's about a five-hour hike from the pass to the village.

Side trip: The ruins of the pre-Inca site of **Kuntur Wasi** show strong Chavín influence in the remains of a triple-terraced pyramid which once supported a temple. The site has recently been cleared and there is now a museum. To get to the ruins walk down the main road from San Pablo to Pueblo Nuevo (about 45 minutes). You'll see the sign to 'Kuntur Wasi' on your right.

San Pablo is a typical colonial village, with its small streets and carved wooden balconies. By the plaza at the lower end of the village is an attractive church with no fewer than three bell towers. On Sunday there is a market on the main street and the locals from the surrounding villages come to barter or sell their produce. The village has a simple hotel and several well-stocked shops. You'll find a few basic restaurants so can indulge in the usual post-hike eating orgy.

Kuntur Wasi, above.

THE CHACHAPOYAS REGION *Telephone code: 041*

Updated by Rob Dover and Charles Motley from the original text by Tom Gierasimczuk

The northern department of Amazonas, with its virgin cloudforest, contains such plentiful ruins and ancient cities that it has been lauded as the richest archaeological zone in South America and has recently been christened 'The Machu Picchu of northern Peru'. These are the remnants of the pre-Inca Chachapoya culture (AD600 to AD1500).

Although the area is slowly being cleared, many structures – even entire settlements – are still hidden under thick vegetation and camouflaged by epiphytes, vines and relentless undergrowth. Some sites, though, have been studied by national and international archaeologists, including such well-known names as Switzerland's Henri and Paula Reichlen, American Gene Savoy and the Peruvian archaeologist Federico Kaufmann-Doig; excavation projects live and die with the availability of funding.

Remarkably, despite its attributes the area is only now opening up to tourism. Not only are there spectacular ruins, but the cloudforest here is particularly rich in orchids, bromeliads and other epiphytes, making it a rewarding area for botanists and natural history enthusiasts. This ecological zone is picturesquely known as *ceja de selva*, the 'eyebrow of the jungle'.

There are no long treks in this forested region, but for walkers there is a wonderful variety of day or half-day hikes with ruins or waterfalls as their objective.

CHACHAPOYAS The region's main town and provincial capital is a friendly place with whitewashed colonial homes and a traditional atmosphere. Improved road access from the coast and ongoing upgrades to hotels and restaurants are facilitating the growth of tourism which is centred around the extraordinary ruins of Kuelap (page 140).

The town itself, with its agreeable climate, makes a pleasant base for exploring the surrounding countryside and the many ruins.

There is a **museum** at the Direccion Regional de Cultura on the plaza (Grau and Ayacucho), which has some Chachapoya pottery and a few dishevelled mummies.

History The Chachapoya culture is one of the most enigmatic in ancient America, appearing in modern-day northeast Peru sometime around AD500. They occupied a territory flanked by the great Marañon River to the north and west and the Huallaga River to the east. Their preference for building their settlements on ridges and hilltops has lent the Chachapoya the popular name of 'cloud people'. The finest example is Kuelap. Unlike the Incas, this was no authoritarian regime but existed as loose-knit chiefdoms, coming together for war but just as easily raiding each other's supplies when crops failed. The empire, it is believed, numbered almost 300,000 at its zenith, its roads, villages and fortresses – now so remote and solemn – all teeming with life. After successfully keeping at bay the expanding Wari, the Chachapoya were finally conquered around 1470 by the Incas, whose strategy was always to weaken the cultural, as well as the military, will of its opponents. Finally, betrayed by the Spaniards who had initially helped them fight the Inca, the Chachapoya disappeared. With such historical ambiguity, it has been easy to give in to imaginative speculation such as the Inca and Spanish descriptions of the Chachapoya as 'white and tall'. Since then, theories about their origin have run the gamut – everything from the lost tribes of Israel to Vikings who took a wrong turn.

Getting there and away There are currently (2013) **no direct flights** to Chachapoyas. The recommended route is to fly to Tarapoto and take a bus to Pedro Ruiz (six hours) then on to Chachapoyas.

The road between Cajamarca and Chachapoyas is in poor condition, so although there are **buses** running along this route, it is not an easy journey. Movil Tours (*www.moviltours.com.pe*) and Transportes Virgen de Carmen both run daily services from Cajamarca to Chachapoyas for 70 soles.

There are several comfortable **overnight buses** from Lima that do the journey in 20–24 hours for around 120 soles. **GH Bus** (*www.ghbus. com.pe*) and **Movil Tours**; throughout the week, leaving Lima in the late afternoon and arriving in Chachapoyas around the same time the next day. They stop, *en route*, at Pedro Ruíz from where you can access the various waterfalls of the region (page 146). **Cifa** (*www.cifainternacional. com*) run similar services. If you want to break the journey up, or if you're coming from Ecuador direct overnight buses run to Chachapoyas from Chiclayo and back, with a one-way journey taking about nine hours (42 soles). **Transervis Kuelap** and Movil Tours leave Chiclayo at 19.30 and arrive in Chachapoyas early the next morning.

The problem with these buses, as you will have spotted, is that they do the most spectacular part of the journey, from the coast up to Chachapoyas, at night thus depriving you of the scenery. And during the rainy season there are frequent landslides which may halt the bus for several hours. And, what's more, even if you break the journey in Chiclayo, the buses from there still run during the night so you don't really achieve anything.

Getting around As in most Andean towns, there is a reliable, albeit seemingly chaotic, network of minibuses that go just about anywhere at least once a day. In Chachapoyas, this nerve centre is on Jiron Grau, where it passes the market. From early morning until the late afternoon, transport of all shapes and sizes leaves for the nether regions of the Chachapoyas realm. Prices vary but expect to pay an average of 8 soles for every hour travelled. Taxis charge about 140 soles for the entire day for up to five people.

 Where to stay There is now a reasonable choice of accommodation and restaurants in and around Chachapoyas, as well as in Tingo, the gateway town for Kuelap, and by the ruins themselves. New lodges are also being built near the waterfalls.

Budget

🏠 **Hostal Kuelap** Amazonas 1057. A budget hotel & it shows. In the same area is …

🏠 **Hotelito Tingo** Jr San Juan, block M, lot 16, by the entrance to El Tingo. 11 soles dbl.

🏠 **DRC Hostal** Just below Kuelap ruins. The guard, Gabriel, & his family have 30 years' experience at the site. The family prepares simple meals & sells drinks & snacks. Very basic. 14 soles.

🏠 **Chachapoyas Backpackers** Dos de Mayo 639; ☎ 478879. Some en-suite rooms available. Wi-Fi & kitchen. 17 soles for a shared room.

🏠 **Albergue Leon** Jr San Juan, block M, lot 16 (in the same area as Hotelito Tingo, above) Very basic but adequate. 20 soles.

🏠 **Hostal Amazonas** Plaza Grau; www. hostalamazonasperu.com. Good value, helpful staff. 28/42 soles sgl/dbl.

🏠 **Hostal La Petaca** On the plaza, Leymebamba; Good, clean, cheap rooms with hot water. 28–42 soles.

Mid-range

🏠 **Hotel Vilaya** Jr Ayacucho 734; ☎ 477664; e hotelvilaya@hotmail.com; hotelvilayachachapoyas.com. A highly recommended 3-star hotel with good beds & glorious hot water. US$30–36.

🏠 **La Casona del Leymebamba** Leymebamba; ☎ 830106. Owned by Julio

Meyer, who can help with the trek to the Laguna de Condores (page 145). US$60 dbl with private bath, US$35 sgl.

Something special

The listings below all offer something a bit different & so deserve to be listed separately:

🏠 **Choctamal Lodge** Reservations (from the USA; toll free) ☎ 1 866 396 9582; m 995237268; e lostambos@msn.com; www.marvelousspatuletail.com. Ideally located in the community of Choctamal for a trek to Vilaya & Kuelap with a great view of Kuelap clear across the valley. For birders this is the best place to see the iconic marvellous spatuletail hummingbird (one of David Attenborough's favourite birds). Buses run here from Chachapoyas. US$40–50.

🏠 **Hacienda Chillo** 5km past El Tingo on the main road to Leymebamba; ☎ 832140 (Magdalena), 01 2659158 (Lima); e estanciachillo@hotmail.com. A rustic yet comfortable & charming hacienda run by local couple Oscar & Ada Arce, both well versed in local information. Oscar built & designed the place himself & the hacienda itself is worth a tour. US$50pp inc dinner & b/fast.

🏠 **Villa Kepno Organic Coffee Farm** Shipasbamba; m 965006233; e villakepnocafe@gmail.com; villakepno. webstarts.com. A few shared rooms are offered at this coffee farm. Juhani (from

Finland) & Maria will be building a sauna & there are also plans for an orchid garden near the village lake. Various tours are offered & you can even learn about coffee growing on a 3-day course. 28 soles inc b/fast with, of course, freshly roasted coffee.

✕ Where to eat and drink

✕ **Cafe Fusiones** Chincha Alta 445. A recommended escape, serving local organic coffee, b/fasts & sandwiches.

✕ **El Tejado** Avda Grau 534; ☎ 777654. Particularly good for lunch.

✕ **Restaurant Batan del Tayta** La Merced 604. A great mix of international, national & fusion dishes. Highly recommended.

✕ **Restaurant Chacha** Plaza de Armas. Recommended for delicious regional & national food at low prices. This popular local spot gets busy.

Useful addresses
Tourist information

🛈 **Direccion Regional de Cultura** Cnr of Grau & Ayacucho

🛈 **iPerú** In the council building on Amazonas

Tour operators

Chachapoyas Travel Jr Grau 565; 🖷 941715623. Tours to the main places of interest in the region.

Turismo Explorer Jr Grau on the plaza. Daily tours to Kuelap & Gran Vilaya.

Vilaya Tours ☎ 477506; 🖃 info@ vilayatours.com; www.vilayatours.com. Englishman Rob Dover has lived in the area for years. He offers multi-day trips & is very knowledgeable.

HIKING AND TREKKING OVERVIEW If you are planning to explore the region on foot, then buy your **maps** at the IGN in Lima (page 128). You'll need sheets 1358 (13-h) *Chachapoyas* and 1357 (14-h) *Leimebamba*. Peter Lerche, a German ethnohistorian, has written a detailed **guide** to hikes in the Chachapoyas region but it is currently only in Spanish.

A **must-read** about the area is *Warrior of the Clouds* by Keith Muscutt (*University of Mexico Press; www.chachapoyas.com*). It is out of print but you may find a secondhand copy. Keith's vivid account of living and exploring Chachapoyas is as historically pertinent as it is poetic. The book *Antisuyo*, by Gene Savoy, is a great – although embellished – source of information if you can get hold of it (it is also out of print). Works by local archaeologists can sometimes be found in Chachapoyas, as can *Chronicles of Peru's Cloud People* by Charles Motley which is also available from Amazon.

EXPLORING THE RUINS AROUND CHACHAPOYAS

Most of the Chachapoyan and Inca ruins described here involve a certain amount of walking; some are relatively easy to visit and some require a trek of a day or more.

THE RUINS OF KUELAP (*08.00–18.00; entry fee 17 soles*) Kuelap was first discovered in 1843 but remained in relative obscurity until recently, when adventure travellers and archaeology *aficionados* realised its sheer magnitude and BBC Television introduced a larger audience to its splendours. It has been described as the continent's largest ancient stone-built complex, dwarfing even Machu Picchu.

So just how big is Kuelap? The oval-shaped city stretches out for 600m in a perfect north–south trajectory on a ridge in the cloudforest some 3,000m above sea level. It is 110m wide and entirely enclosed by a massive defensive wall that soars up to 18m. The single structure covers 6ha. The two eastern entrances and one western entrance display an optical illusion of sorts: the massive limestone walls taper inwards forming an ever-narrowing corridor as you penetrate the citadel, until eventually there's only room for one person to enter at a time.

Once inside, you marvel at not only the view – of terraced plots of land resembling giant quilts and jagged peaks and deep valleys – but at the mind-boggling Chachapoya city planning. Natural contours of the land are incorporated, not levelled, and the lack of hard angles gives the entire area an organic feel. The citadel is composed of an upper and lower town. Over 450 roundhouses – common buildings and kitchens – are testament to the communal living practised within Kuelap. A peculiar conical building at the southern end served, it is believed, as a solar observatory that kept track of the seasonal passage of the sun – and therefore was an oracle of sorts for ancient farmers.

The general consensus among archaeologists is that Kuelap was built continuously from AD600 until sometime before the arrival of the Inca (contemporary reports of the region make no mention of Kuelap). However, the new empire grew within Kuelap's walls, with the citadel playing the role of market town, residence, solar observatory and sacred site. Agriculture on the surrounding fertile hillsides swelled the population to around 3,000 to 4,000 in Kuelap proper, judging by the concentration of roundhouses that today pepper the site like decomposing mushrooms.

Visiting Kuelap Kuelap lies about 75km from Chachapoyas and 189km from Celendín. Roads have been improved recently and an Interpretative Centre and toilets have been built near the entrance to the ruins. Local families sell drinks, snacks and even full meals so visiting Kuelap isn't the expedition it was only a few years ago.

Most visitors choose to arrange transport and a guide from one of the agencies in Chachapoyas, but others recommend making your way there independently so you can soak up the feeling of mystery without the distracting presence of other people.

Kuelap is best visited in the dry season (May to November). In the rainy season the paths are slippery and muddy, although some circuits

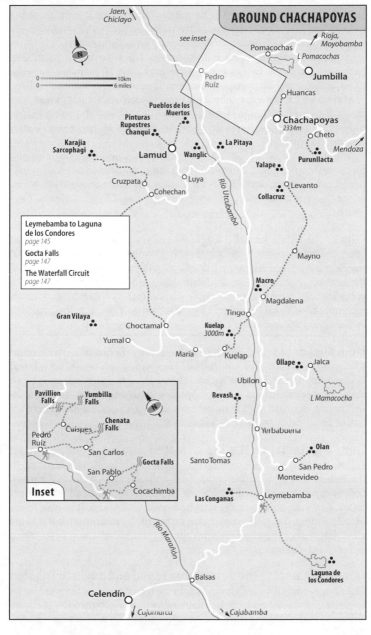

AROUND CHACHAPOYAS

Leymebamba to Laguna
de los Condores
page 145

Gocta Falls
page 147

The Waterfall Circuit
page 147

Jaen,
Chiclayo

see inset

Rioja,
Moyobamba

Pomacochas

L Pomacochas

Jumbilla

Pedro
Ruíz

Huancas

Pueblos de los
Muertos

Chachapoyas
2334m

Cheto

Pinturas
Rupestres
Chanqui

Mendoza

Karajia
Sarcophagi

Lamud

La Pitaya

Purunllacta

Wanglic

Yalape

Luya

Cruzpata

Cohechan

Levanto

Collacruz

Mayno

Gran Vilaya

Macro

Magdalena

Choctamal

Tingo

Kuelap
3000m

Yumal

Maria

Kuelap

Ollape

Jalca

Ubilon

L Mamacocha

Revash

Yerbabuena

Pavillion
Falls

Yumbilla
Falls

Chenata
Falls

Santo Tomas

Olan

Cuispes

Pedro
Ruiz

San Carlos

San Pedro
Montevideo

San Pablo

Gocta Falls

Cocachimba

Inset

Las Conganas

Leymebamba

Rio Marañón

Laguna de
los Condores

Balsas

Celendín

Cajamarca

Cajabamba

are possible if you're prepared. Be warned, though, that even seasoned trekkers are surprised at how tough the trails can become. Even in the dry season you need to be reasonably fit to cope with the steep trails.

A few years ago it was a four-hour trek from Tingo to the citadel but a new road now brings you to a car park only 20 minutes from the ruins. If using public transport the nearest approach is from the village of **María**, which is accessed by daily minibuses from Chachapoyas. You can still trek from **Tingo**, taking the obvious trail at the stone bridge over the Utcubamba River. It works its way up to the ruins, short-cutting the road.

You should allow at least three hours to look around the complex and three hours to get back down to Tingo. You can break the trek up into two days by staying at the Kuelap (DRC) hostal. Doing so will allow you to see the citadel at sunset and sunrise, both magical spectacles in good weather.

RUINS AND TREKS BEYOND KUELAP Among the interesting ruins and hikes scattered around the surrounding countryside is **Gran Vilaya**, publicised by Gene Savoy in 1985. Gran Vilaya is remote and isolated, though some campesinos cultivate land around there. They are a good source of information, and if you do one of these hikes you are recommended to take a guide. Organised tours of the area are provided by Turismo Explorer (page 139).

From Kuelap to Choctamal (*3,000m; 5–6hrs*) Follow the road behind Kuelap to the village of Choctamal. Here you can stay in Choctamal Lodge or alternatively there is a basic hotel; local families will cook you a meal. Some campesinos will happily work as guides, so ask around. You will need a guide to see the many ruins in the Choctamal area; there are lots of small paths and getting lost is easy.

From Choctamal to the top of Mount Shubet (*3,700m; 7–8hrs*) Follow the trail between the two bridges in Choctamal. This leads up to the **Yumal** pass (alternatively you could get public transport to the pass). Follow a not-too-obvious trail along the ridge to the head of the next valley. Crossing a ridge to the west by a good trail you will be able to see Mount Shubet. There are some ruins on top of the mountain, but it is the view that makes the climb worthwhile. It gets cold at the top, so take a jacket, food and water.

From Choctamal to the pass of Abra Yumal and down to Tribulon (*3,300m; 4–5hrs*) It's a two-hour walk to the top of the pass for good views towards Choctamal and Kuelap, then a downhill walk through the lush, although increasingly deforested, valley. Tribulon is a small community with friendly people. Here you can stay with a family who will supply you with basic meals and guide you around the **nearby ruins**, which include Las Pilas, Machu Llaqta, Santa Cruz, Pueblo Alto, Ojilcho and Santa Maria. All of the ruins are hard to get to, through dense cloudforest with no paths. Don't risk going without a **guide**. The return route from Tribulon to Choctamal takes six to seven hours.

From the pass of Abra Yumal to Vista Hermosa (*7–8hrs*) A steep, difficult path through lush cloudforest. The small community of Vista Hermosa offers basic accommodation and meals with a family. Nearby are the ruins of **La Plazuela**, a steep climb up from Vista Hermosa, and a bit further on are the ruins of **La Mesa** and **La Pirquilla**. You need a guide to visit these sites.

From Vista Hermosa to Chachapoyas (*allow 2 days*) First, you walk over to **Congon** where a steep trail takes you up to the beautiful valley of **Huaylla Belen**. This is a great place to camp beside a small meandering stream. Next day head up to **Tilla pass**, where you can avoid the modern road and carry along a horse trail to the village of **Cohechan**. Take plenty of water with you as there is none once you've left the Belen River. From Cohechan walk to the village of **Cruzpata** (30 minutes beyond are the sarcophagi situated on the mountain slope called **Karajia**).

OTHER SITES AROUND CHACHAPOYAS

Levanto Lying about 30km (by road) from Chachapoyas, this is a small, friendly mountain village with some excellent nearby ruins. Levanto was the Spanish regional capital for a while, before the capital was relocated at the present-day Chachapoyas. The town was an important Chachapoya settlement and, not satisfied with proving their superiority on the battlefield, the Incas reconstructed their version of the Chachapoya roundhouse just southwest of Levanto. This Inca Military Garrison guarded a major intersection of the empire's roads: the north–south road connected Cusco

👁THE SARCOPHAGI OF KARAJIA

Karajia is an extraordinary site two to three hours' drive northwest of Chachapoyas. Here are five enigmatic stone figures, gazing east from their perch on the cliff face. Behind them are tombs (long-since looted) that used to hold human remains.

Although it's possible to get a colectivo to the start of the track that leads to the sarcophagi, finding one back can be a problem. It's better to take a tour from Chachapoyas.

with Quito, and east–west was the ancient Moche road from the coast to the jungle where they acquired feathers, jaguar skins and gold.

The site, called **Collacruz**, was reconstructed again by Morgan Davis, a Canadian architect, in the early 1990s. His Levanto team built the famous house in Kuelap, the only restored house there. To see the site, follow the Chachapoyas road for five minutes and then take a left at the first large path (flanked by houses to the left). If in doubt, just ask for Collacruz. There are two **hotels** styled after Chachapoya roundhouses. Prices range from 14 soles to 28 soles, depending on the season. You can also find accommodation with a family if you ask around, or you can camp. Basic meals are available at the small shops or with a family.

To **get to Levanto** take a truck or taxi early in the morning from Chachapoyas, which takes about two hours. You can also do it on foot but the path – an unrestored Inca road – is very steep so it's better to get a vehicle up to Levanto and walk back, downhill. This normally takes four hours. The stone-paved Inca road is easy to follow, and normally a guide is not necessary.

Yalape Just above Levanto, this is another massive ancient city – second in size only to Kuelap. It was probably a residential complex – the Chachapoyans' largest metropolitan area – and includes many well-preserved examples of typical Chachapoya architecture. Some beautiful friezes have survived but the site is now very overgrown.

Lamud Situated 37km northwest of Chachapoyas, a two-hour colectivo ride along a good, yet heart-stopping road. The Hotel Kuelap is cosy and the area is crammed with little-known archaeological gems. A worthwhile **half-day trek** takes you to **San Antonio** some 5km from Lamud. You can see *chulpas* (pre-Columbian sarcophagi) and Kakta, which has buildings with pictographs, a 45-minute walk each way. In Lamud, there is a tourist office where you can ask for local guides.

Pueblos de los Muertos North of Lamud, about a three-hour walk from town through unusually barren pasture lands, is this impressive site with mummy casings, caves and cliff dwellings overlooking the stunning Utcubamba River from 2,250m. Gorgeous scenery makes trudging along the narrow path worth it. Organise a guide in Lamud as it is easy to get lost.

Wanglic This site consists of roundhouses built on a ledge halfway up a very narrow sandstone canyon. To get across the canyon you need a head for heights and cross a chockstone bridge. The path starts from Tinkas on the Chachapoyas–Luya road. It can be hot and as few people visit the site, in places you may need to push through scrub (a guide would be helpful here).

TREKKING ROUTES AROUND LEYMEBAMBA Leymebamba is a gorgeous Andean town blessed with a myriad archaeological sites and trekking opportunities. The town gets its name from the Quechua term Raymi Pampa, Field of Festivals, after the conquering Inca army defeated the Chachapoya here during their Festival of the Sun. **Buses** and **cars** run to Leymebamba from Chachapoyas at various times during the day, taking about two hours. The recommended **hotel** is La Casona del Leymebamba (page 138), but there are others.

Rob Dover writes: 'There are many hiking possibilities starting from Leymebamba including a well-preserved Inca trail going south. Also Leymebamba is the starting point for a trek to the Laguna de los Condores (see below), a beautiful and mysterious lake where over two hundred mummies were found in 1997.'

An impressive **museum** 3km south of Leymebamba (see below for directions) houses the Laguna mummies and more than 2,000 artefacts recovered from the site. Tucked among a verdant valley and built completely by hand, the museum is one of the prettiest in Peru. Guides are available to show you around and a 17 soles per person entrance fee helps fund the ongoing studies at the museum.

There is also a 2½-hour hike from Leymebamba to the ruins of **Las Congonas**, a Chachapoya site. There are three sites here, originally on hills or mounds, two of which have now been levelled. A conical mound remains, with various decorated round stone houses and a watchtower. The ruins are covered in brambles and thick undergrowth, but the views are wonderful. Get clear directions before setting out from Leymebamba or use a guide. The classic tour takes all day and visits the remains of Molinete, Cataneo and Las Congonas.

Guides here are as knowledgeable as they are plentiful. They charge 22–28 soles/day and can arrange horses for 28 soles/day. IGN sheet *Leymebamba* (14-h) covers this area. You can also pick up a 1:60,000 map at Fusiones café (page 139) or at the Leymebamba Museum for about US$10.

From Leymebamba to Laguna de los Condores

Distance	About 40km (round trip)
Altitude	2,800–3,700m
Rating	Difficult
Timing	8–10 hours (each way)
In reverse	Possible
Start of trail	Leymebamba
Transport at the end	Buses back to Leymebamba from Chacapoyas (60km)
Maps	IGN sheet *Leymebamba* (14 h)

Route description Follow the main trail out of the village (south) through the annexe of Dos de Mayo, taking the short cuts towards the museum. The path follows a mule track and intersects the **Leymebamba–Celendín highway** before passing behind the museum. Follow the wide trail past some farms for about 45 minutes. After dropping down into lush cloudforest, you'll cross a bridge and see a sharply climbing path on your left. Take it. An ascent of 700m follows before the path levels off somewhat. There is a barely visible trail to follow as you work your way southeast so a guide from Leymebamba is essential. The path alternates between steep climbs and level ground before you come to a windswept plain with gorgeous rock outcrops. Be especially careful as the path is riddled with holes in the porous limestone. After 1½ hours of fending off Mother Nature's booby-traps, you're rewarded with a 700m climb to a 3,900m pass before dropping down into the stunning lush forests surrounding the lake. The descent to the lake is slippery, with exposed rocks as the only working trail.

There is a **basic lodge** on a moraine above the lake (*22 soles/night*) where you can sleep. You must bring your own food. The next day is spent exploring the lake and overlooking cliff tombs. Gazing out from the cliffs on to the remote, cloud-shrouded lake, it is easy to see why the Chachapoya chose this place to immortalise their royalty. You return to Leymebamba on the third day.

> **Note:** This hike is not recommended when it is raining. Permission to walk here must be granted beforehand from the landowner, Julio Ullilen, owner of La Casona del Leymebamba (page 138).

THE WATERFALLS *Additional information by Charles Motley*

Gocta Falls, northwest of Chachapoyas, has been on the tourist map for some years but a recently developed **Waterfall Circuit** offers an even better mixture of nature and hiking with several 'new' waterfalls.

GETTING THERE FROM CHACHAPOYAS There are two routes to the waterfalls, one via Cocachimba and one via San Pablo (both 45 minutes by car from Chachapoyas) but most people take a tour from Chachapoyas to avoid the extra hike from the main road.

 WHERE TO STAY

⌂ **La Posada del Cuispes** www.laposadadecuispes.com. Located in an unspoiled village close to the waterfalls – this is a lovely, friendly place to stay. The owners will prepare food & offer guided walks to the falls. 50–170 soles/room (sgl–4pp).

⌂ **Gocta Hotel** On the edge of San Pablo village; http://hotelgocta.com. Situated at the head of the trail to the Gocta Falls.

Set to open in 2014, this hotel will offer room service, laundry & restaurant. Dbls from US$60 per night inc buffet b/fast. Camping is currently available for 10 soles/night, with hot showers & facilities for handwashing clothes. See advert, colour page 30.

🏠 **Gocta Lodge** Cocachimba; www. goctalodge.com. Wonderful location with a view of the waterfalls. The lodge is built at the start of the 2hr trail to Gocta.

GOCTA FALLS (*entry fee 5 soles; 6km; 2hrs*) A day trip to the falls combines a moderate to strenuous walk with gorgeous scenery. The waterfall is reputedly the third highest in the world if the boffins ever decide on how a waterfall should be measured, and tumbles down in two falls of 231 and 540m. The falls have water year round and are definitely more impressive after a storm when you can be blown off your feet if you get close to the pool at the bottom. The hikes to Gocta take you through small fields (where the locals grow pineapples, sugarcane and yucca) and then forest where you might be lucky enough to see the cock-of-the-rock and just possibly the yellow-tailed woolly monkey, an endemic species to the cloudforests of northeastern Peru. The entrance fee goes to the community for path maintenance and social projects and there is a local guides' association who can walk with you but they are not always well informed and their fee tends to be quite high. However, the route is clear and you don't need a guide to find your way.

Gocta Falls via Cocachimba (*2–2½hrs*) This is the more popular of the two routes, taking you to the base of the second (lower) fall. It's a hilly walk, and you are advised to start the hike at 08.00 from Cocachimba to be ahead of groups and increase the chances of seeing cock-of-the-rock. The path can be wet and muddy, and you are recommended to hire a horse to take you up the steep path to the falls.

Gocta Falls via San Pablo (*2–2½hrs*) Fewer people take this route, which arguably has the best view of Gocta on the way as well as some pictographs. It runs to the base of the first (upper) fall. There is a trail that connects the two main trails; it is steep and care should be taken.

THE WATERFALL CIRCUIT (*15–20km; 1–2 days*) Gocta is not the only waterfall in the region. Further north with access from the village of **Cuispes** (where there are two new lodges) is the cascade of Yumbilla which, at 895m, is higher than Gocta. There are also several other spectacular waterfalls. One of Peru's newest nature reserves has been created to protect the cloudforest above these falls.

Volunteers have cleared and marked trails to the various falls, making a wonderful one- or two-day hiking circuit (15–20km), and provided shelters and toilets. In the forests you may see the cock-of-the-rock, the marvellous spatuletail hummingbird, or the tiny long-whiskered owlet which is the size of a wren. You could also see spectacled bears and even a yellow-tailed woolly monkey. So for the wildlife alone, this is a truly wonderful trip. To help save these endangered species volunteers have created a nursery of several thousand wildlife-friendly trees and shrubs to plant along the trail and to reforest the pastureland below.

Getting to the trailhead
The main town of the area is **Pedro Ruíz** which has a good selection of **accommodation** of various prices. The best is probably the Amazonense (*Avda Marginal, 146 Jazan*) by the police station on the main highway, but for something different try Villa Kepno, a coffee farm owned by Juhani Jarner, from Finland, which has some rooms available at the nearby community of **Shipasbamba**. He also offers tours of the circuit.

Long-distance buses from the coast stop here, if you don't want to go all the way to Chachapoyas.

At the time of writing the trail starts in Cuispis, but will soon begin in San Carlos, going past both Chenata and Yumbilla Falls. All *moto-taxis* (tuk-tuks) will take you to Cuispis for 10 soles (where you buy your admission ticket for the trail from the municipal building) and for an extra 5 soles will take you up to the end of a 5km road to where the trail crosses.

Magali in Pedro Ruíz is a recommended **guide** who speaks English.

Route description
From a distance you can see that there are several rock ledges along this mountain ridge that are nearly level. The trail follows one of these ledges, with cliffs soaring 300m above and below. The water crashes on to this ledge in its fall. The trail is protected by a cliff so is normally dry.

The first waterfall on the one-day circuit is reached after 1km going to the right. This is the **Pavillion Fall**, the most beautiful of this zone. Where it hits the trail there are huge rounded golden sandstone boulders and the waterfall spreads out into multiple falls; the grass is vibrant green from the mist. From there you backtrack on the same path to the road and the 5km trail is on the right of the road to the next waterfall, **Yumbilla**, which falls 895m in a series of drops and was only discovered in 2007.

A further waterfall, **Chenata**, is accessed from the village of San Carlos. At the time of writing, volunteers are clearing a path to these falls and others in the area, and are also creating a botanical garden near Shipasbamba.

! **Updates website:** For the latest updates go to www.bradtupdates.com/perutrekking. You can also post your feedback here – corrections, changes or even new hikes. Your information will be put on our website for the benefit of other travellers.

above left A newly built trail in the Chachapoyas region gives hikers a chance to experience the flora and fauna of the cloudforest, as well as some dramatic waterfalls, such as Yumbilla (pictured here) (HB) page 148

above right This impressive monolith at Kuntur Wasi shows the influence of the Chavín culture (WH/PP) page 135

below You can still find yourself alone in the seldom-visited pre-Inca ruins of Kuelap, known as the 'Machu Picchu of the north' (LG/PP) page 140

above   Alpamayo, considered by many to be the most beautiful
mountain in the Andes (S/GA) page 173

left   The snow peak of Taulliraju, seen from below the pass of
Punta Unión on the Santa Cruz trek (HB) page 182

below   The hair-raising pass of Punta Yanayacu, in the Cordillera
Blanca (HB) page 187

above   Scenes like this from the San Antonio pass are typical of the isolated and spectacular Huayhuash range (MM) page 208

below left   Lake Carhuacocha, Cordillera Huayhuash, is characteristic of the glacial lakes of this region (S/M) page 206

below right   New views open up at every turn in the Cordillera Huayhuash (S/M)

above   Nevado Ticlla in the central Andes — here you can almost guarantee to have the trails to yourself (GP) page 217

below   The broad valley of the Río Taparaco makes an ideal camping spot on the Inca Royal Road (MW) page 226

above   Huánuco Viejo, important but little-visited Inca ruins on the Inca Royal Road (MM) page 221

below   Inca road leading towards the Waga Punta pass at 4,400m, shortly after leaving Castillo on the Royal Inca Road (RO) page 226

above   **Trekkers heading for lunch in the beautiful valley of Machapampa, Lares** (MS) page 277

below left   **A moment's rest on the Abra Huillquijasa before the steep descent to Cuncani, Lares** (MS) page 275

below right   **Pack animals (horses or donkeys) are used whenever possible in the mountains of Peru. The one exception is the Inca Trail which is only suitable for porters.** (KJ)

above Built to last. The zigzag ruins of Sacsayhuamán still dominate the plain above Cusco. No-one is sure why the Incas built it. Probably it was a fortress; maybe a temple. The mystery is part of the appeal. (Y/DT) page 257

below Chinchero is the beginning of several excellent walks into the Sacred Valley. Best known for its vibrant Sunday market, it also has some well-restored Inca terracing. (JF) page 268

above left On the Choquequirao trail. Treks in the Cordillera Vilcabamba are typified by deep, wooded valleys. (SS) page 313

above right The Inca ruin of Wata on the little-known Moyoc Circuit in the Cordillera Vilcabamba (MS) page 311

left Representations of animals in stone are a rarity in the Inca culture. An exception is this llama at Choquequirao. (H) page 317

below On the trail to Soraypampa in the Cordillera Vilcabamba, with Salkantay ahead (TS) page 301

above   The Ausangate Circuit: the classic trek of the Cordillera Vilcanota (MOM) page 321

below left   'We've landed on Mars!' Hikers on Yauricunca in the Cordillera Vilcanota (KD) page 338

below right   The Ausangate Lodge Trek allows you to walk through the magnificent Cordillera Vilcanota while spending the night in comfortable accommodation (S/RMG) page 337

above left   On the steep descent before climbing to Huiñay Huayna on the Inca Trail (SS) page 296

above right   The stone paving on the Inca Trail is one of the most perfect surviving examples of their road-building skills (HB) page 290

below left   The end of the Inca Trail. Walking down to Machu Picchu from Intipunku. (S/RMG) page 297

below right   The route to the summit of Putucusi — 'a hot, sweaty, slippery struggle' (L) page 293

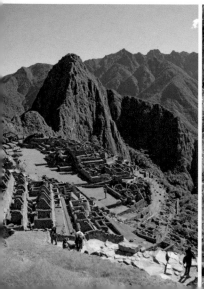

above Volcán El Misti, near Arequipa — no technical climbing skills are needed to make the ascent (CK/C) page 351

below left The majestic Colca Canyon: the reverse of other treks in this book — the descent comes first (S/P) page 354

below right Andean condors catch the thermals above Colca Canyon (TR/MP/FLPA) page 354

8

The Cordilleras: Negra, Blanca and Huayhuash

This is an incredible trekking and climbing area, with fascinating flora and fauna, and the remains of several pre-Inca cultures as well as some Inca ruins. The focal point – or rather line – of the area is the **Callejón de Huaylas**, the name given to the **Río Santa Valley**, which separates the Cordillera Negra (west) from the Cordillera Blanca (east) in the department of Ancash in Peru's northern highlands. The department capital, Huaraz, is at the southern end. A paved road runs the length of this valley, linking the villages and providing spectacular views of the nevados Huandoy and Huascarán.

THE CORDILLERAS: AN OVERVIEW

There are three *cordilleras* (mountain ranges) in Ancash: the Cordillera Negra, the Cordillera Blanca and the Cordillera Huayhuash. The cordilleras Negra and Blanca face each other across the Río Santa, and the Cordillera Huayhuash lies about 50km to their southeast. All three are excellent for trekking and draw enthusiasts from all over the world.

As its name implies, the Cordillera Negra is not snow-covered (although 'black' is an exaggeration) but it's a shame that few trekkers take the time to explore this seldom-visited range. It is worth a visit if only for the stunning views of the cordilleras Blanca and Huayhuash, the highest of the country's astonishing total of 20 glaciated mountain ranges. The largest concentration of tropical-zone glaciers in the world (70%) is found in the Cordillera Blanca, including Peru's highest mountain, Huascarán, at 6,768m. The second-highest mountain, Yerupajá (6,634m), is in the Huayhuash.

The campesinos who cultivate land up to about 4,000m and graze cattle and sheep almost to the snowline, are mainly *mestizos*, although they speak Quechua as their first language. The Indian culture is still alive, but less so than in the Cusco area, perhaps because this was never an Inca

LIST OF HIKES AND TREKS IN THIS CHAPTER

stronghold. Not many Inca ruins of importance are found here. The pre-Inca site from the Chavín culture, Chavín de Huántar is important and warrants a visit, and archaeologists are constantly finding more pre-Inca remains throughout the Cordillera Blanca.

CORDILLERA NEGRA Because few hikers want to spend much time in this snowless range we have given it less coverage than its more popular neighbour, but there are some good hikes and the best views of the whole Cordillera Blanca range are from the Cordillera Negra. It is worth exploring this range while acclimatising in Huaraz. Hikes are fairly easy, the highest pass being around 4,500m and the highest peak at 5,187m (Rocarre, in the northern part of the range).

CORDILLERA BLANCA This is Peru's best-known mountain region. Only 100km from the Pacific Ocean, and 180km long, it provides a barrier between the desert coast and the wet Amazon Basin. On the west side of the Cordillera Blanca the Río Santa drains into the Pacific, while on the east side the Río Marañón drains into the Atlantic. If you count the multi-peaked mountains, 33 peaks rise above 6,000m, crowned by **Huascarán**

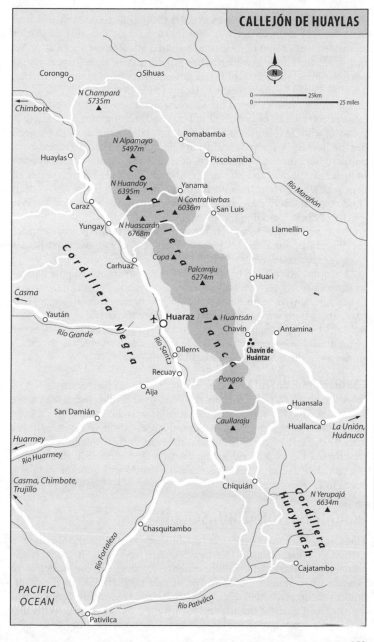

CALLEJÓN DE HUAYLAS

Corongo

Sihuas

N Champará 5735m ▲

← Chimbote

0 ——— 25km
0 ——— 25 miles

Pomabamba

N Alpamayo 5497m ▲

Huaylas

Piscobamba

Río Marañón

N Huandoy 6395m ▲

Yanama

N Contrahierbas 6036m ▲

San Luis

Caraz

Yungay

N Huascarán 6768m ▲

Llamellín

Copa ▲

Palcaraju 6274m ▲

Huari

← Casma

Yaután

Cordillera Negra

Río Grande

Carhuaz

Huaraz

✈

Huantsán ▲

Chavín

Antamina

Olleros

Chavín de Huántar

Río Santa

Recuay

Pongos ▲

Aija

Huansala

San Damián

Caullaraju ▲

Huallanca

La Unión, Huánuco

← Huarmey

Río Huarmey

← Casma, Chimbote, Trujillo

Chiquián

Cordillera Huayhuash

N Yerupajá 6634m ▲

Chasquitambo

Río Fortaleza

Cajatambo

PACIFIC OCEAN

Río Pativilca

Patívilca

Cordillera Blanca

153

(6,768m). The range is an important hydrological reserve, as much of the extremely arid coastal area directly to the west depends on glacier meltwater, from some of its several hundred glaciers, for survival. Snow melt from the Cordillera Blanca has provided Peru with its year-round water supplies, while 80% of Peru's power comes from hydro-electricity, now threatened by the retreating glaciers (page 19).

The range includes seven life zones, which gives it great biodiversity (almost 800 species of flora, 112 of birds and ten of mammals). There is plenty of wildlife to look out for, though most of the mammals have been heavily hunted in the past and so are hard to see. The spectacled bear, puma, mountain cat, white-tailed deer and the vicuña are important indigenous species, and the north Andean huemul, a rare species of deer, is also found here. Among the birds are the puna hawk, the Andean condor, giant coot, giant hummingbird, ornate tinamou and various species of duck, including the entertaining torrent duck.

These days the glaciers rarely reach the 5,000m point. Below them are the grasslands, puna, usually grazed by cattle. There are very few llamas or alpacas in this region.

One of the advantages of hiking here is that the range is quite narrow so all trekking routes are easily accessed from roads. Most run from west to east, crossing the cordillera at a high pass and descending again to a road. These trails were created centuries before the arrival of recreational trekkers, being the main thoroughfare for the Andean inhabitants. Some of the trails have recently been made into roads for vehicular traffic. A summary of the trekking routes is on pages 171–2.

CORDILLERA HUAYHUASH This compact range is just under 30km in length from north to south, and yet it has seven peaks over 6,000m, the highest of which is Yerupajá at 6,634m. Many trekkers consider it even more spectacular than the Cordillera Blanca, and it is certainly more remote and challenging. The peaks all seem to have towering, vertical ice-covered faces on all sides. The classic trek described in this chapter is a complete circuit of 164km around the Cordillera Huayhuash, taking seven to 12 days (pages 198–210).

PARQUE NACIONAL HUASCARÁN

Huascarán National Park was established in 1975, and became a UNESCO World Natural Heritage Site ten years later. It includes the whole area of the Cordillera Blanca above 4,000m, with the exception of Nevado Champará (5,735m) at the extreme northern end of the range, and covers in total 3,400km². Conservation and sustainable development are the main goals of the park administration; it sometimes seems that development is winning, with roads being constructed through some of the most beautiful areas. Tourism is growing rapidly in Peru, especially adventure tourism, so the pressures on Huascarán National Park are ever increasing. The most popular areas for conventional tourism are the Lagunas Llanganuco and the Pachacoto Valley, and the most popular trekking route is the Santa Cruz–Huaripampa–Llanganuco circuit.

Whatever your plans, try to visit the park's most spectacular living thing: the *Puya raimondii* (page 20). These incredible plants grow in the valley of Pachacoto, 57km south of Huaraz and in the Cordillera Negra near Caraz. You may not be lucky enough to see them in flower, but even so they are an unforgettable sight. Organise transport to the village of Pachacoto and hike up the valley to the park station (*2½hrs*). You'll find the puyas up the road from there, to your right. Organised day tours go to this area and then on to the (retreating) glacier of Pastoruri.

PARK FEES The park office (*SERNAMP; www.sernanp.gob.pe/sernanp/*) is on Jiron Federico Sal y Rosas 555, in Huaraz (\ *043 422086;* ⊕ *08.00–13.30 & 14.30–18.00 Mon–Fri, 08.30–12.00 Sat*). All visitors to the park should register at one of the park offices – there are also rangers at trek start points – and pay the entrance fee of 65 soles per person for a month, or of 5 soles for one-day entry. The fee helps with conservation projects. If you only want two days, you have to pay for the full month. If buying your permit at the entry point, you should carry the correct change and, if re-using a month-long ticket you must show your passport to the authorities.

> **Note:** There are rumours that in 2014, park rules may change to make any trek possible in Huascarán only if accompanied by an authorised guide. Check www.bradtupdates.com/perutrekking for the latest information.

GETTING THERE AND AWAY Although most people wish to make Huaraz their first stop in the cordilleras, many will choose to leave from other towns so we have covered all options here.

By air to Huaraz It's 400km from **Lima** to Huaraz (Anta) and there are daily, hour-long flights with **LC Peru** (*Huaraz office: Avda Luzuriaga No 904;* \ *043 424734;* e *Huaraz@lcperu.pe; www.lcperu.pe;* ⊕ *08.30–18.30*) all year, with a 15kg limit for checked baggage and 5kg for hand baggage. Fares are from US$100 return. Flights are currently at 06.30 from Lima and 07.30 from Huaraz.

By road to Huaraz By **bus**, from **Lima**, the journey takes eight hours and costs from 33 soles for the cheapest seats, up to 98 soles for a luxury bus with reclining seats. The road is paved all the way and as it is used by several mining companies taking ore to Lima, it is generally kept in good

8

condition. Recommended luxury bus companies are **Cruz del Sur** (*www.cruzdelsur.com.pe*), **Movil** (*www.moviltours.com.pe/portal*) and **Oltsura** (*www.oltursa.pe*). Try to travel Lima–Huaraz during the day, and sit on the right side of the bus to enjoy the beautiful scenery.

Huaraz may be reached **from the northern coast** via three routes; the visual impact of approaching the cordilleras this way is unforgettable. Travelling from **Casma** to Huaraz (150km) takes three to 3½ hours, and it takes around ten hours (185km) from **Chimbote** via Huallanca, the Río Santa Valley, Cañón del Pato and Caraz to Huaraz on a good new road. Buses with Linea, Movil Tours, Yungay Express, Cruz del Norte and Alas Peruanas do this route.

Transport within the region
There are many local transport options through the **Río Santa Valley**, and to the towns on the eastern side of the cordillera. Colectivos run the 66km between Huaraz and **Caraz** daily, between 03.30 and 21.00. They leave whenever they fill up, every five to ten minutes or so, from their departure point in Huaraz on block 1, Avenida Fitzcarrald (the main road leading out of town over the bridge) on the corner with Jiron 13 de Diciembre. The full journey takes about two hours – they stop at every village along the way: Monterrey (*20mins*), Marcará (*45mins*), Carhuaz (*1hr*), Mancos (*1½hrs*) and Yungay (*1½hrs*).

Heading **south** from Huaraz to **Olleros** (29km) or **Recuay** (36km) takes about 45 minutes; on to **Catac** (11km) 30 minutes more; on to **Pachacoto** (9km) 15 minutes. Colectivos leave from Octavio Hinostroza y 27 de Noviembre.

Buses to **Chiquián** (111km) leave from Bolognesi 261.

Routes to the **eastern side of the Cordillera Blanca** are mostly dirt roads going over the high passes of the cordillera. In the dry season trucks and some buses run daily. In the rainy season, road conditions are poor and there's little transport.

It takes 40 minutes to travel the 7km between **Macará** and **Vicos** by colectivo. Travel from **Carhuaz**, up the **Ulta Valley** and down to **Chacas** (75km) takes three hours on a tarmac road. A tunnel opened in 2013 so the road no longer goes over Punta Olimpica. Colectivos and taxis now pass this way frequently. Huaraz to **Huari** takes four to five hours (148km).

Journeying from **Yungay**, up the **Llanganuco Valley** and down to **Yanama** (58km) takes four hours. Vehicles leave daily at 07.00. Most transport continues on to **San Luis** (61km), an extra three hours, but not always. There are also frequent minibuses from Yungay that run to the **Lagunas Llanganuco** in 1½ hours during the tourist season.

The 110km journey from **Chavín** to Huaraz takes three to four hours; several buses a day run with Sandoval, Río Mosna, Empresa de Transportes Turismo Cahuish and Turismo Chavín Imperial for 12 soles per person. The road is only tarmac for part of the route.

The route from Huaraz to **Piscobamba** and **Pomabamba** is 157km; it takes eight to nine hours to Piscobamba, one hour more for Pomabamba. Buses leave twice daily (early morning and evening) with both Renzo and Transportes Veloz; it costs approximately 30 soles.

Travel between **Caraz** and **Cashapampa** (22km) is possible via shared taxis at a cost of approximately 6 soles per person. The journey takes one to two hours.

Pick-ups leave Huaraz from Las Americas and Avenida Gamarra to **Pitec** whenever they fill up (about every 30 minutes, between 07.30 and 17.00), but note they go only as far as **Llupa** (the journey takes 40 minutes). Ask the driver to drop you off at the footpath up to Pitec; from there it's a 1½-hour walk to Pitec.

The journey from **Catac** to **Chavín** (98km) takes 3½ hours; on to **Huari** (38km) a further two hours, and on to **San Luis** (61km) three

FARMING IN THE CORDILLERAS   *Roberto Arévalo*

In the cordilleras Blanca and Huayhuash the pastures are administered by local communities, principally for the grazing of animals: cattle, sheep, donkeys, mules and horses, in order of importance. Grazing is extensive; a rotation system is practised whereby during the rainy season (January to April) animals are moved to lower pastures, and during the dry season (May to November) they are grazed in higher areas. This allows the grass to rejuvenate and maintains the quality of grazing. While the animals are being grazed on higher ground, some of the villagers will move up with them and spend several weeks at higher altitudes watching over the animals. They will usually stay in simple stone houses with ichu roofs, known as tambos.

Ecologically the high forests and scrublands help to collect and store the water from rainfall and glacier meltwater, as well as conserving the soil, and inhibiting erosion. In the dry season, the stored water is of vital importance for the lower regions, for agriculture and for village water supplies.

The biggest problem faced in the cordilleras in terms of conservation of grass and shrub lands is overgrazing and burning by local farmers. The ichu grass is burned every few years to stimulate new growth and produce a softer plant for livestock to eat. Burning has a high impact on all the plants in the vicinity, decreasing the number of seeds available, and reducing the fertility of the soil, often destroying trees and shrubs, thereby preventing forest regeneration. Overgrazing prevents adequate plant re-growth leaving soil exposed to erosion.

hours. Flag down passing Lima–Chavín and Huaraz–Lima buses, several daily (see pages 155–6 for details).

Huaraz to **Huallanca** (140km) takes four hours; three daily buses do this route with El Rápido/Paraiso Natural. From Huallanca there is transport on to **La Unión** (*1hr*) and **Huánuco** (*4hrs*).

HUARAZ *Telephone code: 043*

Situated at 3,050m, this thriving small town has a lovely climate and lively atmosphere. It exudes energy: there's a bustling market and most of the gringos you meet here are either planning a trek or climb or have just returned from one, so it is easy to get information. There are lots of tour operators, shops, hotels, restaurants, nightlife, and all the attractions designed to encourage the visitor to stay as long as possible.

WHERE TO STAY Huaraz is awash with accommodation, but it's definitely worth booking in advance if you are there from June to September. Simple **budget accommodation**, usually with shared bathroom, ranges from 17 to 42 soles per person (*US$6–15pp*). **Mid-range options** usually include private bathroom, Wi-Fi, breakfast and often cable TV with prices from US$25 to US$50 per person. **Luxury accommodation** is restricted to the Llanganuco Lodge in the Yungay area, and Cuesta Serena in Anta, both right in the heart of the Cordillera Blanca, where the price tag (up to US$280) reflects the level of comfort and surrounding views.

There are several other villages in the Río Santa Valley which offer a good **alternative to staying in Huaraz** itself. These villages are the access points for many of the treks described below, and you will find them friendly places with lively markets. What's more, they are less used to gringos than Huaraz.

Budget

Jo's Place Jr Daniel Villarzan 276; 425505; e josplaceHuaraz@hotmail. com; www.hosteltrail.com/josplace. Cosy guesthouse owned by an Anglo-Peruvian couple, 7mins from the centre, with a lovely garden. B/fast (bacon & eggs) available at extra cost. Dorms from 15 soles, camping from 10 soles.

Alojamiento Soledad Jr Amadeo Figueroa 1267; 421196; e ghsoledad@ hotmail.com; www.lodgingsoledad.com. Charming, family-run guesthouse with home-from-home feel. Dorms from 28 soles.

Albergue Churup Pedro Campos 735, directly below the Iglesia Soledad; 424200; e info@churup.com. Welcoming, lively place, informative, & very popular, 10mins' walk from the centre. If full, has a second hostal around the corner. From 33 soles.

Mid-range

Olaza's B&B Julio Arguedas 1246, Soledad; 422529; e info@andeanexplorer. com; www.olazas.com. Family house in a safe, residential area. US$25–35.

Morales Guest House Pasaje Ucanan No 232, Barrio de Jose Olaya; 421864;

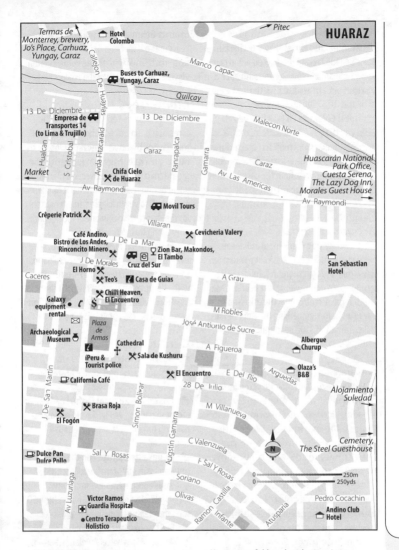

The map shows:

Termas de Monterrey, brewery, Jo's Place, Carhuaz, Yungay, Caraz

Hotel Colomba

Pitec

Manco Capac

Buses to Carhuaz, Yungay, Caraz

Callejón De Huaylas

Quilcay

13 De Diciembre
Empresa de Transportes 14 (to Lima & Trujillo)

13 De Diciembre

Malecon Norte

Avda Fitzcarral

Hualcan

S Cristobal

Market

Caraz

Ranrapalca

Gamarra

Caraz

Av Las Americas

Caraz

Huascarán National Park Office, Cuesta Serena, The Lazy Dog Inn, Morales Guest House

Chifa Cielo de Huaraz

Av Raymondi

Av Raymondi

Movil Tours

Crêperie Patrick

Villaran

Cevicheria Valery

Café Andino, Bistro de Los Andes, Rinconcito Minero

J De La Mar

Zion Bar, Makondos, El Tambo

J De Morales
El Horno

Cruz del Sur

Teo's

Casa de Guías

A Grau

San Sebastian Hotel

Caceres

Chilli Heaven, El Encuentro

Galaxy equipment rental

Plaza de Armas

M Robles

José Antiunio de Sucre

Archaeological Museum

Cathedral

iPeru & Tourist police

Sala de Kushuru

A Figueroa

El Encuentro

E Del Rio

Arguedas

Albergue Churup

Olaza's B&B

Alojamiento Soledad

California Café

28 De Julio

Brasa Roja

El Fogón

J De San Martin

Simón Bolívar

M Villanueva

Agustín Gamarra

C Valenzuela

N

Cemetery, The Steel Guesthouse

Dulce Pan Dulce Pollo

Sal Y Rosas

F Sal Y Rosas

Soriano

Olivas

Ramon Castilla

Ramon Infante

0   250m
0   250yds

Pedro Cocachin

Victor Ramos Guardia Hospital

Centro Terapeutico Holistico

Atusparia

Andino Club Hotel

8

m 94307736; e reservas@
moralesguesthouse.com; www.
moralesguesthouse.com. Small & cosy
guesthouse. US$25–55.

San Sebastian Hotel Jr Italia 1124,
426960; e andeway@terra.com.pe;
www.sansebastianHuaraz.com.

New, peaceful hotel with nice views,
terraces & clean rooms. From US$40pp
for a dbl.

The Steel Guesthouse Alejandro
Maguina 1467; 429709. New guesthouse
with character & good views. En-suite rooms
US$40–80 inc b/fast.

As a treat

🏠 **Andino Club Hotel** Pedro Cochachin 357; ☎421662; e andino@hotelandino.com; www.hotelandino.com. Terrific ambience & service. Suites have jacuzzis & the best views in Huaraz. US$75pp upwards.

🏠 **Hotel Colomba** Jr Francisco de Zela 210; ☎421501; e colomba@terra.com. pe; www.huarazhotel.com. A characterful hacienda with a large & tranquil garden full of plants, 5mins' walk from the centre. Suites & family rooms available. From US$80.

Further afield
Around Huaraz

🏠 **The Lazy Dog Inn** About 10km east of Huaraz, at the foot of the Valley Walks; www.thelazydoginn.com. A carefully designed ecolodge, way off the beaten track, which is great centre for acclimatisation & day hikes before embarking on some serious treks. Around US$100 per night. See advert, page 149.

👁 **Carhuaz:** Carhuaz is a small town with many modern amenities. It is a good base if you prefer somewhere smaller, lower and warmer than Huaraz. The **market** on a Wednesday and Sunday morning is a great opportunity to see (and buy) plenty of local produce, including honey, cheese and *manjar blanco* (thick, sweet milk). It's a colourful occasion as many traditionally dressed local traders come from the mountain villages into town.

🏠 **Cuesta Serena** Anta, near the airport (north of Huaraz); ☎400038; cuestaserena. pe. An intimate new boutique hotel with just 7 rooms set in spacious grounds & terrific views of Huascarán. It is run by

Mariana Gonzales, a Limeña who lived many years in the USA. From dbl US$180 (with b/ fast) to US$240 for 'the suite with panoramic views of Huascarán & all the peaks'.

Monterrey

🏠 **Hotel Baños Termales** ☎427690; e realhotelmonterrey@yahoo.com. In 1973 this was one of the very few hotels in the Huaraz area & *the* place to stay for all climbing groups (pages 178–9). Now decidedly run down but there are rumours that it might be renovated, so worth keeping an eye on if only for the chance to soak in one of the hot baths after a long trek. 100 soles/room.

🏠 **El Patio** On the main road in Monterrey; ☎424965; e reservas@elpatio. com.pe; www.elpatio.com.pe. Hacienda with charming gardens, away from the bustle of Huaraz – which some visitors find inconvenient. Dbl about US$45pp.

Carhuaz

🏠 **Hostal La Merced** On the Plaza. A long-established, comfortable hostal. Sgls about 17 soles.

🏠 **Hostal Residencial Carhuaz** Avda Progreso 586; ☎794312. An old colonial building full of character. Sgls about 17 soles.

🏠 **La Casa de Poncha** On the road to Hualcan, 3km out of Carhuaz; ☎761885; e lacasadepocha@yahoo.com; www. socialwellbeing.org/lacasadepocha.htm. 50 soles inc meals of organic farm produce.

🏠 **El Abuelo** 9 de Diciembre 257; ☎(043) 39445; www.elabuelohostal.com. Calm, relaxing with beautiful gardens. Owned by guidebook writer & cartographer, Felipe Diaz. Sgls or dbls from 100 soles.

Yungay

🏠 **Llanganuco Lodge** e hello@ llanganucomountainlodge.com; www.

llanganucomountainlodge.com. A wonderful eco-lodge on the edge of the national park, & set in spacious grounds. English-owned by Charlie Good, who is usually on hand to give advice. Camping is usually permitted in the grounds, or splash out on one of the luxury rooms. US$100–250. See advert, colour pages 22–3.

✖ **WHERE TO EAT AND DRINK** There are dozens of restaurants in Huaraz. For those whose stomachs have already adapted to local food, check out the market for variety and excellent value (◔ *06.00–18.00*). There are many restaurants in the streets near the market offering great value, with menus starting from just 4 soles for soup, main and sometimes pudding, lots of *pollerias* for chicken and chips and the ubiquitous Chinese for ample portions at cheap prices.

There are several great, slightly more expensive restaurants if you feel like some more upmarket food, some run or owned by expats – a selection is included below.

Restaurants popular with locals

✖ **Brasa Roja** On Luzuriaga 915; ◌427738; www.labrasarojaperu.com. Deservedly one of the most popular restaurants In Huaraz, with both locals & tourists. Basically chicken & chips, but of good quality & with plenty of other options.

✖ **Cevicheria Valery** Avda Agustín Gamarra 492. Nice terrace, serving chocho & ceviches, which the locals love, at very reasonable prices.

✖ **Chifa Cielo de Huaraz** Avda Fitzcarrald 388. Good Chinese food, cheap & lavish helpings, prompt service.

✖ **El Encuentro** (2 to choose from) Jr Julian de Morales 650 & in Parque del PeRíodista. Tasty food, from pizza, pasta, salads & grills to local dishes. Good wine & drinks list.

✖ **Rinconcito Minero** Julian de Morales 757. With dishes starting at 10 soles upwards, this local haunt is a cracking place to sample local cuisine, with its own *cevicheria* next door too.

✖ **Sala de Kushuru** Simón Bolívar 926. This restaurant serves real local specialities such as *kushuru* (algae), *ceviche de chocho* (lupin seeds) & cuy,

✖ **Teo's** Jr Simon Bolívar 615B. Recently opened, with great dishes available on each of its sliding-scale *menu del dias* ranging from 8 to 20 soles. Expect a friendly, efficient service, too.

As a treat

✖ **Bistro de Los Andes** Julian de Morales 823. Good mix of local & international dishes such as burgers & pasta. Reasonably priced, with good views of the Plaza de Armas.

✖ **Chilli Heaven** Parque Ginebra; ◌221313. Great curries from India & Thailand, plus Mexican, pizzas & fajitas. Moderate to expensive.

✖ **Crêperie Patrick** Avda Luzuriaga 424. French cuisine with good crêpes & desserts. Moderate to expensive.

✖ **El Fogón** Avda Mariscal Luzuriaga 928, 2nd floor; ◌421267; www.elfogon.com. pe. Maybe the best eatery in town, a perfect treat after a long hike.

✖ **El Horno** Parque del PeRíodista No 103; ◌424617. Big, tasty pizzas from 13 soles upwards, & some of the best-tasting & value steak in town. Very popular.

Cafés

☕ **Café Andino** Jr Lucar y Torre 530, 3rd floor; ☎ 421203; www.cafeandino.com. Offers great home-roasted coffee & fine teas with lovely views. Book exchange, trekking maps for sale, & tasty food.

☕ **California Café** Jr 28 de Julio 562; www.huaylas.com/californiacafe. Home-roasted coffee, games & lovely food.

☕ **Dulce Pan Dulce Pollo** 1010 Jr San Martin; ☎ 423111. Cracking selection of take-away or eat-in cakes, pastries, sweets. At night, converts into a tasty restaurant.

USEFUL ADDRESSES
Banks and foreign exchange

There are several banks & exchange offices on Luzuriaga & around the Plaza de Armas.

Charities and volunteering

Local NGOS that may have opportunities for volunteers include:

Lazy Dog and Andean Alliance www.andeanalliance.org/. A grassroots NGO with volunteer positions for teachers & in small business development in the Huaraz area.

On Belay www.onbelayty.org/On_Belay_TY/Home.html. This organisation works towards improving safety in the mountaineering environment.

Semillas de la Vida www.facebook.com/pages/Semillas-de-Vida/168883563205387. Volunteer positions for educators in this community-founded school.

Teach Huaraz www.teachHuarazperu.org. Positions for teachers.

Turmanye (Arco Iris) www.turmanye.org/. Works with disadvantaged families in the Huaraz area.

Communications

There is a profusion of internet offices & telephone boxes all over Huaraz, for making cheap calls or browsing the web. Many hostals & hotels now offer free Wi-Fi.

Telefónica Block 6 of Avda Luzuriaga. Telephone & internet.

Bars and entertainment

♀ **El Tambo** Opposite Makondos. A popular gringo disco, also busy towards the end of the week.

♀ **Makondos** Jose de la Mar y Avda Simon Bolivar. Popular, rocking w/end disco, Latino beats mixing with international favourites. Male gringos may have to pay 10 soles to get in.

♀ **Zion Bar** Jose de La Mar. Intimate, reggae-influenced bar whose DJ keeps the beats going until late. Fabulous Pisco sours.

Emergencies

High Altitude Rescue Unidad de Salvamento Alta Montana; ☎ 493327, 493291, or Yungay ☎ 493333

Tourist police Avda Luzuriaga 724; ☎ 421351; ⏰ 08.00–13.00 & 17.00–20.00 daily. Basically in front of the Plaza de Armas. Friendly & helpful, some officers speak English. Contact them if you are robbed or in the event of an accident in the mountains. When closed go to PNP Police on Calle Sucre Block 5 (off Luzuriaga, opposite Plaza de Armas).

Health

✚ **San Pablo Clinic** 172 Huaylas, Independencia; ☎ 428811; ⏰ 24hrs

✚ **Victor Ramos Guardia Hospital** Luzuriaga Avda Block 8; ☎ 421290

Shopping for provisions

The best place to buy supplies is at the main produce market, between Calle Tarapaca

& de la Cruz Romero. There is also a small supermarket on Luzuriaga, the main street of town, where you will also find pharmacies, restaurants, trek agencies & kit rental. See also *16 things to do in Huaraz*, overleaf.

Tatoo Parque Ginebra, opposite the Casa de los Guías; ☎422966; e huaraz@tatoo.ws; ◷ 09.00–20.00 Mon–Sat. Sells hiking gear & equipment.

Spanish school
Langway Avda Luzuriaga 975, 2nd floor, office 203; ☎424286; www.huaraz.info/langway
Teach Huaraz www.teachHuarazperu.org

Tourist information and other useful organisations
🖸 **Casa de Guías** (Mountain Guide Centre) Parque Ginebra 28-G; ☎427545; e informes@casadeguias.com.pe; www.casadeguias.com.pel; ◷ May–Sep 09.00–13.00 Mon–Sat, & 16.00–20.00 Mon–Fri. Home to the Peruvian Mountain Guide Association. This is a good place in Huaraz for information on trekking & climbing, local or private transportation, guides, cooks, porters, arrieros & mules. They can also advise you on organised trips & put you in touch with their qualified mountain & trekking guides. They are happy to chat about weather conditions & have some useful books & maps for sale. Good place to meet other trekkers & climbers.
🖸 **iPerú** Plaza de Armas, Pasaje Atusparia, oficina 1; ☎428812; e iperuHuaraz@promperu.gob.pe; www.peru.travel; ◷ 09.00–18.00 Mon–Sat, 09.00–13.00 Sun. Friendly staff who speak English & are full of information from colectivo times & prices to tour ideas.
🖸 **The Huaraz Telegraph** www.thehuaraztelegraph.com. An interesting

read on & offline. You can pick it up in Huaraz at hostels, hotels, iPerú, the tourist police & at language centres. Some of the cafés also have copies available to read.

Tour operators
Recommended tour/trekking companies include:

Andescamp Lodge ☎423842; m 943 563424; e andescamp@gmail.com; www.andescamplodge.com. Peruvian-owned trekking & accommodation company offering fully equipped group treks & other adventure activities. Also Backpackers' Hostel with low rates. See advert, page 150.
Café Andino Jr Lucar y Torre 530, 3rd floor; ☎421203. A lovely café that, as well as having good coffee & snacks, also sells maps, provides information & organises climbing & trekking. Ask for Chris Benway.
Explore Andes Avda Agustín Gamarra 835; ☎428071; e info@exploreandes.com; www.exploreandes.com
Huaraz Treks and Climbs Pasaje Bello Horizonte 777; ☎220152; e info@huaraztreks.com; www.huaraztreks.com. Run by UIGM guide Rodolfo Oropeza. See advert, page 150.
Montañero Andean Experience Parque Ginebra 30-B; ☎426386; e andeway@terra.com.pe; www.trekkingperu.com. Also rent out equipment.
Pablo Tours Avda Luzuriaga 501; ☎421145; e pablotours@terra.com.pe; www.pablotours.com
Peruvian Andes Adventures Jr José Olaya 532; ☎421864; e info@peruvianandes.com; www.peruvianandes.com. Top quality tours. See advert, colour page 31.
Pyramid Expeditions Contact Eudes Morales Flores, Las Americas 314;

With additional suggestions from Alberto Cafferata

1 Visit the brewery Spend the afternoon watching the making of Sierra Andina beer, from fermentation to pouring, at the brewery a five-minute taxi ride from town (*Avda Centenarío 1692, Cascapampa;* ✆ *221419;* e *info@sierraandina.com; www.sierraandina.com;* ⏰ *15.00– 22.00 Tue–Sun*).

2 Eat and shop in the market Located on Avenida Raymondi, this indoor market has everything from day-to-day clothes to fruit, veg, meat, handicrafts and a lively food and drink area (⏰ *daily*).

3 Learn about the past The archaeological museum (Museo Archaeológico) is in the centre of town and has some interesting exhibits from the Chavín and Recuay cultures: ceramic, mummy and lithic (carved rock) figures (⏰ *08.30–17.15 Tue–Sat, 09.00–14.00 Sun*).

4 Massage, sauna, mud and more Appointments are necessary at Centro Terapeutico Holistico where a one-hour massage costs from 80 soles (*Avda Villo 756;* ✆ *427194; www.centroterapeuticoholisticoperu.com*).

5 Take a hot bath Take a taxi (5 soles) or a colectivo (1 sol) to Monterrey and soak away the aches and pains (⏰ *07.00–18.00 daily; entry fee 4 soles*).

6 Salsa the night away If you want to dance the night away, Makondos on Jose de la Mar y Avenida Simon Bolivar is *the* place (page 162), especially at weekends after midnight. Locals flock here to salsa and strut and drink the speciality *Gin con Gin.*

7 Drink a Pisco sour or eat a guinea pig El Fogón is the best place to try Peru's national cocktail, with a choice of more than 50 Piscos. It is also one of the best places to eat in Huaraz so, after warming up with a Pisco, why not try a cuy (pages 66–7).

8 Take a one-day bike trip in the cordilleras Negra or Blanca The biking in this area is phenomenal; there is enough variety for all levels of experience, with stunning views along the way. Try Chakinaniperu (✆ *424259;* e *julio.olaza@terra.com.pe; www. chakinaniperu.com*) with prices from US$70 to US$150 per person including bike hire and guide.

9 **Get on a horse** The Lazy Dog Inn (page 149), 12km from Huaraz, offers a variety of horserides. Book ahead to discuss levels and prices.

10 **Try rock climbing at Hatun Machay** Some 75km south of Huaraz, these stunning rock formations are a must for rock climbers. There is a refuge there so you can stay the night. For more information, ask at the Casa de Guías (page 163).

11 **Visit Paron Lake** The largest body of water in the Cordillera Blanca, 31km east of Caraz. Hike along its north shore to see the perfect pyramid of Mount Artesonraju, thought to be the inspiration for the Paramount film company's logo.

12 **Experience the Cañón del Pato** A real favourite with adventurous drivers, this road follows the often very narrow canyon cut by the Río Santa as it plummets its way down from the cordilleras Blanca and Negra passing through over 25 narrow tunnels on the way.

13 **Take a trip to the Pastoruri Glacier** Witness the global warming effect on the Cordillera Blanca – and see some *Puya raimondii*.

14 **See the sunset at the *Puya raimondii* at Winchus** In the Cordillera Negra, 36km east of Caraz, at 4,200m. You can see the golden and purple colours of the 140km Cordillera Blanca to the east, and a few minutes later, an amazing sunset above the clouds over the Pacific Ocean when facing the west.

15 **Paddle a kayak on Purhuay Lake** This huge lake, 8km east from Huari, is surrounded by eucalyptus forest. You can hire a kayak, take a hike along the shore of the lake and even enjoy fried trout in the shade of the trees.

16 **Eat a Pachamanca** Enjoy this traditional Inca feast. A fire is lit in a hole which is then filled with meat and vegetables before being covered over with earth to cook slowly. The result is delicious and must be eaten with your hands only; no cutlery! The Rancho Chico at Tingua is one of the best places to enjoy it.

423443; e moralesf@speedy.com. pe, moralesf@terra.com.pe; www. pyramidexpeditions.com. Works with UK & US tour operators. See advert, colour page 25.

Quechuandes Avda Luzuriaga 702, Pasaje Atusaría; m 943562339 ; www. quechuandes.com. Day tours & longer expeditions also.

Santa Cruz Expeditions (In partnership with UK agency Andean Trails) e info@ santacruzexpeditions.com; www. santacruzexpeditions.com. Operate climbing & trekking trips. Also rent mountaineering equipment.

Sky Line Adventures Pasaje Industrial No 137, Cascapampa; 427097; e info@skyline-adventures.com; www. skyline-adventures.com. US-run agency. Pre-arranged treks, climbs & bi-weekly mountaineering courses May–Sep. Must call or email ahead.

FESTIVALS These are just a few of the many fiestas in the region held during the winter (trekking season) months. Check with the tourist office for any that coincide with your visit.

1 May	Fiesta del Señor de la Soledad. Religious parade.
Early May	Fiesta de San Isidro. San Isidro is the patron saint of agriculture, and his festival is held during the first two weeks of May all over Peru.
End of June	Semana del Andinismo, a six-day celebration of the mountains with costumes and dancing.
6–8 July	Santa Isábel y la Virgen de las Cosechas, Callejón de Huaylas. Parades, costumes, dancing.

CARAZ *Telephone code 43*

Situated at the northern end of the Río Santa Valley about 67km from Huaraz, this is the access town for treks in the northern Cordillera Blanca. At a much lower altitude than Huaraz, Caraz is a pleasant, untouristy town with a warm climate and welcoming atmosphere. There are plenty of really nice places to stay and some good options for day trips as well as easy access to Cashapampa and Hualcayán for trekking.

WHERE TO STAY AND EAT
Accommodation

🏠 **Perla de Los Andes** Jr Daniel Villar 179, Plaza de Armas; 392007. Their best rooms have a balcony facing the Plaza de Armas. Nice small restaurant. Sgl or dbl from 50 soles pp.

🏠 **Pony's Lodge and Pony's Expeditions** Jr Sucre 1266, Plaza de Armas; 391642; e info@ ponyexpeditions.com; www. ponyexpeditions.com. Run by outdoor enthusiasts Alberto Cafferata & Aide Caballero. Can organise trekking, climbing & mountain biking. Camping gear for rent. Also 4x4 for private transfers from/to Lima or Trujillo, with English-speaking driver. En-suite sgls or dbls at 50 soles pp, inc b/fast & Wi-Fi.

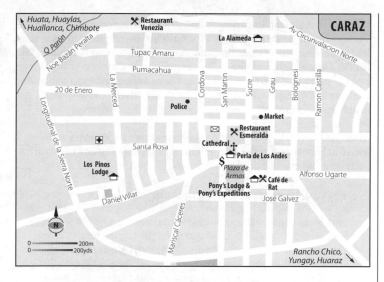

🏠 **La Alameda** Avda Noe Bazán Peralta 262 (at the junction with Jr Sucre); ☎391177; e jctorres-2009@hotmail.com; www.hotellaalameda.com. Run by sisters, clean, peaceful twin rooms for 90 soles.

🏠 **Albergue Los Pinos** Parque San Martin 103 (Jr Daniel Vilar, 6 blocks from main square); ☎391130; e apuaventura@terra.com.pe, lospinos@apuaventura.com. An old *casona* (country house) with a variety of rooms or camping. Great location on a quiet square with views. Rooms 100–150 soles. The owner Luis Gerardo Rojas Lara (a former Inca Trail guide from Caraz) has also opened the agency **Apu Aventura** (☎ *391130; www.apuaventura.pe*).

Restaurants

✕ **Café de Rat** Jr Sucre 1266, Plaza de Armas (upstairs, no sign). Run by Alberto & Aide of Pony's Expeditions. Delicious b/fasts, muesli, salads, vegetarian food, pizza & pasta, fondue (on request), as well as free Wi-Fi, book exchange & dart board.

✕ **Rancho Chico** In Tigua, on the west side of the Huaraz–Caraz road. Serves traditional Peruvian food outdoors, inc *pachamama*.

✕ **Restaurant Esmeralda** Jr Alfonso Ugarte, right behind the church. Serves good *comida criolla* & a great-value set meal.

✕ **Restaurant Venezia** Avda Noe Bazán Peralta; ⏰ Mon–Sat. Good Italian dishes.

TOUR OPERATORS Both **Pony's Expeditions** and **Apu Aventura** (see *Where to stay and eat*) can organise treks and other adventures in the local area.

TREKKING AND BACKPACKING OVERVIEW

For more general information, see *chapters 3 and 4*.

WEATHER Although the dry/wet season pattern is more reliable than the weather in temperate climates, you should not be surprised to have rain, hail or snow in the dry season (mid-June to mid-September), nor some bright, clear weather in the rainy season (early October to late May). Bear in mind that in bad weather it is unrewarding and even dangerous crossing the high passes, which will be cloud-covered, and you may get caught in a blizzard.

ACCLIMATISATION Read the discussion on this subject on page 103, and spend at least two or three days in Huaraz before doing any hiking trips, then do a few practice day hikes.

AVALANCHE AND LANDSLIDE HISTORY

This region is particularly prone to catastrophic landslides. From time to time the water levels build up in the high mountain lakes, causing them to breach. When an avalanche lands in a lake, or when an earthquake dumps half the glacier there, a huge wall of water, mixed with snow, ice, mud, rocks and other matter, breaks the weak moraine wall of the lake, and flows down the mountain taking everything with it. Since 1702 there have been numerous catastrophic events of this kind. The worst was in 1970, when a massive earthquake devastated much of central Peru and the town of Yungay in the Santa Valley was completely buried by a huge avalanche caused by ice-fall from Huascarán, killing almost all of its inhabitants. It is thought that almost 20,000 people died there.

A government organisation, INGEMMET (Instituto Geológico Minero y Metalúrgico), was formed to try to prevent such future disasters. Artificial lakes were built and many of the natural lakes were dammed to try to absorb any falling debris. This was initially successful, with no major floods as a result of glacial lake breakouts for many years. However, in April 2010 a 500m chunk of ice snapped off one of the glaciers on the mountain Hualcan, tumbling into Lake 513 (one of the artificially created lakes) above the town of Carhuaz, creating a tidal wave 23m high that swept over the dam wall and down through five villages, causing widespread destruction.

As Peru's glaciers retreat, the frequency and size of ice avalanches increase. The drainage channels and dams built in the aftermath of the 1970 disaster may not work in the future unless they are rebuilt. A bigger ice-fall could have much worse consequences.

GUIDES There is no shortage of guides in Huaraz, and the Casa de Guías (page 163) has around 100 approved guides in its association. It is also worth getting recommendations from other hikers. In the high season there is a set price of 140 soles per day for one to three people, or 170 soles per day for a group of four or more. It is normal practice to write up a contract between yourself and your guide. However, unless the rules change, you do not need a guide for the hikes described in this chapter. In general the trails are clear, and if you do get lost it's no great disaster assuming you are carrying sufficient food. Nevertheless, you should carry – and know how to use – a topographical map and compass or GPS.

ARRIEROS AND THEIR ANIMALS, PORTERS AND COOKS Many hikers use mules or burros (donkeys) to carry their camping equipment and food. The advantages are great; you can walk with just a daypack (which you will appreciate on those long uphill stretches to the passes), and you can take more food and clothing, both of which help considerably with the strenuous days and cold nights. A good arriero knows the route and the possible variations, and thus serves as a guide. He will also help bridge the gap with local people that you meet along the way, help you buy food where possible, and could be invaluable in the case of an emergency. The arrieros have organised themselves into an association, and the prices are set: at the time of writing an arriero will need to be paid 42 soles per day and a burro 22 soles per day. A horse costs 33 soles per day. Plus you are responsible for providing all meals for the arrieros and their helpers, and should check that they have shelter for the nights, otherwise you may need to provide that as well. Settle all conditions beforehand and pay half at the start of the trip and the other half at the end. If you are planning on going above the snowline or on some of the treks where passes are too rocky for donkeys you may need to hire porters. Porters and cooks in this area generally charge 70–85 soles per day.

MOUNTAIN REFUGES (REFUGIOS) Based in Macará, just south of Carhuaz, is the Italian charitable organisation, Don Bosco (✆ 043 443061). Working in association with the Italian Alpine Club, they train young men from impoverished villages to work as guides, cooks etc. They have also built five *refugios* in the Cordillera Blanca for climbers tackling the main peaks. These well-built places are hostel-style, with bunk-bed dorms, and have hot water and sometimes even a restaurant. Check their website for further details (*www.donbosco6000.net*) or enquire at Casa de Guías (page 163) for individual bookings.

ENTRANCE TO THE VALLEYS Most of the valleys where the trails start have locked gates at their entrances. This is to stop thieves from stealing the animals that graze in the valleys. The campesinos who own the animals and farm the land at the foot of the trails operate a toll system for hikers with burros. You have to pay for the gate at the start of the trail to be opened; and, if returning the same way, you will have to pay to exit. If you have an arriero with you he will deal with this. Make sure you discuss this in advance, as gatekeepers may need advising of your plans ahead of time. The fee is expensive – from 28 to 42 soles – but does not apply to backpackers who can climb over the gate. For further information check at the Casa de Guías (page 163).

RENTING EQUIPMENT All trekking, climbing and general camping equipment – boots, clothing, tents, stoves, ropes, ice-axes, helmets, crampons, etc – can be rented in Huaraz (page 163), at reasonable prices (eg: sleeping bag 8–14 soles per day, stove 6–8 soles per day). There is

i **TREKKING POSSIBILITIES IN THE CORDILLERA NEGRA**

Recommended by Nick Ward, veteran Peru trekker and explorer
These treks are for the more adventurous hiker with time on their hands. Nick recommends finding a guide that knows the area, just choosing where to start and where you would like to end, and picking your own route following the line of the watershed. You are likely only to see the indigenous people, who will at times be most inquisitive and sometimes rather concerned that you may be prospecting.

Camping points will be determined by where you can find good water – most days this isn't a problem, there are streams and lakes.

Nick's suggestion is that you climb out of the Santa Valley westwards and walk along the high ridges northwards or southwards, climbing over as many peaks as you like. You can spend one or more nights at each camp, allowing time to explore the many Inca sites, enjoy stunning views across to the Cordillera Blanca and to see the *Puya raimondii* growing along the route. There are no supplies along the way. A recommended guide to off-the-beaten-track routes in the Cordillera Negra is Victor Lliuya Lliuya (e *alpamayo_46@hotmail.com*).

Two places of special interest are the **Bosque de Rocas**, an impressive stand of huge eroded boulders, west of the lake of Conococha at the southern end of the Callejón de Huayalas, and the *Puya raimondii* at the northern end of the canyon, 36km west of Caraz. The former is shown on the Austrian map of the south Cordillera Blanca. For the puya you need to follow a dirt road to reach the pass of Huashta Cruz at 4,200m, and Winchus (or Huinchus) where the plants grow.

an increasing number of hire shops in Huaraz but during peak season demand is high and you may not find any equipment of good quality. There are shops selling imported kit, but it is very expensive and for emergency purchases only. Several of the trekking organisations in Huaraz rent out equipment (page 163).

FOOD AND SUPPLIES Huaraz is the best place to buy food for your trip. In the smaller towns you can get fresh food from the market, but the choice is limited. Up in the mountains, you might be lucky to find a señora willing to cook a meal for you, or you might find very basic food at some tiny shop. You cannot rely on this, however – mostly the campesinos have barely enough to feed themselves – so bring enough for the whole trip, plus some extra. The market in Huaraz has a good selection of trail food, and there are several small supermarkets dotted around the main town centre, with the best of these on Luzuriaga.

MAPS You are advised to take a map if you are hiking independently. The relevant IGN map is listed in the route information, but there are other trekking maps available around Huaraz.

Cordilleras Blanca y Huayhuash by Felipe Diaz is readily available in Lima and Huaraz (about 28 soles). This useful map shows the routes and roads in the valleys, giving you an overview of the whole area.

The Austrian Alpine Club publishes three good maps – 0/3a covers Cordillera Blanca North, 0/3b covers Cordillera South, and 0/3c covers Huayhaush, available in the outdoor shops, some cafés (most notably Café Andino, page 163) and agencies for 85 soles upwards. These are mentioned under individual treks as Alpenvereinskarte. When planning a new route bear in mind that the glaciers have receded a lot since the area was last surveyed.

Skyline Adventures has published three separate 1:75,000 maps of Cordillera Blanca North, South and Huayhuash, priced around 33–42 soles each. These are probably the most up to date and accurate of all the trekking maps.

TREKKING ROUTES IN THE CORDILLERA BLANCA

The following treks have been selected for their views, their variety, or because they are relatively easy. We begin with an acclimatisation hike near Huaraz, and then describe the longer treks beginning at the northern end of the range and working south:

- A day hike outside Huaraz (*6km; 3–4hrs*); page 172
- The Alpamayo Circuit (or semi-circuit) (*About 83km; 6–10 days*); pages 173–80

- The Santa Cruz Trek: Cashapampa to Colcabamba or Vaquería (*45km; 3–4 days*); pages 181–3
- The Lagunas Llanganuco and Laguna 69 (*About 12km; 5–6hrs*); pages 183–6
- Climbing Pisco (*About 40km; 2–4 days*); page 185
- Quebrada Ulta to Chacas, Yanama or Colcabamba (*About 42km; 4 days*); pages 186–8
- Quebrada Ishinca (*38km; 1–2 days*); pages 188–9
- Pitec to Collón via quebradas Quilcayhuanca, Cojup and Ishinca (*About 67km; 4–8 days*); pages 189–90
- Four valley walks near Huaraz:
  - To Laguna Churup via the quebrada (*7km; 4–6hrs*). page 191;
  - To Laguna Shallap via the quebrada (*16km; 7hrs*), page 192;
  - To Laguna Rajucolta via the quebrada (*38km, 16hrs*), pages 192–4;
  - Up the Quebrada Quilcayhuanca to the lagunas Tullpacocha, Cuchillacocha and Paqsacocha (*39km, 4 days*), pages 194–5
- Olleros to Chavín (*37km, 2–3 days*); pages 195–8

A DAY HIKE OUTSIDE HUARAZ This is an easy hike outside Huaraz, so ideal for acclimatisation and to enjoy the views of the city, and the cordilleras Blanca and Negra.

Distance	6km
Altitude	3,150–3,650m
Rating	Easy
Timing	3–4 hours
In reverse	Possible
Start of trail	Plaza de Armas in Huaraz
Transport at the end	Not necessary (return to Huaraz on foot)
Maps	IGN sheet *Huaraz* (20-h)

Route description Head south from the Plaza de Armas on Avenida Luzuriaga until the intersection with Avenida Villón. Turn left and walk up Avenida Villón until the **cemetery**, then right and left again and follow the obvious dirt road uphill then curving to the right. Follow this road all the way to the pass, taking short cuts where possible.

The road drops into the valley on the other side of the pass, with some spectacular views from the **large cross** which overlooks the city. Stay on this side of the valley, following the footpath which goes along the mountain ridge and finally drops down in the direction of Huaraz again. The path meets up with the start of the trail at the cemetery.

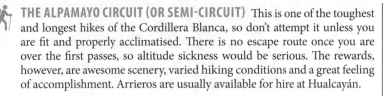

THE ALPAMAYO CIRCUIT (OR SEMI-CIRCUIT) This is one of the toughest and longest hikes of the Cordillera Blanca, so don't attempt it unless you are fit and properly acclimatised. There is no escape route once you are over the first passes, so altitude sickness would be serious. The rewards, however, are awesome scenery, varied hiking conditions and a great feeling of accomplishment. Arrieros are usually available for hire at Hualcayán.

Distance	About 83km
Altitude	2,800–4,850m
Rating	Difficult
Timing	6–10 days (depending on side treks)
In reverse	Possible
Start of trail	Hualcayán
Transport at the end	Passing trucks will take you back to the Santa Valley. Buses run to Huaraz
Maps	IGN sheets *Corongo* (18-h) and *Pomabamba* (18-1); Alpenvereinskart *Cordillera Blanca Nord* (0/3a), Skyline *Cordillera Blanca Northern Treks*

Route description Take the path that heads straight out of Hualcayán up the hillside. Your first destination is Laguna Cullicocha, a long, hard climb via a series of switchbacks with an altitude gain of about 1,800m. This will take five or six hours. The trail crosses the remains of a 1970 earthquake landslide, then climbs slowly past two dry (most of the time) creeks, and comes to a meadow atop a little hill. This is a possible camping place, with great views. A canal provides water. It is another 7km of moderate climbing to **Laguna Cullicocha**. Continue up the switchbacks, passing a creek, before the trail goes up a ridge where you get the first glimpses of the *nevados* (snowfields). The trail climbs to the right and comes to a fork. Here you're at about 4,450m and are 14km from Hualcayán.

> ! **Getting to the trailheads:**
> Several treks in the northern Cordillera Blanca start in **Cashapampa** or **Hualcayán**. There are daily buses, colectivos and taxis from Caraz market to Cashapampa, from 06.00 to 15.00 but there is no public transport to Hualcayán; you need to catch a colectivo to Cashapampa and then hike three hours, or take a **taxi** for 100 soles.

The trail to the left goes to Laguna Cullicocha (called Laguna Atuncocha on the IGN map) and the one straight ahead to Laguna Yuraccocha, at the foot of Nevado Santa Cruz. There is an **ElectroPeru hut** nearby. If

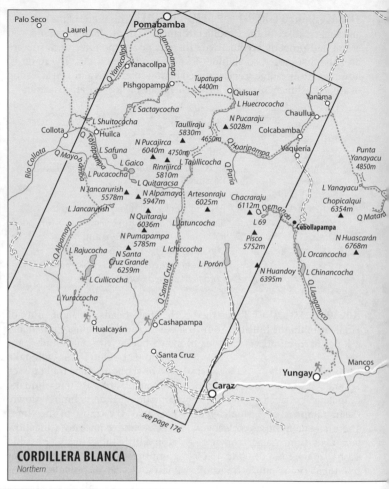

CORDILLERA BLANCA
Northern

❗ Note: Place spellings and the heights of peaks and passes vary according to which map you use. Where possible we have taken them from the Austrian Alpine Club maps.

you need shelter for the night ask the guardian if you can sleep there. If you want to take a side trip to Laguna Yuraccocha, it is 9km with little change in altitude.

The trail to Laguna Cullicocha continues climbing to 4,650m, about 3.5km from the trail fork. There is another, higher, lake, **Rajucocha**, but it is difficult to reach. The best campsites are found at the little **Laguna Azulcocha**, just north of the outlet from Laguna Cullicocha.

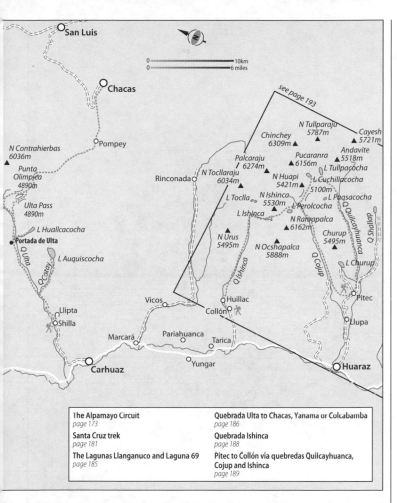

see page 193

The Alpamayo Circuit *page 173*	Quebrada Ulta to Chacas, Yanama or Colcabamba *page 186*
Santa Cruz trek *page 181*	Quebrada Ishinca *page 188*
The Lagunas Llanganuco and Laguna 69 *page 185*	Pitec to Collón via quebradas Quilcayhuanca, Cojup and Ishinca *page 189*

Now head towards Alpamayo. The trail starts about 40m below Laguna Cullicocha, crosses some granite rock, and climbs up to the pass of **Osoruri** (4,860m) and then a second pass, **Los Cedros** (or Vientunana) at 4,800m, about 3km from the lake. You can camp between the first and second pass – there is water here. From the pass a long descent begins into the Quebrada de Los Cedros/Alpamayo via a series of switchbacks. Near the bottom the trail forks. The trail to the left continues down to the hamlet of Alpamayo, and the main trail (yours) to the right crosses a stream and descends to the east to meet the river where there are some indeterminate ruins and terraces. Quebrada de Los Cedros (which

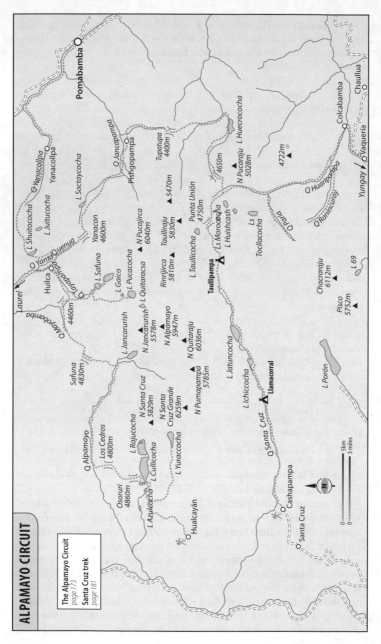

The Alpamayo Circuit
page 173

Santa Cruz trek
page 181

becomes Quebrada Alpamayo at about this point) is at 4,000m, 10km from the pass. There are lots of good camping spots here, but it's best to move on up the quebrada to **Laguna Jancarurish** for the superb views of Nevado Alpamayo. 👁 base camp, below.

👁 **Side trip:** If you are still full of boundless energy you can make the 10.5km climb of about 500m from the valley to the **base camp** used by climbers of Alpamayo (5,947m) and Santa Cruz (6,259m).

The trail continues to the pass of **Safuna** – also known as Garagara or Caracara (4,830m) – crossing the streams below Laguna Jancarurish, and climbing north to the right of two creeks to some small lakes. Continue up the slopes of loose rock towards the pass (on the right side of the crag at the top). The trail is faint until higher up on the moraine. Take great care in bad weather when it may be difficult to find this route. In good weather the views behind are inspiring, looking over the moraines to the immense glaciers and peaks of Alpamayo (5,947m), Jancarurish (5,578m), Quitaraju (6,036m), Pumapampa (5,785m) and Santa Cruz Grande (6,259m).

From the pass it's a steep descent into **Quebrada Mayobamba**, but on a much better trail. This is a beautiful quebrada, with many good camping spots.

Continue towards a ridge on the east side of the valley. A faint path goes to the top of the ridge at a small pass (4,460m) then descends into **Quebrada Tayapampa**. 👁 Lagunas Safuna, below.

The main trail (now a dirt road) follows Quebrada Tayapampa for two hours to the small community of **Huilca** at 4,000m. It's about 5.5km from the lake.

👁 **Side trip:** Turn right (south) at Quebrada Tayapampa for **two Lagunas Safuna** just below the multi-peaked Nevado Pucajirca (6,040m is the highest) on the far side of the valley. This trail soon joins a dirt road leading to **Laguna Safuna Baja**, which lies at 4,250m with good campsites. **Laguna Alta** is 1km further on and has no campsite. Another trail takes you 5.5km to **Laguna Pucacocha**, which lies at 4,500m. To reach it take the path that leads to the middle of the canyon, passes tiny Laguna Kaiko, and comes to a crude cabin above Laguna Pucacocha. Above the next moraine you find **Laguna Quitaracsa**, directly below Nevado Alpamayo.

To Pomabamba Now there are two possible routes to Pomabamba. The first is via the village of Laurel. Follow the road, along the quebrada and down to the valley which runs to the north of Huilca. It's about 3km. From here the road climbs up to a small pass at 4,300m. Coming down the other side you'll see some small lakes, about 12km from the valley. At this point the road and the trail separate. The road continues to Palo

Seco and the trail goes southeast to **Laurel**. The trail descends about 6km through a narrow valley to Laurel at 3,500m. From Laurel you can find buses to Pomabamba, or continue to the north and return to Huaraz via the **Cañón del Pato**.

The second choice is longer, via Yanacollpa, but goes direct to Pomabamba. The trail climbs steeply from Huilca, heading northeast, to

HOW IT ALL BEGAN

On 3 June 1973, almost exactly 40 years ago, I was sleeping on the front lawn of the Hotel Monterrey near Huaraz. Our tent had been stolen, so we'd bought a shower-curtain which we rigged up as a crude shelter. I wrote about our trip in letters to my parents: 'There was long soft grass about the place so we slept very comfortably. This morning we were woken by hordes of Indians trotting past on their way to the market. They wore brightly coloured embroidered skirts in great quantities, and high-crowned straw hats with tassels, and embroidered shirts trimmed with lace. The babies on their backs were swaddled, biblical style, bound so tightly they could only move their heads. They looked like little wooden dolls and their mothers looked rather doll-like too, they were so stiff with clothes.'

It turned out that the Monterrey was a climbers' hotel. A Canadian team were preparing to scale a 6,400m peak in the Cordillera Blanca. They pointed it out on an old German topographical map from the 1930s that was pinned to the wall in the hallway. It was the first detailed map of the region we'd seen and we studied it carefully. 'There's a footpath marked which goes over the mountains and ends up at some ruins we were intending to visit'. I wrote: 'We plan to walk it, providing it still exists, which it most likely does. It should take us about four days and goes up to 14,500ft so I hope we'll be warm enough. We're at 9,000ft here so it's not too much of a climb'. This low-key statement of fact belies the heated argument that took place in front of the map, with George saying how lovely it would be to hike that trail and me saying we had no tent, no boots, no map and – in my case – no motivation. He won the day.

It took us all morning to find a truck going to Olleros. Once there we asked an astonished local man if the path continued to Chavín. He nodded. 'Nueve horas'.

'Hay muchos gringos aqui?'

'Nunca'.

So we were the first backpackers they'd seen who wanted to walk to Chavín. I liked that, even though nine hours seemed a bit optimistic.

the first pass at 4,280m. You'll see **Laguna Shuitococha** ahead. The trail continues east to the second pass at 4,350m, about 6.5km from Huilca. It then drops down into **Quebrada Yanacollpa**, passing a few small lakes. Here you are faced with another choice of two routes. If you decide to go to the village of Yanacollpa continue down through the meadows to the stream. Follow its left bank until a bridge where you can cross the stream,

It was a beautiful walk. We took our time, explored the surrounding area, and slept in deserted shepherd's huts. 'The next morning we woke to find a man squatting in the doorway watching us and whistling. It wasn't his hut, he was just curious, so George made him a cup of tea and he talked at great length about how he used to work for a "patron" and life was very hard but since the agrarian reform four years ago he's been part of a co-operative and "free". His parents had died when he was very young but his elder brother made sure he got some schooling, which was probably why he spoke good Spanish.'

Mostly we found the trail easy to follow apart from an agonising time when we had to cross an ice-encrusted bog in the early morning, barefoot to keep our shoes dry. I was crying with the pain of it. 'We walked over 12 miles today but through constantly changing scenery. Lots of glaciers and jagged snowy mountains, and bare mountains all different shades of red and brown. The Indians have been amazed to see us. The women have hidden in their huts and the men rarely returned our greeting. Mostly they just stared.'

Chavín, once we got there, was initially a disappointment. 'Just heaps of earth with tunnels inside them which were too small to walk through. But then we found a guide who unlocked a couple of doors leading to inside chambers, and there were these *terrific* stone carvings!'

Getting back to Huaraz was a trial. 'We finally found a truck that was leaving "Now" (it was 3 o'clock) but it finally got going at 5. We rode in the back, sitting on sacks of coca leaves, with pigs riding in the rear section. There were quite a few of us, women with babies, a couple of men and a chatty policeman. We thought it would take around two hours (it looked about 50 miles on the map) so we didn't believe the policeman when he said it would be eight hours. But he was right. We rolled into Huaraz at 1am, frozen absolutely solid after going over a 15,000ft pass (but beautiful with a full moon lighting up the snowpeaks).'

And that was how it all began. I discovered that trekking in Peru wasn't so bad after all, and when we reached Cusco and learned about an old Inca road that led to Machu Picchu there was no argument about whether to try hiking it.

8

and descend to **Yanacollpa** (3,700m). It's about 8km from the pass. To continue to Pomabamba you then drop down to the river and look out for an **irrigation canal**. Follow this all the way (about two hours) to the dirt road, where you may be able to catch a colectivo to Pomabamba. The distance from Yanacollpa to Pomabamba is about 12km.

The alternative route from the small lakes is via Quebrada Jancapampa. At the small lakes you can see a path going up the slopes to the south; follow it until the pass at 4,350m, from where it goes steeply downhill on a faint path until the upper end of **Quebrada Jancapampa**, just below the nevados Taulliraju and Pucajirca. From here it's an easy descent (10–12km) over the meadows to the start of the quebrada, following an **aqueduct**. Continue down to the Río Shiulla and from there to Pomabamba.

Pomabamba is a nice little town with friendly people and an ATM. You can stock up on some supplies here, find accommodation, and give yourself a good feed in one of the basic restaurants before returning to Huaraz by bus. The journey takes about eight hours. Sit on the right-hand side of the bus for the best views.

To Vaquería The trail heads southeast from Huilca, following the Quebrada Yanta Quenua for about 4km, until you start the steep climb taking you to the next pass, Yanacon, at 4,600m, from where you look down over wooded slopes of quenual forests to the picturesque **Laguna Sactaycocha** far below. Pucajirca towers above the pass. A beautiful long descent brings you to the vast flat open valley of **Jancapampa** (3,500m) at the foot of Taulliraju (5,830m) and Rinrijirca (5,810m). There are plenty of camping places in this dramatic spot, with glaciers above, waterfalls cascading to the valley and farming communities dotted around the slopes below. The following day cross the broad grassy pampa heading south, towards the houses of **Pishgopampa** on the far side of the valley. From here continue to climb out of the valley, heading southwards, towards the pass of **Tupatupa** (4,400m), one of the most stunning viewpoints on the trek. The Cordillera Blanca is spread out before you. The views stay with you as you descend to the village of **Quisuar** (3,800m) – from here you can hike out along the river to Lucma, where there is transport to Pomabamba.

To continue hiking head west from Quisuar, a gentle start up the valley towards the Pucaraju pass. Leave **Lake Huecrococha** to your left. The climb steepens considerably as you near the pass at 4,650m, but the spectacular panorama of snow-capped peaks makes all that climbing worthwhile. There may even be condors soaring in the Quebrada Huaripampa below. The jagged top of Taulliraju (5,830m) is impressive to the west. Ahead of you both peaks of Huascarán fill the view. From here it's all downhill. Carefully descend the steep and loose zigzag path to join the Huaripampa Valley. There are camping places in the valley bottom at **Tuctubamba** (3,800m). The final day is a gentle stroll down the valley to the road at **Vaquería**.

THE SANTA CRUZ TREK: CASHAPAMPA TO COLCABAMBA OR VAQUERÍA

This is the classic trek of the Cordillera Blanca and the most popular – deservedly so, but it does become very crowded in peak season. Nevertheless, nothing can diminish the impact of the spectacular views as, following the route clockwise as described here, you hike gently up Quebrada Santa Cruz where giant, snow-covered peaks tower above you on both sides of the valley.

The number of arrieros currently working out of **Cashapampa** gives an idea of just how crowded it is: there are well over 70. They have formed a collective and charge a flat rate of 17 soles per animal and 33 soles per arriero per day. You must also pay for them to return to Cashapampa at the end of the trek.

There are established campsites and pit toilets at regular intervals (every three to four hours) along the route which reduce the damage to the environment and should be used, even if some have fallen into slight disrepair.

Distance	45km
Altitude	2,900–4,750m
Rating	Moderate
Timing	3–4 days (excluding side trips)
In reverse	Possible – see *Clockwise or anti-clockwise?*, below
Start of trail	Cashapampa
Transport at the end	From Vaquería there is (infrequent) transport to Yungay and Huaraz or to Yanama and San Luis
Maps	IGN sheets *Corongo* (18-h) and *Carhuaz* (19-h); trekking map *Llanganuco to Santa Cruz* from the SAE; Skyline *Cordillera Blanca Northern Treks*.

Clockwise or anti-clockwise? Opinion is divided on which is the best direction to do this hike. Starting in Cashapampa gives you the gradual acclimatising ascent on the first day, which suits unfit trekkers. Backpackers using public transport may, however, prefer the anti-clockwise direction, that allows sufficient time to walk to the campsite on the first day, thus giving a good start on the high pass the following day. Then, at the end of the trek, it is easy to hike out by midday and catch one of the early-afternoon colectivos from Cashapampa.

You should have no problem reversing the directions for Cashapampa to Vaquería, but take care at the beginning of the trail if you want to bypass Colcabamba. From the bus stop at Vaquería drop straight down to a creek, cross it, and follow the path, taking the left-hand trail over a small hill/pass and descending into the next valley. Here you follow or cross the river up to the park boundary.

Route description The trail starts just outside the village of Cashapampa where you can hire arrieros and burros or horses if you need them. There is camping in a grassy field near the start of the trail (for a small charge) and a kiosk where you can buy soft drinks and some basic supplies.

It is a steep, gravelly climb up the **Quebrada Santa Cruz** for two hours, following the right bank of the river. The path is pretty obvious, and flattens out for the last two to three hours, taking you all the way up to the first pampa, about 6km from the village, which makes a suitable camping place for the first night, being four to five hours from Cashapampa. This campsite (with toilet) is known as **Llamacorral**.

The next day continue up the Santa Cruz Valley, with spectacular mountain views on both sides, until you reach **Ichiccocha** (Laguna Chica) – which is now frequently dry – and, a bit further up, **Jatuncocha** (Laguna Grande) at 3,900m. This lake is about 11km from Cashapampa, and some three to four hours from the campsite. Continue along the main trail for 40 minutes, and where the path splits, a signpost indicates the trails. 👁 Alpamayo base camp, below.

The main trail continues along the left bank of the river, climbing gently. In 1997 a lake breached the wall of the terminal moraine on the south side of the valley, depositing a massive amount of sand and boulders into this valley. Cross the river via a **small bridge** an hour after the junction, arriving at the meadows of **Taullipampa** beneath the peak of Taulliraju (5,830m). There is a toilet block here and plenty of space to camp. On day three it's a steep and long climb up to the pass of **Punta Unión** at 4,750m, about 15km from **Jatuncocha** and a seven- to eight-hour walk from there, or two to three hours from the Taullipampa campsite.

The view from the pass, looking back at the Santa Cruz Valley, is one of the finest in Peru. The majestic peak of Taulliraju guards the pass, its glaciers calving into the turquoise lake of Taullicocha. Further down the valley the snows of Chacraraju (6,112m), Huandoy (6,395m) and Huascarán (6,768m) form the backdrop.

👁 **Side trip:** There is a rewarding walk to the **Alpamayo base camp** and Laguna Arhuaycocha from here which takes about one to 1½ hours each way. To visit the base camp, take the path climbing steeply to the left (northwest). You don't have to come all the way down again to continue the main trek, but can cut across the valley side, traversing to the campsite at Taullipampa (4,200m).

Side trip: The energetic can hike up **Quebrada Paría** and, further down, up Quebrada Ranincuray. Both are on your right, and get you closer to those magnificent mountains.

After gazing for the last time at the view, prepare yourself for the steep, slippery descent into the valley on the other side, keeping to the right and passing the **Lagunas Morococha** on your right, with the peak of Nevado Pucaraju (5,028m) ahead of you. The trail makes a right turn, descending into **Quebrada Huaripampa**, a lovely valley of meadows and small lakes. Keep to your right, following the river, until you reach the junction of **Quebrada Paría** (named Q Vacaria on some maps), about 11km (*3–4hrs*) from the pass. There are plenty of excellent camping places here, with the glaciers of Artesonraju (6,025m) providing a spectacular backdrop. Quebrada Paría, above.

Continuing down the valley, turn right to descend to the river and cross. On the far side the path splits, the left fork going on down to the village of **Colcabamba**. Here, there are the rewards of a small village including basic accommodation and meals. From Colcabamba there is a path leading up to the road for transport back to Yungay, via the Llanganuco lakes, and Huaraz or to Yanama on the eastern side of the cordillera. Alternatively, take the right fork, climb a few minutes over the ridge, down the far side, cross the river and summon your energy for a final steep, hot ascent to the road and the village of **Vaquería** where you can enjoy a cold drink. From here there is (infrequent) transport throughout the day to Yungay and Huaraz or to Yanama and San Luis.

THE LAGUNAS LLANGANUCO AND LAGUNA 69

The valley of Llanganuco is spectacular for the views of Chopicalqui (6,354m), double-peaked Huascarán (6,768m and 6,655m) and Huandoy (6,395m). The walk from Cebollapampa to the unimaginatively named Laguna 69 provides a lovely glimpse of this beautiful place without the necessity of camping. The lake itself is glacial, so bright turquoise in colour and is surrounded by snowpeaks and fed by waterfalls. A day ticket is currently 5 soles and if you plan to stay longer you have to pay 65 soles for a month-long ticket, regardless of the number of days.

Getting to the trailhead

A dirt road runs from Yungay, past the Llanganuco lakes, up and over the pass (Portachuelo de Llanganuco) to Yanama on the eastern side. This provides access for locals, and trekkers heading to the start of the Santa Cruz trek at Vaquería and gives you easy access to the start of this walk. There are also several colectivos a day from Yungay, during the tourist season, that only go as far as the first of the Llanganuco lakes, Chinancocha. They are specifically for tourists and after driving up, hang around for an hour or so to give you time to

8

Distance	About 12km (round trip) from Cebollapampa
Altitude	3,840–4,450m
Rating	An easy hike, not steep, with beautiful scenery
Timing	5–6 hours
Start of trail	Quebrada Llanganuco, accessible by colectivo from Yungay
Transport at the end	Public transport available over the Punta Unión pass (although buses tend to be quite full, it is possible to get on), or arrange to be picked up by taxi
Maps	IGN sheet *Carhuas* (19-h), Alpenvereinskart *Cordillera Blanca Nord* 0/3a, Skyline *Cordillera Blanca Northern Treks*

visit the lakes, and then head back to Yungay. The jumping-off point for walking to Laguna 69 is a few kilometres beyond this, so if you are going that way either ensure you get a colectivo that is going on over the pass or negotiate with your driver to take you to Cebollapampa. Some people prefer to share a taxi from Huaraz (*3hrs*).

Route description Below the lakes there is a park office checkpoint where you have to pay your entrance fee. It is possible to walk from the park office up the valley, but most buses will be going higher up. A trail climbs up to the Llanganuco lakes from the checkpoint, taking short cuts across the dirt road. It's about 6km or two hours to the lakes. First you'll pass the smaller **Laguna Chinancocha**, and then the bigger **Laguna Orcancocha**. It's best to cross the **stream** at the upper end of the **Lagunas Llanganuco** where the path continues up the valley, crossing the road several times. Don't forget to look back at the superb views. About 3km above the lakes, at the first major bend in the road, a path descends to the meadows of Cebollapampa beside the stream in the **Quebrada Demanda** (3,900m). If you've brought a tent, this is a good camping spot with excellent views of the nearby peaks of Huascarán Norte (6,768m) and Chopicalqui (6,354m). There are a couple of toilet blocks at the site, which by the end of the season inevitably end up quite disgusting.

This is the start of the trails up to Pisco base camp and Laguna 69. For Laguna 69 follow the trail up Quebrada Demanda to the right of the river. The path is obvious and the scenery is beautiful. You will pass some huts and then the trail peters out. Stay on the right side of the valley until you cross a stream coming down from your right. Follow the path up the far side of this stream and then up the steep zigzags on the valley side.

As you climb high above the valley you look down on open pasture and have a beautiful view of a large waterfall over on the left. The path takes you round and above this waterfall, passing a small lake before dropping into an open meadow. You can camp here but the inquisitive cows can be irritating. They have a penchant for eating clothing left out to dry and knocking over stoves. Continuing across the plain you will find a sign indicating that Laguna 69 is 3km away toward the left (north) and that the Glacier Broggi is 2km ahead (east). Both trails are obvious.

After Laguna 69, backpackers have the option of continuing up to Punta Unión and completing the Santa Cruz circuit (page 182), but

🥾 CLIMBING PISCO

Distance	About 40km total
Altitude	3,900–5,752m
Rating	Strenuous and technical; requiring ice-axe and crampons
Timing	12–16 hours each way, walking and climbing over 2 or 4 days
Start of trail	Cebollapampa. By colectivo Huaraz–Yungay then Yungay–Cebollapampa, or taxi from Huaraz
Maps	Alpenvereinskarte *Cordillera Blanca South* 0/3b

This 'trekking peak' of 5,752m is the most popular in the Cordillera Blanca, and although it is non-technical it should not be attempted by inexperienced mountaineers unless they're fully equipped (crampons, ice-axes, harness, rope) and accompanied by a fully qualified mountain guide. Contact the Casa de Guías in Huaraz (page 163) for recommendations and help in organising this trip. You need to allocate two or three days, including the ascent.

From Cebollapampa cross the river and head northwest steeply up the valley side on the path signed to Pisco. With a full backpack it's a good three-hour trek up to base camp. Donkeys can usually be hired at the bottom to help, and at 20 soles per animal and 30 soles a day for an arriero this is a small price to pay to make the climb a bit easier. The views of surrounding peaks improve as you climb, and from base camp itself the panorama is superb. There is a large mountain refuge at Pisco base camp (42 soles a bed) and plenty of space for camping, with fresh water from a spring. Book your bed through Don Bosco in Marcará (page 169), the organisation that runs the *refugios*.

8

day hikers have the choice of returning to the road and catching a lift to Colcabamba or Yanama, or returning the way they came.

QUEBRADA ULTA TO CHACAS, YANAMA OR COLCABAMBA This isn't a popular trek, which is one of its big advantages, but it has plenty of other things going for it too, including marvellous views of the snowpeaks looming above the valley on either side of the quebrada, and some great side trips. There's also the opportunity to be terrified as you come over one of the cordillera's most dramatic, nerve-racking passes. If you are scared of heights don't do this one.

This trek provides one of the best opportunities in the Cordillera Blanca for seeing condors.

There is a paved road all the way up the Quebrada Ulta and down the other side to Chacas, but in the past it has carried relatively few vehicles because of the difficulty in getting over the pass. A new tunnel through Punta Olimpica avoids the high pass and thus traffic may increase. At least this road can be used to save you some climbing, and it does nothing to destroy the superb views. Buses run regularly from Huaraz to Chacas along this route.

Distance	About 42km
Altitude	3,050–4,900m
Rating	Generally easy, except for the passes, which are tough going
Timing	4 days (excluding side trips)
In reverse	Possible, and can be done as an extension to the Santa Cruz trek
Start of trail	Shilla, or higher up the quebrada
Transport at the end	Public transport back to Huaraz once or twice a day
Maps	IGN sheet *Carhuas* (19-h); Alpenvereinskart *Cordillera Blanca Nord* 0/3a

Route description You may decide to take transport higher up the quebrada to save some of that climbing (there are regular buses; the best place to get off is when the road starts to zig-zag). If you are starting from **Shilla**, follow the main footpath to **Llipta**; it crosses the road several times. After about 7km you come to the entrance of the **Quebrada Auquiscocha** (called Catay on some maps) to the right. 👁 Quebrada Auquiscocha, opposite.

The main trail continues climbing up the valley until the **Portada de Ulta** (the entrance of the valley) at 3,600m, about 3.5km from Quebrada

> **Side trip:** It's a 3km walk up **Quebrada Auquiscocha** to its lake at 4,300m. There are not a lot of camping possibilities at the lake, but a large cave hidden behind the underbrush just to the right of the outlet stream will give you shelter.

> **Side trip** At the portada, Quebrada Huallcacocha leads off to your right, with a pleasant walk of about 3.5km to **Laguna Huallcacocha** (4,350m).

Auquiscocha, where a Huascarán National Park ranger will check or sell the required entry ticket.

◉ Laguna Huallcacocha, left.

The main route splits into several trails at the portada, running through the meadow and up the valley. The snow-covered summit of Chopicalqui appears to the left with Quebrada Cancayapampa (Matará). If you are looking for somewhere to **camp**, there are some super places in the meadows of this quebrada at 4,350m, about 4km from the entrance of the valley. The massive cliffs of nevados Huascarán (6,768m) and Chopicalqui (6,354m) loom above.

You have a choice here: if you can't face the drama of the Yanayacu pass, there is an easier route which follows the road to the right up to the pass of **Pasaje de Ulta** (a tunnel beneath the Punta Olimpica). It climbs to the right of a little ridge, crosses the pass, and brings you down to Pompey and then Chacas.

The more adventurous trail to Yanama continues north towards Nevado Contrahierbas (6,036m) at the head of the quebrada at 4,100m, just under 2km from the Quebrada Matará. It passes above the shallow **Laguna Yanayacu** (possible campsites, and the last water for 8km), turns up the valley to the east, and climbs to the pass of **Punta Yanayacu** at 4,850m, about 8km from the start of the quebrada. This is the dramatic one. The narrow path is cut into the side of the mountain, with a rock cliff on one side and a sheer drop on the other. Having survived this, you descend to a very high and cold lake full of icebergs, below the glaciers of Contrahierbas. If you are well equipped for freezing conditions, this is a marvellous campsite, with rumbling avalanches during the evening and night. The path continues down the valley and soon reaches the valley floor and good campsites.

Keep to the left side of the stream, crossing it near the lower end of the valley, and you have reached the junction of the Colcabamba trail and the Yanama road at 3,350m,

> **Note:** Don't camp close to the villages in this area, and watch your belongings.

about 10km from the pass. Take the left trail to Colcabamba, which climbs steeply for about 500m. It then levels out and traverses the ridge before dropping to the village of **Chaullua**. Here it meets the Colcabamba–Yanama trail. Take this to the left, making a short climb to where the trail splits; the upper trail leads to Quebrada Morococha and the Portachuelo de Llanganuco, and the lower trail to **Colcabamba**, about 6km on what is now a dirt road.

 QUEBRADA ISHINCA This is a beautiful **up-and-back hike** up the valley of Ishinca, with an interesting side trip to the Ishinca glacier. There are great views all the way, and the hiking is easy. This is the route for climbers going up to Ishinca, Urus or Tocllaraju. Ishinca and Urus are 'trekking peaks' that can be climbed by suitably equipped trekkers (crampons, ice-axe, harness, rope) with a qualified guide. Ask the Casa de Guías for details and recommendations (page 163). There is a refuge at Ishinca base camp (contact Don Bosco in Marcará to book, page 169) and a second unattended refuge at Ishinca moraine camp, two hours above the main one. You get the key from the main refuge.

Distance	38km (round trip)
Altitude	3,200–4,950m
Rating	Easy to base camp, a steep climb to the lake
Timing	1–2 days from Collón or Huillac to Ishinca moraine camp
Start of trail	Taxi or colectivo from Huaraz to the small village of Collón, 3km from the main road
Transport at the end	There is public transport to the road head, or alternatively organise transport in advance from one of the agencies in Huaraz
Maps	IGN sheet *Huari* (19-i), Alpenvereinskart *Cordillera Blanca Süd* 0/3b.

Route description Walk on the road out of Huillac to where a rock is painted red with 'Ishinca' and an arrow. Follow the trail to the right for two hours to the portada, where a Huascarán National Park ranger will check or sell the required entry ticket. This is the entrance of the **Quebrada Ishinca**, at 3,850m, about 7km from Huillac. Camping is possible around here.

The trail continues through a series of meadows to the head of the valley. Good campsites abound. A clear path passes by a **waterfall** on the south wall, and after an easy climb of 2km it crosses the stream and reaches the **Ishinca climbers' base camp**, at 4,400m, about 8km (*4hrs*) from the entrance of the valley. There is a large refuge here, and plenty of camping spots.

Beyond the base camp the trail begins to climb the south wall, at times quite steeply, before passing a swampy meadow and making the final

Side trip: From Ishinca base camp there is a possible 1½-hour side trek up to **Laguna Toclla**, below Nevado Tocllaraju (6,034m). An alternative side trip is to the base camp for Nevado Urus: a trail climbs up from the head of Quebrada Ishinca to this small base camp at 4,980m, about 2½ hours. There are a few small camping spaces and beautiful views of the nevados Ishinca (5,530m), Ranrapalca (6,162m) and Ocshapalca (5,888m).

climb to **Laguna Ishinca**, at 4,950m. This is about 3.5km (*2hrs*) from base camp.

From here it takes about an hour to the Ishinca glacier, following the moraine on the right side of the lake. Laguna Toclla, above.

Return the way you came.

PITEC TO COLLÓN VIA QUEBRADAS QUILCAYHUANCA, COJUP AND ISHINCA
Done in its entirety, this is a challenging but infinitely rewarding route only to be undertaken by experienced hikers, preferably with a guide. However, there are shorter, there-and-back variations.

Distance	About 67km from Pitec to Collón, via the Ishinca Valley
	25km from Pitec to Laguna Paqsacocha
	23km from Laguna Paqsacocha to Ishinca base camp
	19km from Ishinca base camp to Collón
Altitude	3,850–5,100m (Huapi pass), 5,350m (Ishinca pass)
Rating	Moderate–difficult
Timing	4–5 days Pitec to Huaraz via Cojup Valley (moderate)
	8 days Pitec to Huaraz via Ishinca Valley (difficult, requires crampons and ice-axes)
Start of trail	Pitec
Transport at the end	Bus to Huaraz
Maps	Alpenvereinskart *Cordillera Blanca Süd* 0/3b

Route description Follow the directions for **Laguna Cuchillacocha** on page 195. The path to Laguna Paqsacocha goes southwest from the pampa below Laguna Cuchillacocha. There are a few cairns if you look carefully, but it's a bit of a steep scramble for 30 minutes, then becomes slightly easier as the gradient levels slightly. A further 45 minutes, following the cairns, will bring you out to a spectacular plateau, with two small lakes, one of which is **Laguna Paqsacocha** at the base of the nevado Huapi (5,421m).

8

There is a 360° panorama from here, one of the best views of the Cordillera Blanca. You can see Pucaranra (6,156m), Chinchey (6,722m),Tullparaju (5,787m), Andavite/Chopiraju (5,518m), Cayesh (5,721m), Maparaju (5,326m), San Juan (5,843m), and Huantsán (6,395m). This plateau is a good spot to camp, though pretty cold. There is nowhere else above this suitable for tents, and over the pass it's a long way down the other side until you find any flat land. It takes 1½ hours from Paqsacocha to reach the pass (5,100m). It's mostly boulders with no clear path, just sporadic cairns to mark the way. The route becomes unsuitable for donkeys, so if you are organising porterage of equipment you'll need porters from here on. There are unsurpassable views from the pass of a dozen peaks. As well as those mentioned above you can see Ranrapalca (6,162m), Ishinca (5,530m), Palcaraju (6,274m) and Huapi (5,421m).

From the pass there's no path down the other side, just sections of **animal track**, steep and rocky in places, muddy and slippery in others. Care is required; hiking poles definitely help the knees. Aim for the building of **ElectroPeru** about three hours below. You can camp nearby or sleep in the hut if it's open. From here it's a four-hour walk out down the Cojup Valley to Llupa, where you can pick up a bus to Huaraz (*40mins*).

Cojup to Ishinca The pass (5,350m) on this trek is permanently glacier-covered. Only take this route if you have suitable equipment (ice-axe, crampons, rope, etc) and experience of crossing glaciers (or are with a qualified guide). From the hut of **ElectroPeru** it's a steep four- to six-hour climb up to the next pass between the peaks of Ishinca and Ranrapalca. Head up the valley side on animal tracks, zigzagging up steep grassy slopes. Look out for **cairns** to give you some guidance, but generally aim upwards (north) and above Lake Perolcocha, until you reach two **small lakes** after two to three hours. From there a further two hours pretty much straight up the rocky moraine of the valley headwall, keeping to the right of the stream, brings you to the ice just below the pass. Ranrapalca looms large to your left and Ishinca to your right. A few minutes on the ice will bring you to the pass. If you look down the other side to your left you can pick out the path on the wall of the moraine below. That is where you are heading. Watch out for crevasses as you descend the glacier. A 15-minute descent brings you out on to the moraine, from where you can follow the path down to **Ishinca moraine camp**, two hours below. Some stretches of this path are vertiginous so care should be taken, especially on wet rock. There is a basic refuge just above the moraine camp, and a few spots to camp by Laguna Ishinca at the base of the mountain.

From the moraine camp it is a long walk out to the village of Collón. Follow the path down to base camp for two hours and then on down the valley for another two hours. From Collón you can find transport back to Huaraz.

FOUR VALLEY WALKS NEAR HUARAZ All these routes are close to Huaraz, making them ideal warm-up hikes for something more ambitious. Some are short hikes from Huaraz, like Churup, and some are spectacular valleys where you can spend a few days and do some side trips. All end at beautiful lakes, but **you must return the way you came**.

The starting point of most of the hikes is Pitec, a scatter of houses east of Huaraz. You can rent a private vehicle or taxi to get you all the way there (15km of rough road, 90 minutes' drive, 220 soles one way for a taxi), or take the regular combi just part way (to Llupa) and then walk along the obvious path.

To Laguna Churup via the quebrada

Distance	7km (round trip)
Altitude	3,850–4,600m
Rating	A steep climb, sometimes off trail
Timing	4–6 hours round trip if acclimatised
Start of trail	Pitec
Transport at the end	Arrange transport in advance, or walk from Pitec to Llupa from where there are minibuses to Huaraz
Maps	IGN sheets *Recuay* (20-i) and *Huari* (20-h); Alpenvereinskart *Cordillera Blanca Süd* 0/3b

Route description The simplest and most direct route from Pitec to the lake is to follow the obvious path along the left side of the long ridge (moraine) heading up behind the **national park information board** at the Pitec car park, where a Huascarán National Park ranger will check or sell the required entry ticket. The path is obvious for the first two hours and then it splits in two. The path to the right goes round the hillside to a flat area with a **waterfall** ahead. From here the last 40 minutes or so are a real scramble up the left of the waterfall. Tree roots and boulders provide plenty of hand and foot holds, but in wet conditions the route can get slippery and be quite intimidating. You will need to use some basic rock-climbing techniques so don't go this way if you don't feel confident about a bit of scrambling – although there are some metal cables to help at the trickiest junctures. There is also a route up the right side of the waterfall, but it is also extremely steep and can be slippery, and there are no cables to help. If you take the left-hand fork back at the junction, continuing on up the ridge, although you end up climbing considerably higher than on the other (right) path, you avoid the scrambling altogether.

Churup is a jewel of a lake, deep blue in colour and half encircled by Nevado Churup (5,495m).

To get back, return the way you came.

 To Laguna Shallap via the quebrada This is one of the valleys beneath the immense peak of Huantsán (6,395m) and is used by mountaineers to approach the peak from the northwest.

Distance	16km (round trip)
Altitude	3,800–4,300m
Rating	Easy–moderate
Timing	About 7 hours (round trip)
Start of trail	Jancu
Transport at the end	Public transport to Pitec
Maps	Alpenvereinskart *Cordillera Blanca Süd* 0/3b

Route description From Jancu, at the entrance to the quebrada, walk uphill into the valley ahead on the right-hand side of the river. You'll see a **bridge** to the left, cross that, and then continue up the left-hand side of the river, to the portada where a Huascarán National Park ranger will check or sell the required entry ticket. This marks the entrance of the Quebrada Shallap at 4,000m and about 4.5km (two hours) from Pitec. The President of Shallap has the key to the gate. Ask at the Casa de Guías (page 163) if you are travelling with pack animals and need the gate to be opened.

The path ascends the valley, through some pleasant meadows and past waterfalls, until the lake's moraine. Pass the old **INGEMMET** (the government agency responsible for the glacial lakes) **hut** and you reach Laguna Shallap, which is now dammed, at 4,300m. This is 6km (three hours) from the portada. It lies just below Nevado San Juan (5,843m). There are some exposed campsites at the lake; better camping is found in the *quebrada*.

Return the way you came.

 To Laguna Rajucolta via the quebrada
Route description This is an exceptional hike because of the way Nevado Huantsán dominates the view so you hardly notice the beautiful cliffs and waterfalls *en route*. From **Macashca** follow the river up to the first gate (about three hours) on a dirt road, where a Huascarán National Park ranger will check or sell the required entry ticket. Cross

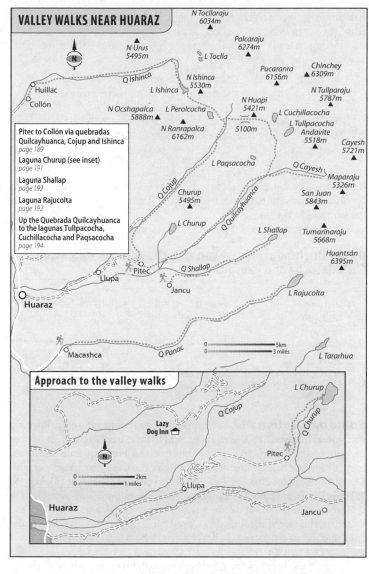

VALLEY WALKS NEAR HUARAZ

N Tocllaraju
6034m

Palcaraju
6274m

N Urus
5495m

L Toclla

Pucaranra
6156m

Chinchey
6309m

Huillac

Q Ishinca

N Ishinca
5530m

Collón

L Ishinca

N Tullparaju
5787m

N Ocshapalca
5888m

L Perolcocha

N Huapi
5421m

L Cuchillacocha

L Tullpacocha
Andavite
5518m

**Pitec to Collón via quebradas
Quilcayhuanca, Cojup and Ishinca**
page 189

N Ranrapalca
6162m

5100m

Cayesh
5721m

Laguna Churup (see inset)
page 191

L Paqsacocha

Q Cayesh

Maparaju
5326m

Laguna Shallap
page 192

Q Cojup

Churup
5495m

San Juan
5843m

Laguna Rajucolta
page 192

L Churup

Q Quilcayhuanca

L Shallap

Tumarinaraju
5668m

**Up the Quebrada Quilcayhuanca
to the lagunas Tullpacocha,
Cuchillacocha and Paqsacocha**
page 194

Q Shallap

Huantsán
6395m

Llupa

Pitec

Jancu

L Rajucolta

Huaraz

Macashca

Q Panac

0 ———— 5km
0 ———— 3 miles

L Tararhua

Approach to the valley walks

L Churup

Q Cojup

Lazy
Dog Inn

Q Churup

Huaraz

Pitec

0 ———— 2km
0 ———— 1 miles

Llupa

Jancu

8

to the left bank (north) of the river within the first hour. About ten minutes beyond the gate you will find excellent camping. The next day continue on to a second gate and then to the base of the canyon wall, where you follow the track along the stream and up to the lake. **Laguna**

Distance	38km (round trip)
Altitude	3,800–4,250m
Rating	Easy–moderate
Timing	16 hours (round trip)
Start of trail	Macashca. Colectivos run there from Huaraz (corner of Octovio Hinostruza and 27 de Noviembre)
Transport at the end	Colectivo from Macashca to Huaraz.
Maps	Alpenvereinskart *Cordillera Blanca Süd* 0/3b

Rajucolta lies at 4,250m, a perfect glacial lake backed by the majestic **Nevado Huantsán** (6,395m). It is about 6.5km (one to two hours) from the portada to the lake.

To return you will need to retrace your steps.

 ## Up the Quebrada Quilcayhuanca to the lagunas Tullpacocha, Cuchillacocha and Paqsacocha

Distance	39km (round trip); 19.5km to the lakes
Altitude	3,850–4,650m
Rating	Easy–moderate
Timing	4 days
Start of trail	Pitec
Transport at the end	Public transport in Pitec
Maps	Alpenvereinskart *Cordillera Blanca Süd* 0/3b

Route description The dirt road from Pitec continues to the **Portada de Quilcayhuanca**, at 3,850m, about 3km from Pitec. Go through or over the gate and follow the trail up the valley on the left-hand side. This is an easy hike to the head of the valley, through green, marshy meadows with lots of cattle, ascending slowly. The distance is about 8.5km (*3½hrs*), to 4,050m. There are plenty of camping places.

The nevado in front of you is Andavite/Chopiraju (5,518m), the valley to your right is Quebrada Cayesh and the one to your left is the continuation of Quebrada Quilcayhuanca, which brings you to the lakes Tullpacocha and Cuchillacocha. 👁 Quebrada Cayesh, opposite.

To reach the lakes in the Quebrada Quilcayhuanca, you'll see a well-marked path heading north from where the two valleys join. After 15 minutes on this path you reach a long grassy meadow, **Llupanapampa**. The path fades, but continue in the general direction you're going, aiming for the top end of the pampa. The trail to Laguna Tullpacocha

Side trip If you want to go up **Quebrada Cayesh** – and you should, for a closer view of the dramatic nevados – look for the little **bridge** over the river, hidden to your right. Cross and climb up the small ridge to the meadow. Across the meadow is another stream. Cross at a shallow place, and enter Quebrada Cayesh. The first part is green meadow; cross to your left, where you'll find a path bringing you to the head of the valley, passing through queñoa forest (*8km; 2½hrs*). Good campsites (but look for a dry place) and great views of the needle-like Nevado Cayesh (5,721m) to the left, Maparaju (5,326m) in front of you, and San Juan (5,843m) and Tumarinaraju (5,668m) to your right. For an even better view climb up the mountain slope to your right. There are remains of an Inca path up here if you can find it. It leads up to the Maparaju glacier, about two hours ahead.

heads up through the bushes, curving around to the right, passing the old **INGEMMET hut**, and continuing up the small canyon until it reaches the lake at 4,300m, about a half hour's walk from the start of the trail. **Laguna Tullpacocha** is right underneath Nevado Tullparaju (5,787m), which feeds the lake with its calving icebergs.

For Laguna Cuchillacocha take the path back from Tullpacocha, past the huts, and continue until you cross a **stream** (Cuchilla). You'll clearly see the path you're aiming for on the mountainside ahead, climbing steeply in a series of switchbacks to the top of the ridge. The path was once used by workers from INGEMMET so is well worn. After an hour you'll reach the **meadow** of Cuchillapampa, where there are a few small stone circular constructions, good for shelter. If you look to your right you'll see a path climbing up the slope, making a few switchbacks, until it reaches a little meadow with the old INGEMMET camp. It takes around 40 minutes to get up to **Laguna Cuchillacocha** at 4,650m, about 500m from the start of the trail.

The head of the valley provides good campsites and super views of nevados Huapi (5,421m) unmarked on most maps but just to right of the pass, and Pucaranra (6,156m) in front of you, with Chinchey (6,722m), Tullparaju (5,787m) and Cayesh (5,721m) to your right.

For even better views, climb up the mountain slope on a rather sketchy path (some cairns appear every now and then) to your left (as you face the mountains) until you reach **Laguna Paqsacocha** in about 1½ hours.

From Cuchillacocha there is a rough, cross-country route to Quebrada Cojup (page 190) or you can return the way you came.

OLLEROS TO CHAVÍN

This is the walk that led to the founding of Bradt Guides, so I (Hilary) understandably have a special affection for it. It is an underrated walk, which consequently sees relatively few tourists, but it has some excellent views and exciting pre-Inca stonework. It also takes you

Distance	37km
Altitude	3,200–4,700m
Rating	Moderate
Timing	2–3 days
In reverse	Yes. With the new road from Chavín part of the way up to the pass, you could get a colectivo (or taxi) to Chichucancha, and reduce the first day's climb.
Start of trail	Olleros. Take a combi from corner of Octovio Hinostruza and 27 de Noviembre in Huaraz
Transport at the end	Bus or colectivo from Chavín (page 156).
Maps	IGN sheet *Recuay* (21-i); Alpenvereinskart *Cordillera Blanca Süd* 0/3b

◉ CHAVÍN

This rather ordinary small town is made exciting by its superb ruins, Chavín de Huántar (a World Heritage Site). Chavín, which has an enormous new **bus station**, is popular with Peruvians, and many buses a day come from Huaraz. There are a few hotels including the **Hostal Chavín** (30 soles) on Calle San Martin about 100m from the Plaza de Armas, and the more central Hotel Inca on the plaza (✆ *044 754021*). Don't miss the excellent museum (Museo Nacional de Chavín) just outside town.

CHAVÍN DE HUÁNTAR (⏱ *ruins & museum 09.00 to 17.00; museum: free entry, ruins: entry fee 10 soles; guides for the ruins can be hired for 30 soles on site*) Experts vary in their estimate of the age of the Chavín culture, but most agree that it flourished between 1300 and 400BC, spreading from the coastal areas to the northern highlands, and reached its zenith around 500BC, when the temple at Chavín de Huántar was built. Chavín appears to have been a predominantly religious culture with various animalistic deities. Highly stylised feline forms are a common feature of the sculptures and carvings, along with eagles or condors, and snakes. It's a fascinating place. The enormous and enigmatic stone heads and finely carved reliefs have a strength and beauty unrivalled by the Incas, who left little in the way of representational art. The seven underground chambers have the finest stonework and an impressive sacrificial stone placed in the middle of the complex.

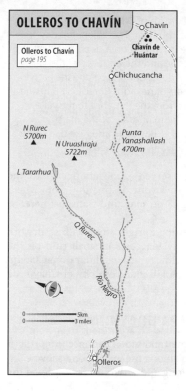

OLLEROS TO CHAVÍN

Olleros to Chavín
page 195

to one of Peru's most interesting archaeological sites, Chavín de Huántar. Some people attribute this trail to the Incas, because of the stretches of fine stone paving, but it almost certainly pre-dates the Inca Empire. The trip is made much more exciting and dramatic by taking two extra days and visiting Laguna Tararhua, tucked in-between three glaciated peaks.
◉ Laguna Tararhua, overleaf.

There is an established arriero in Olleros who charges 20 soles per day for his mule and 30 soles per day for himself.

Route description From Olleros (3,420m), where a Huascarán National Park ranger will check or sell the required entry ticket, go past the plaza and after 100m take the **dirt road** downhill to the right and across the river. The trail goes straight up the valley to the right of the **Río Negro** at first passing through clusters of **adobe houses** with characteristically blue-painted doors. After an hour of walking the track leaves the settlements and passes through open fields. Keep following the road, taking obvious short cuts, until you pass the entrance to **Quebrada Rurec** after three hours of walking. The trail drops into a long plain – marshy in the wet season. About eight hours from Olleros you reach the head of the plain where there is a shallow lake dammed by a low moraine with some good campsites. Here you will be faced with **three valleys**; the one to the far left has orange and black vertical rock layers, the one in the centre has well-developed scree slopes and the one straight in front of you is hummocky and rocky. This is the valley you want. The main trail may be difficult to find but head up the right side of this valley and you will soon encounter an obvious and wide **pre-Inca trail**.

This rises steeply with good views of glaciated peaks opening to the north. There are several lakes and two false passes before you reach **Punta Yanashallash** at 4,700m, about 14km (*4–5hrs*) from the moraine lake at the bottom of the valley. From the top of the pass the pre-Inca

8

road switchbacks down on well-preserved stone abutments to the settlement of **Chichucancha**, 9km from your destination, from where a new road has been built to Chavín. You may find transport here, or walk the three hours to the town.

If walking, look out for an interesting upright stone with stonework around the base, also for a seemingly inaccessible small ruin on the opposite side of the river canyon on a cliff about a half hour from **Chavín**. This was probably a lookout station for the ancient city of Chavín de Huántar (page 196).

TREKKING IN THE CORDILLERA HUAYHUASH

The Huayhuash Circuit is the sublime trekking experience in northern Peru, combining a feeling of isolation among the magnificent snowpeaks, and accomplishment since this is a long and arduous hike (if doing the entire circuit).

GETTING THERE AND AWAY The major town and traditional starting point for hiking was, until recently, Chiquián, but a new mining road now brings hikers deeper into the Huayhuash to the next village, Llamac, and on past Pocpa. The usual starting point these days is **Matacancha**.

By **public transport** you still are best to go to Chiquián and then take another bus or colectivo from there to Llamac and, maybe, on to Matacancha. Chiquián can be reached from Lima in eight hours by **Cavassa bus** (*www.turismocavassa.com.pe*). In **Lima** buses leave from Jr Raimondi 129, La Victoria (☏ 4313200) or Jr Montevideo 618 (☏ 4277663, 4261418) and cost 30

soles. Buses **from Huaraz** take 2½ hours to Chiquián, operated by El Rápido. In Chiquián buses depart from Bolognesi 421 (☏ 722887) and in Huaraz from Jr Lucar y Torre 324) leaving at 05.00 and 14.00 daily (do check bus times before travel as they can change).

Note: there is no ATM in Chiquián.

WHERE TO STAY AND EAT There are no hostels in Llamac, Pocpa, Huayllapa or Pacllón.

Chiquián *Telephone code: 043*
Hostal Los Nogales Comercio 1301; 447121; www.hotelnogaleschiquian.com. A colonial place, with big rooms around a courtyard full of flowers. From 20 to 35 soles pp.
Hostal Huayhuash 28 de Julio 400; 447049. En-suite rooms with hot water. From 28 soles pp.

San Miguel Jr Comercio 233; 447001. Rooms round a courtyard. A bit overpriced at 40 soles pp.

Cajatambo *Telephone code: 01*
Hostal Tambomachay Jr Bolognesi 110; 2442046. Basic.
Hostal Miranda Tacna 151; 2442030

BACKPACKING OR TREKKING THE HUAYHUASH CIRCUIT This trek circles the entire range, and is arguably the most scenically exciting hike in Peru. The most dramatic scenery of the walk is around the east side of the cordillera, where a chain of lakes reflects the towering white peaks. The whole circuit involves 120–186km of walking (depending on your start and finish points) between altitudes of 2,750m and 5,000m, which represents a serious endeavour, so this is only recommended for hikers in excellent physical condition. The circuit with no side trips can be done by the very fit in seven days, or you can take up to 12 days, exploring and taking it more slowly. There are shorter variations, however, if you use a different access or departure point.

The route is fairly obvious most of the way, although a well-worn trail is not always present. This is a remote area, so if hiking independently carry (and know how to use) the IGN maps. Because of the popularity of this circuit, garbage and other human waste is beginning to mar the enjoyment of some camping areas. Toilets – some flush, some pit latrines – are available at all designated campsites, so please use them. Don't add to the litter problem, and better still help clean up after other people. Pack all of your litter out. Do not make campfires since there is very little wood left in the area.

You can **hire burros** here for about 15 soles per day (20 soles for a horse) with 35 soles per day for the arriero – ask around in Llamac or – safer – at the Casa de Guías in Huaraz (page 163).

There are lots of **entry fees** to pay as you hike around Huayhuash – around 180 soles per person in total. Most are between 10 soles and 25 soles, so carry lots of small notes as change is not always forthcoming. Keep hold of all receipts, as you may need to show them more than once. The fees contribute to the local communities and upkeep of toilets, etc.

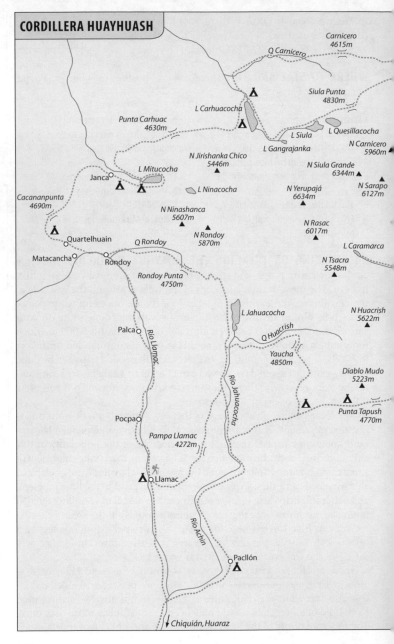

CORDILLERA HUAYHUASH

Carnicero
4615m

Q Carnicero

Siula Punta
4830m

L Carhuacocha

Punta Carhuac
4630m

L Quesillacocha

L Siula

L Gangrajanka

N Carnicero
5960m

N Jirishanka Chico
5446m

N Siula Grande
6344m

N Sarapo
6127m

L Mitucocha

L Ninacocha

N Yerupajá
6634m

Janca

Cacananpunta
4690m

N Ninashanca
5607m

N Rasac
6017m

L Caramarca

Quartelhuain

Q Rondoy

N Rondoy
5870m

N Tsacra
5548m

Matacancha

Rondoy

Rondoy Punta
4750m

L Jahuacocha

N Huacrish
5622m

Palca

Río Llamac

Q Huacrish

Yaucha
4850m

Diablo Mudo
5223m

Pocpa

Río Jahuacocha

Punta Tapush
4770m

Pampa Llamac
4272m

Llamac

Río Achin

Paclión

↓ Chiquián, Huaraz

200

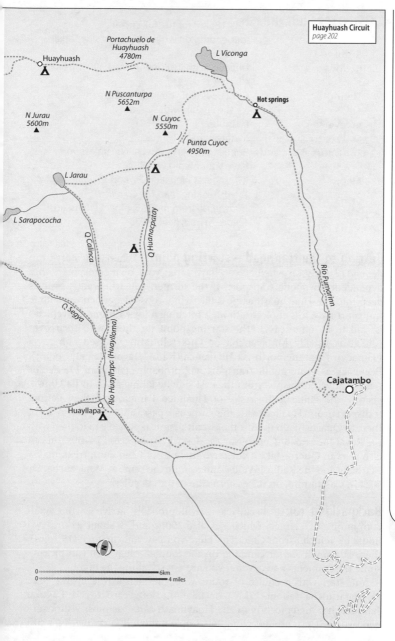

Huayhuash ○
▲

*Portachuelo de
Huayhuash*
4780m

L Viconga

N Puscanturpa
5652m ▲

Hot springs
○
▲

N Jurau
5600m ▲

N Cuyoc
5550m ▲

Punta Cuyoc
4950m
▲

L Jarau

▲

Q Huanacpatay

Río Pumarinri

L Sarapococha

Q Calinca

▲

Q Segya

Río Huayllapa (Huaylloma)

Cajatambo
○

Huayllapa
▲

N

0 ———————— 6km
0 ———————— 4 miles

Distance	120–186km for the full circuit (depending on whether you do side trips)
Altitude	2,750–5,000m
Rating	Difficult, with just under 6km (5,998m) of climbing
Timing	6–12 days (6 if you leave at Cajatambo; 12 for the circuit, with side trips)
In reverse	Possible
Start of trail	Matacancha or Llamac
Transport at the end	Public transport from Llamac unless you have your own vehicle
Maps	IGN sheets *Chiquián* (21-i) and *Yanahuanca* (21-j); trekking map *The Cordillera Huayhuash* from the SAE; Alpenvereinskart *Cordillera Huayhuash* 0/3c

Getting to the trailhead – starting points Where you start from depends largely on whether you have hired your own transport or are dependent on public transport. If the former, you will want to get as deep into the Huayhuash as possible, while those dependent on public transport have less choice (although hitching a lift with mining vehicles is said to be quite easy). The starting point for those with their own vehicle is usually **Matacancha** or **Quartelhuain**, accessed either via Llamac or from the north via Huallanca (Kathy's favourite entry point). Backpackers using public transport will probably start from **Llamac** or – more adventurously – from the east side by taking a bus to **La Unión**, visiting the fantastic Inca site of Huánuco Pampa, and then getting transport from Huallanca to the Cuncush pass, and walk down from there to Quartelhuain to start the circuit. It is also possible to join up with the Royal Inca Road (Capaq Ñan) as described on pages 224–30. You can also start in **Quero** (take a colectivo there from Chiquián), trekking via Marhuay and the Radiash Valley and joining the route at Matacancha. Or start in **Cajatambo**, on the eastern side of the cordillera.

Backpacking route Backpackers will probably arrive in the small community of Llamac, which lies at 3,250m and is about 21km (two hours by vehicle) from Chiquián. Here you pay your first fee (15 soles); there is a small fee for camping on the football pitch. You can pick up some refreshments here, even if you are not spending the night.

You start with a choice of route: walk or hitch a ride up the road to Matacancha (about 17km) or take the longer route via **Laguna Jahuacocha**, the epicentre of the Huayhuash as far as most visitors are concerned. If you are not going to complete the full Huayhuash Circuit but are leaving at Cajatambo you are strongly recommended to take this route. Those doing the full circuit will be seeing some of that dramatic scenery on their way back.

The long route to Matacancha Take the path south from Llamac (ask in the village for directions). About ten minutes from the edge of the village the path rounds a spur and doubles back, climbing diagonally to the left towards an obvious cleft in the mountain horizon. Climb steeply up the eroded mountainside to a false pass, then for a further hour (enlivened somewhat by an Inca wall) to the real pass, **Pampa Llamac** (or Macrash Punta on the Austrian map) at 4,272m, which is on the right of a round, loaf-shaped hill. You follow the route of the **water pipe** that supplies the valley with fresh water from Jahuacocha. The ascent is a struggle, but it really is worth it. I (Hilary) experienced one of my moments of purest exhilaration on the pass. In front lies the western face of the Cordillera, giant dragon's teeth of glistening white: **Rasac**, **Yerupajá**, **Jirishanka**. As a further reward, the trail turns into a proper Andean path, winding gently through queñoa trees and lupins, past waterfalls and rocky overhangs to the valley of **Río Jahuacocha** below. In another two to three hours (if you haven't decided to camp on the way) you will arrive at **Laguna Jahuacocha**. A local family may offer to sell you Coca-Cola or beers. Resist the temptation to buy trout, if offered, since the lakes are over-fished.

When you are ready to leave the lake and rejoin the main trail, **do not cross the river** but take the path along the left (north) side of the lake, which then swings to the left and begins to go uphill. **Fill up with water** before you start on the pass – there are no streams for several hours. It should take three hours to reach the top, but it took our group four hours; not because it was so difficult, but because it was so beautiful, you keep stopping to stare. You seem to be almost on top of Rondoy's glacier, and look down into a milky, blue lake. The serious business starts below a long scree slope: the pass is to the right of a set of jagged grey teeth, obvious on the skyline above you. The path goes directly to the left of the teeth, then traverses across to the 4,750m pass at Rondoy Punta. After two to three hours descending you will reach the small settlement of **Rondoy** on the road. Matacancha is less than 2km away.

The direct route to Matacancha From Llamac continue along the dirt road to the smaller community of Pocpa (*entry fee 10 soles*), at 3,450m, an easy 45-minute walk, with good camping spots before Pocpa. The climb continues up the valley (the new road making the walk easier, though still hard on the feet), passing another small community called **Palca**, the mine camp (three hours from Pocpa), and finally you arrive at the entrance of **Quebrada Rondoy** at 4,000m, about 11km (*5hrs*) from Pocpa. From here you get the first glimpse of snow-capped mountains,

8

Side trip: If you want to get closer to those snowpeaks, an enjoyable hike can be made to the lake at the end of **Quebrada Rondoy**, below nevados Rondoy (5,870m) and Ninashanca (5,607m).

and there are some good camping spots at **Matacancha**. There is traffic on the mining road throughout the night – the rumbles aren't avalanches! ◉ Quebrada Rondoy, left.

Trekking route From **Matacancha** the road continues north to **Quartelhuain** where the trekking route branches off to the right, just before the bridge across the **Río Llamac**. If you have spent the night at Matacancha a trail starts above the toilets at the campsite, intercepting

---

HIGH-ALTITUDE TREKKING
Dr Chris Fenn

People live in an astonishing range of environments, where external temperatures may be tropical or below freezing. Our bodies make the appropriate adjustment so that we are able to maintain an internal temperature that only fluctuates by a few degrees. An altitude of 5,820m seems to be the limit at which humans can live for any length of time. The guardians of the Aucanquilcha mine in northern Chile work at an altitude of 5,985m, but return to slightly lower levels to live. It is, of course, possible to climb higher, but your body cannot sustain the changes it needs to make in order to survive. Although you can cope with the intense cold, it is the thin air at high altitudes that you cannot cope with. It forces your lungs to fight for oxygen. It is not the amount of oxygen that changes as you go higher, it is the pressure at which the oxygen molecules are forced into your lungs. At sea level the atmospheric pressure is 1 atm. Take a hike up to 5,500m and the atmospheric pressure is about 50% less. Essentially the air has fewer particles per cubic inch or, in scientific terms, has a lower density at higher altitudes. With less oxygen being forced into your lungs, your body sets about making a few adjustments that will improve this situation. Firstly, the sensors in your neck detect the reduced oxygen level in the blood and stimulate an increase in breathing rate. This is noticeable at altitudes above 3,500m, but is only a short-term measure to ensure that the body is supplied with enough oxygen – it can't be kept up for long. Anyone who climbs above 8,000m is able to survive the summit attempt by hyperventilating. The highest breathing rates ever recorded were in climbers on Mount Everest, at 6,340m. Their average respiratory rate was 62 breaths per minute, which has the effect of shifting 207 litres of air every minute. Imagine their rate of breathing on the summit at 8,796m! This puts a heavy burden on the intercostal muscles (found between your ribs), and working these muscles just to

the one from Quartelhuain. It leads to the first pass of **Cacananpunta** (4,690m), running up the valley just above the river on its east (right) for 100m. It then strikes up the valley side, heading above and to the left of a couple of stone houses and round sheep corrals. If you look at the hillside above you, you should be able to make out the route you need to follow. You should reach the pass about three hours after leaving the road. From the pass, the trail drops down through a wide marshy valley to the junction of **two rivers** (*2hrs*). Continue to the right, past the settlement of **Janca** (entry fee *40 soles*) and up the Río Janca for about 1½ hours to **Laguna Mitucocha** (4,300m), where there are fantastic views and plenty of camping places. A secondary route from just below the pass takes

keep breathing at high altitude accounts for 10% of the oxygen you need – simply at rest.

In order to make use of every precious molecule of oxygen that comes into the body, polycythemia (marginally easier to spell than pronounce!) also occurs. This is the increase in red blood cell manufacture and is considered to be one of the classic and most rapid responses when you take your body trekking in thin air. With a greater number of red blood cells, the oxygen-carrying capacity of the blood is improved. However, so is the stickiness of the blood and its tendency to clot, so if you have a history of heart disease or stroke, it may be wise to enjoy trekking at sea level.

Despite these efforts by the body to supply the blood with enough oxygen, the brain and central nervous system are particularly sensitive to a reduced oxygen supply and don't function quite as well as usual. At extreme altitude (5,500m), climbers complain of strange goings on in terms of hallucinations, tunnel vision, lack of co-ordination, memory loss and mood swings. Even simple tasks, like tying boot laces, need far more attention and concentration than usual.

A lack of oxygen to the brain also affects co-ordination and balance. Trying to walk, heel to toe, along an imaginary straight line is one of the tests for acute mountain sickness. If you find you sway off your path your brain and body are struggling to adapt to the high-altitude environment. This activity may look amusing, but suggests you have acute mountain sickness (AMS), not much fun. Surprisingly little is known about why some people suffer from mountain sickness and others don't. Even within the same person, there is a variation with repeated exposure to altitude.

The symptoms of AMS and treatment are covered in *Chapter 5, Health and Safety*.

8

Side trip: From Mitacocha you can continue up the valley to **Laguna Ninacocha**, at the foot of Jirishanka Chico (5,446m). It's a steep climb, but not difficult, over a moraine. It takes about 1½ hours each way.

you direct to Laguna Mitucocha, bypassing Janca. Laguna Ninacocha, left.

The next pass is **Punta Carhuac**, at 4,630m, 7km (*3hrs*) from the start of this day's trek. Beware of aggressive dogs in the valley on the way down. On the descent follow the river to the **Laguna Carhuacocha** (*2hrs*) at 4,100m. This is a gorgeous place with some marvellously scenic campsites, one of the best being above the lake on the pampa with fantastic views of the east sides of Yerupajá (6,617m) and Siula Grande (6,344m). There is a little community situated below the lake at the top end and another at the bottom end. You can camp near either.

From here the pack animals will take a longer, less interesting route, but trekkers usually opt for the more spectacular one described below for an additional charge of 15 soles. The climb is a steep one in places, and, although the path is good most of the way, you must be able to read a map as you can get lost in low cloud.

From Laguna Carhuacocha to Huayhuash Walk along the southern edge of Lake Carhuacocha and then along the east side of **lagunas Siula** (4,300m) and **Quesillacocha** (*2hrs*) which lie nestled below the towering east face of Nevado Siula Grande (6,344m), the mountain which features in Joe Simpson's famous book (and film) *Touching the Void*. At the top of Quesillacocha, pass a **waterfall** coming down from the left, and after a few minutes start to climb steeply, on a narrow zigzagging path. Continue to climb steeply for an hour before the gradient flattens out with a **huge boulder** marked Mirador (viewpoint)

Standard (donkey) route from Laguna Carhuacocha to Huayhuash: This is the easier route used by pack animals. Cross the river below the lake on the **new bridge** and follow the Carhuacocha Valley down for 20 minutes then climb steeply up the **Carnicero Valley** to your right (south), passing dry lakes and where there's a good chance of seeing vicuñas, to the pass of Carnicero, at 4,615m, about 8km (*3–4hrs*) from Laguna Carhuacocha. The trail, clear all the way, comes down between **two lakes**. Good campsites but cold nights. The trail continues its descent, passing a little settlement, to the community of **Huayhuash**, at 4,350m, 4km from the lakes, entry fee 15 soles. The village is situated at the bottom of the valley, with a junction of another valley to the right. This is a popular camping spot and can get quite dirty by the end of the season. It is also renowned for robbery, so keep a careful eye on your belongings.

making a great stopping point. The views behind of three glacial lakes and sharp snowpeaks are astounding, some of the best on the circuit. Cross a flattish grassy corrie and then climb steeply again up the rocky slope ahead for 45 minutes to reach the **pass** (Siula Punta; 4,830m). You will see a cairn from below. There is no really distinct path down the other side for large periods, but stay to the left of the lakes ahead and below. It's boggy; two to three hours will bring you on to the donkey path to **Huayhuash**, and your camp; entry fee 15 soles. ⊛ Donkey route – Laguna Carhuacocha to Huayhuash, opposite.

From Huayhuash to Laguna Viconga and the hot springs

The trail continues up the valley (south), with good camping places and some small lakes on the right, to the pass of **Portachuelo de Huayhuash**, 4,780m, 5km (*3–4hrs*) from Huayhuash. Ahead are spectacular views of the Cordillera Raura. The trail drops down from the pass to **Laguna Viconga**, 4,500m, 5km (*1hr*) from the pass. If you decide to stay the night here, camp above the lake. The path continues to the lower end of the lake, where there is a dam and a building for a hydro-electric project. Beware: the water flow of the river is controlled by the dam on Laguna Viconga, and when the water is released it is virtually impossible to cross the river. Check but it seems that usually water is released during the day and the flow stopped at night.

You can ignore the usual campsite at Viconga and walk 20 minutes to the hot springs (camping and entry fee 20 soles in total). This small campsite has nice views, cold drinks for sale, and of course, the hot springs. Bring biodegradable soap, as one small concrete lined tub is for washing, the other for relaxing. Not the best hot springs in Peru, but after several nights camped above 4,000m you are not going to be fussy!

The route to Cajatambo
The path to the hot springs is also the point where you can leave the Cordillera via Cajatambo; the town lies at 3,400m, about 22km (*8–9hrs*) from the lake and has basic accommodation and buses to Lima (check the latest timetable with the SAE club before leaving Lima). There is little alternative transport.

The main route to Huayllapa
The trail continues from the dam and climbs up the valley to your right to the pass of **Punta Cuyoc** at 4,950m (a more impressive 5,000m on some maps making it the highest pass on this hike), a good four hours from Laguna Viconga and the hot springs. Glancing behind as you ascend you should see the Cordillera Raura, and ahead the multi-peaked nevados Puscanturpa (5,652m being the highest) and Cuyoc (5,550m), which features some beautiful cornices. The pass lies quite a bit above and to the left of the ridge's low point below Cuyoc and Puscanturpa Sur (5,550m). A small **lagoon** signals the

Side trip: Climb **San Antonio** pass, for breathtaking views of Laguna Sarapococha, Siula Grande, Sarapo, Jurau and Yerupajá. After descending from Cuyoc pass, and from the pampa, look for a large waterfall to the right. Cross the pampa, and pick up a good path to the right of the waterfall. It's a good two to three hours to the head of the falls, and the last 30 minutes is very steep, but the views from the top are a real highlight. You will really get to appreciate the enormity of the Huayhuash range from here, how the huge mountains rise steeply and how their glaciers drape and feed into the beautiful lakes below.

You can retrace your steps, and go back down the valley to Huayllapa, or descend the path on the other side of the pass (steep) and turn left to Quebrada Calinca, heading down the valley towards Huayllapa. You will miss the Huanacpatay campsite descending this way.

approach of the pass, and the vegetation disappears as you approach the **cairns**, giving way to stone and gravel. At the top – the 360° of all 360s – you'll see Yerupajá, Siula, Sarapo and more to the right, Cuyoc right next to you, the Raura behind and the Blanca in the distance.

A steep, slippery trail descends to the pampa on the far side where there are good campsites (San Antonio, above), then down the narrow valley of Quebrada Huanacpatay to **Río Huayllapa** (Huaylloma on some maps) 4,000m, about 12km (*4–5hrs*) from the pass, with camping available at Guanacpatay.

As you reach the end of the Huanacpatay Valley the **path divides**. If you are planning to go directly to the village of Huayllapa, the left bank of the river is better (extremely steep, somewhat vertiginous and not passable for burros which should go down the right side). If you wish to take the side trip to lagunas Jurau and Sarapococha (below), stay to the right of the river. There is a dramatic (300m) waterfall just before Quebrada Huanacpatay meets the Río Huayllapa, which makes a wonderful shower.

The main trail descends alongside **Río Huayllapa**, passing the entrance of the long Quebrada Segya which leads to **Laguna Caramarca** below nevados Rasac (6,017m) and Tsacra (5,548m). This can be another side trip to the small village of Huayllapa, at 3,600m. In the village you will

Side trip: To reach the **lagunas Jurau** (4,350m; *7km, 3–4hrs*) and **Sarapococha** take the trail heading up the right bank of the Río Huayllapa to the base of the moraine in front of Laguna Jurau. Some steep, rocky trails climb to the right of the outlet stream to the barren, beautiful lake lying below nevados Jurau (5,600m) and Carnicero (5,960m). It is easy to cross the stream near the lake and take the path across the moraine heading toward Sarapococha. Another small lake, Ruricoltau, lies to the right directly below the face of Nevado Sarapo (6,127m). You can descend back to Río Huayllapa from Laguna Sarapococha. This side trek will take one day.

find a couple of shops where you can stock up on some basic foods. Entry fee for this part of the trek is 35 soles.

From Huayllapa to Llamac
Here you have another chance to leave the Cordillera via **Cajatambo**.

The main route continues north up the valley to your left as you climb back out of Huayllapa (right if coming down from Quebrada Huayllapa and a ten-minute hike above the village), climbing quite steeply up to the pampa, where there are good campsites, in about two to three hours. From the pampa stay on the left-hand side of the valley until a high valley appears to your left after about an hour – stay on the walking path or follow the mining road. That's the route up to the next pass of **Punta Tapush**, 4,770m, 8km (*5hrs*) from Huayllapa.

The first summit is not the top of the pass – you come out on to a large **plateau**, which you cross for 30–45 minutes, following either the path or the gravel road. From the cairned top the trail descends; keep to the left of two small lakes (good camping spots, though cold) to a **valley junction** (a valley comes down from your right), about one hour from the pass.

The trail straight ahead goes to the village of **Pacllón** (colectivos to **Chiquián** 1½ hours), but if you started from Matacancha you will want to make the diversion to **Laguna Jahuacocha**. This trail climbs east up the right-hand valley for about 2½ hours to the obvious pass of Yaucha or Llaucha, 4,850m. From the pass the trail descends to the left (north) into the **Río Huacrish**, and along the river to its junction with Río Achín/Jahuacocha just below the southern shore of Laguna Jahuacocha, 4,050m (*12km, 4hrs from Punta Tapush*). If you are brave enough to swim, there is a lovely pool here at the foot of the waterfall. It's a ten-minute hike up to the lake from the river junction. The lake is the focal point of the Cordillera Huayhuash, and the many visitors have left far more than footprints. Make sure you leave the place cleaner than you find it (pack out all rubbish); entry fee 15 soles.

The trail back to Llamac and Chiquián goes down the north bank of the **Río Achín** below the lake. It's not a clear path to begin with, but stay on the right, passing the settlement of **Jahuacocha**. Follow the path from the village, along the top of the covered irrigation channel and then, where it splits not long after the village, gradually begin to climb. This is a good path, winding gently through queñoa trees and lupins, past waterfalls and rocky overhangs up the valley side for about two hours until you reach the pass. Cross the pass, have a good last look at the view of the Huayhuash peaks, then head down the steep gravelly path until you reach **Llamac** in about two hours, following the pipeline of water. An alternative, easier route out of Jahuacocha is to follow the **irrigation canal** all the way. Donkeys aren't allowed to take this route and must go over the top. This water channel provides water for Llamac's irrigation

8

From here you can take a colectivo (leaving at 11.00) to Huaraz, or arrange private transport.

It's another six hours' hike from Llamac to Chiquián. Jahuacocha to Pacllón and Jahuacocha to Matacancha, above.

9

The Central Andes

This part of Peru covers the departments of Huánuco, Cerro de Pasco, Junín, Huancavelica and Ayacucho and for many years was under the awful shadow of the Sendero Luminoso (Shining Path) terrorist group, most of whose thousands of victims came from this region. There are still some security issues, so if you are thinking of heading into remote areas, especially in Ayacucho department, take care: terrorism has not completely disappeared. You should check the current situation with the South American Explorers in Lima (page 128) or locally, in Huancayo, with one of the agencies there (see page 217) before planning adventurous excursions. Outsiders are sometimes suspected of being part of a government intelligence organisation group and a gringo is likely to be thought to be from the DEA (Drug Enforcement Administration).

HUANCAYO   *Telephone code: 064*

The region's capital is a large, ugly town spread out across the fertile Mantaro Valley. It is the excellent markets and the second-highest train in the world (the highest before the opening of the Qinghai–Tibet Railway in 2006) that put Huancayo on the tourist map. There are fascinating daily **markets** full of fresh local produce on Avenida Huancas and a Sunday market on Avenida Huancavelica with stalls selling crafts, food, clothes and pretty much anything else you can think of. The **Andean Train** runs only once or twice a month from April to October, operated by Ferrovias Central Andina (FCCA), a private company that primarily transports minerals.

Huancayo merits a stay of several days, using the town as a base to explore the interesting nearby villages and for treks into the cordilleras Central and Huaytapallana. The **craft villages** are spread around the Mantaro Valley, and each village specialises in a type of craft (page 215). They are straightforward to explore using public transport. The people of

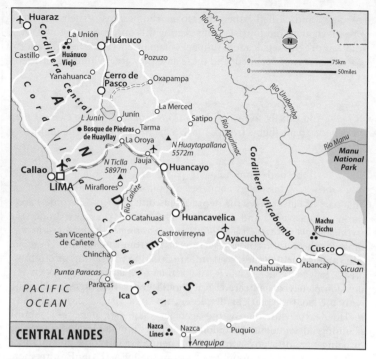

CENTRAL ANDES

LIST OF HIKES AND TREKS IN THIS CHAPTER

Huancayo have a reputation for being particularly welcoming and they are proud of their traditions and gastronomy. All Peruvians like a party, but in Huancayo there are more festivals than days of the year.

HISTORY The town gets its name from the original inhabitants, the Huanca. By all reports they were a fearsome tribe, ruthless towards their enemies and subjecting to Inca rule reluctantly and temporarily – they sided with the Spanish at the time of the Conquest.

In the 1980s the lives of the people in and around Huancayo were blighted by the terrorist activities of the Maoist Sendero Luminoso, which originated in Ayacucho. They blew up power plants, murdered officials and killed unco-operative campesinos. Their activities effectively deterred tourists from visiting this once-popular town. With the capture of their leader Abimael Guzman, in 1992, the influence of the organisation declined, and these days they are no longer considered a threat.

GETTING THERE AND AWAY

By air You can **fly** to nearby Jauja from Lima. **LC Busre** (*www.lcperu.pe*) operate daily flights from Lima to Jauja from US$120. The flight takes 45 minutes.

By bus The **road** from Lima is paved and in good condition and the journey by bus takes about seven hours. You have a choice of bus companies; offices listed below are all based in Lima.

Cruz del Sur Avda Javier Prado 1108 ; www.cruzdelsur.com.pe. Excellent services, buses with toilet, food included in the price. From 55 to 85 soles.
ETUCSA Avda Paseo de la República 646, also at Nicolas Arriola 535, La Victoria.

A reasonable standard of bus, with toilets & reliable departures. From 42 to 55 soles.
OLTURSA Avda Aramburú 1160, San Isidro; www.oltursa.pe. Another good option; very good service. From 55 to 85 soles.

There are many other bus companies leaving from the Lima bus terminal in Yerbateros; they are used by locals (from 28 soles) but the quality is less good. The ten-hour journey to/from **Ayacucho** is dramatic and costs around 30 soles with **Expreso Molina Unión**.

By train The **passenger train service** from Lima run by Ferrovias (*www.ferrocarrilcentral.com.pe*) is currently running approximately once or twice a month (check locally before travel). It takes 11–13 hours for the 345km journey and costs US$44 *Clasico* and US$87 *Turistico*. Their website gives the next departure and details on how to buy tickets.

The normal train service to and from **Huancavelica** is cheap and regular, leaving Huancayo from Estación de Trenes de Chilca (*Libertad;* ☎ *217724*). Tickets can be bought on the day, an hour before travel.

GETTING AROUND
Most visitors get around on foot or by taxi for a few soles.

WHERE TO STAY
Budget

Hotel Baldeón Amazonas 543 y Giráldez; ☎ 231634. Very small bedrooms, shared bathrooms, shared kitchen available

for use. Family run, safe & friendly. About 14 soles.
Casa de la Abuela Prol Cuzco 794, cnr with Jose Galvez 420; ☎ 234383;

e casadelaabuela@incasdelperu.org; www.lacasadelaabuela.org. A backpackers' place with prices inclusive of b/fast. The owner, Lucho Hurtado offers a 10% discount to carriers of this book & students. Secure parking for vehicles, & luggage can be stored while you are trekking. From 28 soles pp. See advert, page 16.

🏠 **Bed and breakfast Peru** Andino Pasaje Juan Antonio 113, near Parque Tupac Amaru; ☎223956; www.peruandino. com. A friendly & popular place. The owners can also organise tours & Spanish classes. From 40 soles.

Mid-range

🏠 **Hotel Presidente** Calle Real 1138; ☎231275; www.huancayo.hotelpresidente.com.pe. This is a good 3-star hotel with safe parking, café, solar energy & hot water. US$40 dbl.

👁 SEVEN THINGS TO DO AROUND HUANCAYO

With additional information from Lucho Hurtado

1 Take a weaving course Weaving, gourd carving, embroidery and silverwork are just some of the crafts typical to this part of central Peru. Incas of Peru (*www.incasdelperu.com*) organise a variety of craft classes including gourd carving over a total of 15 hours (*3hrs a day*) for US$150. Learn to use traditional back-strap looms from pre-Hispanic times, collect plants and herbs with locals to create natural dyes, or make your own Andean jewellery using colourful ropes and beads.

2 Study Spanish Huancayo is an excellent town in which to stay and study some Spanish. There are few tourists here so you'll have plenty of opportunity to practise your newly learned skills. Classes cost from US$150 for a five-day course (*3hrs a day*) with accommodation (*Incas of Peru; www.incasdelperu.com*).

3 Visit Chupaca Market Situated some 11km from Huancayo (*take the bus opposite Plaza Vea on Avda Ferrocarril; 25mins*) and held on Saturdays. Once you've had enough of the bustle, you can also walk to Laguna Ñahuimpuquio (3,400m) and the beautiful archaeological remains of Arwaturo (3,460m) built by the Huancas (AD1200–1450). The walk takes about one hour and offers great views towards the glacier Huaytapallana.

4 Go bike riding in the Mantaro Valley Hire a bike, or take a guided bike tour. The Mantaro Valley offers a fabulous range of routes for mountain biking. Incas del Peru hire out full suspension mountain bikes and provide helmets, maps and advice. They have guided tours for US$55 per day and rent bikes for US$25 per day.

✖ WHERE TO EAT AND DRINK

Restaurants and cafés

✖ **Antojitos Pizzeria** Jr Puno 599. Good-value pizzas, live music.

✖ **Chicharronería Cuzco** Jr Cusco 177. Really excellent *chicharrones* (fried pork ribs). Basic but cheap & delicious.

✖ **El Viejo Madero** Jr Puno. Good chicken & chips.

✖ **Govindas** Jr Cusco 289. Vegetarian.

▭ **Juliette** Avda Giraldez 594. An excellent coffee shop just off the main square.

▭ **Koki´s** Puno 298. Great café/bread shop with good coffee inc cappuccino.

✖ **La Cabaña** Avda Giraldez 652. Pizzeria, *peña* & restaurant, traditional food & pizzas. Live folk music with dances & live bands Thu–Sat, starting at 21.00.

✖ **Restaurant Nuevo Horizonte** Ica 578. A vegetarian restaurant with a nice atmosphere & decent food.

5 **Visit a trout farm** Take a local bus to Concepcion (*30mins north of Huancayo; local buses for Jauja & Concepcion depart from Calixto S; approx 3 soles pp*) and then ask locals where to take the bus to the small town of Ingenio (*20mins*). Here you can enjoy the various walking trails before enjoying a delicious meal – a true gastronomic treat, great for sampling the local trout dishes. Walk up to the Criadero de Truchas (trout farm), continue on paths alongside the river as far as you like, there are plenty of trails heading into the mountains.

6 **Visit the Mantaro Valley craft villages** Many of the villages surrounding Huancayo specialise in particular crafts and are well connected by buses from Huancayo itself. Visit **Cochas Chico** for gourd carving (*45mins east of Huancayo*), **Hualhuas** for traditional weaving (*20mins north*), **San Jeronimo** for silver filagree (*25mins north*), Aco for ceramics (*55mins northwest*) and **Molinas** for woodcarving (*near Jauja; 1hr 20mins from Huancayo*).

Local buses to these villages cost just a few soles each way, or you can join an organised tour that will combine a number of villages. Buying directly from the artisans is of great benefit to the local economy.

7 **Visit Jauja** A breath of fresh air after Huancayo, this small town is set in very pretty countryside, offering plenty of lovely walking opportunities. Take a walk round **Laguna Paca** on the edge of the town. Take a bus from the centre of Huancayo (*cnr of Calixto & Omar Yali*) to Jauja, some 45 minutes away. The historical centre is currently being restored. Jauja has several hostels and restaurants, so makes a good base for walking.

Bars and entertainment

Some of the restaurants listed above also have live music, La Cabaña being particularly popular with tourists & locals alike.

USEFUL ADDRESSES
Banks and foreign exchange

Money Gram & Western Union are available at Real Plaza shopping centre, plus many ATMs. *Casas de cambio* are on Lima St, just 1 block from Plaza Constitución. Travellers should be careful as although some offer good rates they also offer forged notes.

Charities and volunteering

Incas del Peru www.incasdelperu.com. A range of volunteer postions.

Tinkuy Peru www.tinkuyperu.com. Most of the opportunities are teaching, mainly maths & English, in a school where 75 children from aged 5 to 16 study.

Communications

There are dozens of **internet** places in town, mostly near Plaza Constitución on Real & Giráldez. Most restaurants & cafés have Wi-Fi.

✉ **Post office** Serpost, Plaza Huamanmarca. Very efficient. When sending a parcel abroad they can provide you with a box, & there's a system for tracking it online.

Emergencies

National police Avda Ferrocarril 555; 📞211653, 200230, 200758

Tourist police Avda Ferrocarril 580; 📞219851

Health

✚ **Clínica Ortega** Avda Daniel A Carrión, 1124; 📞235430; www.clinicaortega.org.pe.

♀ **Galileo** Paseo La Breña. Upmarket bar with live music.

♀ **Karaoke Torre Torre** Plaza de la Constitución. Good Pisco sours.

♀ **Taj Mahal** Avda Huancavelica 1052. Upmarket disco.

Run by Dr Felix Ortega, who speaks some English.

✚ **Clinicon** Pasaje San Jorge 125; 📞214305; m 964631091. Dr Fernando Mendoza works with tourists.

✚ **David A Carrion Hospital** Avda Daniel Alcides Carrion 1552; 📞222157, 232222; ⏰ 24hrs for medical emergencies.

✚ **Dentist** Lucho Mendoza, Pasaje Elena Tovar de Chipoco 181; 📞239133. There's no sign. It is advisable to call for an appointment.

✚ **Optician** Alfredo Traverso, in the same building as Óptica Santa Lucia (selling & repairing glasses) Calle Real 775

Laundry

Lavanderia Chic La Breña 154. The best laundry service.

Shopping for provisions

Casa del Artesano Plaza Constitución. A good selection of all the local crafts under 1 roof.

Craft market Paseo La Breña, 1 block from Plaza Constitucion. Small craft market.

Real Plaza Ferrocarril 1057. A modern shopping centre with fast food, chemists, shoe shops, clothes shops & Plaza Vea large supermarket, that stocks just about everything.

Sunday Market (Feria Dominical) Huancayo has a rather famous Sun market selling everything from a huge selection of crafts to antique sewing machines to grapefruits.

Tourist information

ℹ Regional Tourism & Industry Office
Calle Real 481; ☎ 233251

Tour operators

AndiAmerica La Florida 280; ☎ 215041; www.andiamerica.com. Organise courses in weaving, spinning, gourd carving, etc, & offer volunteer work at their school. They run a hostel in the centre of town (Peru Andino) & also offer a wide range of excursions.

Dargui Tours Jr Ancash 367, Plaza Constitución; ☎ 233705; www.darguitours.com. Conventional tours offered.

Discover Peru Centro Comercial, Visual Center S7, 2nd floor, Cusco 310; ☎ 200453. Local tours.

Incas del Peru Avda Giraldez N 652; ☎ 223303; e luchoh@yahoo.com; www.incasdelperu.org. Lucho has been expertly running tourist operations in Huancayo for many years. Language courses in Spanish & Quechua. Also weaving, natural dyes, Peruvian cooking & traditional music. Tours, courses, treks in the Mantaro Valley, the Huaytapallana area & cloudforest of Chanchamayo. Also mountain biking. See advert, page 16.

Peru Andino Pasaje Juan Antonio 113, nr Parque Tupac Amaru; ☎ 223956; www.peruandino.com. Organise some tours & Spanish classes.

Peruvian Tours Plaza Constitución 122, 2nd floor. They offer half- & full-day city tours from US$5.

FESTIVALS Huancayo is known for its many festivals, those listed below are just a sample; ask at the tourist office for a festival around the time of your visit.

20 January	San Sebastián and San Fabián. La Tunantada (The Rascal) dance, Jauja and Yuayos.
2 February	Virgen de la Candelaria
15 June	Virgen de las Mercedes
8 September	Virgen de la Natividad
3–13 December	Virgen de Guadalupe

THE CORDILLERA CENTRAL

Updates from Nick Ward and John Biggar

The Cordillera Central, which lies only about 180km inland of Lima, is an excellent trekking destination. The routes are much quieter than the popular treks in the cordilleras Blanca and Huayhuash, and ideal for backpackers looking for solitude away from groups. The weather is generally better, too. The dry season runs from May to September and this is the best time to trek. The highest peak in the Cordillera Central is Ticlla (5,897m), and a circuit trek around this dramatic snow-covered peak is described here. A brief description is also given of a much shorter variation along an interesting bit of Inca Road.

HIKING THE TICLLA CIRCUIT Highlights of this circuit include some exceptionally beautiful high-altitude lagoons, interesting wildlife and

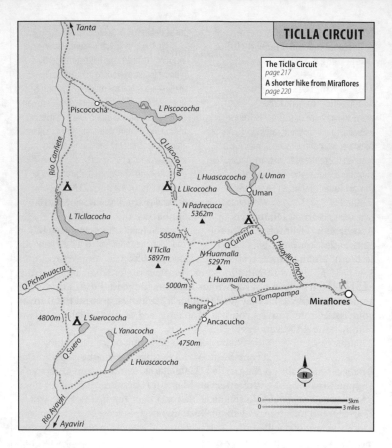

The Ticlla Circuit
page 217
A shorter hike from Miraflores
page 220

TICLLA CIRCUIT

friendly local people. The easiest place to start this trek is from the village of Miraflores at the southeast corner of the range, but a similar route could be followed by starting from Ayaviri (to the west) or Tanta (to the northwest).

The village of Miraflores is a friendly place at an altitude of 3,650m. There are only a few very small shops, but bread is usually available. Accommodation, donkeys and any other basic tourist facilities can be found here; try asking at the mayor's office on the southwest corner of the square or just sit and wait in the square itself and ask the locals who come past.

There are plenty of walking options in this area, so if you come from Lima and are not acclimatised it is a good idea to stay in Miraflores and do some day walks, or camp a few kilometres along the trail, before embarking on the longer trek.

Distance	About 80km
Altitude	3,650–5,050m
Rating	Moderate–difficult
Timing	5–6 days
In reverse	Possible
Start of trail	Miraflores, occasional public transport from Huancayo
Transport at the end	Bus from Miraflores to Huancayo or Lima
Maps	IGN sheets *Huarochiri* (25-k) and *Yauyos* (25-l)

Getting to the trailhead There are two main ways of approaching Miraflores: from **Huancayo** or from Lima via the coast and Cañete. Approaching from high-altitude Huancayo has a big advantage for acclimatisation.

From **Huancayo**, travel by (infrequent) bus via Angasmayo and San Jose de Quero to Miraflores; or you may prefer to arrange private transport – it's a five-hour drive on a reasonable road. From **Lima**, take a bus to Yauyos which may well stop for a few hours in the coastal town of Cañete. From **Yauyos** you will probably need to hire a pick-up – two bumpy hours to Miraflores.

Route description From Miraflores, cross back over the river to the west side and walk up the trail on the south side of the deep **Quebrada Tomapampa**, bright with flowers and cacti. It is possible to camp in high pastures at **Ancacucho** (also called Rangra) near the head of the valley after three to four hours' walking with wonderful views of the dramatic southeast face of Ticlla. From Ancacucho make the short climb over the pass (*1hr*) of 4,750m to the west and then descend steeply to the long **Laguna Huascacocha** (4,250m) under the south slopes of Ticlla (*2hrs*). You will be on some original Inca trail for parts of the route. There are good campsites at the near (northeast) end of this scenic lake. The trail continues down the south side of the lake where there are also camping places. Cross the outflow stream and begin gradually ascending the hillside on the north side of the valley of the **Río Ayaviri**, again on an original Inca trail. This leads up and round into the **Quebrada Suero** and it's a short walk up this valley to the scenic **Laguna Suerococha**, where camping is possible (*3–4hrs*).

From Laguna Suerococha climb the grassy slopes to the northwest and cross a pass at about 4,800m (paths are indistinct). Go down the valley on the other side of this pass until it begins to steepen and then traverse to the right (make sure you do this!) on animal tracks over open slopes to the head of the **Quebrada Pichahuacta** (*2hrs*). Climb a steep side valley

Side trip: Walk up to the end of the valley on the north side of the lakes to the spectacular mountain cirque under the northwest side of Ticlla. From the campsites at the outflow walk down the headwaters of the Río Cañete to the north for about 7km (*2hrs*) until another wide valley joins from the right. From this junction it is possible to walk to the small settlement of **Tanta**, just an hour to the north, where you can purchase some basic supplies. You can start or leave the trek at Tanta, though it might be difficult to arrange transport (the only public transport is reported to be a once-a-week colectivo to Jauja).

to the north and a pass of 4,750m with views of the beautiful curving Laguna Ticllacocha. It is a steep two-hour descent to the north to reach the campsites at the outflow stream of this lake. ◉ Tanta, above.

From the valley junction turn into the right-hand valley and walk up the broad, sometimes swampy valley bottom to a small settlement at the west end of **Laguna Piscococha**. Continue (*3hrs*) on a trail along the hillside immediately south of the lake. There are nice campsites at several points on or near the south shores. From the far end of Piscococha walk for two to three hours up the swampy **Quebrada Llicococha** to the south (there is a good path on the right-hand side) to the blue-green waters of the scenic **Laguna Llicococha**. Just beyond this lagoon the path climbs steeply up and over the highest pass of the circuit, at 5,050m, then descends steeply to the **Quebrada Cutunia** at 4,600m (*2–3hrs*). This section of trail is very well made and may be of Inca origin. Walk out down the Quebrada Cutunia probably passing many herds of llamas, to the small settlement of **Uman** at the valley junction. ◉ Lagunas Uman, left.

Side trip: It is worthwhile deviating to the impressive **Lagunas Uman** to the north (*2hrs inc return*), where you may well see flamingos and *taguas* (giant coot).

From Uman the valley drops slowly southwards then suddenly descends the steep and narrow **Quebrada Huayllacancha** by a rocky path, which bends and twists among boulders and beautiful queñoa trees on the right-hand (west) bank of the stream. You rejoin the original route out of Miraflores for the last hour. It will be a total of about four to five hours from the Quebrada Cutunia to Miraflores.

A SHORTER HIKE FROM MIRAFLORES If you are short of time, this two- or three-day trek is a great alternative to the Ticlla Circuit. Follow the description above out of Miraflores and up the **Quebrada Tomapampa** but just before the **Ancacucho camp** (Rangra on the IGN map) look for a trail heading up the north side of the valley. This takes you over a 5,000m pass with great views of the huge east face of Ticlla. Keep to the left here and the trail soon turns into a spectacular and well-made trail high up on

The Cordillera Huaytapallana (from Quechua, meaning 'place where flowers are collected') is a beautiful and still largely unexplored glaciated range which forms a part of the Cordillera Central.

The range lies just 30km northeast of Huancayo and has many peaks over 5,000m. The highest peak in the range is the **Nevado Huaytapallana** at 5,572m, but Huaytapallana is famous, not just for its size, but for the rate at which its glaciers are retreating. It was recently reported that the Huaytapallana glacier shrank an astonishing 50% between 1986 and 2006 and that the remaining ice could completely melt by 2030, with a devastating effect on the lives of the people of Huancayo and the Mantaro Valley.

The range has three parts to it: the northwest or Marairazo sector with five ice-covered peaks, 4,800m to 4,943m, relatively unexplored by mountaineers; the western or **Putcacocha** sector with five ice peaks, 4,850m to 5,059m, some climbed (access to these two parts of the range is by bus, Huancayo–La Concepción–Comas); and the eastern or main sector with some 30 peaks, 4,850m to the 5,572m of Nevado Huaytapallana, slightly better known. The approximate length of this glaciated area is 18km, north to south, and 6km at its widest.

There are **day trips** organised by local companies (page 217) into the eastern part of the range where you find the greatest concentration of high peaks, usually **trekking** 10km to lagunas Carhuacocha and Cocha Grande and back. The treks generally start from the road pass 'Virgen de Las Nieves' (where there is a bar) at 4,595m and this would be a good point to start exploring independently. There is great potential for trekking in the area, so long as you are well equipped.

the north side of the **Quebrada Cutunia**. This trail joins the trek described above just below the **Llicococha pass**. It is worth going up to the pass for the view. Then follow the description opposite down to Miraflores.

OTHER PLACES OF INTEREST IN THE REGION

CERRO DE PASCO A very chilly mining town at 4,338m above sea level, but there are some interesting hikes in the surrounding mountain areas. Just 45km from the town is the amazing **Bosque de Piedras de Huayllay** (Huayllay stone forest), a protected area of rock formations and beautiful lakes.

Nearby is **Lake Junín** (known also as Chinchaycocha Lake), which is good for birdwatching. There are **buses** from Lima, Huancayo, La Oroya and Tarma to Cerro de Pasco. Many buses also pass by on the way to the Amazon cities of Tingo Maria and Pucallpa. There are several **hotels** with hot water and Wi-Fi. **Jimenez**, **Horizonte** and **Altavista** are decent and there are some other cheaper options, but hot water is important in this cold city!

TARMA (SANTA ANA DE LA RIBERA DE TARMA) A welcoming mountain village situated in a beautiful valley, at 925m Tarma has a very pleasant climate and there are exceptional hiking possibilities in the surrounding mountains, with ruins, lakes and caves. **Tarmatambo**, an important Inca ruin, is just 6km from Tarma on the **Capaq Ñan**.

HUANCAVELICA *Telephone code: 067*
A very pretty mountain town with good crafts and local festivals (see pages 48–9), Huancavelica is waking up to tourism. There are some interesting hiking possibilities in the surrounding mountains.

Getting there and away There is a regular **train** service between Huancayo and Huancavelica (*www.ferrocarrilcentral.com.pe; 128km; 4–5hrs*) currently running on Monday, Wednesday and Friday departing at 06.30. Huancavelica to Huancayo is on Tuesday, Wednesday and Saturday, departing at 06.30. You get a buffet and numbered seat for 14 soles; First Class is 8 soles. This is the only train in Peru that is not privatised, so it's still very cheap and has an old-fashioned charm (which means it quite often breaks down). The train was reputedly known as 'El tren macho' because it 'came when it wanted to'. The station in Huancavelica is on Avenida Leoncio Prado near Jr Huancavelica.

 Where to stay There are various hotels in Huancavelica, including:

Hotel Tahuantinsuyo Jr Carabaya 399. Well-lit rooms with tables & chairs. Shared & private showers. 8–11 soles.

Hotel Ascención Plaza de Armas. Hot showers, shared & private rooms. 8–28 soles per room.

Hostal Camacho Jr Carabayo 481. Hot water, clean & well looked after. 11–17 soles per room.

Hostal Charito Jr Victoria Garma 334; ☎451237

Hostal La Portada Jr Virrey Toledo 252; ☎451050. Dbls 45 soles with private bath.

Hotel Presidente Plaza de Armas; ☎452760. Dbls 45 soles with private bath.

Hostal Ascensión Jr Manco Cápac 485; ☎453103. Dbls 50 soles with private bath.

Moving on from Huancavelica to Ayacucho and Cusco or Lima
This is a very scenic route that can be taken by a series of colectivos.

Huancavelica to Lircay takes 2½ hours, Lircay to Julcamarca 2½ hours and Julcamarca to Ayacucho 2½ hours. **Lircay** has hotels with basic facilities and **Julcamarca** is notable for its impressive colonial church.

From Huancavelica to Lima there are several buses leaving in the evenings; the journey takes about ten hours.

AYACUCHO   *Telephone code: 066*

This was once famous as the birthplace of the Sendero Luminoso (page 5) but today it is regaining its prominence as an important centre with notable crafts and festivals. There are plenty of hiking possibilities in the surrounding mountains, with some interesting ruins, and Ayacucho is becoming an increasingly popular stopover place for travellers taking the eastern route to Cusco. To see some of the best weavers, walk to **Barrio Santa Ana**. The daily **market** is always rewarding with plenty of action, cheap meals and a great variety of fruit juices.

If you're up for a challenge, try visiting all 33 churches of Ayacucho, seeking out the condor and the hummingbird in the religious iconography. Ayacucho has the most flamboyant Holy Week festival in all of Peru.

Visiting the village of **Quinua**, 37km from Ayacucho, makes for a good day trip. Local buses run there from near the market. Quinua has superb ceramics and reputedly the best deep-fried guinea pig in Peru. The Pampa de Quinua nearby is where Peru secured its independence at the Battle of Ayacucho in 1824.

Getting there and away There is a good **bus** service operating between **Huancayo** and **Ayacucho**, which take about ten hours and costs 30 soles; **Expreso Molina Unión** is the best option since it runs during the day, so you can see the fabulous scenery. Sit on the right side of the bus for the best views. An alternative is to take the **train** from Huancayo to Huancavelica (page 213) and then catch various local buses or colectivos from there to Ayacucho. The whole trip could take two to three days and is highly recommended. yacucho to **Cusco** on Expreso Los Chankas is a 20-hour trip on a semi-cama bus. They also have services to **Andahuaylas** where you are recommended to break your journey. You can also **fly** between Ayacucho and Lima; see www.lcperu.pe for details.

⌂ Where to stay and eat

⌂ **Hostal Florida** Jr Cusco 310; ☏812565. Comfortable & central with courtyard garden. 42–55 soles dbl.

⌂ **Hostal Tres Mascaras** Jr Tres Mascaras 194; ☏312921; e hoteltresmascaras@yahoo. com. Lovely mid-range place, with excellent b/fasts & pleasant gardens. 42–70 soles dbl.

✖ **Via Via Café** www.viaviacafe.com. Centrally located on the Plaza de Armas serves good local food & is popular with tourists & locals alike – great views too. This is also a mid-range hotel, from US$75 for a dbl.

Updated with help from Michael Woodman; original text by Ann Spowart-Taylor and John Pilkington

This hike gives a wonderful insight into Andean rural life as it passes through many small farms and villages. What makes it special, however, is that it follows what was once the principal highway of the Inca Empire, Capaq Ñan. Soaring and diving for 2,500km along the spine of the Andes, this was the greatest road in the medieval Americas. Castillo to Yanahuanca is one of its finest stretches, and halfway along the walk you'll come upon the extraordinary Inca citadel of Huánuco Viejo, a major archaeological site which has the added bonus of being visited by very few tourists.

Route finding is generally easy – the Inca road stretches out clearly before you – but you should carry a compass and GPS in case of poor weather together with the IGN sheets listed below. The walk divides into two roughly equal parts with an opportunity to rest and re-supply at the small town of La Unión, just off the route in the valley of the Río Vizcarra. Water is readily available except on the 6km and 7km stretches noted in the route description. It is sometimes of dubious quality, so carry a means of purification and fill up where possible at the cleanest sources.

Food supplies are available in Huari, La Unión and Yanahuanca but the choice is limited; anything out of the ordinary should be brought from the cities of Huaraz, Huánuco (not to be confused with Huánuco

Distance	About 160km
Altitude	3,200–4,470m
Rating	Moderate
Timing	10 days, including a rest day at La Unión
In reverse	Possible
Start of trail	Castillo. Taxis and occasional trucks and minibuses from Huari if approaching via the northern part of the route, or Chavín. The southern end of the route can be accessed from Chiquián in the Cordillera Huayhuash.
Transport at the end	Buses and minibuses leave daily from Yanahuanca for Huánuco and Cerro de Pasco.
Maps	IGN sheets *Huari* (19-i), *La Unión* (20-j) and *Yanahuanca* (21-j) and perhaps *Recuay* (20-i)

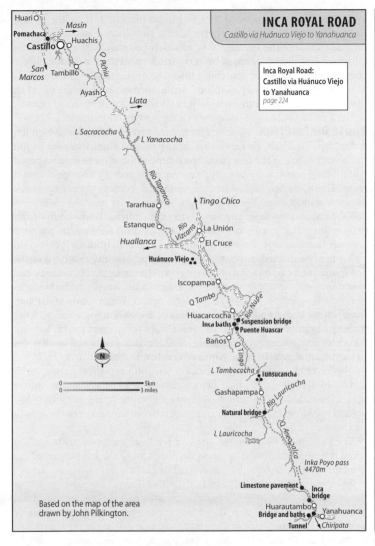

INCA ROYAL ROAD
Castillo via Huánuco Viejo to Yanahuanca

Inca Royal Road:
Castillo via Huánuco Viejo
to Yanahuanca
page 224

Huari

Masín

Pomachaca

Huachis

Castillo

San Marcos

Tambillo

Ayash

Llata

L Sacracocha *L Yanacocha*

Q Pichiu

Río Taparaco

Tararhua

↑ *Tingo Chico*

Estanque

Río Vizcarra La Unión

Huallanca El Cruce

Huánuco Viejo

Iscopampa

Q Tambo

Huacarcocha

Río Nupe

Inca baths **Suspension bridge**
Puente Huascar

Baños

Q Tingo

L Tambococha **Iunsucancha**

Gashapampa

Río Lauricocha

Natural bridge

L Lauricocha

Q Anegalca

*Inka Poyo pass
4470m*

Limestone pavement **Inca
bridge**

Huarautambo

Bridge and baths Yanahuanca

Tunnel ↘ *Chiripata*

0 ————— 5km
0 ————— 3 miles

Ⓝ

Based on the map of the area
drawn by John Pilkington.

Viejo) or Cerro de Pasco. It may be possible to buy some bits and pieces
as you go along but you can't depend on it.

GETTING TO THE TRAILHEAD If you do the walk from north to south
you'll make your approach via Huari, a small town perched on a ledge
above the valley of the Río Huari. There are several places to stay

including the recommended El Dorado at Bolívar 341, or the Hostal Paraíso further up the hill. There's also a tiny indoor market for last-minute supplies. The quickest way to reach the start of the walk in the village of Castillo (3,200m) is by taxi. Trucks also leave occasionally for Huachis via Castillo; or you could take one of the regular minibuses to Masín and ask to be dropped at the Castillo turn-off by the river. (The last option will leave you with a tough 5km climb.)

ROUTE DESCRIPTION Walk up the main street of Castillo and turn left at the top. This path becomes the Inca road and climbs steadily uphill for several hours to the first pass. From time to time there are fine paved stretches, and as you gain height splendid views open up back towards Huari and the mountains to the north. Four hours from Castillo the valley opens out at a place called **Tambillo** – there's good camping here and also beyond the pass. The route crosses the river and then climbs steeply and stonily to the pass of **Waga Punta** at 4,400m, from where it descends gently on the southwest side of a valley. After making a brief detour up a side valley it climbs to a second pass at 4,100m, before turning south and descending steadily past a school and small farms to the village of **Ayash** on the banks of **Quebrada Pichiu**.

> **Note:** The route from this pass is incorrect on IGN sheet 19-i. At grid 769500 it shows the main highway turning slightly north of east towards Pichiu village. The correct trail is the one marked as a dashed line going south to the edge of the sheet.

This trail descends into Ayash on magnificent Inca paving, then climbs to a conspicuous nick before resuming its southeasterly course up a steep-sided valley. After two hours the valley opens out into broad upland meadows. There's good camping here and for most of the way to La Unión.

The path now follows a stream and leads gently upwards towards a small lake then continues in the same direction to the lowest part of the horizon where it crosses the gravel road to **Llata**.

The crossing is technically a pass at 4,400m. Don't be tempted to follow the gravel road, but instead continue on a course slightly east of south. The route is ill-defined near the crossing but gradually becomes clearer again. The Inca road now maintains its altitude across rolling uplands to the broad headwaters of the **Río Taparaco**. An excellent campsite may be found here beside the stream just south of the village of **Lliulla**.

Walking down this valley is delightfully easy. The Inca road, in places 6m wide, is grassy and leads steadily downhill, keeping to the left of the river. High above are two lakes, large but unseen. The road goes straight through a farm where it is possible to cross the river with little difficulty.

The valley then narrows, forcing the track to the river's edge until suddenly the scenery opens out again at a left-hand bend and the start of a superb section which follows the river's right bank for the next 12km. You'll pass through a **large village** with a school and 30 minutes later will come to the last really good campsite, on the riverbank. (It's four hours from here to the Río Vizcarra and the road to La Unión.) After 15 minutes the village of **Tararhua** is reached, from where the road climbs steadily up the right-hand valley side, giving spectacular views of the river below. Eventually it levels off, passes through a village called **Estanque**, and 4km further on begins its dramatic descent into the Vizcarra Valley. Look out for the ruins of Huánuco Viejo, just visible across the valley in the middle of a plain.

A couple of minutes beyond the Vizcarra bridge you'll come to the **Huallanca–La Unión road**, with regular public transport to the easy-going riverside town of La Unión, 7km downstream. This makes a good stopover. There's **accommodation** at the basic Hostal Gran Turístico (*Comercio 1300*), or the even more basic but friendly El Domaino (*Dos de Mayo 359*). Soothe your aching limbs in the hot baths at **Tauripampa**, 3km up the valley. It is possible to camp by the river near the road then have a short day going up to Huánuco Viejo and camping at a good official site nearby.

This is a perfect base for exploring the sprawling ruins of **Huánuco Viejo**, one of the most important cities of the Inca Empire. The site boasts superb stonework and its crowning glory is a huge *usnu* or ceremonial platform in the middle of a vast central plaza. North and east are temples, dwellings, military barracks, storehouses and a palace for the visiting Inca, approached through a sequence of fine stone arches.

The ruins are on a high plain south of La Unión, a tough two-hour walk away. Take the steep path starting behind the market and climb towards a prominent cross; then continue through a village on a wide path. Ahead and to the right you'll see the corrugated iron roof of what turns out to be a chapel, with the ruins beyond. Alternatively, you can take an Iscopampa minibus and get off at El Cruce from where it's a level 30-minute walk.

No trace is left of the Inca road shown on the IGN map between the Río Vizcarra and Huánuco Viejo. If you'd like to prove this for yourself, leave the main road 1km east (downstream) of the point where you joined it and pick your way up the ancient scree slope spilling out from a narrow side valley. Although steep, the route isn't difficult, and as you enter the valley you'll find yourself on a clear path which leads all the way to the top. The entrance to the ruins is 2km east–southeast from here, an easy walk across the level plain. Allow 1½ hours from the main road.

From Huánuco Viejo, by contrast, the **Royal Road** is almost continuously clear and easy to follow as far as Yanahuanca, four days'

9

walk away. Start from the east gate of the ruins and head up a prominent valley, keeping the stream on your left. Pass through a farm and under a power line, then cross the stream and climb steadily up the left-hand valley side, first across open land and then through a field. This is one of the few sections where the route isn't obvious, but it levels out to the right of the power line. After picking it up again you'll pass above the village of **Iscopampa**, then climb gently to 4,000m before dropping down to **Quebrada Tambo** where there's good water and a place to camp.

The road undulates for the next hour to the hamlet of **Huacarcocha** and a little further on it begins a long descent to the **Río Nupe** at 3,350m where waters from hot springs have been fed into a couple of rough open-air baths. The first of these is close to where you join the main valley road; the second is 300m downstream, near the river. The Inca is said to have bathed regularly in the latter during his journeys along the Royal Road.

Only a crumbling abutment remains of the original river crossing, so to continue south you have to make a detour to a **suspension bridge** downstream. Walk northeast along the main road for 11–12km, then follow a broad footpath down to the river. You'll rejoin the Inca road at a log bridge across Quebrada Tingo; this is known locally as **Puente Huascar** after one of the last Incas. If the water is low, it may be possible to wade across the river and reach Puente Huascar directly. Don't take any risks with river crossings though.

Now begins a fabulous section, climbing steeply alongside Quebrada Tingo before heading across a high plain and finally climbing again to 4,050m. As you near the **summit**, glimpses of the Huayhuash range gradually appear until the entire cordillera is visible. In the dry season, after crossing a stream where the road begins its final ascent, there'll be no further water until you reach **Laguna Tambococha** 6km ahead.

This beautiful lake lies in a broad marshy valley, which in the rainy season presents a serious obstacle. John Pilkington recommends wading the river just below the outlet: 'The ooze spread for miles in both directions, so I chose what looked like the narrowest bit and waded in. It was rather scary to be up to my waist at one point, flailing about and sinking; but I managed to extricate myself somehow and emerged dripping and gooey on the other side. The Inca road crossed this marsh on a causeway which has sunk without trace.' John adds reassuringly that he made the crossing in April, at the end of the rainy season. From June onwards it shouldn't be too bad. In the dry season, when we did it, there was no great problem. The donkeys had to make a detour of a few kilometres upstream but we were able to find a way over slightly marshy ground just west of the sunken Inca causeway.

Your reward for these tribulations comes less than 1km further on in the shape of the eerie Inca ruins of **Tunsucancha**, also known as

9

Side trip: If you have a day or two to spare you could explore more of the **Royal Road**, climbing steeply south from the tunnel to a village called Chiripata from where a well-preserved section follows first Quebrada Ranracancha and then the Cerro de Pasco road for 14km to the village of Tambopampa, before striking out across the vast, lonely Plateau of Bombón.

Tambococha. Many *tambos* or staging posts have been found on the Inca road network but this seems to have been rather a special one, having three long barrack buildings as well as accommodation for the *chasquis* or relay runners who carried the king's messages.

Continue south, joining a dirt road that climbs a ridge before passing through the village of **Gashapampa** at just under 4,100m. There's little evidence of the Inca road here but it picks up again after the village, keeping to the left (east) of a broad plain. Don't be tempted to follow the dirt road which contours round the west side of this plain. The route descends, first gradually and then more steeply, into the deep gorge of the **Río Lauricocha**, which is finally reached after a breathtaking section round a rocky buttress. Tunsucancha to the river is about four hours.

The river is wide and the Inca bridge has long since disappeared, but there is a new bridge across to the far bank. Ascend from here by the Inca stone staircase and continue along the highway with superb views of the gorge and its impressive limestone cliffs.

Now begins a steady climb to a minor summit at 4,250m, with distant views to the snow-capped Cordillera Huayhuash in the west, followed by a drop into another valley and a long, gentle ascent of the upper reaches of **Quebrada Aneopalca** alongside a river which, with its many joining streams, provides numerous good camping sites. But be aware that after the prominent stream 1km before the summit the route enters a limestone area and there's **no more water for 7km**. The valley finally steepens to culminate in the spectacular 4,470m pass known as **Inka Poyo** or 'Inca's Resting Place', a high point in every sense of the word.

From the summit the terrain falls away into a huge basin studded with rocky outcrops. The Inca road descends its left flank, passing farms and crossing minor ridges to reach, after 5km, one of the most perfect limestone pavements to be found anywhere in the world. The whole landscape here is surreal, with great sinkholes to the west and cliffs ahead towering over the precipitous gorge of Quebrada Huarautambo. A truly special place, and luckily after a dizzying 20-minute descent down an Inca staircase you'll find a perfect campsite where the road joins the valley floor.

The final stretch to Yanahuanca is idyllic. The Inca paving is stunning and soon you'll reach a beguiling multi-spanned Inca bridge across the ever-growing quebrada. Oddly, the Inca road doesn't cross the bridge but remains on the left bank of the river, descending steadily to the prominent village of **Huarautambo** where it eventually gives out in the village square. A stone water spout and trough here may be of Inca origin, and there's a beautifully preserved Inca building with eight niches 50m to the north. Villagers will point the way.

! **Updates website:** For the latest updates go to www.bradtupdates.com/perutrekking. You can also post your feedback here – corrections, changes or even new hikes. Your information will be put on our website for the benefit of other travellers.

From Huarautambo a road of recent origin zigzags down a narrowing chasm to the valley of the Río Yanahuanca, and unfortunately its builders seem to have destroyed what was left of the Inca road. You can avoid the zigzags by following a path, first left and then right of the river. At the bottom you'll be just 20 minutes from Yanahuanca and the end of the walk. But before you saunter down the valley road we recommend a **small diversion**. Walk a few hundred metres up the Río Yanahuanca, cross the bridge, and return the same distance to a riverside cliff through which has been hewn an impressive pedestrian tunnel. Although just off the Royal Road this may well be of Inca origin; local people certainly think so. There are **commercial baths** fed by hot springs near the bridge.

Yanahuanca is a small but lively town with basic accommodation in and around the main square. 👁 Royal Road, previous page.

10

Cusco and the Vicinity

Cusco lays claim to being the oldest continuously inhabited city in the Americas. It was the religious and administrative capital of the far-flung Inca Empire, and the equivalent of Mecca for the Inca's subjects: every person of importance throughout the empire tried to visit Cusco once in his lifetime.

Tourists feel the same way. Cusco is indisputably the most beautiful and interesting town in Peru, and one of the finest on the whole continent. Nowhere else do you find the combination of splendid Inca stonework and elegant Spanish colonial architecture, Quechua and *mestizo*, traditional and modern. The tourist boom that started in the 1980s has ensured that homesick gringos can munch their way through chocolate cake and pizza as well as cuy and *papas*, and luxuriate in top-quality hotels as well as backpacker hostals. And as one who remembers Cusco from 1969 I cannot say the town has been spoilt by tourism. For one thing it smells a lot better!

HISTORY OF THE INCAS

The Inca legend tells us that Cusco was founded by the son of the sun, Manco Capac, and the daughter of the moon, Mama Occllo, who materialised on the Islands of the Sun and Moon in Lake Titicaca and journeyed together to Cusco, 'the navel of the earth'.

The Incas built their empire on the achievements of earlier cultures: the coastal peoples that they conquered left an artistic legacy richer than the Incas'. It was in the field of conquest and social organisation that the Incas really excelled. At the time of the conquest the empire stretched from the present-day Ecuadorian/Colombian border to the River Maule in southern Chile, bounded in the east by the Amazon jungle and in the west by the Pacific Ocean.

It is unknown exactly when Cusco was founded, but it is generally agreed upon that expansion began around 1438 with the Inca ruler

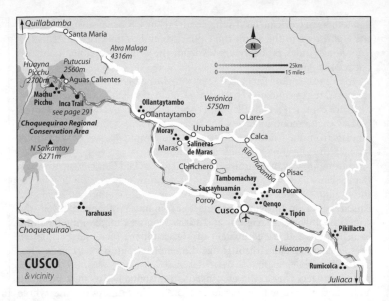

Pachacuti (Pachacuti Inca Yupanqui), who was largely instrumental in defeating the Chanca, long-time enemies inhabiting the region northwest of Cusco.

It is thought that Pachacuti laid the plans for Tahuantinsuyo, the Inca Empire. The name Tahuantinsuyo means 'the four quarters of the earth'. Cusco was the heart of it, and its exact centre was considered to be the sun temple of Coricancha. To the north lay the Chinchaysuyo, to the west the Contisuyo, to the south the Collasuyo and to the east the Antisuyo. The name Andes probably comes from the original inhabitants of this region, the Antis.

Topa Inca, son of Pachacuti, continued to extend the empire and his efforts were consolidated by Huayna Capac of the following generation. The Inca conquered and ruled by a combination of conciliation and force. Nobles of the conquered groups were given important positions, and officials from the Cusco area settled in the remote reaches of the empire to teach the Quechua language and customs.

The empire was in decline before Pizarro reached Cajamarca, however. Before Huayna Capac died he divided the unwieldy empire in two: his son Atahualpa was to rule the north, whilst the south was under the control of Huáscar. Rivalry between the two half-brothers exploded into a civil war, which Atahualpa eventually won around the time that the Spaniards reached the Peruvian coast. The story of what happened when they arrived in Cajamarca is told in *Chapter 7*.

The victorious Spaniards marched into Cusco and began to destroy it although, according to the chroniclers, they marvelled as they smashed. Gold was stripped from the walls and the great stones were broken up to be used for Spanish buildings. What the conquistadores began, rebellion and natural disasters completed. An insurrection by Manco II left much of colonial Cusco in ruins, and a devastating earthquake in 1650 finished the job. The combined forces of man and nature, however, could not destroy the great Inca stone walls, which stand to this day.

Subsequent centuries were punctuated with uprisings against Spanish rule, the most important one being led by the mestizo rebel Túpac Amaru II in 1780. Peru gained independence in 1826.

With the discovery, in 1911, of Machu Picchu by Hiram Bingham, Cusco was back in the limelight again and overseas visitors began to arrive to admire the mysterious ruins. Cusco was added to the list of the world's cultural heritage by UNESCO in 1983, which has been instrumental in conserving the visible remains of that great empire.

CUSCO   *Telephone code: 084*

You will see various spellings: Cusco, Cuzco or Qosqo (the Quechua spelling), but they all mean 'navel of the earth' or – more prosaically – centre of the empire. Some historians say that the Incas built Cusco in the shape of a puma, with the River Tullumayo (which now runs underground) forming its spine, Sacsayhuamán the head, and the main city centre the body.

Visitors should spend at least two days here getting used to the altitude (3,350m). Make the most of it – there is something for everyone: excellent shopping for handicrafts, the best Andean music, good food, fine colonial buildings, and of course the awe-inspiring Inca stonework. The crisp air, hot sun and clear blue sky of the winter dry season make it an ideal town for pottering around and there are plenty of coffee shops and juice bars to collapse into when you get tired.

GETTING THERE AND AWAY

By air Flights are heavily booked and more expensive around school holidays (*Jan–Feb & Jul–Aug*) and national holidays, especially around Independence Day and Christmas.

For airport information, call ✆ 222611 or 222601. It is no longer necessary to reconfirm flights.

It takes one hour to fly **to Lima** and there are daily services with **Star Peru**, **Lan Perú**, **Peruvian Airlines** and **Taca**. Prices vary but there are often special offers out of season. Expect to pay between US$100

INCA STONEWORK

'How did they do it?' is the question most frequently asked by tourists admiring the perfectly cut and fitted stones that constitute the empire's most famous legacy. The seeming impossibility of cutting and dressing lumps of granite without the use of metal tools has provoked some fanciful theories. The explorer Colonel Fawcett speculated that the Incas knew of a substance that would soften the stone to a clay-like consistency, thus facilitating a perfect fit. More serious archaeologists have suggested that discoveries of parabolic mirrors of gold and silver indicate that the Incas used amplified rays of sunlight to cut stone. In the 1980s, however, Jean-Pierre Protzen, an architect at the University of California at Berkeley, demonstrated that using only materials available to the Incas it is not difficult to cut and position stones to the highest standards. He built his own 'Inca' wall to prove it.

Protzen selected a quarry of andesite rock that had not been worked since Inca times for his researches. Evidence showed that stones were selected out of rock falls or prised out of a rock face. The Incas had no metal tools, so used simple river cobbles as hammerstones. These, although of the same hardness as the andesite being worked, do not shatter on impact. Protzen used a 4kg hammer-stone to shape a block of andesite. He found that it was necessary only to drop the hammer-stone at the required angle, letting gravity do the rest. Using this technique it took only 20 minutes to dress one side of the stone. Protzen then turned his attention to creating a hole through stone, such as those used to secure the roofs at Machu Picchu. Hiram Bingham, who famously rediscovered the ruins of Machu Picchu in

and US$180 to Lima or **Arequipa**. It's just 65 minutes (via Juliaca) to Arequipa and there are daily flights with Taca (direct) and Lan Perú. Lan Perú also runs a daily flight **to Juliaca** which takes one hour. You can fly **to Puerto Maldonado** to access the Tambopata reserve via daily flights with Lan Perú, Star Peru and Taca; the flight takes an hour.

✈ **Lan Perú** Avda El Sol 627-B; ✆ 255552, 255553, 255554; www.lan.com. More expensive for non-Peruvians.
✈ **Peruvian Airlines** Calle del Medio 117; ✆ 254890; www.peruvian.pe

✈ **Star Peru** Avda El Sol 627, Office 101; ✆ 262768, 253791; www.starperu.com
✈ **Taca** Avda El Sol 602-B; ✆ 0800 18222; www.taca.com. More expensive for non-Peruvians.

By bus Cusco has a bus station, *terminal terrestre*, in Prolongacion Pachacutec (✆ *224471*). This makes land transport an easy business as most buses leave from and arrive here. Cruz del Sur now has its own

1911, speculated that the Inca stonemasons bored holes by rotating a bamboo between the palms of their hands, using sand as an abrasive, but Protzen believes that they were pounded out from each side; the conical shape at each end of the hole supports this theory.

The Incas generally cut the top face of each stone to receive the shape of the stone to be laid above it, so that the upper courses of stones project into the lower course. Protzen proved that, through trial and error, it was possible to achieve a perfect fit. The Incas had an abundance of manpower and time, as chronicled by the Spaniard José de Acosta in 1589: '[The stones] fit together with incredible precision without mortar. All this was done with much manpower and much endurance in the work, for to adjust one stone to another until they fit together, it was necessary to try the fit many times, the stones not being even or full.'

Visitors to Ollantaytambo marvel at the way huge rocks were transported across the Río Urubamba. Again, this seemingly mighty feat was in fact relatively easy if the great stones were slid over the small stones on the river bottom. With enough people working together almost anything is possible. The Inca Pachacuti, under whose rule the greatest buildings were created, imposed a labour tax to supply this manpower.

Many of mankind's greatest works have this in common: they were constructed for the glory of God. The Incas were no exception. Without their worship of the sun and absolute obedience to his deputy on earth, the supreme Inca, the awe-inspiring temples and fortresses that draw us to Peru would never have existed.

10

terminal (*Av Pachacutec 510;* 720444), with buses to Lima, Arequipa and Puno. Alternatively **Turismo Mer** (245171; *www.turismomer.com*) is an upmarket tourist bus service to Puno with guided stops on the way. From Cusco, buses stop at Andahuaylillas, Raqchi, La Raya and Pukara. Costs 140 soles, departures at 07.30. A similar company is **Inka Express** (*www.inkaexpress.com*).

There are daily buses running the 344km **to Juliaca**; services take four to five hours. Continuing on to Puno (an additional 44km) takes a further 45 minutes. Bus companies include **Power** (227777; *17 soles; departures every 2hrs from 08.00 to 22.00*). There is a good colectivo system between the two towns.

Civa (*01 4181111; www.civa.com.pe; from 42 to 72 soles; services at 06.45, 16.45 & 20.00*) runs services **to Arequipa** which take ten hours (longer in the rainy season) to travel 521km. Buses leave in the late afternoon.

Note: Always check the political situation in the central Andes before travelling by road through these areas.

Travel **to Abancay** (195km) takes four hours and onward travel from there **to Andahuaylas** (135km) takes a further seven hours (both journeys are longer in the rainy season). The following companies run this service: **Civa** (*details as above*) and **Wari** (01 2020600; *www.expresowari.com.pe*), with

i THE TOURIST TICKET

The Cusco Tourist Ticket or Boleto Turístico is essential for anyone visiting the area. The Boleto Turístico General costs 130 soles or 70 soles for students with an international student card. It is valid for ten days and is available from the Galerías Turísticas (*Avda El Sol 103 Oficina 101*) or from the sites themselves. The ticket includes entry to 17 sites in and around the city. Note you can only enter each site once – officials will stamp your ticket to make sure. You must also write your name and passport number on your ticket and may be asked to present your passport. They do not want people sharing tickets.

Sites in Cusco:
- Art Museum and Santa Catalina Monastery
- Museum of Contemporary Art
- Regional History Museum
- Coricancha Site Museum
- Museum of Folk Art
- Centre for Native Art
- Pachacutec Monument
- Sacsayhuamán
- Qenqo
- Puca Pucara
- Tambomachay
- Tipón
- Pikillacta

departures at 06.30, 13.00 and 20.00 for 20 soles (an Ortursa service leaves at 16.00). At busy times, booking may be necessary.

Buses running on **to Ayacucho** (252km) from Andahuaylas take ten hours (they can take longer in the rainy season), but road conditions are poor. Cusco to Ayacucho takes 21 hours.

By train Since the privatisation of the railways in 2000, tourists have not been allowed to travel on the colourful local trains to Machu Picchu. Owing to limited availability and in order to stop companies block-buying tickets, you will need your passport details when booking tickets; you will also be asked for photographic documentation on the trains themselves.

Remember to buy your tickets as far in advance as possible, especially at peak times.

To Puno **PeruRail** is the only company running trains from Cusco to Puno at present. For the latest times and prices check their website at www.perurail.com; for reservations email them on e reservas@perurail.com. In Cusco, tickets are available from travel agents or direct from the Wanchaq station on Avenida Pachacutec s/n (☏ *238722, 221992*). If you want to do it in style, the **Andean Explorer** service costs US$255 one way (*710 soles*).

Sites in the Sacred Valley.
* Pisac
* Ollantaytambo
* Chinchero

Alternatively there are three **partial tickets** available, again giving one entry to each site. A Boleto Turístico Parcial costs 70 soles; there is no student discount. You have a choice of three different circuits: Circuit 1 is valid for one day, circuits 2 and 3 both for two days.

* Circuit 1: Cusco City (Regional History Museum, Coricancha Site Museum, Art Museum, Pachacutec Monument, Santa Catalina Monastery, Centre for Native Art)
* Circuit 2: Sacsayhuamán, Q'enqo, Puca Pucara, Tambomachay
* Circuit 3: Sacred Valley (Pisac, Ollantaytambo, Chinchero)

A different ticket, the **Boleto Religioso**, is needed if you want to visit religious buildings, including the cathedral and the church of San Blas.

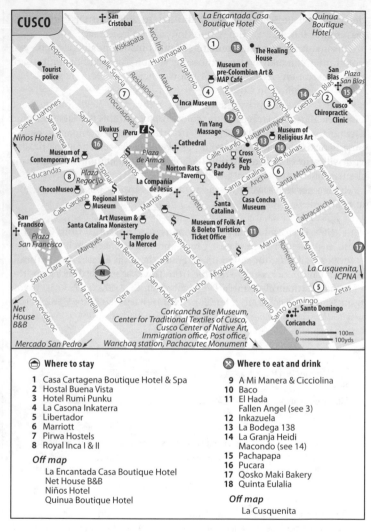

CUSCO

To Machu Picchu Until recently trains for Machu Picchu left from the San Pedro station in Cusco, with the first part of the journey memorably via a series of (literally) switchbacks, so that the train could negotiate the steep hill out of town. Then the railway line was damaged, and Poroy, some 15 minutes by road from Cusco, became the starting point. Whether San Pedro will ever regain its former status is unknown, but assume that trains depart from Poroy or Ollantaytambo, in the

Sacred Valley, and check www.bradtupdates.com/perutrekking for the latest news.

After ten years of having only one train company in Cusco, there are now three (all expensive) operators serving Machu Picchu (or rather its nearest station, Aguas Calientes, now officially called Machu Picchu Pueblo), with offices in Cusco.

〰 **Inca Rail**   Plaza de Armas, Portal de Panes 105; ☏ 233030; www.incarail.com. A new company, with 4 different services running all year round at a price of 115–155 soles. They will accept bookings, but you can also turn up on the day & hope that tickets are still available. There is also a First Class service at 280 soles one way that only runs on special holidays & from May–Oct, & to crown it all a Presidential Service which can be chartered. All trains depart from Ollantaytambo.

〰 **Machu Picchu Train**   Avda El Sol 576, just across from the Qoricancha; ☏ 221199; www.machupicchutrain.com. Tickets available from 140 to 175 soles one way & with 3 departures per day. Check their website for special offers. All trains depart from Ollantaytambo.

〰 **PeruRail**   On the main square in Portal de Carnes 214; ☏ 581414; www.perurail.com. The oldest privatised train operator in Cusco with over 15 years of taking travellers to Machu Picchu & back; they also have the highest frequency of trains & the most variety of services, from the backpacker service at 95 soles one way & the posh Vistadome around 210 soles one way. They also have a luxury service called the Hiram Bingham, which includes b/fast, dinner with music, fully restored cabins & a guided tour around Machu Picchu. The inclusive price is US$658 (*1,830 soles*).

ℹ️ **THE BACK DOOR TO MACHU PICCHU**

For those on a budget, you can now do a tour to Machu Picchu which takes you over the Abra Malaga pass, down into the high jungle and on to the town of **Santa Teresa**. It takes about eight hours and costs around 55 soles. This can be organised with any of the agencies around the main square.

When you get to the hydro-electric plant you can either walk the 8km along a path beside the railway to **Aguas Calientes** or catch one of the trains which takes about 45 minutes. The first train departs at 07.56 and the last one is at 16.35.

Although it's easier to do this as an organised tour, you could do it independently by taking a bus from Cusco towards Quillabamba, getting off at Santa María (one hour before Quillabamba) and then getting a colectivo to Santa Teresa. However, this costs almost the same as organised transport from Cusco and probably takes two hours more. Much more interesting, of course, is to trek there with a choice of two routes (see *Chapter 11*).

GETTING AROUND The beauty of Cusco is that you can walk almost anywhere you will need to go with all major sites and tourist facilities concentrated in the historical centre. Nowhere will take you more than 15 minutes on foot. If you do need to head out of the centre then a reasonably priced taxi is a good option. All taxis, whether licensed or not, cost 3 soles for all daytime fares within the city centre and 4 soles after 22.00; if you call a licensed taxi to your hotel, it will cost slightly more. Try **Okarina** (✆ *247080*) or **Aló Cusco** (✆ *222222*).

 WHERE TO STAY You are spoilt for choice in Cusco, from luxury hotels to the basic backpackers' places. Prices are lower outside the tourist season and good deals can be expected at the upper- and mid-range hotels around that time. Foreigners are exempt from taxes, but always check, and remember that prices given here are a guide only; they are likely to have gone up. There are many hostels available in Cusco; most have a very young crowd and a bar, restaurant and range of activities. Prices are

ON BEHALF OF CHILDREN

Jolanda van den Berg with her boyfriend, from the Netherlands, were typical backpackers. They travelled independently, as cheaply as possible, with the goal of seeing the pink dolphins of the Amazon. Stuck in Cusco for a few days, they at first resented this delay. The Inca ruins were fabulous, of course, but it was another aspect of the city that caught their attention. 'We had seen them before, of course. Children trying to sell us things at traffic lights, wanting to shine our shoes, carrying loads which looked too big for an adult, cute little girls and boys, always snotty-nosed, always dressed in dirty, torn clothes. But all of a sudden we saw only children.' Titus and Jolanda bought more postcards than they could possibly write, had their shoes shined twice a day and started playing with the kids, drawing pictures with them, kicking a football around, trying out a few words of Quechua.

At 08.00 one morning they attended Mass in the cathedral in the Plaza de Armas. At that hour they were the only gringos. The service was in Quechua, the temperature in the great building close to freezing, but the atmosphere of spirituality was overwhelming. For nearly an hour afterwards neither of them spoke, and then Jolanda said quietly 'I'm going to do something for those children'. Two days after that the backpackers flew to Iquitos and swam with the dolphins.

Six months later Jolanda came back to Cusco, alone, and rented a room. Within a few months she had two street boys living with her. Then four more … until there were 12! To support them, the Niños Unidos Peruanos Foundation was created in Holland.

higher in Cusco than other parts of Peru. Expect to pay from about 25 soles/US$9 for a dormitory to several hundred dollars a night for all-out extravagant luxury.

Lower mid-range

🏠 **Pirwa Hostels** www.pirwahostelsperu.com. 4 available in Cusco with dorms from 25 soles.

🏠 **Niños Hotel** Calle Meloq 442; 📞231424; www.ninoshotel.com. A 20-room hotel, which helps train the street children of Cusco in tourism skills. Each room is named after a child & decorated by his or her paintings or stories. All profits are put back into the charity Niños (see below). What a wonderful opportunity for readers to give something back! 64/128 soles sgl/dbl with communal bathroom, 140 soles dbl with private bathroom.

🏠 **Net House B&B** Calle Unión140; 📞245445; www.nethouseperu.com. Clean & central. Kitchen available. From 70 soles for a private room.

🏠 **Hostal Buena Vista** Pumacurco 490; 📞255672; www.hostalbuenavistacusco.com. Central, with a nice patio area. From 98 soles.

The boys were mostly 11- and 12-year-olds except for little Oscar who was three. 'I had to take Oscar,' said Jolanda, 'his mother was in jail for the murder of Oscar's father. Self defence.' Apart from the obvious lack of food, shelter and education, the street kids of Cusco were poor in something else: self-esteem. They were aggressive and often violent. Karate lessons became as important a part of their day as school attendance and helping with the chores. Then came the idea to open a hotel. It was a way of giving financial support to the project and at the same time providing employment for the older children. A benefactor came up with the money and a beautiful colonial house was purchased. It took almost a year to convert it into a hotel but the two star Niños Hotel opened in 1998. It was an immediate success, and the hotel has enabled Jolanda to open the first Niños Restaurant where the children receive regular health checks, daily showers, education and tons of love and attention. Today, 600 children get two daily meals in the five restaurants for children that Jolanda has started over the years, where they can also play safely, do their homework and acquire social skills. Now the project includes three hotels: Hotel Meloc, Hotel Fierro and the Hacienda and 17 years later, Jolanda is following her mission, and the Foundation's mission, to create a better life and a better future for as many neglected children in and around Cusco as possible.

For more information, go to: www.stichtingninos.com.

Mid-range

🏠 **Hotel Rumi Punku** Choquechaka 339; ☎221102; www.rumipunku.com. A splendid Inca doorway, good service, spa & restaurant available. Very close to the main square. From US$80 per night.

🏠 **Quinua Boutique Hotel** Pasaje Santa Rosa A8; ☎242646; www.quinua.com.pe. Really stunning: each apt has a different theme from pre-Inca to modern but there

are some serious stairs to get there. From US$95 for a dbl.

🏠 **Royal Inca I and II** Plaza Regocijo; ☎231067, 234221; www.royalinkahotel. pe. Very central. An old colonial building maintaining a lot of character inc original paintings. US$95 dbl.

🏠 **La Encantada Casa Boutique Spa** Tandapata 354, San Blas; ☎242206; www. encantadaperu.com. A new hotel very simply

⊙ THE CENTER FOR TRADITIONAL TEXTILES OF CUSCO

One of the highlights of my (Hilary's) last visit to the Cusco area was a weaving demonstration at the Center for Traditional Textiles of Cusco (supported by Cultural Survival in America), which took place in an adobe-built compound not far from Calca. Our guide was the dynamic director, Nilda Callañaupa, who grew up in Chinchero so has seen for herself how traditional weaving practices are giving way to synthetic materials and less time-consuming methods. The history and diversity of weaving in Peru is astounding. Some designs and techniques date back over 2,000 years, and each Andean village has its own favoured patterns. Collecting and documenting these is one of the goals of the centre.

Our visit began with a talk by Nilda explaining the spiritual significance of weaving to the descendants of the Incas, as well as their traditions and techniques. The weavers, dressed in the traditional clothing of their villages, were kneeling on the ground (a position that I would find agonising after a few minutes!) in front of their looms. The intricate designs grew in front of our eyes and I shot a roll of film in a few minutes. In a corner were a group of men knitting *chullos*, the traditional hats of the region. Their big, stubby fingers manipulated the tiny needles with enviable dexterity. Peruvian weavers use the indigenous backstrap loom (modern, pedal-operated looms are not used in the Andes), either working on broad textiles to make ponchos or mantas, or creating narrow belts, or beautiful tubular 'ropes'.

Before we left there was some serious shopping to be done. It was good to know that we were helping to support the work of the centre, as well as purchasing a particularly beautiful souvenir.

Most tour operators should be able to arrange this visit. For more information see the website www.incas.org, or www. textilescusco.org/eng.

decorated, with restaurant & spa, & great views of Cusco from the front rooms. US$100 dbl.

As a treat

🏠 **Libertador** Calle San Agustín 400; ✆231961; www.libertador.com.pe. In a beautiful colonial building. Lots of communal spaces. Part of the Libertador Luxury Collection. US$240 dbl.

🏠 **Marriott** Calle Ruinas 432; ✆582200; www.marriott.com. The newest hotel in Cusco, with a restaurant & spa. US$435 dbl inc b/fast.

🏠 **Casa Cartagena Boutique Hotel & Spa** 2 blocks from the main square; ✆224356; ww.casacartagena.com. A new 5-star hotel in Cusco. Oxygen-enriched rooms (!) & a Royal Suite. From US$530 dbl.

🏠 **La Casona Inkaterra** Plaza Nazarenas; www.inkaterra.com. Another new hotel in Cusco. Very safe & quiet. Only 11 suites available. Prides itself on privacy. From US$600 dbl.

🍴 **WHERE TO EAT AND DRINK** Most visitors will want to try typical Andean dishes rather than international fare, although the taste of home is often welcome after a long trek. You can eat all day: enjoy the bizarre décor of Fallen Angel, a slap-up *novo-Andina* meal at Baco and round off with an ice cream from El Hada. And that's just on the first day.

For large plates of **local food** at reasonable prices try **La Cusquenita**, a traditional *picanteria* on Avenida Tullumayo 227 which also has authentic folk dancing, and **Quinta Eulalia** Choquechaca 384, which is only open for lunch.

As you'd expect in the tourist capital of Peru, there is a good choice of **bars** and other **entertainment**. There is a nightly **folklore show** at Centro Qosqo de Arte Nativo, Avenida Sol 6044. **ICPNA Cusco** (*Avda Tullumayo 125*) has frequent theatre and musical performances.

Restaurants and cafés

🍴 **A Mi Manera** Triunfo 393; ✆243629. Nice décor & great, beautifully presented Peruvian food. You can also take cooking lessons by arrangement.

🍴 **Baco** Ruinas 465. Sister restaurant to Cicciolina. Good food & wine selection, English menus & service. Good for a special evening out.

🍴 **Cicciolina** Triunfo 393, upstairs at the back, next door to A Mi Manera. Excellent food from tapas to full menu, white tablecloths. Best wine selection in Cusco. B/fast also available.

☕ **El Hada** Calle Arequipa 167. Delicious organic ice creams & good coffees.

🍴 **Fallen Angel** Plazoleta Nazarenas 221. Amazing décor & ambience, best at night for drinks & partying. Also has a guesthouse with 4 individually designed funky suites.

🍴 **La Bodega 138** Herrajes 138. Excellent pizza, pastas & delicious salads in a modern setting. Always busy, & very reasonably priced.

🍴 **La Granja Heidi** Cuesta San Blas 525; ✆233759. Extremely good natural/organic food, inc yogurts & cheesecakes. Good-value lunches.

🍴 **Macondo** Cuesta San Blas 571. Popular pub/restaurant with inventive food; great hangout.

✕ **Pachapapa**   Plazoleta San Blas 120. Really good choice of typical dishes. Well known for their *lomo saltado*. Cuy available if ordered 24hrs in advance.

✕ **Pucara**   Plateros 309; ☏ 222027. Been around for years, good tasty Peruvian food at fair prices.

🖵 **Qosko Maki Bakery**   Avda Tullumayo 465. The best bakery in town, set up to help street kids by teaching them skills & giving them jobs. *Pain au chocolat* is a real favourite.

✕ **Restaurant Inkazuela Plazoleta** Nazarenas 167; ☏ 234924. A very popular & friendly place with a menu of tasty, wholesome, traditional casserole dishes.

Bars and entertainment

🍷 **Cross Keys Pub**   2nd floor, Triunfo 350. English-run pub that's an ever-popular hangout for tourists & a few locals.

🍷 **Norton Rat's Tavern**   Cnr of Santa Catalina Angosto with the Plaza de Armas. Serves Cusco's only locally brewed real ale, the excellent Zenith Beer. See advert, colour page 30.

🍷 **Paddy's Irish Bar**   Plaza de Armas 124, entrance on the corner of Triunfo. Very popular pub with lively atmosphere.

🍷 **Ukukus**   Plateros 316. A very lively disco/club with live music from around 22.45 every night. It is always packed with locals & gringos. Several groups play there, a sometimes strange fusion (typical in Cusco) of traditional Andean music with injections of rock, reggae & salsa.

USEFUL ADDRESSES
Banks and foreign exchange

There is a plethora of banks & ATMs & exchange places situated on the top block of Avda El Sol & on the Plaza de Armas.

Bookshops

Opening hours are generally 10.00–20.00; closed 13.00–15.00 for lunch.

Libreria Jerusalen   Calle Heladeros 143
Libreria La Familia   Tullumayo 465
Special Book Services (SBS)   Avda El Sol, opposite & just down from Qoricancha; www.sbs.com.pe

Charities and volunteering

Cusco has more organisations working to alleviate poverty & suffering in the local population than any other town. Many welcome volunteers & all would be grateful for a donation of money or medicines. For a full listing of these organisations see pages 74–6.

Chiropractor and therapeutic massage

Cusco Chiropractic Clinic   Carmen Bajo 184-B, San Blas; 📱 984791288. Dr Howard offers spinal diagnostic & low-force therapeutic methods.

The Healing House   (Maureen Santucci) 555 Qanchipata, San Blas; 📱 984900617. Offers excellent therapeutic massage & other treatments – very relaxing after a long trek – with prices varying between 98 & 110 soles.

Yin Yang Massage   Calle Triunfo 392, Oficina 219; 📱 984939717. This is where all the expats go, it's great – 75 soles for a 1hr massage.

Communications

There are dozens of internet offices, all over town.

✉ **Post office**   Avda Sol, block 5.
🕐 08.00–19.00 Mon–Sat

Conservation and accessibility of Inca ruins

The vulnerability of the Inca ruins around Cusco, including the Inca Trail, has prompted the setting up of several bodies dedicated to protecting them.

COPESCO A government plan to aid poor rural areas by implementing tourist infrastructure. They cover a wide remit, from building bridges & better access roads, through to building toilets & rest stops on trekking routes.

Direccion Regional de Cultura (DRC) Avda de la Cultura 238, Condominio Huascar. 236081; www.machupicchu.gob.pe. They collect the entrance fees to the Inca Trail & Machu Picchu. In theory this money is used to conserve the area.

National Parks Department Avda Sol, between blocks 5 & 6; www.dirceturcusco.gob.pe

Emergencies

Tourist police Calle Saphi 510

Health

➕ **Clínica Paredes** Calle Lechugal 405; 225265; 24hrs. Has some of the best specialists in Cusco.

➕ **Clínica San Jose** Avda de los Incas 1408; 253295; e info@sanjose.com.pe; www.sanjose.com.pe. Represents International Companies of Travellers Insurance & has a network of medical services in Cusco (Machu Picchu, Sacsayhuamán, etc), offering vaccinations, anti-venom serum, malaria prevention, air & terrestrial ambulance, repatriation, laboratory analysis, & clinic.

➕ **Dentist** Dr Virginia (Vicky) Valcarcel Velarde; Avda el Sol 627-B, office 30; 231558. Speaks some English, & has modern equipment.

➕ **Doctors** (private) Dr Oscar Tejada Ramírez; 233836. Dr Jaime Triveño; 225513 .

➕ **Hospital Regional** Avda de la Cultura; 227661, emergencies: 22369, clinic: 239792

Handicrafts

Cusco has a wealth of souvenirs for every price range. There are various handicraft markets, which sell llama finger puppets, fluffily alpaca slippers, chullos, pan pipes & alpaca wool jumpers of varying quality. There is also a whole selection of high-priced jewellery shops, stores selling top-quality alpaca products such as Kuna & Sol Alpaca plus various opportunities to buy Peruvian coffee, chocolate & even coca sweets.

Immigration

Avda Sol, block 5; 08.00–13.00 Mon–Fri

Shopping for supplies

The largest supermarket in Cusco is **Plaza Vea** in the huge shopping mall on Avda de la Cultura; **Mega**, on Avda del Sol, is also convenient.

Tourist information and other useful organisations/clubs

🚗 **Automóvil Club del Perú** Avda Sol 948, office 203; 01 6119999

🚗 **COSITUC** Avda Sol 103, office 102; 261465; www.cosituc.gob.pe; 07.00–18.00 Mon–Fri, 08.30–12.30 Sat. Tourist Tickets 125 soles (students 70 soles).

🚗 **íPeru** 2 offices: airport (Main Hall & Departure Lounge); 237364; e iperucuscoapto@promperu.gob.pe; 06.00–17.00 daily. Also 117 Portal de Harinas 177, Plaza de Armas; 252974; e iperucusco@promperu.gob.pe; 09.00–21.00 daily.

🚗 **Ministry of Tourism (DIRCETUR)** Plaza Tupac Amaru; 223701; e Cusco@dirceturcusco.gob.pe; www.dirceturcusco.

10

gob.pe; ⊕ 07.15–13.00 & 14.00–16.00 Mon–Fri

i South American Explorers Cusco
Atoqsaycuchi 670; ☎ 245484; e cuscoclub@ saexplorers.org; www.saexplorers.org; ⊕ 09.30–17.00 Mon–Fri. The clubhouse offers an excellent travel advice & information service to members. It also has a book exchange, books & topographical maps for sale & is a friendly, relaxed place to hang out where you will meet other travellers. The Cusco clubhouse is often in need of volunteers, so if you can spare a week, a month or more, email or drop in. For membership details see page 51.

Tour operators
Here follows a selection of Cusco-based adventure tour operators:

Amazonas Explorer Avda Collasuyo 910, Miravalle; ☎ 252846; e enquiries@ amazonas-explorer.com; www.amazonas-explorer.com. Cusco-based specialists in rafting & trekking expeditions, run by British Paul Cripps who has over 30 years' experience. Fixed departures for the rivers Apurímac & Cotahuasi in Arequipa. Also runs local trekking & rafting trips alongside these more adventurous, highly specialised options. See advert, page 282.

Andina Travel Plazoleta Santa Catalina 19; ☎ 251892; e sales@andinatravel.

! A note about tour operators: There are dozens of travel agents in Cusco; those listed are some of the better-known ones. They should be able to provide a good service with professional guides and reasonable equipment. Don't sign up for tours on the street, and do make sure you get a proper contract of services and receipt.

com; www.andinatravel.com. With a penchant for less well-known treks, they are rumoured to have some new routes opening up soon.

Apus Peru Cuichipunco 366; ☎ 232691; www.apus-peru.com. Trekking specialists with several off-the-beaten track options.

Aventours (also known as **Ecoinca**) Saphi 456; ☎ 224050; e info@aventours.com; www.aventours.com. Has been the leader in Peruvian trekking for over 20 years.

EcoAmazonia Lodge Calle Garcilaso 210, office 206; ☎ 236159; www.ecoamazonia. com.pe. Operates daily tours to its jungle lodge.

Enigma Jr Clorinda Matto de Turner 100, Urb Magisterial (1st floor); ☎ 222155; e info@enigmaperu.com; www. enigmaperu.com. Upmarket treks & tours with a good reputation.

Eric Adventures Urb Santa Maria A1-6, San Sebastian; ☎ 272862; e cusco@ ericadventures.com; www.ericadventures. com. Rafting & trekking.

Manu Ecological Adventures Plateros 356; ☎ 261640; manuadventures.com. Tours to Manu.

Manu Expeditions Calle Clorinda Matto de Turner 330, Urb Magisterial (1st floor); ☎ 226671; e adventure@manuexpeditions. com; www.manuexpeditions.com. Upmarket company owned by ornithologist Barry Walker, co-author of Bradt's *Peruvian Wildlife*, he is part-owner of the Manu Wildlife Centre, runs trips into Manu, specialises in birdwatching.

Manu Nature Tours Avda Pardo 1046: ☎ 252721; e info@manunaturetours.com; www.manuperu.com. Top end of the market trips into Manu.

Mayuc Portal Confituras 211, Plaza de Armas; ☎ 232666; e chando@mayuc.com; www. mayuc.com. Rafting trips on the Urubamba, Apurímac & Tambopata, some trekking.

Pantiacolla Tours Calle Garcilaso 265, office 12; ☎238323; e pantiac@terra.com.pe; www.pantiacolla.com. Recommended for Manu.

Peru Adventures Paradise (PAP) C H Amauta Bloque G-201; ☎231054 e info@papadventures.com; www.papadventures.com. Very friendly & personalised trekking company. See advert, colour page 24.

Peruvian Safaris Plateros 365; ☎235432; e sales@peruviansafaris.com; www.peruviansafaris.com. Owns & operates Explorer's Inn lodge, 58km up the Tambopata River from Pto Maldonado,

which, as well as being a tourist lodge, is also one of the main research centres for scientific work in the Amazon Basin.

Q'ente Calle Choquechaca 229; ☎222535; www.qente.com. Treks, including daily Inca Trail departures.

Rainforest Expeditions Puerto Maldonado; ☎877 2319251; m 984 705266; e sales@rainforest.com; www.perunature.com. Operates tours to its 2 lodges in the rainforest of Tambopata – the Posada Amazonas Lodge & the Tambopata Research Center (TRC).

◉ FAVOURITE SITES IN CUSCO

As Peru's main tourist centre, the city's sights are well documented and are covered by the Cusco **Tourist Ticket** (Boleto Turístico). Here are my (Hilary's) personal favourites from 20 years of introducing trekkers to Cusco.

THE CATHEDRAL (La Catedral) Particularly rewarding if you can catch an early-morning service, but at any time for the painting of Christ and his disciples enjoying a guinea pig at the Last Supper.

CORICANCHA (Qoricancha) An awe-inspiring example of exquisite Inca stonework (the Temple of the Sun) topped by a Spanish colonial church, Santa Domingo.

THE CHURCH OF SAN BLAS (Iglesia San Blas) This is my favourite religious building in Cusco. From the outside its adobe façade looks unremarkable but inside is some of the best wood carving you will see in Peru. Take a close look at the cherubs holding up the weight of the pulpit. The artistry is marvellous but the physiological knowledge less so – try that position yourself!

CONVENT OF SAN FRANCISCO (Iglesia y convento de San Francisco) Most interesting for its crypt housing a macabre display of skulls and bones.

INCA MUSEUM (Museo Inka) The best of the museums. An impressive and somewhat gruesome collection of mummies and Inca artefacts. Helps put the Inca culture into perspective.

Tambopata Jungle Lodge Calle Nueva Baja 432; ☎245695; www.tambopatalodge.com. A small & basic lodge close to Lake Sandoval.

United Mice Avda Pachacuteq 424 A-5; ☎221139; e reservations@unitedmice.com; www.unitedmice.com. Daily departures for the Inca Trail.

Vilca Expediciones Plateros 359; ☎244751; e manuvilca@terra.com.pe; www.manuvilcaperu.com. Trips into Manu.

FESTIVALS IN AND AROUND CUSCO The area is well known for its traditional celebrations, with most of them having an Inca/Spanish mix. Certainly worth visiting one if you happen to be in the area.

6 January	Ollantaytambo. Reyes Magos (Festival of the Magi), with dancing and parades.
20 January	San Sebastián and San Fabián: Cusco. Procession of saint effigies in San Sebastián district.

◉ TEN THINGS TO DO IN CUSCO

Additional suggestions from Carol Thomas

1 Try paddle-boarding Go paddle-boarding on **Lake Huacarpay**, 35km (*45mins*) south of Cusco on the Sicuani road. Huacarpay is also good for birdwatching. Then visit the nearby village of Lucre, famous for its traditional desserts and the excellent restaurant Quinta Lucre, set in large gardens and serving good local food. On **Laguna Huaypo**, near Chinchero you can try stand-up paddle boarding for a relaxing workout and great views. For the more adventurous, a quick practice on Lake Urcos before attempting the Class 1 and 2 rapids between Mollebamba and Urcos offers a thrill of a life-time adventure.

2 Make a chocolate bar Learn everything there is to know about chocolate, from bean to bar, in a hands-on experience at the ChocoMuseo (page 68) on Garcilaso 210 (*www.chocomuseo.com*). You can also participate in one of the workshops and make your own bar.

3 Admire the view Wander through the San Blas streets to San Cristobal for superb views over Cusco.

4 Visit the past See the star map and mummies at the Inca Museo, just off the Plaza de Armas.

5 Go star gazing Visit the Planetarium (*office at Avda Pardo 800*) for an in-depth discovery of the southern skies. Perfect pre-trek so you

Seven weeks before Easter	Carnival. Celebrated throughout the Cusco area but particularly colourful in Pisac.
Monday before Easter	Cusco. Señor del los Temblores (Lord of the Earthquakes). Religious parade.
3 May	At all mountaintops with a cross on them. Cruz Velakuy –The Vigil of the Cross.
Thursday after Trinity Sunday (one week after Pentecost Sunday)	Cusco. Corpus Christi. Saint effigies from all the churches of Cusco are brought to the cathedral to 'sleep' with the other saints, and paraded the following day.
Late May/early June (50 days after Easter Sunday)	Ollantaytambo. Santisima Cruz de Sennor Choquekillca. Festival of the patron saint of Ollantaytambo. Four days of colourful parades and dancing.

know what you're looking at during those fabulously clear nights on the trail.

6 Consort with the devil Walk or horseride to the Devil's Balcony, known locally as Chacan, just above Sacsayhuamán, 2.5km outside Cusco (page 258). A natural rock bridge crosses a gorge, with a large cavern beneath.

7 Visit a local market Discover the huge variety of local produce in the markets: flowers, un-nameable fruit, delicious fresh juices and large chunks of meat at San Pedro Market (Mercado San Pedro), shop until you drop at the Artisan markets or head (by taxi) to Molino, a huge covered market selling clothes, music, cameras and just about everything you can think of (except fresh food and crafts).

8 Have a massage Enjoy a post-trek relaxing massage at Yin Yang; see page 244.

9 Try guinea pig or *chicharrones* The villages of Saylla and Tipón, on the main road to Puno just before the turn off for Tipón ruins are full of restaurants serving these traditional delicacies.

10 Stop and sit … Take time out of a busy schedule to simply sit in one of the many small plazas or cafés and soak up the sheer diversity of this amazing town.

Early June	Qoyllur rit'i. The 'Star of the Snow' festival at a remote mountain site near Tinqui, north of Ausangate (pages 326–7).
17 June	Fiesta de Raqchi. The festival of Viracocha.
24 June	Cusco. Inti Raymi. The Inca festival of the winter solstice, celebrated at Sacsayhuamán.
16 July	Paucartambo and Pisac. Fiesta de la Virgen del Carmen. Typical dances.
28 July	Independence Day.
15 August	Qoya and Calca in the Sacred Valley. Virgen Asunta. Parades and dancing.
Last Sunday in August	Sacsayhuamán. Fiesta de Huarachicoy. A re-enactment of the Inca manhood rite, performed in dancing and Inca games by the boys of the local schools.
8 September	Chichero and other villages. Virgen de la Natividad. Parades and dancing.
14 September	Huanca. Fiesta del Señor de Huanca. Religious pilgrimage to the shrine of El Señor de Huanca.

MOUNTAIN BIKING IN THE CUSCO AREA   *Paul Cripps*

A great way to get off the beaten track in Peru is by taking to two wheels and exploring the maze of Inca trails, mule paths and dirt roads that criss-cross the Andes. Monster downhills, lung-bursting uphills, some of the best technical single tracks in the world, incredible scenery and friendly locals are just some of the joys of cycling in the Andes.

Mountain biking in and around Cusco and the Sacred Valley has really taken off in the past few years, largely based around downhill racing, the most famous of all being the Inca Avalanche (*www. incaavalanche.com*), which runs from the 4,600m Abra Malaga to just outside Ollantaytambo at 2,800m. It attracts pro-riders from all over the world and has the joy of a mass start to create total chaos!

To really get away from it all you need to bring your own bike, although a variety of hire bikes are available in Cusco. The more you pay, the better the quality – many companies will not rent out just bikes for fear of damage but will only rent them as part of a guided trip. Do consider hiring a guide or joining an organised trip – there are an increasing number of local guides who know the area well and can choose the route trip for you that you'll almost certainly never find on your own. Plus, you'll have the peace of mind of a support vehicle to carry all your camping gear, plus cooks, spare bikes and of course yourself – should you get tired.

| 1 November | Fiesta de Todos los Santos and Día de los Muertos. All Saints' Day. Celebrated everywhere with bread dolls and traditional cooking. |
| 24 December | Cusco. Santuranticuy. 'The buying of saints', a massive celebration of Christmas shopping Cusco style. |

HIKING, TREKKING AND BACKPACKING

WEATHER The weather here is typical for the central Andes, with a dry season (April to October) and rainy season (November to March). If you can only visit in the rainy season don't be downhearted. Apart from the really wet months of January and February you are likely to have some sunny days, and mornings are often fine. Most days are clear and sunny in the dry season but you should still be prepared for rain or – more likely on the high passes – snow. Note that the Inca Trail is closed in February.

ACCLIMATISATION Adjusting to the altitude is no hardship here. Take time to see the marvels of Cusco and the Urubamba Valley before you set off for the mountains.

There are countless trails and routes in and around the Cusco Valley – from a three-hour road ride around the ruins to amazing off-road loops that visit rarely explored places and will challenge the very best of riders. People in the know rate the 'Milky Way' as possibly one of the best rides in the world!

Probably the most famous day ride in the region is Chinchero–Moray–Maras–Urubamba – mainly downhill on a great mix of dirt road, single track and mule trail. This ride offers awesome views of the Sacred Valley and the chance to visit the cool circular ruins of Moray and the even cooler salt mines of Maras. It is a great day out and doable by most fairly fit cyclists. A beautiful road ride along the Sacred Valley of the Incas is also possible.

Further afield, the dirt roads behind Ollantaytambo, Calca and Pisac provide a variety of multi-day options up and over the final passes before a monster descent into the Amazon jungle. There are also many single tracks that join these routes, hard to find but rated as some of the best off-road mountain biking in the world. For those looking for a more cross-country experience, consider joining a group cycling from the shores of Lake Titicaca, following rarely used dirt roads all the way back to Ollantaytambo in the Sacred Valley.

10

GUIDES, ARRIEROS AND PACK ANIMALS Apart from the Inca Trail, which you can only do as part of an organised trek, you do not need a guide for most of the trails described here and in *Chapter 11*, but if you are venturing off the beaten path you would do well to hire one as much for security as to find the way. There is plenty of choice, so try to get a recommendation from a reliable local person or another traveller. Clarify all details before you set out, pay half the money in advance, and sign an agreement.

RAFTING IN PERU   *Paul Cripps*

Peru is home to some of the best whitewater runs on the planet, from extreme rafting through the world's deepest canyon to jungle float-trips through the Amazon rainforest. Using specially designed rafts and accompanied by experienced guides, you can access spectacular locations away from roads, villages and human contact whilst enjoying this exhilarating and adrenalin-pumping sport – this is the deepest darkest Peru of Paddington Bear fame (you may even glimpse one of his relations if you are lucky).

But before you jump on the first raft trip available it is worth bearing in mind that the very remoteness that makes these rivers so special also brings with it logistical and safety problems should anything go wrong. Every year accidents, including fatalities, do happen and you should be aware that your dream raft trip does hold certain inherent dangers. Don't be put off – there are all types of trips to cater for all types of people, but if it is extremes of adrenalin or wilderness you are looking for be sure to seek out the experts, as going with the wrong company can seriously endanger your life.

It is highly recommended to pre-book your multi-day rafting adventure before leaving your home country, as many of these expeditions have very infrequent departures and you could find yourself waiting for ages to get a group together. Prices vary dramatically, as do quality of equipment, food, experience of guides and safety records. Be sure to shop around. Day trips are easier to organise direct from Cusco.

RÍO URUBAMBA (*year round, Class 2–4, 1 day*) The Urubamba is probably the most rafted one-day river trip in Peru but avoid the sewage infested section around Ollantaytambo and the Sacred Valley of the Incas and head for the much more fun and cleaner sections of Cusipata (Class 2–3) and Chuqicahuana (Class 3–4) which mix exciting rapids with outstanding scenery and wildlife. Inflatable canoes and family rafting trips can also be enjoyed on the lovely Piñi Pampa section, just outside Cusco (Class 1–2). These trips are all best

Pack animals can be organised in Cusco through a trekking agency, but if you speak Spanish it will be cheaper to do it yourself in the village at the trailhead. Around Cusco, as elsewhere, most arrieros are members of an organisation and there are set prices: arrieros 33 soles a day and burros 33 soles. Remember you have to pay for their return journey, too. Prices can vary from area to area and may well have gone up by the time you read this. Note that it's not always that easy to turn up and find animals or arrieros.

accessed from Cusco but can be combined in a long day from the Sacred Valley if necessary.

RÍO APURÍMAC (*May–Oct, Class 3+ & 5+, 3 days*) One of the top ten rafting rivers in the world and the true source of the Amazon, the Apurímac run is rapidly becoming known as the best short whitewater rafting adventure in Peru if not in the whole of South America. A short drive from Cusco into a 3,000m-deep canyon of spectacular rock formations, rare wildlife and outstanding white water, this is one trip not to be missed by lovers of adventure and wilderness.

CUSCO/AREQUIPA RÍO APURÍMAC, BLACK CANYON (*May–Oct, Class 3+, 3–4 days*) This lovely 'family-friendly' version of the more scary commercial section (see above) of the Apurímac is a classic wilderness raft trip for anyone looking for a fun but not too frantic rafting adventure. It can be run in four (or at a pinch three) days and the outstanding Apurímac scenery combines fun Class 3–4 rapids with Inca ruins, huge beaches to camp on, waterfalls to explore and a genuine wilderness experience. Suitable (with the right company) for families from about age 12 and up, this is a gem of a river and well worth exploring. There are very few departures a year so book well in advance.

CUSCO/PUNO/MADRE DE DIOS RÍO TAMBOPATA (*Jul–Sep, Class 3–4, 8–9 days*) The Tambopata is home to over 800 species of birdlife, 1,200 species of butterfly and countless endangered mammals from rare giant otters to jaguars and black caiman to giant anteaters. Using a raft to access this area is the perfect way to experience a true rainforest adventure far off the beaten track. This trip ends near the world's largest macaw lick; it's a short flight back from Puerto Maldonado to Cusco.

Paul Cripps has over 30 years' experience of running whitewater and other adventure trips in Peru.

RENTING EQUIPMENT It is best to bring your own equipment if you can because what's available in Cusco is limited and not of great quality. Several trekking agencies in Cusco rent out camping gear and there are some dedicated equipment rental shops to be found on Calle Saphi. Check all items carefully before paying your deposit. Approximate prices per day: tent 8 soles, sleeping bag 6 soles, stove 8 soles.

FOOD AND SUPPLIES Buy all your trail food in Cusco as variety is extremely limited in trailhead villages. Between the markets and supermarkets the selection in Cusco is very good. Buy sufficient extra supplies for your arriero if you are hiring pack animals or using porters.

MAPS AND BOOKS Plenty of maps are available for this area, including some good trekking ones. The best IGN topographical maps are *Urubamba* sheet 27-r for Lares, Ollantaytambo, Urubamba and the start of Inca Trail; *Santa Teresa–Machu Picchu* sheet 27-q for Machu Picchu, Salkantay and Choquequirao treks; *Pacaynata* sheet 27-p for Espíritu Pampa; and *Ocongate* sheet 28-t for the Ausangate Circuit (see *Chapter 11* for these treks).

The best map of the Inca Trail is from the South American Explorers (SAE) (page 246). They also publish a good map of the Ausangate Circuit and have IGN maps which members can look at and sometimes buy. Copies of IGN maps can also be bought from shops that sell town plans in front of the university on Avenida de la Cultura.

Look for the most informative and best-written guide to the area: *Exploring Cusco*, by Peter Frost, which is currently being updated.

HIKING ROUTES AROUND CUSCO

The area around Cusco is a delight for hikers. Here you can step back in time and see a rural way of life that has hardly changed for 400 years: women spin wool as they walk along the trails, carrying babies in their brightly coloured woven mantas; herds of llamas and alpacas peer at you curiously; donkeys and mules are driven round and round over the freshly cut wheat or barley to separate the grain from the chaff; and the earth is still dug using the ancient Inca foot plough.

In the valleys near the thatched huts of the descendants of the Incas, and high on the hills far from human habitation, are the marvellous remains of that mighty empire: stone walls and temples of a grace and strength unique in the Americas and backed by a range of snow-covered mountains.

The hikes detailed on the following pages are just a beginning and there are lots of other possibilities. If you do go out exploring by yourself, do respect the culture, make contact with the local people and ask permission when you want to camp on their land or take a photograph.

Do not be the instrument of change, environmental or social. Your responsibility is to keep these places as they are. The following local hikes are described in this chapter:

Local hikes
- Inca ruins around Cusco (*Tambomachay to Cusco; 7.5km; 4hrs inc time to explore the ruins*); pages 255–8
- Sacsayhuamán to Chacan and the Devil's Balcony (*7.6km; 3hrs*); pages 258–60
- Tambomachay to Pisac (*25km; 1–2 days*); pages 260–3
- Cusco or Sacsayhuamán to Lamay via Huchuy Qosqo (*31km; 2 days*); pages 263–5
- Lamay to Cusco (*31km; 2 days*); page 265
- Patabamba to Huchuy Qosqo and Lamay (*21km; 1 day*); pages 265–6
- San Jerónimo to Huanca (*15km; 7–8 hours*); pages 266–8

Chinchero–Urubamba Valley hikes:
- Chinchero to Urquillos and Huayllabamba (*8km; 3–4hrs*); pages 269–70
- Chinchero to Maras (ruins of Moray), Salinas and the Urubamba River (*27km; 8–9hrs*); pages 270–1

INCA RUINS AROUND CUSCO *Updated by Mark Smith*

For most people Sacsayhuamán and the nearby ruins are their first introduction to Cusco's Inca past – and the breathtaking effects of its altitude. Doing this trek from the top down makes for a fairly gentle and very nice acclimatisation walk and is certainly much better than travelling by bus.

Distance	7.5km
Altitude	3,300–3,755m
Rating	Easy
Timing	4hrs (including time to explore the ruins)
In reverse	Possible, but much harder (uphill)
Start of trail	Tambomachay: either take a taxi from Cusco, or take a bus or combi heading to Pisac; they go from Puputi and Tullumayo. Alternatively take the Señor de Huerto combi from Rosaspata market.
Transport at the end	Not necessary (walk ends in Cusco)
Maps	IGN sheet *Calca* (27-s)

Route description You will need a Cusco tourist ticket (pages 236–7) to visit the sites but technically you can walk past them without one,

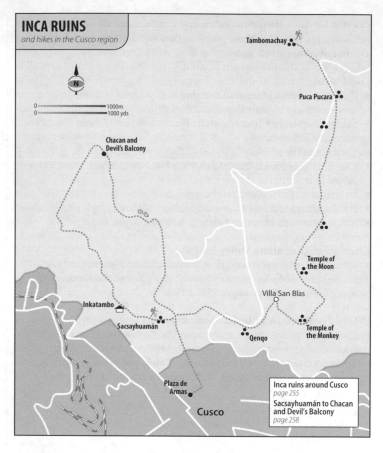

INCA RUINS
and hikes in the Cusco region

Tambomachay

Puca Pucara

Chacan and
Devil's Balcony

Temple of
the Moon

Villa San Blas

Inkatambo

Sacsayhuamán

Temple of
the Monkey

Qenqo

Plaza de
Armas

Cusco

0 ━━━━━━━ 1000m
0 ━━━━━━━ 1000 yds

Inca ruins around Cusco
page 255
Sacsayhuamán to Chacan
and Devil's Balcony
page 258

although you will probably get hassled by park guards, especially near Sacsayhuamán.

At the start, take time to visit the Inca Baths of **Tambomachay** which are well worth seeing. Inca 'baths' were to do with ritual bathing rather than washing, and this is an excellent example of the Inca fascination with water and their ability to direct it where they wanted. Water is channelled through three stone outlets and is pure enough to drink. After visiting Tambomachay it is time to start walking. Head right down the road to **Puca Pucara**, the large reddish Inca site at 300m. This is said to have been a tambo or resting place, or control point. Carry on along the road and at 600m a track cuts left, some 100m before the village of Huayllarcocha. Follow the track behind the lake noting the carved rocks at 800m, once a place where the Incas made offerings. Carry straight on past the **football**

pitch at Km1.06, then straight away the path drops down into a valley beneath a stand of eucalyptus trees in a south–southwesterly direction.

After you've walked just under 2km, soon after you see a large rock on your right, the path bends around to the left. You need to cross the marshy area across to the obvious path running down the right-hand side of the valley. If, instead of crossing to your right at the marshy areas, you were to carry straight down and slightly left you will pass some ruins which are currently being restored. The path through them is currently not finished but eventually you will be able to take this alternative path to the Temple of the Moon.

Keep heading down the path you are on in a south–southwesterly direction. Ahead in the distance you will see the small village of Villa San Blas, which you will pass close to on your way to Qenqo later. But first you need to visit the solitary rocky hill, home of the Temple of the Moon, which you can see to your left. A bit over 3km from the start your path crosses another marshy area to reach the vehicle track. Turn left on this to reach the **Temple of the Moon**. Take some time to explore its cave, carved altar, sundial and very eroded puma sculpture. Your route now turns right, heading along the right side of the Temple of the Moon towards the straggly eucalyptus and a few houses 200m in front of you. In 150m you reach the wide, grassy Inca trail and follow it down to your right to reach the carved rocks of **Cusilluchayoc** (part of the Capac Nan), the Temple of the Monkey. Explore its rocky maze, keeping an eye out for the monkey carvings, then take the leftward trending faint path which goes up the hill behind. You'll soon reach the houses of **Villa San Blas**, which you saw earlier but from the other side. Carry ahead on the road, noting the rocky site of Qenqo to your left before taking the path off to the left at Km4.55 to **Qenqo** itself. This huge limestone rock, naturally eroded and skilfully carved both on top and within its caves, is full of enigmas too. The rock monolith in front could have had a phallic significance (unlikely, as the Incas seem none too impressed with the phallus as a symbol of power), or could be a desecrated carving of a puma … or what you will. The delicate zigzag carvings on top of the rock were probably ceremonial channels for *chicha*, and the beautifully carved cave must surely have been associated with Pachamama, Mother Earth.

After visiting Qenqo carry on along the road, taking care with traffic, until you reach the sign pointing the way to **Sacsayhuamán** along the road to the right. Follow this, passing a few souvenir shops, until a path heads off to the left. Take this and shortly follow the path that cuts across right to arrive at the green-roofed toilet block in the **Sacsayhuamán car park**.

Everything that is 'known' about the origin and purpose of Sacsayhuamán is pure speculation. Every tourist guide has a different story. Some claim that it is pre-Inca, others that it is very early Inca. To the casual visitor, it scarcely matters why the massive zigzag walls (attributed to defence – in the event of an attack the enemy would expose his flank – or to the deities of lightning or the puma) were built. They are one of the wonders of Peru, and the most accessible example of massive Inca stonemasonry. Climb to the top of the mound to see the 'reservoir' or astrological structure, built in a circle with 12 radiating 'spokes'. Most likely this was the foundation of a tower, with an underground system of water channels. Opposite the giant walls, across the 'parade ground' that is now used for the spectacle of Inti Raymi on 24 June, are naturally eroded rocks, some with Inca carvings. This is popularly known as the Inca's Throne, and the rocks make good slides for both young Inca descendants and gringos.

Women bring their llamas for a highly profitable graze in the parade ground. They are extremely photogenic and well aware of their current worth. Bring plenty of change, and don't be conned into paying more than the equivalent of a dollar for a photograph.

After exploring the impressive monoliths of Sacsayhuamán simply head down the steps that run from the car park in a straight line for 1km until you reach the Plazoleta Nazarenas. Turn right here and carry on down to reach the Plaza de Armas, 7.5km from your start.

SACSAYHUAMÁN TO CHACAN AND THE DEVIL'S BALCONY *Mark Smith*

Chacan is a huge natural rock bridge over a gorge. In this easy hike you can explore the fantastic cavern through which the stream runs and visit the precarious Devil's Balcony, perched high up the cliff. The adventurous can continue along a faint trail where there are lots of Incan features, or you can simply retrace your steps.

Distance	7.6km (round trip)
Altitude	3,590–3,765m
Rating	Easy if you return the same way, but there is a more adventurous option available
Timing	3 hours
In reverse	Possible
Start of trail	Sacsayhuamán
Transport at the end	Not necessary (walk ends in Cusco)
Maps	IGN sheet *Calca* (27-s)

Route description The route description starts from Sacsayhuamán, but you could also start by walking up from Cusco. Or to avoid paying the tourist ticket, take a taxi to just above Sacsayhuamán, and ask for the turn-off to Chacan.

Start with your back to the small ticket checking booth in the Sacsayhuamán car park at 3,590m. There are two – the one you want is the higher one. Do not confuse it with the main entrance on the road. Look up to your right across the Incan site and across the road and you will see a **large purple sign** saying 'Sacsayhuamán' (though you cannot read that from here). Head for this, then take the **small set of stairs** directly in front of you and follow the trail which climbs to the right. Go past an area of caves and tunnels and past the **amphitheatre** on your left. Looking across the **amphitheatre** you will see an area of smoothed rocks known as **Los Rodaderos**, used by generations of children as a slide.

Note: If you don't have a tourist ticket to the ruins you can ask the taxi to drop you at this sign.

Carry on the path through an Inca area passing above the intricately carved rock and you will come out on the road, 200m from where you started. Go right on the road for 50m and come to the sign to Sacsayhuamán which you saw from below. Chacan is also signposted here but rather than following the road it is much nicer to take the right-hand path towards Huchuy Qosqo.

The path climbs steeply and after 200m you will see a large overhanging rock hidden in the trees to your left. Carry on for another 200m until you crest the hill and can see the wider path running straight ahead of you, which you take. In 400m the main path turns right. You leave this and go slightly left up the small rise. In 300m arrive at a **pair of lakes** on your right at 3,727m. Carry straight on and into the village. At the village path junction the track you are on bends down to the left. Ignore this, you need to go right. At your feet you will see the start of a **concrete water channel** and you must follow this all the way to Chacan.

In about 400m you will see a river valley running across your path. This is the site of Chacan. If you decide to do the circular trip instead of retracing your steps, you will eventually head downstream along the far bank of this, so sight your line now, and look for the path that runs just below the large jumbled stone blocks.

At 2.5km from the start, you arrive at **Chacan** (3,765m), directly above the stream. There are various carved rocks here and the **Devil's Balcony** is a few metres down to the right; look for an opening into a small platform that opens out into the cliff face. If you descend to the right you will see a large red wall of rock and the stream running through a cave at the bottom of it. Whether you enter it depends on water levels, as it gets quite small at the far end. There are also many Incan sites further upstream for those who wish to explore – you can see them as you approach Chacan.

You can either retrace your steps from here back to Sacsayhuamán, or take a more adventurous, less obvious route onwards. While the path is not precarious it is very narrow and you will get a few scratches from the bushes that overgrow the path; it is not that easy to follow. If you decide to continue, from the end of the Chacan natural bridge you will see a path going left. This is yours. The main path follows the water channel to the right. Within 2m your path splits. Do not take the one that goes up to the village but take the lower, traversing one, and aim for the jumbled blocks of stone that you should have seen earlier.

You pass below these stones and here you need to lose a couple of metres height as your path continues from the top corner of the small agricultural field. The path is now rather faint and narrow but it is there. Carry on traversing until you enter an area of low-growing queñua trees that almost hide the path. Emerge from the trees after 100m. You will see some small agricultural terraces to your left and a large rock down on the opposite stream bank below you. You will eventually end up at the rock but do not try and go direct. Instead, go 50m to your right, diagonally down towards the edge of the eucalyptus trees.

Where the queñua meets the eucalyptus there is a slightly **sunken stony path** entering the eucalyptus. Pay attention now and count 50m along this path and you will come to a very indistinct junction. It is actually a **three-way junction**. Take the path that cuts back leftwards and downwards, to arrive at the stream beneath the large rock. You can see remains of Incan walls at the base of the rock. Cross the stream and climb up the other side to the wide track which bends back around behind the rock and carries on. After 15 minutes you come to a wide grassy area to the left of the path and there is another track of the same width as yours coming in from behind you slightly to your right. This joins your path and you just keep heading straight on the unified path.

In five minutes you reach a junction of the by-now stone track, with the **Inkatambo hotel** on your left. Turn left and in 300m you'll reach the tarmac road and 100m along to your left is the main Sacsayhuamán entrance control. There are toilets here. If you have a tourist ticket, then cut across the flat grassy area of Sacsayhuamán and carry on down to Cusco in 40 minutes. If you don't have a tourist ticket, head down the road to the right and in 15 minutes you will be able to cut down through old streets into the Plaza de Armas.

 TAMBOMACHAY TO PISAC This long day or two-day hike takes you across the mountain range behind Cusco, dropping down the other side to Pisac in the Urubamba Valley. The varied sights and scenery include an Inca ruin, typical villages and traditional agriculture.

Route description The trail starts about 100m down the road from the **Tambomachay** ruins. Take the well-worn trail up the hill, then through farmland passing a few farmhouses, and climb the slope to the pass, admiring the views of Cusco from the top. This should take you about one hour.

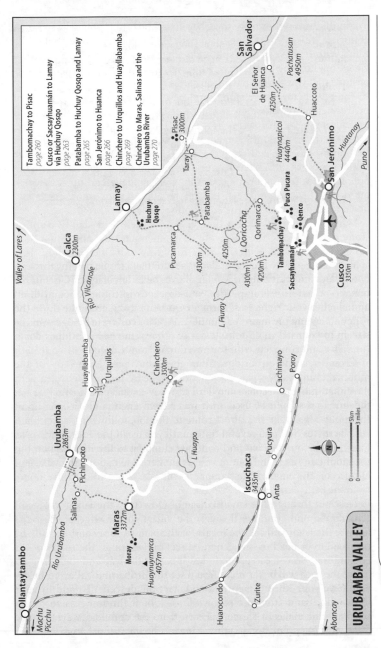

URUBAMBA VALLEY

Tambomachay to Pisac
page 260

Cusco or Sacsayhuamán to Lamay via Huchuy Qosqo
page 263

Patabamba to Huchuy Qosqo and Lamay
page 265

San Jerónimo to Huanca
page 266

Chinchero to Urquillos and Huayllabamba
page 269

Chinchero to Maras, Salinas and the Urubamba River
page 270

San Salvador

San Jerónimo

Pachatusan ▲ 4950m

El Señor de Huanca 4250m

Huaccoto

Huaynapicol 4440m ▲

Pisac 3000m

Taray

Patabamba

Puca Pucara

Qenco

Tambomachay

Sacsayhuamán

Cusco 3350m

Lamay

Huchuy Qosqo

Calca 2300m

Pucamarca

L Qoricocha

Qorimarca

4250m

4300m

4300m   4290m

Río Vilcanote

Valley of Lares

L Huray

Huayllabamba

Urquillos

Chinchero 3500m

Cachimayo

Poroy

Pucyura

L Huaypo

Urubamba 2863m

Pichingoto

Salinas

Maras 3372m

Moray

Huaynuymarca 4057m ▲

Río Urubamba

Ollantaytambo

↑ Machu Picchu

Iscuchaca 3435m

Anta

Huarocondo

Zurite

↓ Abancay

Hualanay

Puno →

N

0   5km
0   3 miles

Distance	25km
Altitude	3,500–3,900m then down to 2,930m
Rating	Long in distance but fairly easy hiking apart from the steep descent to Pisac
Timing	1–2 days
In reverse	Possible, but more difficult, with a steep climb up from Pisac
Start of trail	Tambomachay. Take a tour which culminates in Tambomachay, or the bus or colectivo towards Pisac, leaving from Cusco's Avenida Tacna. Get off at the ruins – about 15 minutes from Cusco.
Transport at the end	There are frequent buses from Pisac back to Cusco
Maps	IGN sheet *Calca* (27-s)

Follow the path to the right, along the mountain slope, passing through two valleys and climbing to a ridge above the little village of **Qorimarca** below – about 45 minutes. The path descends into the valley, with an **aqueduct** to your right. Pass through Qorimarca and continue down the valley, following the main road until you reach a **concrete bridge** over the stream to your left in 45 minutes or so. The main road continues down the valley and connects with the paved road from Cusco to Pisac.

Cross the concrete bridge. Your goal from here is the top of the mountain range.

A road has been constructed all the way to the pass to service the pipeline that supplies Cusco with water from Laguna Qoricocha up in the mountains. Take the direct route to the top, following the footpath which crosses the road several times until you reach the edge of the lake. Pass the lake on your left and continue climbing to the highest point of the mountain range in front of you. From here you can see the village of Qoscco on the edge of the pampa. It will take about four to five hours from the bridge to here.

Descend through the small village of Qoscco to the larger village of **Patabamba** and continue through the village to the edge of the ridge (stay to the right and ask the locals for the path to Taray and Pisac). The dirt road does head in this general direction (although the road doesn't end in Pisac) so you can opt to follow it part of the way and then drop off it, but the path will be far nicer. You'll see the Urubamba Valley far below you. Give your knees a pep-talk and start the descent. To add to your misery fine sand from the soft white rock of the mountainside covers the trail and makes it slippery. Learn from the crab: sideways may be safer. At some point stop to admire one of the Inca's most amazing feats:

canalising the Río Vilcanota so it runs dead straight for over 3,000m, probably to conserve the farmland on the sides. Once the trail levels out, continue up the valley towards **Pisac**, passing through the small village of **Taray**. It takes about two hours from Patabamba to Pisac.

CUSCO OR SACSAYHUAMÁN TO LAMAY VIA HUCHUY QOSQO

This is a treat of a walk, taking you through lovely countryside and over the mountains just outside Cusco, with spectacular views and interesting and seldom-visited Inca ruins, then down the Urubamba Valley. If you do not have a tourist ticket you will need to start via the path to the left of Tambomachay described in the text, as you will not be able to pass either Sacsayhuamán or Tambomachay ruins without one. Unless of course you get past these sites before the guards start work (before 07.00).

Distance	31km
Altitude	3,350–4,350m then down to 2,930m
Rating	Moderate, with 4 high passes.
Timing	2 days
In reverse	Possible (see page 265)
Start of trail	Cusco, Sacsayhuamán or Tambomachay
Transport at the end	Bus to Cusco
Maps	IGN sheet *Calca* (27-s)

Route description You can either hike or take a taxi up to the ruins of **Sacsayhuamán**. If you are walking from Cusco, start at the left-hand side of the cathedral steps and take the street on the left, Cuesta del Almirante. You will reach Plaza Nazarenas after five minutes; turn left here and head up the hill (Pumacurco). After 20 minutes the street comes to some shops and meets the road. You may want to buy a freshly squeezed juice before continuing through the Sacsayhuamán entrance gate and heading on up the stepped path. After 200m there is a split in the path; both end up in the same place. Some 45 minutes after starting your hike you come to the car parking area for **Sacsayhuamán**. If coming by taxi, you can start here. Follow the path up to the road, where you turn right. After about 150m, just before the house, turn left following a small footpath up the valley. This widens as you climb. Continue up, passing a **radio mast**, until you come to a dirt road. You can see the Cusco–Pisac road to your right. Cross the dirt road and continue hiking up the hill for a while along the fairly obvious trail which runs parallel with the Cusco–Pisac road.

Another option is to start at the **Tambomachay** ruins. The advantage of this route is mainly saving time and energy: Tambomachay is about 300m higher than Sacsayhuamán. However, this route might be a bit troublesome, as the Tambomachay ruins are part of the Cusco tourist ticket, so ideally you would need to have one even if you are planning just to pass through. There is another trail that leads to the village of Tambomachay, around the site. For those who don't have a ticket, the trail is visible from the checkpoint: it is a path to your left, which goes to the village. If you take this route you will go around the archaeological complex (you will see it to your right). If you meet a security guard just tell him where you are heading. After about 1½ hours walking up the valley you'll see the *andenes* (Inca terraces) to the left of the path. Continue on for 15 minutes and the trail will go left and up, after 15 minutes more you'll reach the first pass.

Follow this trail all the way up to the first pass at 4,200m (*3hrs*). This part is tricky. When you get to the first pass there will be an *apacheta* (stone cairn) and the visible trail continues down to the right and leads to the village of Quesere down in the valley. You have to take the less obvious path that starts from the apacheta and leads up following the ridge. Go down the valley along the left-hand slope until you come to the **stream** at the bottom. The path splits going up on the other side: it doesn't matter which one you choose, they both lead to the second pass at 4,300m, from where you'll see the small **Laguna Quellacocha** lying in the valley in front of you. Descend on the high trail round the north end of the lake, ignoring the path that leads off to the left. Climb east to the third pass at 4,250m (about three to four hours). From the top you can see **Laguna Qoricocha** to your right. There are campsites in both this valley and the next one. Continue along the trail leading northeast over the next ridge and on to the fourth pass at 4,300m. Descend into the valley ahead of you, keeping to the right. Get directions from the campesinos whenever possible – the trail disappears in places.

After a while you'll see the village of **Pucamarca**. Below it the valley forms a steep ravine, and on the right is a platform with Inca walls. Cross this and find a steep, well-preserved **Inca stairway** descending into the ravine. At the narrowest part of the ravine, cross to the left bank. The trail traverses around the mountainside (west) for a spectacular view of the Urubamba Valley. The path leads through an **Inca gateway**: the entrance to the ruins of Huchuy Qosqo.

Huchuy Qosqo means 'Small Cusco' in Quechua. Little is known about this extensive and mysterious site, but it is being restored and there is now an entry fee of 22 soles.

At the main plaza, a long building with six doorways stands above the terrace wall. This is a *kallanka*, a large building that once had a peaked roof covering it. These structures were constructed around the main plazas in the principal towns of the empire to house soldiers, labourers and other transient people. It was from buildings like this one that Pizarro and his men made their desperate charge on the Inca Atahualpa at Cajamarca, capturing him and massacring thousands of his Indian troops.

From Huchuy Qosqo head for Lamay. Take the trail that starts from the **lower plaza** to the right. It is very steep but quite obvious once you find it. Sometimes it forks, but choose the wider one, and try not to be seduced by short cuts, as some of them are treacherous. You should be in **Lamay** in two to three hours. From Lamay's main road (you will hit it eventually) you can catch a direct bus to Cusco.

LAMAY TO CUSCO Reversing the above walk is certainly possible though the climb up to Huchuy Qosqo is a tough way to start the day. Try to do it early enough to avoid the heat.

From Lamay cross the **Urubamba River** via the Huchuy Qosqo bridge and follow the footpath upwards. It is signed to Huchuy Qosqo, with the INC blue arrows painted on to rocks. It takes three to 3½ hours to reach the site on a steep zigzag path.

From here the trail is clear to the village of **Pucamarca** (*2½hrs*). From the village follow the stream into a valley for half an hour until you reach a junction with another stream. This is a good place to camp. The next morning resist the temptation to follow the new stream to the right, but continue up to the pass, keeping close to the original stream bed (which will probably be dry). At the top of the pass your visual aid is **Laguna Quellacocha**, a small lake. You need to pass to the right (north) of it, picking up a trail that will take you over two passes beyond the lake. From the second path you can either join the Cusco–Pisac road or continue on to **Tambomachay** or **Sacsayhuamán**. This second day will take you five to six hours' walking. Wherever you end up you will find transport to take you to Cusco.

PATABAMBA TO HUCHUY QOSQO AND LAMAY This alternative route to Huchuy Qosqo is one of the most beautiful in the Cusco area. It takes you through farmlands and small villages perched high above the Sacred Valley, with lovely views throughout the day. It is an excellent acclimatisation walk if you are planning a longer trek, as your path climbs

Distance	21km
Altitude	3,800–4,200m then down to 3,000m
Rating	Easy
Timing	1 long day
In reverse	Possible but tough
Start of trail	Patabamba
Transport at the end	There are frequent buses heading to Cusco or you can take one to Calca and on to Cusco
Maps	IGN sheets *Calca* (27-s) and *Cusco* (28-s)

to a pass at 4,200m before taking you downwards through an impressive canyon, to the Inca site of Huchuy Qosqo.

Route description You'll need to take a taxi to **Patabamba** (18km from Cusco). The turning is at the Taray junction on the road between Cusco and Pisac, or you can walk from the main road from where an 18km dirt track brings you to this small village where several families offer homestay accommodation. The route to Huchuy Qosqo is marked with painted **blue arrows**, but always ask to be sure. Turn right in the middle of Patabamba on to a wide stony track and follow this as it borders the Sacred Valley way below. After an hour of walking you reach a **viewpoint** – looking down into the valley you can see Pisac to your right, Qoya below and Lamay (where you end up) off to the left. Continue along the track traversing high above the Sacred Valley, until **Sehua**, a very underdeveloped village of adobe houses, with water running through the streets and an air of poverty. Fork left at the end of the village, upwards, still following the blue arrows. Three hours or so after the start of the walk you reach a pass, from where you can see the deep gorge you'll be heading down to get to Huchuy Qosqo. First head left to the village of **Pucamarca**, where the path comes in from Tambomachay. See above for the description of the walk from Pucamarca onwards to Huchuy Qosqo. From here, there's a dirt road with vehicle access to **Calca**, or a steep zig-zag path to **Lamay**. Alternatively, head out of the top right-hand corner of the site and continue upwards to Tauka (near Chinchero), again following blue arrows, for four to five hours (three to four hours up and one down) and from there take a bus to **Chinchero**. Ask the archaeologists or caretaker at the ruins for directions.

SAN JERÓNIMO TO HUANCA The destination for this hike is one of the landmarks of the Sacred Valley. Tour groups from Cusco often ask their guides about the large, red-roofed church which stands, seemingly alone, on the mountainside. This is the Sanctuary of El Señor de Huanca, and pilgrims have been coming here since 1674 when Our Lord made a miraculous appearance before an Indian miner. For good measure he appeared again in 1713, this time shrewdly choosing a rich landowner as witness, hence the handsome church that commemorates the event.

Around 14 September there is a pilgrimage to the sanctuary. The faithful walk through the night to Huanca in order, it seems, to have a thoroughly commercial time bartering their goods at a huge fair set up for the day.

A road has now been constructed linking the two villages, but it carries little traffic and you are mostly on footpaths. Once this was suggested as a two-day hike but the new road makes it easier to leave when you've had enough, so one day is fine. The trail is clear, but steep and rough in places. Always carry plenty of water.

Distance	15km
Altitude	3,300–4,250m then down to 2,950m
Rating	Easy
Timing	7–8 hours
In reverse	Possible
Start of trail	San Jerónimo, a town to the east of Cusco. Colectivos run there every ten minutes from the corner of Avenida Sol and San Miguel, near the post office in Cusco. The journey takes an hour. A taxi will cost around 20 soles.
Transport at the end	It's a half-hour walk from the sanctuary to Huanca where there is transport to Cusco. Walk a further half hour to San Salvador where buses and combis run to Cusco via Pisac (*2hrs*). If you're lucky, you can pick up a combi from the sanctuary.
Maps	IGN sheet *Urubamba* (27-r)

Route description Although the new road takes away some of the beauty and remoteness in this mountain area, you will be following the footpath, which only crosses the road a few times.

Start from the **San Jerónimo plaza** on the right-hand side of the church, following the street and turning left at the first opportunity. Follow this road to the end of the village, making a right turn at the end, and continue on the footpath which goes slowly uphill through eucalyptus groves. Ask the locals if you're not sure. The path is an old Inca road, passing some tambos and following an Inca aqueduct up the mountain ridge. It takes about two to 2½ hours to the top of this plateau. You can see a few farmhouses to the right, and the road winds its way up the mountain to the right. After the houses on your left the footpath climbs up in the same direction as the road, but passes the highest point on the left.

At the first pass at 3,700m, which you will reach in about half an hour, you can see the village of **Huaccoto** on the other side of the valley. Descend into the valley and towards the village; a further half hour. Walk through this small, typical Quechua village, taking the well-marked path (with loose stones) up the hill to your right. The path makes a left turn, winding around the mountainside above the village. Soon you reach the top, which has a cross on it. An open pampa stretches in front of you. Continue up the pampa, keeping left, until you reach the pass and the highest point on this hike at 4,250m – about 2½ hours from Huaccoto. The pass gives a spectacular view over the Urubamba Valley. The

10

This extensive Inca site is easily accessible from Cusco, and is well worth a visit. It is relatively unknown and hence not overflowing with other tourists, and is also a good starting point for day walks up into the hills above. There are several tracks that climb the hillside above the site; just pick one and follow it. Tipón is 4km off the main road running to Sicuani from Cusco (21km from Cusco). Catch any of the buses heading south along this road and ask for Tipón.

Tipón was an important Inca site, thought to have been dedicated to the veneration of water. It is extensive, with a series of stonewalled andenes irrigated by a beautifully channelled stream of water, originating from a spring high on the mountainside. To the west of the terraces lie the remains of a settlement, with various buildings of typical Inca stonework, including an *intihuatana* ('hitching post of the sun' – a stone which casts a shadow when the sun falls upon it at a certain point in the astronomical calendar). The terraces, similar to those at Moray, may have been some sort of agricultural experimentation centre.

mountain to your right is called Pachatusan (4,950m). Just a few metres below the pass on the other side, on top of a cliff, you'll see the remains of an Inca building which probably served as a guard post overlooking the Sacred Valley.

As you descend you'll see the church roof below you on the right. A well-marked path descends along the steep slope. The descent takes about one to 1½ hours. Take the time to visit the church and its painted rock, which commemorates the First Miracle and is now part of the altar.

From the sanctuary to the village of **Huanca**, where you can get transport back, is half an hour, or it's a further half-hour walk to **San Salvador**. From here you can get transport back to Cusco via Pisac – a two-hour journey.

CHINCHERO–URUBAMBA VALLEY HIKES These two walks are just a sample of the several which take you into the Urubamba Valley with its many Inca sites and transport options back to Cusco. At the high point there are lovely views over the cordilleras Vilcabamba and Vilcanota.

Chinchero is on the tourist route, but is a perfect example of the resilience of the Andean Indian to outside influences. The Sunday market is still amazingly colourful, full of traditionally dressed women in the regional cartwheel hats, and geared as much to the villagers' needs as to those of the milling tourists. Women sit in groups by their produce, fry fish, or serve chicha from earthenware pots. Others sell handicrafts.

Chinchero is worth visiting, even on a weekday, for the impressive Inca stone wall forming one side of the plaza, and some wonderful terracing with very fine stonework. The town used to be an important Inca centre and there are many examples of their stone carving. Before you leave the village take a look inside the Spanish colonial church, built on Inca foundations (the side chapel has an Inca well and water channels from the temple that once stood here). The church dates from 1607 and has a wonderful painted ceiling and walls. The main figure is of St James, patron saint of the conquistadores.

If you walk down the Inca stairs, which start behind and below the church to the left of the terraces, you'll come to the main trail going down the valley. There are two large rocks near the path, with carved stairs, seats and water channels. Leave the village by noon at the latest (preferably earlier) to be sure of reaching the valley floor before dark. Always carry water on these hikes; the valley is pretty dry and hot, especially in the dry season.

Chinchero to Urquillos and Huayllabamba
This trail is a fine example of an Inca road, with the ruins of a tambo, an Inca posthouse, halfway. It can be combined with a visit to Chinchero market and ruins before you start walking. The walk itself, while steep in places, has some beautiful views as you walk down the canyon to the Sacred Valley.

Distance	8km to Huayllabamba (5km to Urquillos, 2 hours)
Altitude	3,500m down to 2,760m
Rating	Easy
Timing	3–4 hours
In reverse	Possible, but a steep climb from the valley so it will take longer
Start of trail	Chinchero
Transport at the end	Local buses run from Huayllabamba to Pisac where you can take a bus back to Cusco
Maps	IGN sheet *Urubamba* (27-r)

Route description Take the path through the ruins at **Chinchero**, following the signs to Urquillos (follow the **blue arrows**). The path has been newly renovated and passes some superb **Inca stone carvings** and some farmland before starting to descend steeply at the back of the ruins. You pass an Inca lookout on the way down, and a glance up left reveals more Inca remains up high on the hillside. A sign halfway down indicates a detour to a waterfall. After two to three hours you arrive at **Urquillos**

10

(3,077m) and from here either cross the main square and follow the stream to a pedestrian **bridge** over the Urubamba River (20 minutes from the square) from where you can catch a bus, or continue walking along the road leading down the valley to the village of **Huayllabamba**, 3km away (note this is not the same Huayllabamba as on the Inca Trail). At Huayllabamba a bridge crosses the river and puts you on the main road through the Urubamba Valley.

Chinchero to Maras (Moray), Salinas and the Urubamba River
Thanks to Peter Frost for information from his book Exploring Cusco

This hike takes you through interesting countryside and Quechua villages, but its outstanding feature is the three very different but equally impressive ancient sites visited *en route*.

Chinchero has already been described: a classic of traditional imperial Inca stone walls and terraced farmland, with a small colonial church thrown in for good measure (page 268). Moray is quite different: unique in fact. It is not the ruins of a city or a fortress, but an earthwork. The ancient peoples of the region took four huge natural depressions in the landscape and sculpted them into agricultural terraces that served, hundreds of years ago, as an experimental agricultural station for the development of different crop strains. Recent investigations have shown that the terraces are organised into sectors, with significantly different temperatures on each level.

Much of the terracing survives intact, leaving regular concentric layers flowing harmoniously into the land. The largest of each of the circular structures has a diameter of 150m, is 150m deep, and is formed by seven of the above-mentioned concentric rings. The interest here is subtler than the massive walls of the Inca sites; it is a place more for contemplation than admiration.

Distance	27km
Altitude	3,760m up to 4,057m and down to 2,865m
Rating	Easy walking, but a long day unless you take a car for the first part
Timing	8–9 hours
In reverse	Possible if you find transport for the last stretch into Chinchero; otherwise not feasible in one day because of the steep climb
Start of trail	Chinchero
Transport at the end	Flag down a local bus to Urubamba and take a bus back to Cusco from there
Maps	IGN sheet *Urubamba* (27-r)

Salinas, as the name suggests, is a village of salt. A salt river runs down the mountainside, partly underground, and since pre-Hispanic times salt has been collected here in hundreds of artificial salt pans, using a natural process of evaporation.

Route description Leave **Chinchero** in the direction of Urubamba and follow the paved road until the turn-off to Maras after about 11km. If you want to avoid the long road-walk, catch a ride with one of the many buses or colectivos on this route. From the turn-off follow the gravel road to **Maras** (3,372m), about 4km. This is a colonial town which used to thrive on mining the salt deposits in the cliffs to the north. Now it is smaller and you can only expect to buy basic supplies here.

The trail to Moray (Huaynuymarca) leads westwards, away from the town in roughly the same direction you followed from the paved road, at right angles to the main street. Ask the locals for directions, as the path is hard to find.

Follow the path until you reach the first ravine (6–8m deep), cross it on a **log bridge**, and continue until the second ravine (about 30m deep). Cross the bridge again. Don't continue along this main trail up the slope to the right. Take, instead, the path that climbs to the left, almost straight up the slope, passing a farmhouse and two small ponds; you'll be able to see a large **signboard** in the distance bearing the name of the site. Aim for that, crossing the third ravine (about 15m deep), to arrive at **Moray**, about 7km (*1½hrs*) from Maras. Here, as well as the earthwork and terraces described earlier, there are the remains of an irrigation system.

A dirt road connects Maras to **Salinas** (3,385m), about 5km (*1½hrs*) away. Approaching Salinas from above like this is ideal: it is an astonishing and extremely photogenic site. The pans look like a giant white honeycomb, with the small bee-like figures of Indians bustling around the rims harvesting their 'crop'.

To finish the hike, follow the trail down the left side of the valley from Salinas to the **Urubamba River**. If you turn left when you reach the river you'll come to the picturesque village of **Pichingoto**. Nearby are caves – some of which are inhabited. Turn right here and you'll soon reach a footbridge over the river. Cross it and follow the trail another 500m to the main road of the Urubamba Valley about 5km from Salinas. Turn right to reach **Urubamba** in about 6km, or pick up a colectivo on the road.

THE VALLEY OF LARES

Trekking in this area takes you into the remote Lares Valley with the spectacular backdrop of the Urubamba Mountains, which lie to the east of the Sacred Valley. The area has become more popular with trekkers over the past few years as the Inca Trail has become more regulated, with most of the organised trekking groups walking between Lares or Quishuarani and Ollantaytambo. The Lares area offers moderately strenuous trekking through small mountain villages, crossing passes of over 4,000m with spectacular views of the surrounding snow-capped peaks of Pitusiray, Sawasiray and Chicon. The treks described here give you the opportunity to see how the Quechua-speaking people of the high mountain villages live by farming potatoes and oca, and herding llamas and alpacas on the inhospitable flanks of the towering peaks. The Lares Valley is known for its very high-quality, brightly coloured weavings and characteristic upturned hats, many of the popular tourist markets being supplied from here.

There are several variations on this trek which you can do according to how much time you have available. Even in the dry season be prepared for bad weather and take a map and compass for your own safety. Although in this area there are always people not far away, they often don't speak Spanish. If you want to take mules or porters and a guide you will probably have to organise it through one of the agencies in Cusco.

Treks in the Valley of Lares and Ollantaytambo region:
- Huaran to Lares and Paucarpata (*About 60km; 3–6 days*); pages 272–6
- Maucau to Yanahuara via Quishuarani and Huacahuasi (*54km; 3–4 days*); pages 276–8
- Ollantaytambo to Pumamarca (*12km; 4–6hrs*); pages 280–1
- Ollantaytambo to Pumamarca and Lares (*About 40km; 3–4 days*); page 281–2

 HUARAN TO LARES AND PAUCARPATA This is the original route in the Lares region which first opened up the area to trekkers. It is best to start

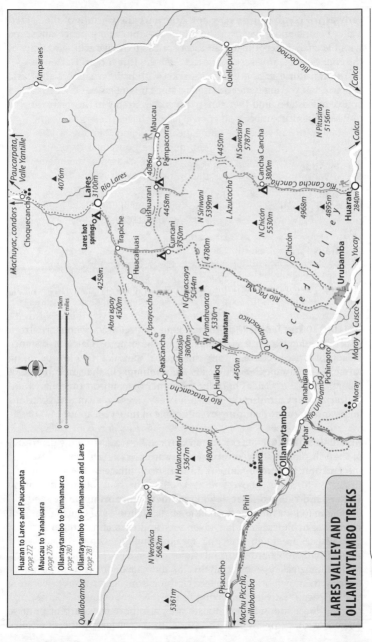

N Pitusiray
5156m

Calca

Rio Qochoq

Quelloputo

Calca

Amparaes

Paucarpata,
Valle Yantille

Machuyac, condors

Choquecancha

4076m

Lares
3100m

Rio Lares

Maucau

Pampacorral

4086m

N Sawasiray
5787m

Quishuarani

4458m

4450m

Cancha Cancha
3800m

Lares hot
springs

Trapiche

Huacahuasi

Quncani
3750m

N Siriwani
5399m

L Azulcocha

N Chicón
5530m

4968m

4895m

Huaran
2840m

4258m

N Cuyacsaya
5C44m

4780m

Chicón

Yucay

Cusco

Abra Ispay
4300m

Ipsaycocha

N Pumahuanca
5330m

Manatanay

Urubamba

Patacancha

Huacahuasija
3800m

4450m

Rio Patacancha

Huilloq

Choquechico

Río Patacancha

Sacred Valley

Río Urubamba

Yanahuara

Pichingoto

Maray

N Halancoma
5367m

4800m

Ollantaytambo

Pachar

Moray

N Veronica
5682m

Tastayoc

Pumamarca

Phiri

Pisacucho

5361m

Machu Picchu,
Quillabamba

Quillabamba

Huaran to Lares and Paucarpata
page 272

Maucau to Yanahuara
page 276

Ollantaytambo to Pumamarca
page 280

Ollantaytambo to Pumamarca and Lares
page 281

0   10km
0   6 miles

N

**LARES VALLEY AND
OLLANTAYTAMBO TREKS**

10

early as the climb can be very hot. You leave the warmth of the Sacred Valley behind and travel over the mountains into a far greener landscape with the chance to bathe in Lares hot springs to revive aching muscles at the end.

You can stock up at the **Calca** market with fruit, vegetables and basic supplies, but you are better advised to stock up in Cusco. Calca also has a couple of hostales, and there are many places to stay in the nearby towns of Pisac and Urubamba.

Distance	About 60km
Altitude	2,838–4,400m
Rating	Moderate
Timing	To Lares 3–4 days, to Paucarpata 5–6 days
Start of trail	Huaran (also possible to trek from Urubamba to Lares or Huaran to Urubamba)
Transport at the end	Lares (2¼hrs by bus to Calca, a few times per day) or Paucarpata (2–3hrs by bus to Calca, not every day)
Maps	IGN sheet *Urubamba* (27-r)

Getting to the trailhead To start your trek get a bus or colectivo from either Avenida Huascar or Calle Puputi heading to **Calca**, a distance of approximately 80km. From the square in Calca take a bus going towards Urubamba and get off after ten minutes in the small village of Huaran. While in Calca check for frequency of transport from Lares and Paucarpata to Calca for the return journey. There are currently various buses and colectivos running every couple of hours till about 16.00.

Route description Set out from **Huaran** (2,840m), climbing gently out of the Vilcanota Valley (directly northwards) on a well-marked trail up the **Quebrada Cancha Cancha** to the small village of the same name, situated a long way above you at 3,800m. The trail follows the course of a mineral-rich red river flowing off the mountains up ahead, and it'll take three to four hours to reach the scattered houses of Cancha Cancha. By now agricultural land has given way to dramatic mountain scenery. The villagers are tough Quechua-speaking Indians who herd llamas and alpacas, and grow hardy, high-altitude crops such as potatoes and quinoa on the steep valley sides. They live as they have for centuries, expertly weaving their own bright-coloured clothing from alpaca wool, celebrating ancient pagan festivals, and living in thatched stone houses. Guinea pigs running loose around their houses are an important source of protein. There is good camping near the school in the village, up the side valley to the left (west) of the village, or at one of the many beauty spots on the way up the trail. Continue walking for 20 minutes up the flat valley bottom beyond the village (northeast). If you look up ahead you will see the trail on the right slope of the valley. Heading north again, the path now begins to climb very steeply towards the first pass, **Pachacutec** (4,450m). Looking down to the left, as you climb, you see the flat pampa where the villagers of upper Cancha Cancha have their houses and stone corrals. The pass is a strenuous two- to three-hour climb from the village. As you look back from the pass, surrounded by the weirdly contorted forms of wind-eroded rocks, the Sacred Valley is visible a long way below and even Chinchero can be made out in the distance. Pachacutec Lake and the peaks of Pitusiray loom out of the swirling clouds. Proceed along the ridge following the trail, now going northwest for an hour, 3km, until the path drops steeply down to the left into a dramatic cliff-lined corrie. There are superb camping sites on the shores of the glacier lakes found in the corrie, and this is an ideal spot for observing Andean geese, caracaras and coots. From the lip of the corrie descend into the next valley, following a series of nine cascading **waterfalls** to the village of **Quishuarani** (3,850m), one hour from the corrie. Camping is possible in the village.

Don't drop down to the bottom of the village, but leave Quishuarani heading directly west, steeply up to the left behind the school. If you were to continue down the valley ahead you would end up in Lares, but miss a beautiful part of the trek. There is a steep two- to three-hour climb ahead, on a good path, to reach the second pass, known as **Kochuyckaza** (4,458m), but marked as **Abra Huillquijasa** on the map. Your walk takes you across grazing areas where large herds of llama are tended by children. Watch out for their protective and sometimes very aggressive dogs; keep a few stones handy just in case. There is a good trail all the way up, but if you happen to lose the trail look out for a **large lake** near the head of the valley, approximately 1½ hours from the village. It is easy to pick up the trail again at the far end of the lake, from where you begin the steep final ascent zigzagging up to the steep rocky slope to the right of the sharp peak ahead. From the pass, there is a stunning view of emerald-green glacial lakes. Drop down to pass the lakes on the right (north) side, cross, from right to left, the waterfall flowing from the corrie and follow the valley down to the village of **Cuncani** (3,750m) in the valley bottom (1½ hours from the pass and one hour from the lakes). You can camp at the lakes or in the valley bottom.

From here it is a three-hour walk down the valley to Lares (3,100m) to the north. It is possible to head south from Cuncani, over the pass of **Pumahuancajasa** (4,780m) and straight down the valley to Urubamba (see overleaf, this can be done in reverse). You should allow two days for this option, from Cuncani. If you set off walking at first light you may be accompanied by local farmers traditionally dressed in bright-red ponchos going to work their fields, singing and playing musical instruments as they go: an unusual sight!

For Lares a clear path follows the right slope of the valley down (northwards) alongside the white, frothy **River Cuncani** until 30 minutes before reaching the village of **Lares** where weary limbs can be soaked in thermal springs (take a swimsuit). Keep a look out to the left below the path for the springs soon after the trail turns to the right (northeast) at Trapiche, after walking 2½ hours. You'll see five **open-air pools** with some small-built changing rooms (*entry 11 soles*). Basic **accommodation and meals** are sometimes available at the springs themselves, but not always. Otherwise Lares has some very basic places to stay and eat. Lares itself is a grey and uninteresting semi-tropical town with little to offer, other than a welcome beer and a chance to restock supplies. However, if you happen to arrive on market day Lares is a colourful hive of activity. There is a hostel (El Paraiso) to stay at on the square if you can find someone to open it for you but there isn't much to hang around for if you don't have to. You may of course have to wait for transport out: approximately 2½ hours to Calca.

If, after reaching Lares, you decide to continue trekking for a few more days, take the road to the north from the bottom of the town towards Choquecancha, three to four hours from Lares, famous for the quality of its weavings. Follow the road down from Lares for two hours through rich vegetation, before turning right after crossing the river and heading steeply upwards on the road to **Choquecancha** (3,200m). A 14-niched Inca wall lines the square of this small ancient village, and a glance up the hillside reveals further neglected archaeological remains. You may be able to camp in the school grounds if you ask the resident teachers, or find a nice spot by the river before climbing to the village. From Choquecancha, head out of the top-left corner of the village, over the ridge to the northeast and out towards Paucarpata. It is a 2½-hour steamy climb to the ridge top, where views of the snow-capped peaks to the north are outstanding. There are some beautiful camping spots here, but no water very near. Andean condors are sometimes seen – they nest in nearby cliffs. From the top of the ridge descend to the northeast for one hour to reach the small village of **Paucarpata** (3,378m), where you will find a shop and perhaps a passing vehicle. It's 2½ spectacular hours from here to **Calca** along the road; again check in Calca before setting off for frequency of transport

MAUCAU TO YANAHUARA VIA QUISHUARANI AND HUACAHUASI
Mark Smith

This is another great trek in the Lares area, and a route that few others will have taken before you. Most trekkers starting at Quishuarani drive straight to the town, or start walking somewhere along the vehicle track that leads from the paved road and continues to Lares. Others stop halfway through the drive from Cusco to walk the couple of hours' journey to the Totora Canyon, before carrying on by bus to camp at Quishuarani. A few years ago, however, we found an alternative starting point which makes for a far better route. By starting at Maucau, you get to pass through traditional farming communities and over a number of high Andean passes before eventually descending into the Sacred Valley.

Distance	54km
Altitude	3,215–4,607m
Rating	Moderate
Timing	3–4 days
In reverse	Possible although transport at the end is less frequent
Start of trail	Maucau, just before Lares
Transport at the end	From Yanahuara there are buses to Urubumba (*10mins*), Ollantaytambo (*20mins*) or Cusco (*1¼hrs*)
Maps	IGN sheet *Urubamba* (27-r)

Getting to the trailhead This trek is best started in the morning. To reach the trailhead, take the bus from the bus station in Cusco to Calca, and from there take the bus heading to Lares. Alight at the community of Maucau which lies some 15 minutes before Lares. The walk starts by the Km18 marker, just past the small waterfall that spills out onto the road.

Route description The start of the trek takes a generally flat path, passing by the giant *Puya raimondii* cactus, more often associated with the Huaraz region, with views of the highest peak in Urubamba range, Sawasiray at 5,400m. Follow the path until you reach the beautiful valley of **Machapampa**. Take care though as the path varies: at some points it diminishes to a narrow sheep track and it can get very slippery when wet.

After lunch follow the path until you reach a big drop to the side, before starting the small half-hour climb to the top of the pass (4,086m). Here, there is a dried-up lake, as well as a five-minute section of rocky ground which requires some careful footing, particularly when wet. After this tricky terrain, the path descends easily to the camp in **Quishuarani**, where you'll find a pleasant enough terraced campsite above the higher of the two schools. If spending the night here, you may be charged a small fee by the community.

Leaving Quishuarani, head east up the side valley climbing above you out of the main valley. Be sure to take in the views back over Sawasiray and the previous pass. After 2.6km, you'll come across the **Laguna Queunacocha**, before meeting the pass (4,458m) after continuing for

10

another 1.4km. From here, you will descend past some beautiful lakes which are often used as lunch spots due to the surrounding scenery. The descent is steep but not exposed – take care on the top section as it follows a zigzag section down which can be tricky at times.

Continue on until you reach the village of **Cuncani** at Km7.3, before descending the valley onto the vehicle track. At Km13.2 turn up into the **Huacahuasi Valley** (3,800m) and continue along the vehicle track until you reach an opportunity to step onto the footpath. There are options to camp in Huacahuasi on the school playing field, or alternatively you could ask at houses. If you're feeling fit, you could continue past Huachahuasi for about 2km where there is a place to camp at Chacchapata (3,973m). Alternatively, there is another camping spot a bit further along at 4,105m. Both are near a stream and have water available.

It's a fairly easy ascent up the Chacchapata Valley from Huacahuasi before a steep hour's climb to the Huacahuasija pass (4,607m). After around half an hour, you should reach the **Laguna Aruruaycocha**, a beautiful turquoise lake which you can walk alongside having descended the zigzag track down a scree slope from the pass. From here, you can pass beneath the snout of one of the Pumahuanca glaciers (5,300m); however, like all the glaciers around here, it has retreated considerably, meaning that it is well above reach. Continue through the native *queñoa* woodland, before reaching **Laguna Milpo**, known to locals as Queuñacocha or Pilcococha, which is a lovely spot to rest or take some lunch with views up to the glaciers of Pumahuanca.

There is a potentially tricky river crossing from the laguna, particularly if it is raining, as the stepping stones tend to be underwater. From here, carry on down a good track through the native woodland, following the stream down the valley where you'll pass a waterfall on your right. There is an opportunity to camp at Mantanay (4,109m). A single family live here so you should ask their permission; they normally sell drinks too. After about 2½ hours you'll come to the Quebrada Chapaschico (3,691m), and from here it is just less than 12km to the trailhead. Yanahuara is a quiet village with decent hotels. If you've organised transport, you can reach Ollantaytambo in 20 minutes or Cusco in one hour and 15 minutes. Alternatively, it is another 2km to the main road, from where you can catch a bus or combi to **Urubamba**, **Ollantaytambo** or **Cusco**.

OLLANTAYTAMBO AND AROUND   *Telephone code: 084*

For Inca admirers, Ollantaytambo is one of the most thrilling places in Peru, and far too often rushed through by tour groups. The town still retains its Inca layout; many of the houses show signs (such as wall niches) of their Inca origins, and many of its inhabitants preserve their traditional lifestyle.

Llanganuco Mountain Lodge

Laguna de Keushu, Yungay, Ancash, Perú
www.llanganucomountainlodge.com
hello@llanganucomountainlodge.com

Traveller´s Choice
—— 2013 WINNER ——
tripadvisor

Llanganuco Lakes & Gorge

The Best Trekking in the Americas

Llanganuco Mountain Lodge (LML) sits a leisurely 30 min walk away from the Huascarán National Park (HNP) entrance, making it the best located trekking lodge in the Americas.

North America has 2 peaks over 5,500m, whereas the Huascarán National Park has over 50. The 3 highest peaks are Huascarán S. & N. & Huandoy. The main attractions are the Llanganuco Lakes, Lake 69, Santa Cruz-Llanganuco trek & Mt. Pisco with LML nestled strategically amongst these at 3503m.

The Lodge

Waterfall at Lake 69

Lake 69 Trek

The reward for those who have acclimatised with us sufficiently, is the renowned world class day trek, Lake 69 (4650m) which is packed with action, emotion & adventure. The rivers, waterfalls & the sheer scale of the towering mountains make it an adventurer´s paradise.

LML is full-board including pack lunches to refuel and provision guests to maximise your enjoyment & success on all of our day-treks. Trekking descriptions & local village guides are also available at Llanganuco Mountain Lodge.

Superior Room

Dining Room

The Perfect Lodge for Tailored Day-Treks & Acclimatisation Plans

Llanganuco Mountain Lodge has over 14 different day treks available, suitable for a range of different ages & levels of fitness, making it the most diverse lodge for trekking in the Cordillera Blanca. Depending on your personal needs & requirements, you are able to tailor your stay exactly as you wish, giving you all the freedom & flexibility you need to maximise your enjoyment & experience of the region.

If you are planning something more adventurous like the Santa Cruz Trek, Mt. Pisco or any other neighbouring peak, the owner will provide you with a tailor-made acclimatisation plan. Being well prepared is the key to successful & safe trekking.

5-Day Personalised Acclimatisation Schedules

Lake & Ruins of Keushu - 3500m

Llanganuco Lakes/Cloud Forest - 3850m

Day 1: The Lake & Ruins of Keushu is the perfect option for those who have just arrived. A relaxing stroll around the lake with great views of the nearby peaks.
Day 2: Head off onto a pre-Inca trail & venture through the cloud forest arriving at the spectacular Llanganuco Lakes. Hire a boat or just relax with your lunch.
Day 3: The Ice of Huandoy is situated very close to the lodge & offers a great days walk up to the bottom of the impressive Huandoy Mountain (6395m).
Day 4: Lake 69 is arguably the hardest & most intense days walk, but most definitely worth it, as the reward at the end is something you will never forget.
Day 5: Get driven up to the Portachelo Pass at the crack of dawn & enjoy one of the most amazing sunrises before descending back down on the pre-Inca trail.

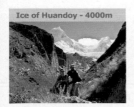

Ice of Huandoy - 4000m

Lake 69 - 4650m

Portachelo Pass - 4760m

What Memories Will
You Take Home?

www.TrekkingPeru.net

Ollantaytambo deserves a stay of a few days, offering as it does a wide choice of accommodation, spectacular Inca ruins and local walks. These days it is also the starting point for most of the trains to Machu Picchu.

GETTING THERE AND AWAY **Buses** leave Cusco every 20 minutes for Ollantaytambo via Chinchero or Pisac; the journey takes approximately 1¾ hours. Cost ranges from eight to 15 soles and there are a variety of buses, combis and colectivo taxis that run from Cusco. A good option is to sign up for a **bus tour** of the Sacred Valley, leaving the tour in Ollantaytambo if you are doing one of these walks. This ensures you get to see all of the Inca sites (recommended).

WHERE TO STAY

🏠 **KB Hostal** e kbperu@hotmail.com; www.kbperu.com. Friendly place just down from the main square just before the bridge.

🏠 **Hostal Las Orquideas** On the road to the railway station; 204032; www.hotellasorquideas.com.pe. Nice, clean, comfortable rooms & has a garden. Recommended. 85 soles pp with b/fast; dinner also available. Turn-off to the station. They can also provide advice as well as walking & biking tours from 60 soles pp.

🏠 **El Albergue** At the railway station; 204049; www.elalbergue.com. An atmospheric, popular place which is very handy for trains. It is now run by the son of the American painter Wendy Weeks & the late Robert Randall who contributed his knowledge of local practices to this book (pages 8–9). US$81–150 per room.

🏠 **Pakaritampu** On the road leading to the railway station; 204020; e info@pakaritampu.com; www.pakaritampu.com. The most comfortable hotel in Ollantaytambo. US$144–193 per room.

👁 OLLANTAYTAMBO: WHAT TO SEE AND DO

The tourist focus of Ollantaytambo is the magnificent **Inca fort and temple** above the town. Get there as early as possible in the morning or late in the evening to avoid tour groups, and buy a locally available guidebook or hire a guide to show you around. The Inca stonework here is as good as you can see anywhere, and there are numerous things of interest, from old mud walls strengthened by guinea pig hair to the *pedros cansadas* ('tired stones') that were cut but then abandoned *en route* from the quarry on the opposite side of the Urubamba. The **Baño de Ñusta** (Princess's Bath) should also be seen.

The **CATCCO Museum** (⏰ 10.00–13.00 & 14.00–16.00 Tue–Sat) at the old parador, one block from the plaza and overlooking the river, is recommended. Set up by the Cusichaca Trust, this exhibition is a must for anyone wishing to understand more about the way of life of the inhabitants, past and present, of the Sacred Valley of the Incas. The museum depends on its entry fees and donations.

✕ WHERE TO EAT AND DRINK There are a couple of restaurants: **Hearts Café** (*www.heartscafe.org*) on the way to the train station does wholefoods well and its profits support local projects which support remote, impoverished highland communities in the area. For more details about the projects check their website: www.livingheartperu.org. **Coffee Tree** does excellent coffee on the Plaza de Armas. Try the market for good, fresh fruit juices.

LOCAL HIKES
Ollantaytambo to Pumamarca

A nice half-day walk into the quiet valley above Ollantaytambo, with the opportunity to get a taxi to the Inca fortress of Pumamarca. You will get a fascinating glimpse into the skill of the Incas and their use of terraces to tame this steep-sided valley for farming, a tradition which is still in place today.

Distance	12km (round trip)
Altitude	2,800–3,400m
Rating	Easy
Timing	4–6 hours (round trip)
In reverse	Possible (catch bus up then walk down)
Start of trail	Ollantaytambo
Transport at the end	If you're doing this walk one way, you can catch a local combi or taxi up to Pumamarca and walk back down or vice versa
Maps	IGN sheet *Urubamba* (27-r)

Route description Leave Ollantaytambo on the road that heads northwards out of the village alongside the **Patacancha River**. Follow this for about half an hour until the last houses in the village of **Munaypata**. Here, cut up a steep path to the hillside above. Follow the trail as it heads eastwards, contouring along the side of the Patacancha Valley. Most of the time now you will be walking through cultivated farmland, fields of maize, potatoes and beans, grown on well-preserved Inca terraces. After 90 minutes or so of walking you will see the stone buildings of **Pumamarca** above you on the hillside. It takes about two hours of walking from Ollantaytambo to reach the site. The site is well preserved and a joy to look around. Its exact function remains something of a mystery, like so many Inca sites. It is thought that Pumamarca was an Inca fortress, strategically located to control access to the Sacred Valley from Antisuyo, one of the four quarters of the empire. The high surrounding walls would support this theory, but then why locate what appear to be food stores outside the main site? You can follow the canal that runs from the site on up the hillside for even better views of the surrounding area.

Ollantaytambo to Pumamarca and Lares

This is a popular trek usually done in reverse by agencies who then take you from Ollantaytambo station to catch the train to Machu Picchu. The advantage of starting in Ollantaytambo is it allows you to finish at the Lares hot springs where you can camp for the night and soak tired muscles.

Distance	About 40km
Altitude	2,800–4,800m
Rating	Moderate
In reverse	Possible
Timing	3–4 days to Lares
Start of trail	Ollantaytambo
Transport at the end	Lares (2¼ hours by bus to Calca, a few times a day)
Maps	IGN sheet *Urubamba* (27-r).

Route description Follow the description above to get to Pumamarca Inca site and from there go out of the ruins at the top of the site and follow the **canal** up and round to the right as it levels out. There is a path alongside the canal. After 1½ hours you pass through a small hamlet **Choquechaca** where the family Laucata live, then continue another 45 minutes or so to an excellent camp spot at a large open grassy area with stunning queñoa forest all around. This is 4½ hours' walk from Ollantaytambo.

Next day continue climbing for three hours to the top of the pass (4,800m) with superb views to Pumahuanca peak (5,330m) to the east, Halancoma (5,367m) to the west, and endless peaks rolling away into the distance including the peak of Nevado Terijuay (5,330m) far to the north. Stay on the ridge traversing round on to a second pass, continuing above the large green **Azulcocha lake** and head downwards past several remote houses to the valley below where you can camp. Local kids will no doubt come and have a peek. There are a couple of nearby houses and plenty of animals grazing nearby, part of the **Patacancha** community. Locally people from this area are known as 'Huayruros' – the name of a red and black seed (*Ormosia coccinea*) thought to bring good luck and the same as the colour of their ponchos. The people in Patacancha and nearby Willoq are well known for their high-quality weavings with intricate designs reflecting aspects of their everyday lives and culture. This is a high mountain day with many alpaca, llamas, Andean geese, condors, puna ibis, Andean flickers, caracaras and coots – and superb scenery. Six to seven hours of walking.

Next day you head upwards again, following the valley gradually, then reaching **Lake Ipsaycocha** after two to three hours. From the lake you climb an hour more to reach the pass at **Abra Ipsay** (4,300m), with stunning views down towards **Lares**, ahead, and back towards the peaks and ridges of the previous day. It is a long trek down into the Lares Valley from here (join the Lares Valley at Huacahuasi), from puna mountain to populated fertile farmland; four hours' more trekking and you can soak your weary limbs in the Lares hot springs. The baths are open 24 hours a day and cost 6 soles.

! Updates website: For the latest updates go to www.bradtupdates.com/perutrekking. You can also post your feedback here – corrections, changes or even new hikes. Your information will be put on our website for the benefit of other travellers.

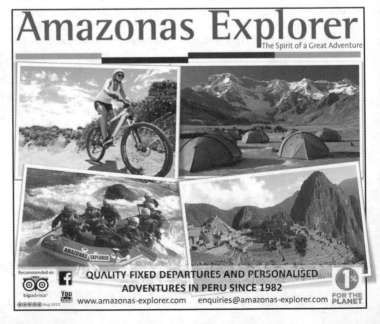

11

The Cordilleras Vilcabamba and Vilcanota

Now you are acclimatised, you are ready to tackle some of the longer walks that are the goal of most of the hikers who base themselves in Cusco. The cordilleras Vilcabamba and Vilcanota offer some of the best hiking on the continent. Not only are there snow-covered mountains, but also subtropical valleys, outstanding Inca ruins, and a traditional way of life that has remained unchanged for centuries. The only downside to this cornucopia of choice is that the adventurous Espiritu Pampa route in the Cordillera Vilcabamba is currently considered too dangerous for backpackers so is no longer described here. The area is overrun with 'narcos' involved in the cocaine trade. The situation is fluid so check with local tour operators who may be running group treks if they deem it safe.

THE VILCABAMBA REGION

The Vilcabamba range, approximately 85km long, is a spectacular part of the Andes, located northwest of Cusco, between the Apurímac and Urubamba rivers. Many people just visit Machu Picchu and go no further, but there are lots of trekking routes to suit all tastes within just a few hours of Cusco. If you don't want an organised trek (and the hordes of people) on the Inca Trail it's even possible to trek to Machu Picchu avoiding the trail altogether if you take the Salkantay route from Mollepata to Soraypampa and on to Santa Teresa (page 301).

Several giant snow-covered peaks rise out of the Vilcabamba massif, often clearly visible from the Lima to Cusco flight (sit on the left side of the plane). Salkantay (6,271m) is the highest peak in the area, towering above all the others. This mountain was revered by the Incas and is still very important to the people living in the Cusco area. Its name in Quechua means 'wild mountain'. The other big snow-covered mountain you'll see is Pumasillo (6,075m), west of Machu Picchu and the highest peak in the mini Sacsarayoc range, seen in glorious close-up on the Choquequirao trek.

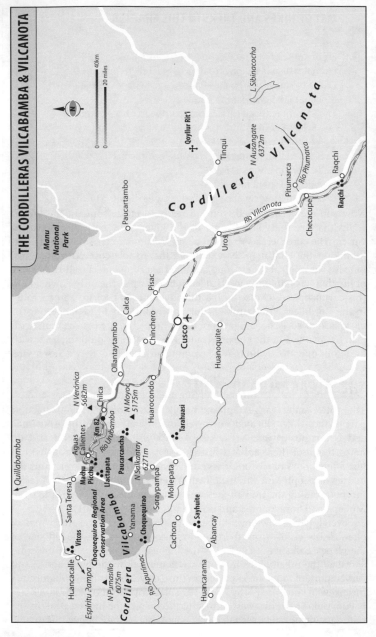

THE CORDILLERAS VILCABAMBA & VILCANOTA

Cordillera Vilcanota

L Sibinacocha

Qoyllur Rit'i

Tinqui

N Ausangate 6372m

Pitumarca
Río Pitumarca
Raqchi
Raqchi

Checacupe

Río Vilcanota

Manu National Park

Uros

Paucartambo

Pisac

Calca

Chinchero

Cusco

Huanoquite

Ollantaytambo

N Verónica 5682m

Chilca

Km 82

N Moyoc 5175m

Río Urubamba

Aguas Calientes

Machu Picchu

Llactapata

Paucarcandha

Huarocondo

Tarahuasi

Santa Teresa

Yanama

N Salkantay 6271m

Soraypampa

Mollepata

Choquequirao Regional Conservation Area

Vilcabamba

Choquequirao

Cachora

Sayhuite

Huancacalle

Vitcos

Espíritu Pampa

Abancay

N Pumasillo 6075m

Río Apurímac

Cordillera Vilcabamba

Huancarama

Quillabamba

40km

20 miles

N

284

Typical of the region is the verdant cloudforest of the rugged eastern side of the Vilcabamba Mountains, and the deep gorges of the **Apurímac** and **Urubamba**. These gorges have been gouged out of granite by centuries of glacier meltwater torrents forcing their way north and eastwards on their way to the rainforest. The area is also rich in Inca history: for nearly 50 years this remote region served as a hideout for the Inca resistance movement as it tried to regain control from the Spanish invaders in the 16th century. The Incas left behind many ceremonial platforms, gatehouses or *tambos*, and a network of beautifully constructed pathways linking its strongholds, the well-known Machu Picchu, and lesser-known but equally important sites such as Choquequirao and Llactapata, and Espíritu Pampa.

AGUAS CALIENTES (MACHU PICCHU PUEBLO)

Telephone code: 084
In the last two decades this little settlement near some hot springs has grown into a sizeable town serving the thousands of tourists who visit Machu Picchu. Unless you are on a day trip to Machu Picchu or are staying at the expensive (but wonderfully located) Sanctuary Lodge, you will spend a night here.

Machu Picchu Pueblo is the ever-sprawling, ramshackle railway town that is the gateway to Machu Picchu. Most people stick defiantly to its old name, Aguas Calientes. It is right on the banks of the Urubamba River, several hundred metres below Machu Picchu. The town is the last stop for the trains from Cusco and buses shuttle people from here up the hairpin road to the entrance to the Machu Picchu site, approximately 4km from the town. It's the sort of place you'll either love or hate, with plenty of character and quite unlike any other town in Peru. It is named after the **hot springs** at the top of the town (15 minutes' walk), which are

WHITE WATER AND INCA TRAIL ON CAR TYRES   *Joyce West*

I wanted to do something a little different for my 70th birthday. After numerous suggestions from various members of the family, my younger daughter suggested a few days canoeing down the Amazon followed by hiking the Inca Trail. I thought 'Why Not?'

It wasn't the big River Amazon but a tributary, the Apurímac, near Cusco, and we were starting near the source. At 3,900m it was bitterly cold. We all spent the first night sleepless in our tents trying to keep warm in our sleeping bags, wearing thermal pyjamas, mittens, scarf, woolly hat and socks. There was ice on our sleeping bags the next morning, my 70th birthday. Jane had secreted a tiny iced cake in her luggage and we were given a steaming mug of coca tea. So my first breakfast at the source of the Amazon was birthday cake and coca.

We were introduced to our inflatable rubber canoes, and after a talk about safety, we had to get ourselves into a wet suit which is similar to trying to put on wet rubber gloves but harder when it's a whole body, especially with arthritic thumbs. The young chaps in the party got very impatient, came across, lifted up the wet suit with me partially inside, and shook me down into it, zipped it up, plonked a baseball cap on top, then a tin helmet.

The first day was relatively easy as the water was shallow and bubbled over the pebbles like an English stream. We learned the basics … right, left, stop, back. On the second day the sides of the canyon had closed in and many tributaries had joined us, so the volume of water had increased dramatically. We were in the rapids!

That day I was bitten by an unseen spider and my feet ballooned and my fingers were like sausages. I couldn't get any shoes on. They said I wouldn't be able to walk the Inca Trail the following week, but I assured them that as I had worked hard to get the oomph, nothing was going to stop me. My oarsman kindly gave me a pair of his sandals made from car tyres. Although they were size 8, and I am (normally) size 5, they did the trick and I was able to continue.

certainly worth a visit if you've just trekked the Inca Trail. Then the hot baths feel wonderful, even though they seem to be in a constant state of refurbishment and don't look particularly clean. Basic changing facilities and showers are available, and there are lockers for your valuables. Swimming costumes and towels can be hired.

The town exists solely for tourists and hence has plenty of hostels, hotels, restaurants, small shops and an avenue of handicraft stalls. Guides to Machu Picchu are available from the agencies along the railway track. Information on the town is available at www.machupicchu.com.

I had just one day in Cusco to get my foot seen to. At the clinic they sliced off a section of the huge yellow blister from the spider bite for a lab analysis and bandaged my leg from hip to toe. I was told to keep it raised on a chair. But the next day we were starting the Inca Trail. When I decided to come on this holiday my main concern was that the youngsters would think 'Whatever is this old biddy doing here?' So from the start, I was determined to prove that I could keep up, despite the handicap of wearing a car tyre on one foot. The other foot had shrunk to a size where I could get a normal shoe on but I was never able to wear my expensive new hiking boots.

I did keep up. At the end of each day everyone was absolutely shattered. Our muscles and joints were aching and the temperature dropped to well below freezing very rapidly. A bowl of hot soup and a good laugh as we all compared notes about the events of the day gave us that last scrap of energy to drag ourselves off to our tents, don our assorted thermal nightwear, and hope that exhaustion would mean a complete night's sleep in spite of the cold.

Every morning we were woken by one of the porters playing his pipe. It was a haunting sound up there in the mountains, with the early morning mists swirling around us. When we heard it, we knew that at any moment a large hand would be thrust through the zip of the tent, with an outsize mug full of very hot coca tea. They would also give out plasters and medication for anyone who required it, and a bowl with just about an inch of water, for us both to share for our morning ablutions.

On the last day of our trek we said goodbye to the porters. We had taken four days to reach this point. They would run back to Cusco in one day in order to pick up the next group. We continued our journey for the remainder of the day, and at sunset were looking across the valley to Machu Picchu. We had made it! Now what will my family dream up for my 80th birthday?

11

GETTING THERE AND AWAY All tourist **trains** between Cusco and Machu Picchu use Machu Picchu Pueblo (for more detailed information see pages 238–9). There is no bus service to the town.

Buses to Machu Picchu leave at the railway end of the only road in town. They depart regularly throughout the day from 05.30, with a rush on departures when the tourist trains arrive. The last bus leaves Machu Picchu at 17.30. Tickets cost US$9.50 each way (US$18.50 return), and are purchased at the little ticket office next to the railway before getting on the bus.

 WHERE TO STAY AND EAT If you are just visiting Machu Picchu (so are not part of a trekking package) it is not usually necessary to book accommodation as there is such a plentiful supply to suit all budgets, and there is a **campsite** in a field by the river, with water and toilets. There are literally dozens of small **restaurants** all along the side of the railway, and lining the pedestrian street that climbs through the town to the hot pools.

🏠 **Gringo Bill's** ✎ 211046; e gringobill@ yahoo.com; www.gringobills.com. A rambling place, with a variety of rooms of all shapes & sizes. One even has an outdoor hot tub. US$47–125pp.

🏠 **Machu Picchu Hostal** By the railway; ✎ 211065; www.hostalmachupicchu.com. Central, clean & comfortable. US$65 with bath & b/fast.

MACHU PICCHU AND THE INCA TRAIL, 1969–73

My (Hilary's) first trip to Peru, travelling solo, was in 1969. Machu Picchu had been my goal ever since seeing a black-and-white photo of the ruins, swathed in cloud. I pinned it up on my kitchen wall.

The train to Machu Picchu was quite posh, even in those days. I took the 'Autowagon' with a glass roof and marvelled at the scenery: 'Without doubt the most beautiful train journey I've been on.' I'd brought my sleeping bag and I, and a Peace Corps volunteer, slept in the first ruin past the entrance, which had a roof and straw on the floor. We walked around the ruins in the light of the full moon 'when we could see almost as well as in daytime. As could the Mad Inca who wanders around all night blowing a whistle and swinging a machete to ward off evil spirits. He chased us back to our sleeping bags.'

In 1973, George and I walked 'The Inca Way' to Machu Picchu. The first mountain we had to deal with was the pile of produce bought by our neighbour on the train: 'Each time the train stopped she'd stand on my feet in order to bargain with the Indians on the platform. One time she bought a live hen and then found it wouldn't fit through the bars on the window. When the train stopped at Km88 it was quite hard to extricate ourselves.'

🏠 **Rupa Wasi** 📞211101; 📧 info@rupawasi.net; www.rupawasi.net. A lovely little ecolodge in a forested area on the end of town with a fabulous restaurant. Rooms US$72–113.

🏠 **La Cabaña** Halfway up the hill; 📞211048; www.lacabanamachupicchu.com. Clean & friendly. Has a spa & a good restaurant. US$130.

🏠 **Machu Picchu Pueblo** 📞211032; 📧 reservas@inkaterra.com; www.inkaterra.com. For that very special treat, it is well worth staying at this elegant & luxurious hotel, situated away from the town in its own private reserve. Bungalows in the forest, with a superb orchid garden, botanic garden & several trails. It's also excellent for birdwatching. From US$550 dbl.

✖ **Cafe Inkaterra** At the train station

✖ **Chullpi Machupicchu Restaurante** Avda Imperio de los Incas 140; 📞211350

✖ **Indio Feliz** Calle Lloque Yupanqui 103; 📞211090. Crêpes, bistro & restaurant. Franco-Peruvian cuisine.

✖ **Tree House** Calle Huanacaure 105; 📧 treehouse@rupawasi.net. High-quality, sophisticated Peruvian contemporary cuisine. Asian, Italian and Latin American styles influence the menu.

FEATURED TREKS IN THE VILCABAMBA REGION

The Inca Trail:
- From Km82 to Machu Picchu (*45km; 4 days*); pages 294–8
- From Km104 via Huiñay Huayna to Machu Picchu (*13km; 5–6hrs*); page 297

It wasn't easy following the trail. Often the path divided and often the most-worn path was the wrong one because of being walked twice: once to its dead-end, and once back again. There was a boggy stretch. We wrote in our book: 'The bog and wet moss will be ankle deep and it's really hopeless to try to keep your feet dry. Just resign yourself to sploshing through.' There was no designated camping. With only four others on the trail it was hardly needed. We slept in Huiñay Huayna, which was almost buried in lush vegetation, and when we arrived in Machu Picchu we hid our packs in the bushes and climbed Huayna Picchu with only our sleeping bags and some plastic. We'd planned to sleep in a cave but it was occupied by 'an evil Englishman' so we slept on the summit. In the rain. But the view at dawn, when the rain cleared and the rising sun turned the puffs and swathes of cloud pink was something I'll never forget.

So was it better in those days? Of course not. Yes, there were very few tourists, but there were copious amounts of litter and some of the Inca stonework was damaged by backpackers lighting fires in the ruins. Favoured camping sites were filthy with human waste. I'm glad for me that I saw Machu Picchu 45 years ago, but I'm glad for Machu Picchu that it is now so well looked after.

Trekking Salkantay:

- Chilca to Huayllabamba via Paucarcancha (*30km; 2–3 days*); pages 298–300
- Mollepata to Soraypampa (*about 16km; 7–8hrs*); pages 301–2
- The Salkantay Glacier Trek: Soraypampa to Chilca (*about 60km; 4–5 days*); pages 302–4
- The Salkantay Trek: Soraypampa to La Playa (or Santa Teresa) or Machu Picchu (*about 50km; 3–4 days*); pages 304–6
- La Playa to the hydro-electric plant and Machu Picchu via Llactapata (*about 12km; 1 day*); pages 306–10

Other treks in the Cordillera Vilcabamba:

- The Moyoc Circuit (*70km; 5–6 days*); pages 310–13
- Cachora to Huancacalle via Choquequirao (*100km; 8 days*); pages 313–20

THE INCA TRAIL

This is deservedly the most famous footpath in South America. It has everything: gorgeous mountain scenery, cloudforest and lush subtropical vegetation with numerous species of flowers, a stunning destination (Machu Picchu) and, above all, the Inca remains that give the trail its name. There are Inca paving stones, Inca stairways, an Inca tunnel, and of course the ruins: **Runkuracay**, **Sayacmarca**, **Phuyupatamarca**, **Huiñay Huayna** (Wiñay Wayna) and **Machu Picchu** itself. The normal, four-day trek requires a good degree of fitness and a willingness to sleep in a tent in around freezing conditions. However, there is a one-day trek from Km104 which gives you a taste of the trail without the camping (see box on page 297).

GETTING ORGANISED In the early part of this century, the Peruvian government instigated changes to the administration of the Inca Trail in an attempt to protect it from further damage by overuse and misuse. The main impact for backpackers was that individuals can no longer trek the Inca Trail on their own, nor can they use the cheap local train service. This means you have to book through an agency licensed to operate on the Inca Trail. They will provide you with a guide and support staff (it is not possible just to hire a guide). The number of trekkers allowed to walk the Inca Trail is limited to a daily maximum of 500 and permits are sold out months in advance, especially in the high season, so it is highly recommended to pre-book your Inca Trail trek before arriving in Cusco. There are around 200 licensed operators in Cusco (see pages 246–7 for specific recommendations). They will buy your Inca Trail permit and will be assigned campsites by the INC (National Institute of Culture) at the same time.

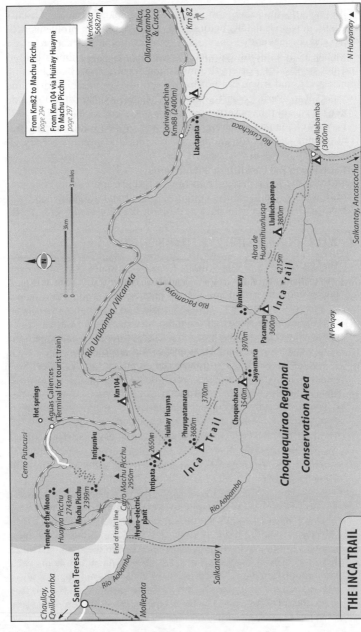

THE INCA TRAIL

From Km82 to Machu Picchu
page 294

From Km104 via Huiñay Huayna
to Machu Picchu
page 297

N Verónica
5682m

Chilca,
Ollantaytambo
& Cusco

Km 82

Qoriwayrachina
Km88 (2400m)

Llactapata

Rio Cusichaca

Huayllabamba
(3060m)

Salkantay, Ancascocha

N Huayanay

Lluilluchapampa
3800m

Abra de
Huarmihuañusqa
4215m

Inca Trail

Rio Pacamayo

Runkuracay

Pacamayo
3600m

N Palqay

3970m

Sayacmarca
3540m

Choquequirao Regional
Conservation Area

Choqueqhaca

3700m

Phuyupatamarca
3680m

Inca Trail

Rio Aobamba

Rio Urubamba /Vilcanota

Km104

Huiñay Huayna

Intipunku

2650m

Intipata
2950m

Cerro Machu Picchu

Hot springs

Aguas Calientes
(Terminal for tourist train)

Cerro Putucusi

Temple of the Moon

Huayna Picchu
2743m

Machu Picchu
2399m

End of train line

Hydro-electric
plant

Chaullay,
Quillabamba

Santa Teresa

Rio Aobamba

Mollepata

Salkantay

N

0   3km
0   3 miles

THE INCA TRAIL

Be very selective when choosing a tour company or guide. Discuss and write down all details beforehand. There have been problems with cheap and consequently poor-quality tours not fulfilling their promises, supplying poor camping equipment and food, leaving rubbish behind and not paying the porters the minimum wage. Be wary of choosing the cheapest, and if you are not happy with the organisation take time to report it to iPerú (tourist protection), INDECOPI (on the Plaza de Armas) or one of the conservation groups in Cusco (page 245).

Be wary of companies telling you that you are on a waitlist for an Inca Trail permit. There is no waitlist, nor do cancelled permits get resold. Any agency telling you otherwise is not a trustworthy company.

Expect to pay at least US$550 (*1,500 soles*) each for a four-day, three-night trek. The price depends on how informed and comfortable you want to be; the quality of the equipment, food and guide; which train service is used to get you back to Cusco; the size of the group; the

 ## WALKS IN THE VICINITY OF MACHU PICCHU

There is no point in reproducing the plethora of information, mostly speculative, about this most famous of ancient sites. The (human) guides know their stuff and help to bring some insight into why and how this place was built, and there is a selection of guidebooks available near the entrance. More than anything, however, this is a place for quiet contemplation and making your own discoveries. Sometimes the sight of an orchid or a lizard can be as enchanting as Inca stonework.

If you still have the energy you can do one of **two walks** while at Machu Picchu – both are well worth doing before heading down to Aguas Calientes, but note that the hikes up the mountains of Machu Picchu and Huayna Picchu each now require a separate permit, which have to be pre-booked at the time of booking your Inca Trail (US$60 each). So make sure you advise your tour company in advance should you wish to add these on.

Once back in Aguas Calientes you can enjoy the valley walk of Putucusi.

 MACHU PICCHU MOUNTAIN This lies just south of the site and overlooking it. It's a 500m climb up a well-made Inca pathway. There are some Inca constructions at the top that were probably for religious ceremonies, given the prominent position of the mountain and they look as though they have been damaged by treasure seekers. Allow two hours each way through lush forest, keeping a lookout for interesting birds, flowers and snakes sunbathing on the path. The path starts from the terraces where the Inca Trail comes in to Machu Picchu at the top of the site.

number of porters; and the experience of the guide. The service should include hotel pick-up and drop-off; a private bus to the trek's starting point; a licensed guide; Inca Trail and Machu Picchu entrance fee; the train back to Cusco; a two-person tent with mats to sleep on; porters to carry camping equipment; and a cook, all meals while on trek (three breakfasts, lunches and dinners) and boiled water for drinking. Expect to pay extra for: sleeping bag hire (US$20), the bus from Machu Picchu down to the train station (28 soles), any meals in Machu Picchu Pueblo, tips, hot springs entrance and porters to carry your personal gear (around 250 soles for four days, although this is sometimes included in the trekking price. A porter will carry a maximum of 20kg including tents and food, and his own gear. Some companies include a porter to carry six or 7kg of your personal stuff but some charge extra for this service – be sure to check when booking. Consider, too, whether you want to do any of the walks around Machu Picchu (see below) for which

 HUAYNA PICCHU MOUNTAIN This is the sugar-loaf-shaped lump which backs all those famous photos of Machu Picchu, and it looks impossible to climb. That is one of its attractions: a very steep, and almost hidden, flight of Inca stone-cut steps winds up the left-hand side of the mountain, hidden among the trees and scrub, and bringing you out at a spectacular viewpoint (though it's hard to ignore the presence of the hotel, and road to the river zigzagging below you). It will take you an hour, with an altitude gain of 200m. The number of hikers allowed to use this route has now been reduced to 400 per day and admission is in two groups, so you will either be starting your ascent between 07.00 and 08.00, or 10.00 and 11.00.

Less popular, under the same permit and an equally beautiful walk, is to the **Temple of the Moon**. There is some high-quality Inca stonework inside a cave, which was obviously a sacred place. This is on the west side of Huayna Picchu, 400m below the summit. For this and the previous walk, head for the path leading out of the north end of Machu Picchu.

 PUTUCUSI The verdant rocky lump on the east side of the river, opposite Machu Picchu, is a challenging climb. Take a guide with you if possible. Most of the ascent is up rickety wooden ladders, with short sections of path in-between. This scramble should only be attempted by serious climbers. From the top the views of Machu Picchu and beyond to Salkantay are pretty spectacular, but be warned: it's a hot, sweaty, slippery struggle to get there.

The Cordilleras Vilcabamba and Vilcanota

THE INCA TRAIL

11

there is an additional fee – it costs US$60 to go up Huayna Picchu or up Machu Picchu mountain.

The Inca Trail is always sold out several months in advance for the dry season (May to September); for this reason it is worth considering going between December and April (except February, when it is closed) even though this is the rainy season. But be warned: the trail can be very muddy and the passes covered in clouds and/or snow. Conversely, you may have beautiful weather and it will be considerably quieter.

WHAT TO TAKE Because so many people with little previous hiking experience do this trail it is worth emphasising the importance of careful preparations. We recommend a few extra snacks. Bring some chocolate and dried fruit or cereal bars for energy. Be prepared for warm days and freezing nights. An alpaca sweater is light and warm so ideal for the Inca Trail. Thermal underwear will help keep you warm at night and weighs very little. A woollen Cusco hat will make a big difference on the cold nights, as will gloves or mittens. A scarf (muffler) takes up almost no room and keeps your neck and chest cosy. Be prepared for rain: carry high-quality waterproofs.

Don't forget a good supply of plastic bags for carrying out your rubbish (although these should be provided by your trekking company). Bring your own toilet roll, and wet wipes or equivalent for washing when water is scarce, and disinfectant hand gel will help avoid diarrhoea when hand-washing facilities are limited.

Bring insect repellent against the very persistent biting flies in the lower areas and at Machu Picchu.

You need to bring your **passport** to show the security guys at the trail entrance. You will not get on the trail without your passport.

 From Km82 to Machu Picchu This is *the* Inca Trail, a four-day trek which starts at Km82 where you will pass through an entrance gate and have your permit and passport checked. The shorter **one-day Inca Trail** starts at Km104 (see box on page 297).

Distance	45km
Altitude	2,400–4,215m
Rating	Moderate
Timing	4 days
In reverse	Not permitted
Start of trail	Km82 (Piscacucho)
Transport at the end	Included in the package
Maps	IGN sheets *Santa Teresa–Machu Picchu* (27-q) and *Urubamba* (27-r)

Route description At Km82 (2,680m) you walk down to the entrance, where your tickets and passports are checked. Sign in here. Cross the bridge and make a right turn following the trail uphill for about 30 minutes, then walk on a rolling path with gentle ups and downs, the so-called 'Peruvian flat' with fabulous views of **Verónica** mountain.

You get a good view from the path over the Inca site of **Llactapata**, which was a supply station for Machu Picchu. Vast retaining walls have converted the steeply sloping hillside into agricultural terraces: a beautiful sight. Just below Llactapata, the Río Cusichaca, a tributary of the Urubamba, takes a spectacular plunge into the ground and runs through a subterranean channel for some distance.

You descend to the **Cusichaca River** and then follow the path up the left side of it until you reach the village of **Huayllabamba** (3,000m). On this first day you trek 10km and climb a total of 320m. By the time you reach Huayllabamba it is likely to be very hot and you will welcome the cold drinks in the village: it makes its living out of Inca Trail hikers.

> **Note:** You must have your **passport** with you – you will not be allowed to enter the trail without it.

At Huayllabamba the trail turns right (northwest) up the Llullucha Valley. After slogging and sweating upwards for about 1½ hours you will drop down to a grassy clearing, popularly known as **The Forks**. There is a designated campsite here. The path then enters woods – first scrub, then beautiful cloudforest where the trees are hung with moss. These fairy-tale woods will help keep your mind off the fact that you are still going steeply uphill with no sign of respite. Eventually, however, the trees become more stunted and you emerge into a meadow, Llulluchapampa. There are latrines with running water and sinks here. Higher up in the meadows there are some pit latrines as well. From The Forks to the meadow is about two hours. This is the last campsite before the pass, aptly named (if you are a female hiker) **Abra de Huarmihuañusqa**, 'Dead Woman's Pass' (4,215m), which you can see ahead of you.

It will take you between 1½ and three hours to climb to the top of the pass, depending on your speed. This is the highest point on the trail, so take heart – if you survive this, you'll survive the other passes. Take time to look around you. You should be able to pick out the circular ruins of Runkuracay ahead, just below the next pass. The descent is steep but not difficult. Just follow the trail on the left side of the valley to the valley floor and the next designated campsite at Pacaymayo (3,600m). Nearby are some huts and toilets built by the INC, that have sinks and running water.

From the valley floor it will take you about an hour to reach **Runkuracay**, a ruin that is not, perhaps, very impressive in itself, but occupying a commanding position overlooking the valley, and at the end of a series of rock-hewn steps that at last gives you a feeling that you are on the trail of the Incas. There is another campsite here.

From Runkuracay the path is clear over the second pass (Abra de Runkuracay, 3,970m) and, excitingly, much of the time you are on **Inca steps**. The descent down the steps is steep, so take care. Just before the trail turns right, you'll see the sign for Sayacmarca. These ruins lie about an hour from the top of the pass and the name, which means 'the Inaccessible' or 'Secret City', is apt. You approach Sayacmarca up a superbly designed stone staircase. This is a diversion (the main trail continues its gradual descent to the right) but don't let fatigue persuade you to miss it.

Like so many Inca ruins, no-one really knows the purpose of **Sayacmarca**, but these are the visible facts: it was built on a precipice commanding a spacious view; there are no agricultural terraces so the complex could not have supported many inhabitants; ritual baths and an aqueduct run around the outside of the main wall; and there are curious stone rings set in the wall by trapezoid openings. For me the mystery adds to the beauty, and it is beauty all the way from here – if you are fortunate with the weather.

The trail continues down to the valley floor. From here it becomes a glorious **Inca road**, being on a raised causeway over marshy ground that then rises up through cloudforest. Stone paving on raised stone foundations, steps and a gentle gradient make for easy walking, and even if it is raining (and it often is) you will marvel at the Inca workmanship. Before the climb to the third pass there is a campsite with toilets. During the ascent you climb through one Inca tunnel, and if it is a clear day you will have the added bonus of a view of Mount **Salkantay** over to your left. The pass (3,700m) is used as a spectacular campsite with, if you're lucky, a view of sunrise on Salkantay. Just below the pass, about two hours from Sayacmarca, are the impressive ruins of **Phuyupatamarca**. Access is down a steep flight of stairs. Clear water runs through the channels cut into the rock that feed five baths, leading one from the other down the hill.

From Phuyupatamarca an **Inca staircase** leads from the west side of the ruins (the far end from the baths) and disappears into the jungle, taking you down a thousand steps. You'll think that your knees will never feel the same again. About 2km beyond Phuyupatamarca you will come to an **electricity pylon**; the trail splits here: on the left it takes you roughly 20 minutes to get to the site of **Intipata**, which is worth a visit, and then on to Huiñay Huayna, but if you take the right-hand fork you go direct to Huiñay Huayna (also spelt Wiñay Wayna).

The end comes in the form of the old trekkers' hostel (now closed), which marks the beginning of the trail to the ruins of Huiñay Huayna (Wiñay Wayna). This is the last camping spot before Machu Picchu and it is almost always full to bursting with tents in very close proximity of each other.

Huiñay Huayna lies just below the campsite, round to the right as you are descending, and is the most extensive of the ruins so far. It has some beautiful stonework (though spoilt by clumsy restoration), a fantastic location, and an air of mystery often lacking in the crowded Machu Picchu ruins.

The trail from the campsite to **Machu Picchu** (1½ hours away) is clearly marked. Most groups try to leave Huiñay Huayna by 05.30 so they can get to Machu Picchu before sunrise. The sky starts getting light by 06.00 and the first rays of the sun reach Machu Picchu around 07.00. The trail contours a mountainside and disappears into cloudforest full of begonias, bromeliads and tree ferns, before coming to a steep flight of stairs leading up to the first Inca gate. The path continues to the main gate, **Intipunku** – 'the Gateway of the Sun' – and suddenly the whole of Machu Picchu is spread out before you. A magical moment.

After drinking in the scene, you can stroll down to the hotel, radiating smugness among the groups of tourists who arrived by train, and enjoy an expensive buffet breakfast or lunch in the Machu Picchu Sanctuary Lodge (*www.sanctuarylodgehotel.com*) or make use of the (also expensive) snack bar near the entrance. You might even take a look at the ruins! There is a place for storing your luggage (for a fee) near the entrance.

Most groups will take the train back to Cusco that afternoon or stay at Machu Picchu Pueblo (Aguas Calientes) (see page 285), although

 ## FROM KM104 VIA HUIÑAY HUAYNA TO MACHU PICCHU

A mini Inca Trail runs from Km104 (on the railway line) up to Huiñay Huayna and then on to Intipunku. It takes two to three hours to Huiñay Huayna, from where it is 1½ hours to Machu Picchu. It's a lovely hike for those who can't face the whole Inca Trail and you will get to walk on original Inca paving and up those narrow Inca stairways, as well as passing a waterfall and masses of orchids on your way to Huiñay Huayna. The trail fee is 130 soles. Take plenty of water as it can be a hot and dusty climb for the first two hours. Be aware of the time as the gate at Huiñay Huayna officially closes at 14.00, so if you arrive later you will be forced to stay overnight. You need to catch the first train in the morning to do it all in one day.

An organised tour through an agency in Cusco costs US$290–450 per person, including transfers, train tickets, entrance fees, guide. **Note:** this is often sold by agencies as the two-day Inca Trail, even though it is really one day of walking – the second day is your guided tour and return transport to Cusco.

some will be booked in at the Sanctuary Lodge, near the entrance to the ruins, which costs US$700 for a double but gives you the exceptional opportunity to explore the site as soon as it opens in the morning. Alternatively you will have arranged to camp by the river. If you still have the energy you can walk down to the railway line (or campsite) from the ruins. Allow an hour, and take the short cuts across the zigzags of the road (these are sign-posted). Machu Picchu Pueblo (Aguas Calientes) and its train station is a five-minute walk down the track.

SALKANTAY HIKES

The cordillera's highest mountain, Salkantay (6,271m), provides an awesome backdrop for these hikes. You have a choice of keeping high, taking the seldom-used but dramatic route beneath the glaciers of Salkantay itself to link up with a trail to Chilca, or dropping down to the subtropical regions to reach Machu Picchu via Santa Teresa. The latter is a far more popular route and now commonly known as The Salkantay Trek. The area is seldom crowded – this is Peru at its most perfect.

Both the above treks share the same route from Mollepata to Soraypampa and the bonus of the opportunity to visit the lovely Inca site of Tarahuasi before arriving at Mollepata, which lies at a subtropical 2,803m. It overlooks a citrus-growing area where flocks of parakeets screech overhead. If you start the trek at Mollepata then the gradual ascent towards Salkantay is made up a valley full of flowering shrubs buzzing with hummingbirds, across streams and past grass-thatched houses, while ahead of you the snow-covered flanks of Salkantay and Humantay gleam in the afternoon sun. A dirt road has been built all the way to Soraypampa so you can skip the first day trekking and travel, instead, by vehicle. At the head of the valley is the tiny settlement of Soraypampa, where there are several choices for camping and even a luxury hotel. From Soraypampa you have the choice of two treks: the subtropical delights and thermal baths of the trail to Santa Teresa and from there to Machu Picchu, or the icy, breathless, stunningly beautiful Salkantay Glacier Trek which takes you back to the Sacred Valley.

An alternative starting point is Chilca, which can be used to access the high route around Salkantay, or be walked as a shorter two-day semi-circuit. This hike is described below.

 CHILCA TO HUAYLLABAMBA VIA PAUCARCANCHA This trail used to be an alternative to the traditional start to the Inca Trail at Km88, intercepting the trail at Huayllabamba. Now the regulations forbidding independent trekking rule this out (unless you are accompanied by a licensed guide) but it is a beautiful, interesting and adventurous hike in its own right, taking you close to the lovely nevados of **Huayanay**

and **Salkantay Este**, sister to the region's highest mountain, Salkantay, to the west, and via the interesting Inca ruins of **Paucarcancha**. It can also be linked with the splendid and seldom-trekked (these days) route around Salkantay (pages 302–4) or the Moyoc Circuit (pages 310–13). Either extension is preferable to finishing at Huayabamba because of the problems of being allowed to hike back to the roadhead, given that this is on the highly regulated Inca Trail.

Distance	30km
Altitude	2,800–4,600m
Rating	Moderate–difficult
Timing	2–3 days
In reverse	Yes, from Paucarcancha if linked with the Salkantay route on pages 302–4
Start of trail	Chilca
Maps	IGN sheet *Urubamba* (27-r)

Route description From Chilca, head due south up the valley opposite the bridge across the Urubamba River, and follow the trail which keeps close to the quebrada, west and northwest. After about five hours you reach the small village of **Ancascocha**. Turn right here (southwest) and head up the valley to your right. There are waterfalls here and some good camping spots. The trail continues towards a pass, skirting left of a small lake and reaching the top at 4,600m, some two to three hours of strenuous climbing from Ancascocha. The two snowpeaks on your right are Salkantay Este and Huayanay.

The trail now drops down towards the village of Quesca, two to three hours away, going to the right of the broad pampa, and down to **Quebrada**

> **𝑖 MOUNTAIN LODGES OF PERU**
>
> Mountain Lodges have built four luxury lodges that allow you to trek the Salkantay route in five-star comfort. They are located at ideal spots along the trail, and offer the complete package, with treks fully guided and supported. The lodges have hot tubs, gourmet food and very comfortable beds. Prices are from US$2,690 in the off-season for a seven-day trek that includes a night in the Machu Picchu Pueblo hotel and a day in Machu Picchu. This trek can be booked through UK and US tour operators or on the Mountain Lodges website (*www.mountainlodgesofperu.com*). They are partnering Yanapana Peru to sponsor the reforestation of Soraypampa in an effort to preserve the ecosystem.

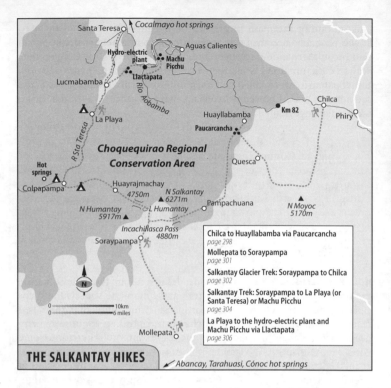

Santa Teresa○ ↑Cocalmayo hot springs

Hydro-electric plant
●● Machu Picchu
Aguas Calientes
Lucmabamba○
Llactapata
Río Aobamba

⛺
La Playa

Choquequirao Regional Conservation Area

Huayllabamba○
Km 82
Chilca○
Phiry○
Paucarcancha

Quesca○

Hot springs ⛺
Colpapampa○ ⛺
Huayrajmachay○
4750m
N Salkantay ▲6271m
▲ L Humantay
N Humantay 5917m ▲
Pampachuana○
N Moyoc ▲ 5170m
Incachillasca Pass 4880m
Soraypampa○

0 ┣━━━━━┫ 10km
0 ┣━━━━━┫ 6 miles

N ⬇

Chilca to Huayllabamba via Paucarcancha
page 298

Mollepata to Soraypampa
page 301

Salkantay Glacier Trek: Soraypampa to Chilca
page 302

Salkantay Trek: Soraypampa to La Playa (or Santa Teresa) or Machu Picchu
page 304

La Playa to the hydro-electric plant and Machu Picchu via Llactapata
page 306

Mollepata○

THE SALKANTAY HIKES

↙ Abancay, Tarahuasi, Cónoc hot springs

Cusichaca and some Inca remains (probably a tambo). Follow the left slope of the valley to **Quesca**. Cross the Cusichaca River and follow its left bank downstream to **Paucarcancha**, a little-known semi-circular ruin in an inspiring position at the junction of two rivers, about two hours from Quesca. Here you have the option of hooking up with the Salkantay Glacier Trek by heading south up the Cusichaca River (recommended), or continuing to Huayllabamba (having checked that you can leave from here) in about an hour.

LIMATAMBO, TARAHUASI AND AROUND If backpacking the route to Sorayampa, I strongly recommend you spend the first night in **Limatambo**, about 10km before the Mollepata turn-off. It is a pleasant, low-lying little town with basic accommodation or camping possibilities. Nearby, at **Tarahuasi**, is an Inca temple with one of the finest examples anywhere of Inca polygonal masonry in a long retaining wall. On the upper level are 28 tall niches, thought by John Hemming to have been for liveried attendants or for mummies. The stonework, in rosette patterns, is orange coloured through its covering of lichen. Tarahuasi was on one of the main Inca roads (Chinchaysuyo) leading to Cusco. It was probably a control gate at the site of a battle between the Spanish and Incas. Hernando de Soto and his soldiers were resting here on their way to Cusco in 1533 when they were attacked by 4,000 Inca warriors; four Spaniards were killed and many injured. This amazing place sees few tourists and at present there is no charge to visit it (although that is likely to change).

About 15km beyond Limatambo the rivers **Apurímac** and **Colorado** meet, at a place called **Airahua**. Just down the river you can visit the hot springs at **Cónoc**. There are also some good routes to explore on foot in this area. You can walk the **Chichaysuyo Inca trail**, which goes towards Cónoc (two to three hours), or take a path going upwards and northwards towards **Rumirumi** and **Minaspata**, from where you have a great view over the Apurímac canyon. The Incas had a hanging bridge over the Apurímac at Maucachaca, just where the Quebrada Honda reaches the Apurímac. This immense bridge was 45m long, and amazed the early chroniclers.

MOLLEPATA TO SORAYPAMPA Most hikers doing the two Salkantay treks do the first part of the route (described here) by vehicle but if you have the time the walk to Soraypampa is scenic, follows paths rather than the road for most of the route, and is a good acclimatisation day. You may be able to hire **pack animals** in Mollepata to take the luggage to Soraypampa: a sensible idea because this gives a good start on that long, uphill first day. If you do succumb to the temptation of public transport there are minibuses from Mollepata to Soraypampa for just 8 soles.

Distance	About 16km (22km if you follow the new road all the way)
Altitude	2,800–3,500m (approx)
Rating	Moderate
Timing	7–8 hours
In reverse	Possible
Start of trail	Transport from Cusco to Mollepata leaves from Avenida Arcopata early in the morning. The 06.00 bus is recommended and the 76km ride takes 2–3 hours.
Maps	IGN sheets *Santa Teresa–Machu Picchu* (27-q) and *Urubamba* (27-r)

Route description Mollepata has improved from the days, over a century ago, when George Squier described it as a 'place unsurpassed in

11

⊙ **Side trip:** It is well worth spending two nights at Soraypampa to experience one of the most stunning parts of the Andes on an unsurpassable day hike to **Humantay Lake**. There is a good path up the valley to the turquoise lake, beneath the imposing 5,917m peak of Humantay. Follow the valley northwest from Soraypampa towards Humantaycocha (Soraypampacocha on some maps). There is a clear path up to the lake which continues on up the valley and back round to the south overlooking Soraypampa. Return the same way.

evil repute by any in Peru'. There is an attractive green plaza, some pretty houses, a few shops and even basic accommodation.

The path heads steeply uphill just outside Mollepata in the direction of the mountains. Ask locals if you're not sure, but it's a pretty obvious trail, going out of the plaza in the northwest corner, then right at the T-junction. Continue up the left side of the valley (northwest), following a cement **irrigation ditch** until the top of a pass 3½ hours from Mollepata. Then, instead of continuing beside the canal, head steeply up to the right. The trail will eventually take you over a pass and into the next valley, **Río Blanca**. Look out for two crosses on the hill (Marcocasa, 3,354m) where there are possible campsites. Below the cross, a difficult-to-follow trail bears round to the right, keeping on high ground, heading northeast through shrubs and bushes. There are many paths through the bushes, all leading to the same main trail, about 45 minutes from the cross. You should be on the west side of the Río Blanca Valley. Continue walking until you join the **dirt road**.

Once you join the road the way is clear and gently uphill, with splendid views of **Humantay** (5,917m) appearing at the end of the valley. From here, **Soraypampa** is reached in about three to four hours of easy and beautiful hiking. The view of Salkantay appears just before Soraypampa and you will see one of the four luxurious lodges of Mountain Lodges of Peru (page 299). There are several camping spots beyond the lodge, and even covered barns where you can camp, giving added protection against the elements. ⊙ From here, visit Humantay Lake, above.

THE SALKANTAY GLACIER TREK: SORAYPAMPA TO CHILCA This is
the spectacular option, but also the toughest, passing high around the flank of Salkantay and visiting some little-known Inca ruins. Since the Inca Trail regulations forbade independent trekking this once-popular route, which formerly offered an alternative starting point to the trail, is not often used – which is part of its attraction. The additional two days to Chilca, however, has added to the challenge. If you do it you're very unlikely to meet any other trekkers.

Route description An hour beyond Soraypampa is the giant V of a moraine spreading down from Salkantay. The trail, not very clear, runs

Distance	About 60km
Altitude	2,800–4,880m
Rating	Difficult
Timing	4–5 days from Soraypampa
In reverse	Possible. Follow the directions from Chilca to Paucarcancha (page 298) and continue to Soraypampa
Start of trail	Soraypampa
Transport at the end	There are regular buses between Chilca and Cusco
Maps	IGN sheets *Santa Teresa–Machu Picchu* (27-q) and *Urubamba* (27-r)

northeast up the right side of the moraine, crossing some streams which run from it. After some steep climbing, the terrain levels out and the trail turns sharply to the right and uphill, near a **big boulder**, and continues along the right-hand bank of a small stream for about an hour (the stream may be dry). Before reaching a flat, boggy meadow, you'll see a **low cliff** (about 5m) hung with icicles formed by the dripping water. Cross the stream below the cliff and climb straight up to the **meadow**. The trail seems to disappear in this boggy stretch, but you can pick it up where the meadow starts to dry out towards the centre and follow the path a little to the left. It's worth making a detour to the **glacier** (if it hasn't receded too far to make this practical). You can see the layers of ice representing annual precipitation, rather like the rings on a tree-stump. Notice, too, the quality of the ice: the old, compact ice is blue and almost clear, while new ice is frosty-looking with trapped air.

Above the plateau the path zigzags up the reddish-coloured scree slope, becoming more conspicuous as it nears the top of the pass of **Incachillasca**, which lies at the top of the scree in the saddle of two minor ridges. This is an impressive 4,880m and it will take you five to six hours to climb here from Soraypampa. The view makes it all worthwhile. The path descending on the other side is quite clear as it traverses the right-hand (east) side of the mountain. There are some good camping places (about 1½ hours from the pass) at the point where the river and trail make a sharp left turn down the valley.

The trail continues down the right bank of the stream to some stone corrals, about three hours from the pass, then crosses the quebrada and follows it down the upper Cusichaca Valley. Keep to the left-hand bank of the river as it turns northeast, picks up speed, and descends through a small gorge. About an hour past the moraine, just past a campesino settlement (**Pampachuana**; you can camp here) on the right-hand bank, the river is canalised for draining the pampa. Shortly after the end of the canal, cross to the right bank via a **footbridge** and follow a good path along the right-hand side of the river down the narrow, steep valley to the **Quesca River** junction and settlement some 1–1½ blister-making hours away.

The seldom-visited Inca fortress **Paucarcancha** stands here. From the foot of the fortress you'll see the trail leading to southeast to Chilca via Quesca and Ancascocha, one or two days' hike away (see pages 298–9). Alternatively, if you have an Inca Trail permit, continue down the valley and join the trail at Huallabamba.

 THE SALKANTAY TREK: SORAYPAMPA TO LA PLAYA (OR SANTA TERESA) OR MACHU PICCHU This lovely and varied hike is now the normal route onwards from Soraypampa. There is one high pass (4,750m) and then it is mostly downhill through forested valleys, above deep ravines, past (or in) a wonderful natural hot bath, until you end up in the citrus groves of Santa Teresa. This small subtropical village used to be linked by rail to Machu Picchu, but both the village and the railway were almost completely destroyed by a landslide in 1998. Santa Teresa was rebuilt and today is an unattractive collection of temporary constructions, mostly wooden houses with tin roofs. The remains of the old town are interesting to visit, and there are excellent hot springs just outside the town. Although the railway to Santa Teresa itself has never been repaired, Machu Picchu can be accessed from the station at the hydro-electric plant (*hidroeléctrica*), a short bus journey away. Alternatively, there is the option of trekking to the hydro-electric plant via the Inca site of Llactapata (pages 308–9).

Distance	About 50km
Altitude	1,500–4,750m
Rating	Moderate–difficult
Timing	3–4 days
In reverse	Possible – but you'd better like walking uphill!
Start of trail	Soraypampa
Transport at the end	Check transport details before you leave Cusco. There's a train from the hydro-electric station to Aguas Calientes, or you can take a minibus to Santa María (*2–3hrs*) on the Cusco–Quillabamba road and from there a bus back to Cusco (*5–6hrs*).
Maps	IGN sheet *Santa Teresa–Machu Picchu* (27-q)

Route description From Soraypampa go up the left side of the moraine at the head of the valley, crossing to the left bank of a stream to pick up a path leading up the side of the mountain. It goes steeply uphill for half an hour, then comes to a series of **zigzags** ('Siete Culebras' is the local name of this stretch). At the top of the seventh switchback the terrain levels out under Salkantay's lateral moraine, and drops gently down to the small **Laguna Soirococha**. The pass you see above is, alas, a false one; the main pass is a little further on, but the view of Salkantay looming above you more than compensates for the effort. The real pass at 4,750m is reached three to four hours from the moraine, and is marked by a **pile of stones**, apacheta, which grows daily as each traveller adds his pebble to thank the apus (mountain gods) for a safe trip.

The trail descends to the left-hand side of the valley, becoming indistinct in swampy areas. If the weather is bad there are caves providing shelter about 20 minutes below the pass. Once the valley narrows there is only one obvious trail to the left of the river. At one to two hours from the pass you'll reach **Huayrajmachay** ('Eye of the Wind'). This is where Mountain Lodges have their second lodge, Wayra Lodge (page 299). You can camp nearby, but just 20 minutes below the lodge is a backpackers' camp maintained by the Regional Government of Cusco. There is water available throughout this day's trek.

You'll leave the beautiful pyramid-shaped peak of Humantay behind as you drop below the treeline, known as *la ceja de selva* ('eyebrow of the jungle'), and walk through groves of bamboo with many orchids and other flowers and lots of hummingbirds. Don't forget to keep looking back at the snowpeaks behind you, framed by bamboo fronds. After about four hours you'll drop steeply down to the bridge across the **Río Chalhuay**. This is a beautiful camping area, but there's an even better one an hour further on. Several of the camping areas are maintained by volunteers. Those trekking with Mountain Lodges of Peru will stay at the nearby Colpa Lodge.

Twenty minutes beyond the tiny settlement of **Colpapampa**, where there is a campsite, you will find the **hot springs**. These were damaged in a landslide, but the rebuilding should have been completed by the time you read this and they should provide a wonderful break from your exertions. To add to the enjoyment you are now walking steadily downhill and pass through several small settlements where refreshments are available.

You are now at the confluence of two rivers, the Totora and the Santa Teresa, and you'll be following the latter all the way down to the town of the same name. After the bridge the trail stays close to the river (ignore a fork to your left) and then, surprisingly (because you were expecting 'downhill all the way'), climbs up to contour round the mountainside through **bamboo groves**. Continue on the footpath on the left side of the river; the dirt road for vehicles is on the right bank of the river, heading from Totora down to Santa Teresa. The landslides that damaged the hot springs have also altered the trail so expect some variation of the route described here. Soon you will come to a **stream** that disrupts the trail. Go up this for about 8m to pick up the trail again on the other side. Carry on uphill to a spectacular **waterfall**. This cascade drops some 300m and the trail crosses it midway. A perfect shower, and the water and air temperature is now warm enough for you to welcome a bath. Following the trail up and down, you come to a second waterfall, with swimming in the pool above. This is an incredibly beautiful stretch, with begonias, purple and orange orchids and strawberries lining the path. Take care on narrow sections and small unstable bridges.

Some three to four hours after the hot springs you'll come to the hamlet of **La Playa** (also known as Sahuayaco). Basic provisions and drinks are available here. Camping in La Playa is the norm as there are shops, private campsites and showers (even hot ones). It can be a little noisy and as there are many people be careful with your belongings. A dirt road reaches La Playa from Santa Teresa, and it is possible to find transport for this 45-minute bus journey. The alternative is a hot, dusty walk from La Playa through citrus, banana and coffee plantations to **Santa Teresa**.

The hot springs at **Cocalmayo**, just outside the town of Santa Teresa, are being rebuilt after the floods of 2011, and are highly recommended after your long hike. In Santa Teresa there are some small shops and basic supplies and hostels. It is a 20-minute bus ride from here to the **hydro-electric plant** from where you can take the train to **Machu Picchu Pueblo**. Alternatively, continue on foot from La Playa via Llactapata as detailed below.

 LA PLAYA TO THE HYDRO-ELECTRIC PLANT AND MACHU PICCHU VIA LLACTAPATA Llactapata is a stunningly located and still rarely visited Inca site, offering the most perfect views (if not cloudy!) across the Aobamba Valley to Machu Picchu, 3km away (as the crow flies). The location is no accident. The explorer and Inca expert, Hugh Thomson, believes that it was 'a place from which [the Incas] could both admire Machu Picchu and take astronomical readings'. The site is set on the side of a steep valley with 6,000m glaciated peaks towering above, and deep river-cut gorges below. Lost for centuries and only rediscovered in 2003, this beautiful place is in danger of being destroyed by grazing cattle and encroaching vegetation as it is unprotected, lying as it does, outside the Machu Picchu Sanctuary jurisdiction. This is an easy extension to the Santa Teresa trek, and recommended if you have the time.

Distance	About 12km
Altitude	1,870–2,800m
Rating	Moderate
Timing	1 day
In reverse	Possible, but unusual
Start of trail	La Playa
Transport at the end	There's a train from the hydro-electric plant to Aguas Calientes or you can walk. Buy tickets for the train back to Poroy station just outside Cusco or to Ollantaytambo in advance in Cusco. From Ollantaytambo you can jump on a bus for 8 soles, for the two-hour ride to Cusco.
Maps	IGN sheet *Santa Teresa–Machu Picchu* (27-q)

Route description Continue walking from La Playa along the dirt road to begin with, then on the right side of the river. Take a right turn after an hour or so at **Lucmabamba** (2,135m) where the path to Llactapata is signposted to your right-hand side. If you continue down the road for another 100m, just past the football pitch is the Lucmabamba campsite with cold showers and fresh water.

The walk up to Llactapata is up an original Inca trail, initially in very good condition but gradually deteriorating. This is a big coffee-growing area and beans can be seen laid out to dry by the wayside. Mountain Lodge's Lucma Lodge is here. As you climb steeply, farms are replaced by virgin cloudforest that is rich in orchids, hummingbirds and butterflies. Get your binoculars out and enjoy the wildlife! After about three hours of hot steamy climbing, you reach the pass (2,800m) and from there it is another 30 minutes down to the amazing Inca site of **Llactapata** and your first sight of Machu Picchu in the distance. Take some time to explore and enjoy the view across the valley to Machu Picchu where ant-like tourists wander through the world famous Inca site.

11

MACHU PICCHU'S OBSERVATORY: LLACTAPATA

© Hugh Thomson 2013

During those heady days of exploration when he cleared Machu Picchu in 1912, Hiram Bingham also visited another Inca site to the west, called Llactapata, about which he published very little (the name Llactapata means 'high town' in Quechua, so is common in the Andes: another Inca site is similarly named at the bottom of the Cusichaca Valley, at the start of the Inca Trail, which often causes confusion).

I first went there in 1982, but the site I saw differed in certain key regards from Bingham's description, as did later reports from other explorers. Over the years, my suspicion grew that we might be dealing with a far larger site than anybody had realised, and that previous explorers had each found a part of a much greater whole. Inca sites often comprise several dispersed sectors.

So in 2003 I organised a large Royal Geographical Society supported expedition, with further help from the Mount Everest Foundation, to do the first thorough investigation of the whole site. Together with the American archaeologist Gary Ziegler, we used infrared techniques to scan the hillside for stone remains from the air. When this failed to work, we led a team of over 40 field-workers and support staff in on foot to try to clear the dense cloudforest cover. Revelation followed revelation. The most unusual feature of the site was a long sunken passageway that ran some 150ft (50m) without access doors to either side. It seemed to have no clear architectural function. This passageway can be seen by visitors to the site today, lying to the far side when approaching from the path, past the plaza. After clearing the vegetation away we emerged at the far end onto a plateau that faced directly towards Machu Picchu. The sight line to the great city, over the valley and in between, was remarkable. Nor was it accidental: Dr Kim Malville, the expert on archaeo-astronomy who accompanied us, calculated that it lay directly in line with sunrise at the June Solstice, which together with the rise of the Pleiades constellation was used in the pre-Columbian Andes to tell the beginning of certain agricultural seasons.

Because the corridor was so long and relatively narrow, when viewed from the far back end the angle of aperture created by the open gateway was precise, and allowed for the rising of the Pleiades and the June Solstice sun to be seen with considerable accuracy: indeed, the dawn sun would only reach the end of the corridor at the time of the June Solstice, as I confirmed on a later visit. This momentous discovery was given further credence by research from source materials about the Incas' study of both the Pleiades and June Solstice elsewhere. It was confirmation of our major finding about the site: that Llactapata was in effect an observatory for Machu Picchu, fulfilling some of the same functions as the Coricancha did for Cusco.

The Incas had built Llactapata as a place from which they could both admire Machu Picchu and take astronomical readings. The layout of the main buildings (in the cleared sector visible today) also corresponded in a remarkable way with the layout used at the Coricancha, the main Sun Temple in Cusco; we know from Spanish chronicles that they used the Coricancha as a template for other sites around the empire.

Overall, the site turned out to be far larger than anyone remotely suspected, with five sectors spread out over the hillside and a two-storey temple above. Most importantly, it also aids greatly with the interpretation of Machu Picchu, to which it is so closely aligned and whose function has been hotly debated in recent years. It is the only Inca settlement in direct sight of Machu Picchu and an Inca road leads from there in the direction of Llactapata, across a drawbridge of logs against a cliff.

The western side of Machu Picchu has always been considered the 'blind side' of Machu Picchu. Bingham could not understand why the Sacred Plaza, the most important grouping of buildings anywhere on the site, was open on that side and faced west: he presumed that the Incas had just not got around to erecting another building that side, whereas in fact they may deliberately have left it open to focus attention towards Llactapata and the distant Mt Pumasillo, with the Sacristy and a curved mirador, a viewpoint, orientated towards it.

There has always been an assumption that Machu Picchu was at the 'end of the line' on the Inca trail from Cusco, a final destination for the Inca emperor and his retinue, just as it is for tourists today. But it seems clear that it was just a stopping point on a much longer trail which would have continued on from Machu Picchu over the 'drawbridge route' and through Llactapata into the heart of the Vilcabamba.

The Llactapata that Hiram Bingham first reported still needs proper restoration to survive the encroaches of the cloudforest; only one sector has been cleared since our expedition's report, and this often suffers from the attentions of cattle, attracted ironically by the small patch of pasture that now surrounds the cleared sector. The site currently lies outside the Machu Picchu Historical Sanctuary and at present receives little protection or conservation, both of which are badly needed.

Hugh Thomson is author of The White Rock: An Exploration of the Inca Heartland, *and* Cochineal Red *(published as* A Sacred Landscape *in the USA). Both have sections on Llactapata. See www.thewhiterock.co.uk.*

Backpackers wishing to do some treks in the Salkantay area without having to carry full camping gear should contact Edwin (m *974229695 (Spanish), or Sara* m *980421554*) who runs a low-cost trek staying at his own basic lodgings. For 30 soles per person he has *hospedajes* in **Soraypampa** (cold shower, common kitchen), **Chaullay** (hot shower, common kitchen) and **Santa Teresa** (hot shower, no kitchen). In a package costing 250 soles he provides food, lodging, and transportation from Cusco to Mollepata (but no guides or arrieros).

The path continues through the ruins, after 30 minutes passing a campsite with magnificent views. Then begins a steep, knee-tormenting descent to the Río Aobamba which will take about two hours. Pass through farms again, always on a good path, to reach a **suspension bridge** over the river. Turn left after the bridge, then right along the Urubamba River, and follow the road for 20 minutes to the **hydro-electric plant** (*hidroeléctrica*) train station (1,870m) where you can have a snack before catching the train to Machu Picchu (remember that you need to have bought your entry tickets for Machu Picchu in advance).

For Aguas Calientes (Machu Picchu Pueblo) see pages 285–9.

OTHER TREKS IN THE CORDILLERA VILCABAMBA

THE MOYOC CIRCUIT *Mark Smith*

Lying just one hour from Cusco this fantastic trek starts with the rarely visited Inca site of Wata before completing a circuit around the lofty peak

Distance	70km
Altitude	2,790–4,750m
Rating	Difficult
Timing	5–6 days
In reverse	Possible
Start of trail	Parpiso, 15 minutes' drive north of Huarocondo (and one hour from Cusco). You can get a taxi all the way, or take a bus to Huarocondo and then take a taxi from there. No buses go to Parpiso itself.
Transport at the end	Train to Machu Picchu from Ollantaytambo, or bus back to Cusco
Maps	IGN sheet *Urubamba* (27-r)

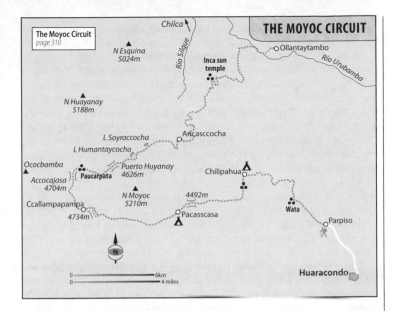

of Moyoc. You camp near traditional farming communities, hike over high mountain passes visited only by sheep and cattle herders, and enjoy stunning views of snow-capped Andean peaks. Finally, you pass through a little-known canyon and follow the course of an Inca canal before coming out high above the Sacred Valley at the site of an Inca temple from where there are stunning views of Mount Verónica, a mountain revered in traditional ideology. You walk down past the old Inca stone quarry to end your trek in renowned Ollantaytambo with its Inca fortress guarding the Sacred Valley.

Route description From the concrete INC sign saying **Parpiso**, climb steadily to the Inca site of **Wata** (3,815m), in two hours and 4km. Only the last 300m is steep. You can explore the ruins and there is shade available (this first part can be very hot). A further two hours (6km) on mainly flat ground brings you to the community of **Chilipahua** (3,748m) where you may be able to camp by the school. There is now a vehicle track as far as the village but it would be a shame to miss out on the Wata ruins.

Follow the stream southward to some thatched houses. There are Inca ruins 20 minutes up on the hill to the left. From the houses, a path climbs easily up on to the ridge on the right. Once on the ridge follow a westward path, which climbs gradually to a **spring** where you could have lunch at 4,316m. It is a further 45 minutes' easy climb to the pass at 4,492m, about three hours from Chilipahua. Enjoy fantastic views across to Nevado Moyoc and down the valley to Nevado Verónica. The path descends to the valley in 30 minutes. Head west up the valley, and you'll soon arrive at a small house known as **Pacasscasa**, four hours and 8km from Chilipahua. There are flat areas to camp that will offer the last views of Verónica before the valley bends out of sight. There are also plenty of opportunities to camp higher up the valley over the next 3.5km. From Pacasscasa continue climbing easily up the valley for 2½ hours (5km) to reach a 4,734m broad pass. Descend to cross the three **streams** marked on the map, before diagonally ascending a scree slope to reach a flat area. Climb the steep zigzags to the pass at the end of valley, 30 minutes from the flat area. The pass lies at 4,753m, 5½ hours and 7.8km from Pacasscasa. Traverse a fine scree slope for 30 minutes, where there may be snow patches, to a third pass (4,671m) 8.4km from Pacasscasa. Descend to a flat area to the left of a stream known as **Ccallampapampa** (4,224m), 10.4km and seven hours from Pacasscasa. There is good camping here.

Cross the pampa and begin a steady climb to a 4,426m shoulder, 1½ hours and 2km from Ccallampapampa with lovely views to nevados Salkantay and Ococbamba. Cross the shoulder and traverse the hillside heading up the valley before arriving at a flat area (4,460m) at the head of the valley after 1½ hours (1.83km from the shoulder). The Accocajasa pass (4,704m) lies on the opposite side of the valley and takes another one to 1½ hours (1km) to reach. From there you'll gaze at impressive views of the glaciers on Nevado Humantay. To descend, first head straight down before turning right, up the valley to the Inca site of **Paurcarpata** where you can camp. This is another 75 minutes (roughly 2km) from Accocajasa pass.

From Paurcarpata, an hour's stiff climb followed by a flattish 15 minutes bring you to **Puerto Huyanay** pass (4,626m) in 1.6km. Take time to admire the views towards the Sacred Valley before descending steadily, with the odd steep bit, passing the small lake of Humantaycocha, then the larger lake of **Soyraccocha**, 45 minutes from Puerto Huyanay (2.4km). Be careful not to miss the fork in the path here: you descend rather than continue to traverse. There are lots of choices for lunch and camping spots from this point on. Pass through the scattered community of Ancasccocha to eventually reach the **Río Silque**. There is a bridge about 150m downstream and a good place to camp across the bridge, just over five hours (8.9km) from Paurcarpata. There are wonderful views of Nevado Verónica from here.

Take the rising path that traverses the right side of valley. At 2km (*1hr*) and 4,063m, the path heads into a valley on the right, keeping on the right side of a dry stream bed until you meet a valley which crosses it in another 30 minutes. Note two distinctive **fingers of rock** above you. Turn left to reach a pass in ten minutes, and look out for a house below with large enclosures; make for this, 2½ hours from the Río Silque (4.3km). See a canyon dipping to the left, and follow the stream to meet another stream which runs into the canyon. Note the Inca canal above. Now your route takes you through the **canyon**, which is about 200m long; unless there has been heavy rain, the stream should pose no problem. The path then traverses the hillside. After a while you'll see Río Silque below, joining your valley. At 8.2km and 3,733m a really stiff climb zigzags to 3,868m. Cross the flat area along the Inca canal to arrive at the **Inca sun temple** lying on a ridge at 3,934m, some 10km from the bridge over the Río Silque. Continue past some Inca buildings, then cross a rockfall to an area that has been flattened into a campsite seven hours from Río Silque (3,588m; 12km). It is a nice place to spend the night or you can just carry on down 5km to cross the Río Urubamba on the old Inca bridge into **Ollantaytambo** where you can either stay the night or take transport on to Machu Picchu or back to Cusco.

CACHORA TO HUANCACALLE VIA CHOQUEQUIRAO
This is a spectacular trek of approximately 100km, with over 5,000m of ascent and slightly less descent. You cross the entire Vilcabamba range in about eight days of trekking, from Cachora through the ruins at Choquequirao (entrance fee payable; see route description on pages 314–20) and on to the last stronghold of the Incas at Vitcos where Manco Inca was murdered.

Your route takes you through an immense range of vegetation and temperatures, with a variety of panoramic views to match, from the ice-capped peaks of the high Andes with their sharp ridges, deep gorges and raging rivers, to the lush flora and prolific wildlife of the subtropical rainforest.

> **Note:** check the security situation in Huancacalle before setting out, as there have been reports of the area being used by drug runners.

Cachora (2,875m) is a small town of around 3,000 people, with stunning views across to the snow-capped peaks of the Vilcabamba range on the far side of the Apurímac. The mountain of Ampay towers above. There are several shops, bars, hostels and hotels, including **Casa de Salcantay** (m 984281171; www.salcantay.com; 85 soles/room) and **Los Tres Balcones** (m 984897566; e juancarlos@choquequirau.com; 140 soles/room). They also organise services for trekkers using staff from Cachora.

You can find **mules and guides** in Cachora, too. Seferina and Celestino Peña, as well as Reynaldo Huaman have been recommended, and seem to be the best known, but there are plenty of others. Expect to pay 30–40 soles a day for an arriero and the same for his animal. You need to pay for them to come back, and also provide them with food and sometimes even a tent. Prices are rising fast in this trekking area so check locally to see what is current. Note, however, that at the time of writing the bridge crossing the Apurímac River from Playa Rosalina to Santa Rosa has been washed out, so mules cannot cross. You can arrange for an arriero to accompany you from Cachora for the first day and can try to contact the arrieros in Yanama to meet you for your second day but communication with the town is intermittent and arrangements made over the phone unreliable.

Distance	100km
Altitude	2,400m–4,600m
Rating	Moderate
Timing	8 days
In reverse	Possible
Start of trail	Cachora
Transport at the end	There is an occasional bus to Chaullay from Huancacalle (*3hrs*), with onward connections to Cusco taking six hours.
Maps	*Santa Teresa–Machu Picchu* (IGN 27-q) available at SAE in Cusco (page 246)

Getting to the trailhead Take the Abancay bus from the bus station (*terminal terrestre*) in Cusco. Buses leave at 06.30, 16.00 and 20.00, and tend to be on time. It's a good idea to buy your ticket the day before. The buses don't stop, so bring a snack and water. Four hours (145km) after leaving Cusco, 45km from Abancay, get off the bus at the road junction (3,695m) for Cachora near the Inca site of Sayhuite (page 316).

Head back up to the road junction, cross the road and follow the dirt track up to the top of the ridge. From here you will see the village of Cachora far below. Well beyond it is the dramatic Apurímac Gorge. From the road junction you can take a colectivo (*5 soles, 30 soles for the entire car; 20–30mins*) or walk to the village (one to two hours of fast downhill walking; you can follow the road, taking short cuts where possible). As well as the colectivos there are buses from Abancay to Cachora in the mornings, the last one leaving Abancay at 11.00.

Route description COPESCO has done a lot of work on the path that you follow to get to Choquequirao. There are signposts and generally it

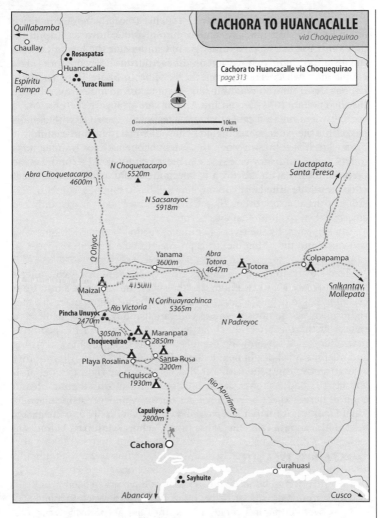

CACHORA TO HUANCACALLE
via Choquequirao

Cachora to Huancacalle via Choquequirao
page 313

0 ————————————— 10km
0 ————————————— 6 miles

Quillabamba
○ Chaullay
●● **Rosaspatas**
○ Huancacalle
Espíritu Pampa
●● **Yurac Rumi**

N

Abra Choquetacarpo 4600m
Q Otiyoc

N Choquetacarpo 5520m ▲

Llactapata, Santa Teresa

N Sacsarayoc 5918m ▲

Yanama ○ 3600m   *Abra Totora 4647m*   ▲○ Totora   Colpapampa

Maizal ○   4150m
Salkantay, Mollepata

N Corihuayrachinca 5365m ▲

Pincha Unuyoc 2470m
Río Victoria

N Padreyoc ▲

3050m ●● Maranpata
Choquequirao ○ 2850m
Playa Rosalina ○ ○ Santa Rosa 2200m
Chiquisca ○ 1930m

Río Apurímac

Capuliyoc 2800m ●

Cachora ○

Curahuasi ○

Abancay ↓   ●● **Sayhuite**   Cusco →

is in excellent condition. From the plaza in **Cachora** take the road that leaves town heading downwards from the bottom-left corner. There is a signpost after about 20 minutes indicating a left turn and from there the path continues to wind its way leftwards along the side of the valley. You need to carry several litres of water with you, as there is little or no water on the route until you reach an old farm house at Chiquisca (17km from Cachora), now converted to a campsite where you can even buy beer, just 3km before you reach the mighty Río Apurímac (20km from Cachora).

After a two- to three-hour walk (10km) from Cachora you reach the edge of a ridge and a picnic/camping spot known as **Capuliyoc** (2,800m). You can just make out where Choquequirao (3,050m) lies, in the distance, slightly above you on the far side of the river. There are a couple of thatch-covered huts on the ridge, from where a further 10km (*2–3hrs*), this time all downhill, takes you to the now-destroyed bridge (washed out in 2011) across the **Apurímac** (1,550m). The crossing is currently by *oroya* – a cable that stretches across the river with a metal basket for the passenger hanging below. There are plans to rebuild the bridge but it isn't known when this might happen. There is water, flush toilets and a cold shower at the **Chiquisca** campsite (1,930m), two to three hours from Capuliyoc, and if you are lucky fruit from the trees at the campsite. The family living here sell basic supplies, some drinks, and also have a toilet. Looking across the river you can see only too clearly the steep climb that awaits you.

You can camp by the river (45 minutes further on from Chiquisca) if you can stand the biting flies. It is possible to take a dip in the river, in calm pools.

Head slowly up the steep zigzags from the river to bring you, after a hot and sweaty 1½ to two hours, to the sugarcane camp of **Santa Rosa** (2,200m, 22km from Cachora). Here you will find plenty of fresh water right down by the houses, where you can also buy bottled drinks and snacks. If there is anybody about they might show you the primitive machinery used for brewing the local rum from sugarcane – a strong and noxious spirit. Right next to Santa Rosa is Santa Rosa Alta, another very attractive campsite with a cold stream running right through it. If you haven't had a shower at the previous campsite, it's a good idea to cool off here. Expect to pay 1 sol per person whenever using shower-toilet facilities. A further steep climb (*1½–2hrs*) takes you to the grassy field at **Maranpata** (2,850m, 25km from Cachora). Just past Maranpata

◉ SAYHUITE INCA SITE

Don't miss the huge carved boulder of Sayhuite (4,000m) and its surrounding site of baths, plaza and carved rocks. Sayhuite has over 200 figures carved into it; they are animals that were important in the beliefs of the Incas such as the jaguar, lizard, monkey and snake as well as anthropomorphic forms and various plants. To get to the site from the main road walk left down an obvious dirt track for five to ten minutes. Pay a small entry fee of 11 soles. Allow at least an hour for your visit. You can buy snacks such as deep-fried pork (*chicharron de chancho*) and maize from the houses by the roadside.

there is a control point where you need to sign in and pay the entrance fee of 38 soles (*students 19 soles with an ISIC*). Views of **Choquequirao** gradually appear ahead, and it's just 90 minutes of relatively flat walking to get there. This last part of the walk is through typical cloudforest, replete with orchids, bromeliads and lichens. There is ample camping space on the extended terraces at the beginning of the site. Camping is free, and there is water and flush toilets, currently shared with the crew working at the site – the site is being restored under the guidance of COPESCO and their team of workers. Approximately 40% of the site has now been uncovered, exposing the many different sectors of Choquequirao.

The ruins comprise the main square, long terraces, a ceremonial platform, palaces, houses and a water canal. Before work began the whole site was almost completely engulfed by the thick vegetation that grows so prolifically at these altitudes. It is believed that Choquequirao was constructed during the reign of the ninth Inca Lord Pachacútec, dedicated to the sun, the water and the apus. Some of the temples have trapezoidal doors and windows typical of the palaces and temples of other Inca sites. Although the stonework doesn't match the precision of other Inca sites, there are some unique features such as the llama mosaics set into some walls. The location is dramatic, views over the Apurímac Gorge are spectacular and in the distance are the snow-capped peaks of Ampay, Panta and Quishuar. Condors are often seen soaring overhead and the men that work on clearing the site claim many sightings of the spectacled bear (*oso de anteojos*). There is rumour of a planned cable car to this site, so go there soon if you want to see it in its near-pristine state.

From the terraced campsite head up towards the toilets where you'll find a trail that goes behind them uphill in the direction of the ruins. When you hit a **T-junction** take a right for a short distance and then a quick left uphill. This trail will reach another T-junction at which you take a left. Head uphill until the junction with a Yanama sign. Take a right up the hill away from the ruins. This trail will take you to the pass.

Alternatively, from the highest cleared point of the site a recently cleared path leads straight upwards for 200m and then joins the main path. Turn left and continue through rich cloudforest on an exposed section for 30 minutes to reach a great lookout point on a sharp ridge with spectacular drops to the Apurímac Gorge. Ahead is a steep grass-covered hillside, down which the path zigzags. Across the valley you can see where you will be heading; there are huts and yet another steep zigzagging climb.

Part-way down the slope is another Inca site, known as **Pincha Unuyoc** or Pinchunío (2,470m), where there is water and extensive terraces probably used for agriculture. The path winds down leftward through the terraces and then heads more to the right to leave this area in the bottom-right corner of the lowest field. This is where the water source is, and some Inca buildings. The path follows the stream of water downwards, the temperature rising as you continue descending to reach the **Río Victoria** (on some maps Río Blanco) at 1,990m where you can have a welcome splash in the cold meltwaters from Corihuaynachina. Don't pollute the water – it is used by villagers further downstream. Take care when crossing the river; there is only a basic bridge and the water can be quite fast flowing. There are camping spots on the far side about 200m downstream from where you emerged, if you can stand the flies which are known locally, and very appropriately, as *pumahuacachi*, 'that which makes the puma scream'.

It is a long steep climb of over 2,000m to the pass of **Abra Victoria** (4,130m). It is possible to accomplish this climb in one day with an early start, but is perhaps better to take it more easily over two days. Be warned that there is only one **reliable water source** on the way up, in **Maizal**, about three hours up from the bottom of the valley, consisting of several small houses mostly inhabited for only part of the year by families from Yanama who grow crops nearby. The enterprising local couple, Valentin Zaca and his wife, have built a campsite, Camping Maizal, with water and showers. As you ascend it is signposted off the main path to the left – about a further 15- to 30-minute walk. There is some very basic food and some drinks for sale here. It is at least another four to five hours to the pass itself, and there is no water on the way. The transition from hot, dry bamboo-rich scrubland through dense cloudforest and then out into typical high mountain *páramo* is remarkable. Even more surprising are the entrance and slag heaps of the Victoria mine, just an hour below the pass, apparently so high in the mountainside and so far from anywhere. This silver and lead mine was successively exploited by Incas and Spaniards alike. From the mine a beautifully constructed Inca road leads to the pass at 4,150m, where a superb view of the impressive snow-capped peaks of the Cordillera Vilcabamba awaits.

The small village of Yanama (3,600m), at the bottom of the next valley, is now your destination. The Inca Trail continues, carved expertly into the cliffside, leading you downwards along an impossible-looking, somewhat vertiginous route. There is water not far from the top of the pass. It is something of a relief to get to **Yanama** in its beautiful setting, and it is one of the most cared-for mountain villages I have seen in the Andes. Typical adobe houses are surrounded by small cultivated plots, there is plenty of water and the village is very clean and friendly. Camping is at the higher end of the village, 20 minutes above the school, with a small fee per tent (2 soles). Some local people also allow you to camp on their property and all have showers, toilets and clean water.

You can hire mules and arrieros here if you need to. The cost is approximately 30–40 soles per animal (the higher price if it is a saddled horse you can ride) and 42 soles per person per day, and you will need to supply food and accommodation for the muleteer. You will also have to pay for the return journey for the team.

At Yanama you have a choice: continue to **Huancacalle** which will take two days or join the route to **Santa Teresa** or Mollepata, giving you the exciting option of finishing this trek in **Machu Picchu** (page 306).

Yanama to Huancacalle Yanama to Huancacalle is a very remote, rarely trekked route taking you to seldom visited ruins. Follow the river downstream, westwards, crossing over a large bridge before heading up the valley known locally as Quebrada de Quilcamachay but named on the map as **Quebrada Otiyoc**. There is no shortage of water on this walk. Follow the path, keeping right at any junction, up this broad U-shaped valley. Look out for the many species of orchid growing in the forests you pass through, especially the rare and exquisite *waqanqi* (*Masdevallia veitchiana*). This three-petalled salmon-pink flower is covered in tiny purple hairs that give the flower the illusion of changing colour depending on how the light hits it. See photo, colour page 6.

Towering granite spires loom on the right, and spectacular mountain vistas appear as you climb. It is approximately six to eight hours from Yanama to the pass **Abra Choquetacarpo** (4,600m). There are plenty of places to camp on the way up the pass. The last few kilometres of ascent are on Inca Trail again, of amazing quality. Some sections are 3m wide, paved beautifully, and have survived the test of time remarkably well. At the pass, after an extremely steep last section, there are cairns constructed as offerings to the apus. From the pass it takes around

👁 IMPORTANT RUINS IN THE HUANCACALLE AREA

It is well worth spending half a day visiting some of the outstanding Inca remains in the area. **Rosaspatas** (also known as Vitcos) lies one hour uphill from Huancacalle, and **Yurac Rumi** (Ñusta Hispana), is less than an hour away. The latter is an enormous carved rock, 5m high, with finely carved steps and angles. All around it there are extensive terraces linked by water canals, probably used for irrigation. If you're lucky, Genaro Quispicusi (page 320) may be available to give you information about these ruins.

The Cobos family, owners of Sixpac Manco, also have a long history of working in the area with explorers (Gene Savoy and Vincent Lee) and are a mine of local information.

11

four to five hours to get to the roadhead at the village of Huancacalle. There are camping spots on the way down. Follow the **Inca road**, then a well-marked path until you reach a dirt road, at which you go left to Huancacalle. The village boasts a couple of *pensiones*, the best known of which is **Hostal Sixpac Manco**, run by the Cobos family (084270298; m 945215039; *28 soles pp, hot water & food available*). Also the **Hostel Ultimo Refugio de Manco Inca** (084 846010), a nice little hostel with hot showers and a kitchen, owned by **Genaro Quispicusi** from the INC in Huancacalle, who is the local official responsible for all the archaeological sites in this area.

There are a few shops and basic restaurants here and also a police checkpoint. Buses and trucks leave for Quillabamba, with regular onward transport to Cusco at 09.00, 13.00 and 16.00, taking five hours and costing 8 soles. A taxi will cost around 55 soles and take just two to three hours.

Yanama to Machu Picchu The easier of the two routes, this is a fantastic way to reach Machu Picchu, and has a number of benefits. You can get the bus out from Totora earlier on, meaning that it has an easier escape. You also have the opportunity to relax at the Santa Teresa hot springs at the end.

By the school at the lowest part of the Yanama community the track splits, one path crosses the river, heading over the shoulder to Huancacalle, and the other, following the river up the valley, is the route now taken by the new road to Totora. The last house, and opportunity to camp before the pass, is about 50 minutes' walk from the school.

From the school it is a four- to five-hour climb to the highest point on the trek at **Abra Totora** (4,647m), using mule tracks which criss-cross the new road following the stream all the way up to the pass. At the top of the pass, if the weather is good, you have unbelievable views of the Cordillera Vilcabamba.

From the pass, walk down to the community of **Totora** (3,380m), again using the paths that criss-cross the road. It is a three-hour walk down to Totora, the last hour of which is on the dirt road. Local families will allow you to camp in their grounds and use their water and showering facilities for a small fee. From Totora there is a colectivo each morning to La Playa and Santa Teresa.

To continue on foot, you must again follow the road for about 45 minutes after which you will come to a small track leading off to the left just after you pass a pipe that passes over the road. This path cuts steeply down and joins the road just before the hot springs at **Colpapampa** after an hour, saving you a two-hour trek along the road. From Colpapampa you join the route of the Salkantay and Llactapata treks described on page 305.

THE VILCANOTA REGION

The Cordillera Vilcanota is named after the Río Vilcanota lying to its west, and is the second-largest glaciated system in Peru (after the Cordillera Blanca), with the largest single glacier in Peru, the Quelccaya icecap. This impressive range of mountains, 80km long and 40km wide, includes the massive Nevado Ausangate (6,372m). Ausangate is the highest mountain in the department of Cusco and, like Salkantay in the Vilcabamba range, was highly revered by the Incas and continues to be sacred today. Offerings are often made by the local communities and individuals seeking good harvests, fertility, health and prosperity. Hiking opportunities here are excellent but they're the toughest in the region, so you need to be fit and acclimatised. The whole area lies above the treeline and is populated with traditionally dressed Quechua-speaking campesinos cultivating the barren altiplano. This is also alpaca country and enormous herds graze in the already eroded valleys. Typical Quechua festivals are popular in this region and you might find yourself drinking the local brew of chicha with the villagers. Their major fiesta is *Qoyllur Rit'i* ('The Ice Festival'), around the second week of June (pages 326–7) and, also in mid-June, there's the fiesta of Raqchi. The most popular hike is the circuit around Nevado Ausangate, but there are many other interesting and spectacular hikes in the area to the south and it is an ideal region for finding your own route, with no regulation and plenty of paths and local people to give you directions.

CONDITIONS This is a remote area, so prepare carefully, particularly if exploring independently off the main route. Always carry enough food and a compass. Camp outside the villages and ask permission when possible. Be prepared for very cold nights (well below freezing) and strong sun during the day. It can be dangerous to hike in this area during the rainy season when clouds and snow cover the passes and hide important landmarks.

FEATURED TREKS IN THE VILCANOTA REGION
- The Ausangate Circuit (*about 80km; 5–6 days*); pages 321–30
- Pitumarca to Laguna Sibinacocha (circuit hike) or Tinqui (*145–160km; 7–10 days*); pages 330–2
- Pitumarca to Tinqui via Chillca (*about 70km; 5–6 days*); pages 332–3
- Raqchi to Pitumarca or Tinqui via Chillca (*50–110km; 4–9 days*); pages 333–7
- The Ausangate Lodge Trek (*about 50km; 5 days*); pages 337–41

THE AUSANGATE CIRCUIT This five- to six-day hike has everything: herds of llamas and alpacas, traditionally dressed Indians, hot springs, turquoise lakes, glaciers, ice caves and even vicuñas. Not surprisingly, it is very popular with trekkers. This route takes you right round the massif of Ausangate and over three high passes before returning you to your starting point, the small village of Tinqui (also known as Tinki and Tinke).

Distance	About 80km
Altitude	3,800–5,100m
Rating	Difficult
Timing	5 days (with pack animals) or 6 days without
In reverse	Possible
Start of trail	Tinqui
Transport at the end	Bus from Ocongate (near Tinqui) to Cusco
Maps	IGN sheet *Ocongate* (28-t); trekking map *Ausangate Circuit* from the SAE or the IGN in Lima

Getting organised Providing you have a map and compass you will not normally need a guide but you must, however, pay the entrance fee to the trekking route (*15 soles*). The ticket-booth is situated at the road turn-off in Tinqui. If you want to organise arrieros, there are two associations with over 100 members at Tinqui, and prices are set: about 36 soles per day for the arriero, and 36 soles per day for a pack animal (a little more for a saddle-horse). Contact them at Hostal Tinqui (see below), or at the South American Explorers in Cusco (page 246). I (Kathy) can recommend Florencio Suclli (m *946662580*) and cook Justo Suclli (m *978641079; Spanish only*), though more for entertainment than his cooking skills – he is one of the star characters in the book *Turn Right at Machu Picchu* by Mark Adams. Those considering **ice-climbing** Campa peak (5,450m) should contact climbing guide Adrian Ccahuana (m *984394957*).

Tinqui Tinqui is near Ocongate, southeast of Cusco. The easiest way to get there is to catch a bus to Ocongate, leaving from the Coliseum in Cusco; the trip takes about three hours along part of the new Panamerican Highway. Tinqui has two basic hostels, **Hostal Ausangate** and **Hostal Tinqui** (*22 soles pp*), and both are great sources of information on the hikes in the area, so worth staying in for that reason alone. If you decide to hire a guide, perhaps if you are planning a variation of the described routes,

> ! **Note:** It is important to check locally for permitted current campsites as the local communities decide where camping spots are and this can change from year to year.

Crispin Cayitano and Teo work out of these hostels and probably know the area as well as anyone.

Route description Take the broad track from the school in **Tinqui** and cross the river via a bridge behind the building. Cross a second, smaller bridge and head up to houses on the right. Continue towards the mountain on a wide trail to open puna with house-sized boulders on the left. Continue on a trail, cross a small stream and head south–southeast across the pampa towards Ausangate. The trail is not always obvious, but keep heading towards Ausangate Mountain. After about two hours, cross a small stream by a **stone footbridge** and ignore the track on the right immediately beyond the bridge. Instead, look for a wide track on the left that climbs gently beyond a group of houses, then crosses an **irrigation ditch** and soon drops down through a green, boggy valley to Upis. It takes about five hours from Tinqui to **Upis**, where there are hot springs, a fantastic view of Ausangate and a great campsite (but beware of theft).

From Upis continue up the valley towards Ausangate, crossing the swampy area as soon as possible to the right of the valley where a faint narrow footpath is found. This continues to a grassy meadow. Cross the meadow and climb to the right to some stone corrals. Here two passes are visible, to the left and right of a yellow/orange hill. Both go to the same place. The lower path is longer but easier, the higher route more spectacular. It's about two to three hours to the top of the pass from Upis.

From the pass descend roughly south–southwest into the valley until you reach a lilac-coloured moraine. From here you can see **Laguna Vinococha**, with a waterfall. Head left (southeast) under the jagged and obvious rocky spires of **Nevado Sorimani** to the top of the waterfall cascading out of the turquoise lake. Hike over the top of a small hillock to the right of the lake and waterfall. From here continue to the right of another small hill on the far right of the lake, and continue roughly east to the base of an obvious red-coloured mountain by **Laguna Pucacocha** – about five hours away from Upis – and a possible campsite. It's worth climbing up the small ridge to the north of the campsite for the close-up views of Ausangate and, if it's clear, far off to the left (northwest) the pyramid of Salkantay can be seen.

Ten minutes from Pucacocha you reach some corrals (**Pucapata**). Head right around a small rocky hill, and continue roughly east on fairly good trails below red cliffs. After about 1½ hours you'll reach the top of a small pass with the main pass to the left (east) and Laguna Ausangatecocha below. Head down fairly steeply and for quite a long way to pasture at the right end of **Laguna Ausangatecocha**. There are some lovely campsites here (4,631m). When you've reached this lake, cross the small stream at the right end and then head northeast on trails behind the moraine, on the east side of the lake. You'll reach this spot about

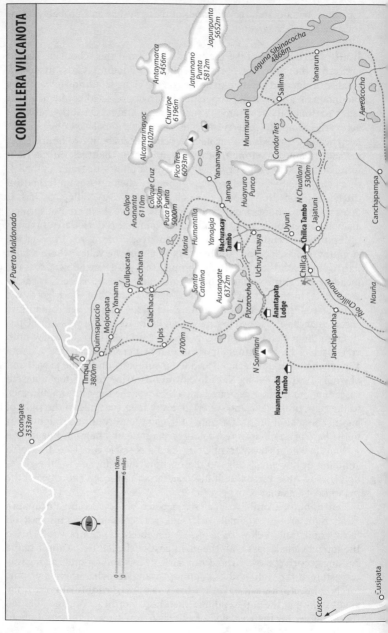

324

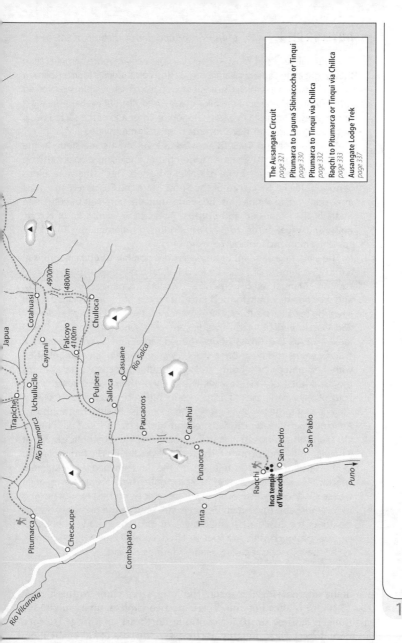

The Ausangate Circuit
page 321

Pitumarca to Laguna Sibinacocha or Tinqui
page 330

Pitumarca to Tinqui via Chillca
page 332

Raqchi to Pitumarca or Tinqui via Chillca
page 333

Ausangate Lodge Trek
page 337

Japua

Trapiche

Uchullucllo

Río Pitumarca

Pitumarca

Checacupe

Cotahuasi

4900m

4800m

Cayrani

Palcoyo
4100m

Chulloca

Casuane

Pulpera

Salloca

Río Salca

Paucaoros

Canahui

Punaorca

Tinta

Raqchi

Inca temple
of Viracocha   San Pedro

San Pablo

Combapata

Río Vilcanota

Puno

11

325

The spiritual beliefs of most Andean campesinos are more complex than they might at first appear. Native campesino communities tend to follow a syncretic religion in which the ancient worship of nature spirits is overlaid with a Christian veneer. At the pilgrimage of Qoyllur Rit'i, perhaps the most impressive Indian fiesta of all, veneration of Christ and of the sacred peak, Ausankati (Ausangate), have become mythically intertwined.

At a breathtaking 4,750m above sea level, on a scree slope in the remote Sinakara Valley sits a stone chapel enclosing a rock outcrop on which is painted a figure of Christ crucified. This is the miraculous Señor de Qoyllur Rit'i (Lord of the Snow Star), the Cusco region's most important Indian shrine and the scene annually, between the Christian feasts of the Ascension and Corpus Christi, of an explosion of colour, noise and ritual as up to 50,000 pilgrims (predominantly Quechua-speaking highland Indians) converge.

The elaborate pageant of timeless devotion has its official origins in a Christian miracle of 1783. Legend tells of a mysterious pale-skinned stranger, Manuel, who befriended Mariano, a native shepherd boy, and was one day transformed into the figure of Christ crucified upon a nearby Tayanka shrub. Mariano witnessed the miracle, died suddenly and was buried beneath an adjacent crag. Churchmen from Cusco looked on as the Christ figure then disappeared, leaving behind a crucifix where the bush once stood. Mariano's crag, later embellished with the painted Christ figure and surrounded by a chapel, today forms the focal point of devotion, while a copy of the cross (crucifix of the Lord of Tayankani) plays an important but secondary role. However, there is a lot more to Qoyllur Rit'i than a simple Christian mythohistory. Anthropologists and historians recognise that this ancient pilgrimage, like many other Andean fiestas, was hijacked by the Catholic Church at a time of rising Indian unrest. The roots of Qoyllur Rit'i lie firmly planted in the ancient animistic religion of the Andean people; and more specifically, in the veneration of Ausangate, the 6,350m snowpeak in whose shadow the festival unfolds. The region's highest mountain, and its foremost apu (mountain deity), is still seen as the primary weather creator of the Cusco area; an ambivalent god whose power can blight crops or bestow health and fertility. His devotees come to appease him, as did the Inca who regularly made offerings of gold.

two hours after leaving Pucapata. The long, steep climb to the highest pass (5,100m) is ahead of you. There are two choices: up a gully to the east (longer, but less steep), or continue northeast up a ridge (steeper, but more direct). Head roughly northeast to the pass of Palomani about

The central day of the pilgrimage is usually Trinity Sunday by which time most of the devotees are gathered at the Sinakara shrine having trekked the 8km from the village of Mawallani, connected by road with Cusco. A scattering of city-dwelling Peruvian pilgrims and quite a few foreigners attend, but it is the sea of colourfully dressed campesinos which dominates the scene. Village dance groups or *comparsas* come from far and wide to render homage to the *taytacha* (little father) through formalised choreography. The *ch'uncho* groups, representing jungle ancestors who long ago migrated to the highlands, wear bright, feathered head-dresses, while the *q'apaq qollas* (symbolising llama herders) wear flat embroidered hats and carry rope whips. And liberally scattered about the heaving crowd are the ubiquitous *ukukus*, or bear-men, sporting brightly coloured woollen masks. Disorderly and anarchic, they speak in bizarre falsetto tones, yet they are the guardians of order. The whip each ukuku carries is not merely a prop, but will be used summarily to punish any devotee found flouting the strict alcohol ban.

The dancing continues throughout the day and most of the night. In the early hours massed ranks of ukukus set off to ascend towards the glaciers, prepared for battle with the malevolent spirits of the damned thought to dwell on the icy slopes. The ukukus plant giant candles, retrieve a cross left there a few days earlier and return to the valley at first light. On Monday morning, a final mass is held as dancing resumes. Throughout the day, a stream of people returns home but a significant number also remain for the overnight pilgrimage which, to the accompaniment of music, retraces the mythical steps of Mariano and Manuel on a 25km trek, interspersed with ritual dance, via Tayankani to the town of Ocongate.

If you want to attend the festival you'll need to check the date of Trinity Sunday; it varies from late May to mid-June. The SAE (page 246) will advise on how best to visit – it's quite a serious undertaking, with a 1½-hour walk to the glacier, a night's camping, and a two-hour wait to get into the church to see those amazing dancers. If planning to stay overnight bring earplugs, as processions march through the camping field just as often as they do in front of the church.

four to five hours from Pucapata. From the pass to the next campsite you can go cross-country, or follow the trail roughly southeast for about one hour through a desert-like landscape under Cerro Puca Punta (which means 'Red Point'). Camping is no longer permitted here, but there is a designated area 90 minutes further on, a lovely campsite hidden behind a small ridge on the left. The locals have built a toilet block but it is locked as it's not currently functioning. (Note that the local communities quite understandably prefer that you do not camp near their water supplies, nor near their houses.)

From **Cerro Puca Punta**, continue east to a broad green valley (Pampa Jatunpata – no camping). Cross a stream (there is a bridge) near some houses and skirt the swampy green valley to the left (northeast), climbing over the hill to the left rather than dropping to the bogs below. Head northeast up **Quebrada Jampamayo**, a valley full of viscachas. You will hear these little animals whistling their alarm calls as they scurry for cover among the rocks. It's best to stay left of the river. At the small community of **Jampa** bear left (north–northwest) around the mountain and arrive at the very small **Laguna Ticllacocha** (4,850m), which is not visible until

THE *CASITA*   Hilary Bradt

When leading a trek in the Ausangate region I had to evacuate a hiker because of altitude sickness. On reaching Ocongate I was anxious to get back to the group so she returned to Cusco alone. Faustino, the arriero, agreed to lend me a horse so we could travel faster, but to spread the journey over two days instead of his customary one. He provided Sambo, a scrawny black pony hung about with flour sacks containing my sleeping bag, etc.

Faustino looked magnificent. Now that he was master, not servant, he'd changed into a splendid multi-coloured poncho, and his bearing and the respect with which he was greeted as we trotted through the town showed that in Ocongate he was a man of considerable status. We trotted through the town, we trotted out of town, and we trotted off the road and along the track towards Pacchanta. I hadn't ridden for several years, and my bottom and knees were screaming for mercy.

I wondered where we were going to spend the night. Since it would be below freezing I hoped we'd be under cover. Yes, said Faustino, a friend of his had a *casita* in the next valley. Here we encountered the friend screaming Quechua curses at a herd of serene-looking llamas and alpacas. He and Faustino disappeared into a grass-thatched hut chattering volubly, and I decided to see if my legs still worked by climbing a nearby hill to watch the evening sun paint golden rings round the alpacas and touch the white bulk of Ausangate with pink.

It was almost dark when I returned to the casita. The interior was lit by one guttering candle and I ducked through the low door and groped my way to a seat by the wall – a remarkably comfortable and well-sprung seat, covered with a sheepskin. My host's daughter gave

you are there. There are some excellent camping places around here. It takes four hours from Cerro Puca Punta to the lake.

Head approximately northwest out of Laguna Ticllacocha and in about an hour you'll come to the pass of **Campa** at 5,000m. This pass used to be almost completely covered with a glacier and the site of a spectacular 100m-deep ice cave. Now, alas, the glacier has receded and although a line of **cairns** guides you up to some small ice caves they lack the drama of their predecessor.

At the pass, the northwest trail heads through the long scree slope of **Quebrada Caycohuayjo** and emerges above and to the left of several lakes. At the final lake, **Laguna Comercocha**, head past a few houses and drop down into the valley below. There's a fairly clear trail which crosses the meandering river via four bridges. Continue on a good and pleasant trail along the left bank of the river, past occasional pools and lakes, until

me a plate of tiny potatoes and I gave them some chocolate. Then I prepared myself for sleep. Father and daughter watched entranced as I laid out my requirements. I unrolled and inflated my Thermarest, stuffed a sweater into a T-shirt for a pillow, and pulled my sleeping bag from its stuff bag. In the background I could hear incredulous squeaks from the daughter punctuating the steady drone of man-of-the-world Faustino explaining what everything was for. When I actually climbed into the blue cocoon of a sleeping bag, it was too much for her. She burst into hysterical giggles and little explosions of laughter accompanied the rest of my preparations. When the show was over, she just curled up on a pile of sheepskins and went to sleep.

The girl was up again at 04.30 to start a cooking fire (inside) with llama dung, and to round up the horses. It was bitterly cold, and dark and eye-smartingly smoky in the hut, and I buried myself in my sleeping bag until it was light enough to see my surroundings. I was rather surprised at what I saw. To begin with, my comfortable seat of the previous evening turned out to be half a sheep carcass with a well-sprung rib cage. There was no furniture, and no windows, but Inca-style niches made useful shelves for more pieces of sheep, half-spun wool, burnt-out candles and a safety pin.

After a breakfast of potatoes we saddled up and set off for the final stretch. After labouring up the 5,000m pass, with Sambo equally breathless on the lead rope beside me, we stopped at a rocky knoll overlooking Ticclacocha. Rumbling glaciers and spiky snowpeaks surrounded me on all sides, with ice cream cornices bulging over the ridges. I was well content to wait there for the group's arrival.

you reach the small village of **Pacchanta**. There's a bridge over the river before here. Pacchanta has two hot springs and good campsites. It takes five hours from Laguna Ticllacocha to Pacchanta.

From Pacchanta you have to cross the river via a bridge and then follow the obvious trail northwest to **Tinqui**, about three hours away.

PITUMARCA TO LAGUNA SIBINACOCHA (CIRCUIT HIKE) OR TINQUI

This very long, rigorous, but infinitely rewarding trek visits the largest lake in the area (18km long), and can be done as a circular hike or joined with the Ausangate Circuit. One advantage is that it is easy to get to the roadhead at Checacupe. You start by walking up a lovely river valley of cultivated fields, gradually gaining altitude, and then climb high to the puna. There are two passes over 5,000m so this is a tough hike.

Distance	About 145km to the lake and back to Pitumarca and 160km to Tinqui
Altitude	3,440–5,300m
Rating	Difficult (very strenuous!)
Timing	7–10 days
In reverse	Possible
Start of trail	Pitumarca
Transport at the end	Taxi/combi/walk from Pitumarca to Checacupe. Colectivo or bus from there to Cusco (*1½hrs*). If ending in Tinqui – bus from nearby Ocongate to Cusco.
Maps	IGN sheet *Ocongate* (28-t)

Getting to the trailhead Take a bus or colectivo towards Sicuani; they leave Cusco every half hour or so. Get off at **Checacupe**, about 1½ hours from Cusco. From here you can catch a combi, take a taxi or walk to the small village of Pitumarca. Before leaving Checacupe, however, try to visit the church (which is often closed but you may find the *portero* who has the key). Unremarkable from the outside, its interior is a lovely example of colonial workmanship with some marvellous paintings, a fine altar and a beautifully carved pulpit.

Route description From **Pitumarca** follow the trail up the valley along the left bank of the river until you reach the small village of **Uchullucllo**, about four hours from Pitumarca. Just before the village is an area of extraordinary eroded rocks. The village lies on the other (south) side of the river, so cross over the bridge. Above the village there are some rather unrewarding hot springs. The trail continues across the courtyard from the school, climbing up the slope and heading towards the village of Anaiso, about three hours away to the east. The trail drops down to the Río Pitumarca again, before reaching the village.

From above **Anaiso**, continue up the right-hand side of the broad valley to where it narrows. Cross a bridge to the left side, then follow the wide path through a narrow canyon, fording the river twice. The canyon opens on to a cultivated area. The path then crosses the river once again, climbing up the valley's right-hand slope, and finally arrives at a broad marshy plain, four hours from Anaiso. The Río Pitumarca changes its name: it is now the Río Yanama ('Black River'). Hike across the marshy plain to the upper end where there is a small settlement. Don't enter the settlement but cross the river to its left side. The trail then curves to the left, heading east over a spur in the valley. Coming off a steep slope, the trail splits and runs along both sides of the river. Stay on the left side and continue up the valley, remaining near the watercourse. The small village of **Canchapampa** lies two to three hours beyond the marshy plain.

From here the trail continues in an easterly direction, leaving the stream and crossing over hilly terrain to **Laguna Aereacocha**, about two hours from Canchapampa. From the lake continue across the plateau before descending on to a vast plain laced with rivers. Follow a path leading over the ridge that lies to the east. Once over the ridge, the path swings north and heads to the southern end of the enormous **Laguna Sibinacocha** (4,868m). It's three to four hours from Laguna Aereacocha to Laguna Sibinacocha. Vicuñas roam this highland region. Spend a day camped at the lake, exploring its shores and the nearby hills. The lake and its surroundings provide an ideal habitat for numerous species of birds. When you are ready to leave, follow the shores of the lake to its northern end.

The mountain ridge that borders the lake's left shore dips low, providing easy access to the village of **Sallma** on the other side. You are now heading south back towards Pitumarca. From Sallma, cross the nearby stream and make your way to the opposite side of the valley, a short distance below the village. Here the trail climbs the slope to a marshy pasture overlooking the valley. Continue to the left of the pasture before climbing to the right of a rocky crag. The pass lies just above 5,050m, and overlooks another broad valley. Laguna Chullumpina can be seen on the far side of the valley. Descend to the left of the open area before heading for the valley below.

Cross the **Río Chumayu** and climb towards **Laguna Chua** (4,900m); there are several houses nearby. Continue past the houses to a different trail that runs along the slope above the lake. Take this trail over the spur of **Nevado Chuallani** (5,300m) on your right. Standing on the spur, you look down into a basin of pasture with a small pond (Laguna Negromutayoc), dry most of the time. Above the pasture to the west you can see the pass leading out of the region around Sibinacocha. The trail crosses the pasture below the pond and then climbs steeply up the mountainside near Nevado Chuallani. This pass also lies at 5,050m and takes one to two hours to reach from the small lake. The trail comes down from the pass through quebradas Lloclla and Misquiunuj, passing the small settlement of **Jajatuni**, until you reach the large valley of the **Río Chillcamayu**, some three hours from the pass. You have two possibilities here: you can hike back to Pitumarca in two to three days, passing through the small community of **Chillca** where you join a dirt road, or you can join up with the Ausangate Circuit trail (page 321) and head for Tinqui, which also takes two to three days.

For the latter, cross to the right-hand side of **Quebrada Chillcamayo** to hike up to its northern end where it becomes the Quebrada Jampamayu, and part of the Ausangate Circuit – about four hours.

 PITUMARCA TO TINQUI VIA CHILLCA This is a shorter variation of the hike above, combined with the Ausangate Circuit. Starting in Pitumarca rather than Tinqui gives you the advantage of easier access, and a chance to get acclimatised as you walk gently uphill along a well-used trail trodden by countless campesinos and their laden llamas heading for Pitumarca. There is a dirt road up to Chillca, but you are only on it for short sections, and mostly on footpaths.

Distance	About 70km
Altitude	3,440–5,000m
Rating	Moderate–difficult
Timing	5–6 days
In reverse	Possible, and less strenuous because you start higher
Start of trail	Pitumarca
Transport at the end	Bus from Ocongate (near Tinqui) to Cusco
Maps	IGN sheet *Ocongate* (28-t)

Route description From Pitumarca follow the trail up the valley along the left bank of the **Río Pitumarca**, passing the village of **Uchulluclo** on the other side of the river, about four hours from Pitumarca. Stay on the left side of the river until you reach **Quebrada Chillcamayo** on your left (the third quebrada from Pitumarca), about one hour from Uchulluclo. Go up this quebrada, following the left bank of the Río Chillcamayu until you reach the village of **Japua**, situated on the other side of the river. Cross the bridge and follow the path along the river, crossing it once more, to the community of **Chillca** at 4,200m, about five to six hours from the start of the quebrada. Chillca is a small village, with a school and a basic shop for supplies. The local people are semi-nomadic, moving around with their large flocks of llama and alpaca. Chillca lies at the confluence of two rivers. Follow the right-hand branch, the Río Chillcamayu, heading northeast, to

Side trip: From **Jampa** you can take a side trip to **Laguna Sibinacocha.** Follow the river valley to your right (northeast) to the community of Yanama, about one hour from Jampa. From here you start the climb to the pass of Huayruro Punco at about 5,150m, passing lagunas Osjollo and Ananía – about three to four hours. From the pass you get a spectacular view over the impressive Laguna Sibinacocha and can marvel at its size. Descend along Quebrada Huampunimayo to the lake (no path) in about two hours. The camping by the lake is beautiful, but cold and windy. An option from here is to follow the banks of the lake south and pick up the trail to Pitumarca described earlier, or to hike back to Chillca (also described earlier) to rejoin the trail towards Tinqui.

the even smaller community of **Uyuni** at 4,400m, about two hours away, and for another four hours up Quebrada Jampamayo to the community of **Jampa** at 4,600m – above. You are now on the **Ausangate Circuit.**

RAQCHI TO PITUMARCA OR TINQUI VIA CHILLCA The southern loop was an accidental discovery during our (Hilary and George's) first trip to the Cordillera Vilcanota in 1979 (page 338) so I have a special affection for it. But note that we have not been able to update the route description since then so you need to tackle it with the same spirit of exploration (though with a map!) that we did all those years ago. The extra bonus of this hike, and the one which enticed us to it in the first place, is the Inca temple of Viracocha at Raqchi (see box, pages 334–5). By combining the southern route with the extension to the Ausangate Circuit you are giving yourself one of the most scenically varied, if strenuous, hikes in Peru. The full trek is a serious venture – about 110km, or eight to ten days of hiking – and you need to be confident of your physical abilities. However, you can make this a shorter trek – as we did back in 1979.

Distance	About 50km or 110km depending on route taken
Altitude	3,440–4,900m/5,000m
Rating	Moderate–difficult
Timing	4–9 days
In reverse	Possible (for both routes)
Start of trail	Raqchi
Transport at the end	Taxi/combi/walk from Pitumarca to Checacupe. Colectivo or bus from there to Cusco (*1½hrs*). If ending in Tinqui – bus from nearby Ocongate to Cusco.
Maps	IGN sheets *Sicuani* (29-t) and *Ocongate* (28-t)

RAQCHI AND THE INCA TEMPLE OF VIRACOCHA

The village is accessible by bus, about 2½ hours from Cusco. Even without the astonishing Inca temple this would be a remarkable village. Centuries ago a violent volcanic eruption spewed black lava all over the area, and this has been put to good use by the resourceful villagers. Numerous walls and corrals have been built from it, and hunks of the stuff still litter the surrounding hillsides. The church in Raqchi is exceptionally attractive, as is the entire village. Perhaps civic pride has something to do with it: once a year, in mid-June, there is a fiesta here which is said to have some of the best costumed dancers seen anywhere in Peru.

THE INCA TEMPLE OF VIRACOCHA (*entrance fee is 11 soles*) The bare facts do nothing to prepare you for the amazing spectacle that greets you as you pass through a little gate to the right of Raqchi church. A long single wall of magnificent Inca stonework is topped by an adobe extension bringing it to a height of 15m. The lower wall is nearly 1.5m thick with typical trapezoid windows and doorways. The remains of a row of stone pillars run on each side of the wall, but only one has retained its adobe top. No other Inca building has pillars and none is as tall. The adobe wall is protected by a recently added tile roof. Beyond the temple are rows of identical buildings made from rough stone, originally topped by adobe, arranged round six identical squares. In another area, towards the road, are the remains of 200 small circular constructions, arranged in lines of 12.

What on earth was it all for? We asked at the archaeological museum in Cusco and we struck gold in the form of George Squier's fascinating account of his travels in Peru, published in 1877. Squier had a meticulous eye for detail. I owe the following information to him, and to subsequent writings by Luis A Pardo in the Revista del Instituto Arqueológico del Cuzco.

The most fascinating aspect of the Temple of Viracocha is the story of how it came to be built. Some people think it was to appease the god Viracocha, after a volcanic eruption. I suppose that's the most logical explanation but I prefer the account by the notoriously inaccurate Inca (he was mestizo, actually) chronicler, Garcilaso de la Vega.

His version is that the temple was built by Inca Viracocha, the son of Yahua Huacac. The father was a mild, ineffectual man with little patience for his son's ambitions and impetuosity, so he sent the prince to the village of Chita, three leagues northeast of Cusco, in honourable exile, to supervise the royal herds pastured there.

After three years the prince returned, saying he'd had a vision. During a siesta in the fields, a white-bearded, celestial being appeared before him saying: 'I am the son of the sun, brother of Manco Capac. My name is Viracocha and I am sent by my father to advise the Inca that the provinces of Chinchasuya are in revolt, and that large armies are advancing thence to destroy the sacred capital. The Inca must prepare. I will protect him and his empire.' Inca Yahua Huacac was unmoved, however, and took no precautions against the coming invasion. When the attack took place, as predicted, he fled to Muyna.

The people, abandoned by their Inca, scattered in all directions, but the prince (who had now assumed the name of Viracocha) arrived with some shepherds of Chita, and persuaded them to return and defend Cusco. Prince Viracocha fought valiantly, though his forces were greatly outnumbered. 'The very stones rose up, armed, white-bearded men, when the weight of the battle pressed hardly on the youthful Inca.' He won, of course, and deposed his father at the request of a grateful people.

The new Inca Viracocha ordered the construction of a marvellous temple, different from any preceding it, at Cacha (de la Vega glosses over the mystery of why the temple had to be built there, rather than at Chita where the vision had appeared, or on the battle site). The temple was to be roofless, with an elevated second storey. It would contain a chapel with the image of the god Viracocha, as he had appeared to the prince. The floor was paved with lustrous black stones brought from afar.

De la Vega's descriptions don't fit with the present ruins, so it's likely that he relied on secondhand reports. However, his sorrowful statement that the Spanish destroyed this magnificent temple in search of gold is certainly true. According to Squier, the churches of San Pedro and Tinta are built of stones from the temple walls, as is one of the bridges across the river Vilcanota. Looking at the present ruins, you can see that the rows of pillars probably supported a slanting roof. The second floor could have been sustained on the columns, with beams running from them to holes in the centre wall.

De la Vega doesn't mention the other ruins, but it's probable that the identical houses were priests' dwellings, or perhaps barracks. The 200 small circular buildings were thought by Squier to be pilgrims' lodgings, but it's more likely they were warehouses or granaries.

There is one other Inca site here, and that is the baths to the left of the temple. You will have to leave the temple area by the gate you came in, and follow the path between stone walls. The baths have some fine water channels, and fresh running water can still be collected there.

Route description The trail starts northeast of the Inca temple in Raqchi, goes past the Inca baths and then climbs steeply uphill to the main trail, which snakes through the lava. Turn right and walk between stone walls until you reach an open area, then continue in the same direction to the foot of a stone-free hill. Turn left here and follow paths up the valley, above some houses sheltered by large trees. Go north up the valley on the right-hand side of the gorge, on a good trail which crosses the stream near the top and climbs over the pass. The path becomes fainter here, but you can follow it into the valley as it zigzags down a scree shoulder towards the village of **Paucaoros**. There is good camping in the area or you can descend to the **Río Salca** through a eucalyptus plantation on the right-hand side of the stream. It takes about five to six hours from Raqchi to the river.

Turn left at the Río Salca and follow it along a good track for about 2km until you see a village on the opposite bank. A kilometre further down you'll find a cable across the river with a small wooden platform dangling below it – and that's how you cross! (This may have been replaced by now.) Once on the other side walk back up the valley to the village of **Salloca** – one to two hours. From here, if you want to terminate the walk, you can hike out to the village of **Combapata**.

To continue the circuit to Pitumarca, when you reach the first houses of Salloca look for a well-marked path heading up the valley. It is exceptionally beautiful, crossing and re-crossing the tumbling river over well-made bridges. There are flowers and flowering shrubs everywhere and plenty of hummingbirds. You'll reach some idyllic campsites about an hour after leaving the Salca Valley.

The first community you come to is **Pulpera**, after about three hours. From here the path curves round to the right, up Quebrada Palcoyo, and after two hours of steady climbing you reach the compact small village of **Palcoyo** at 4,100m. Continue up the valley on a well-used path, probably together with a herd of llamas and/or alpacas, to the small community of **Chulloca**, about three hours from Palcoyo. Just before the village a path climbs up the valley to your left. Follow it to some corrals, and continue climbing steeply to the pass at 4,800m – about two hours. This is 'the stripy mountain', **Yauricunca**, and at the top you may feel, as I did, that you've landed on Mars.

Don't kid yourselves that it's now downhill all the way: you have a 4,900m pass before you can descend to the Río Pitumarca.

Two paths lead down the valley from the pass. One runs to the right (southwest) down the side of the mountain ridge into the valley; the other continues northeast. Take the latter and follow it to a village on the valley floor. The trail traverses a rather nasty scree slope so you may prefer to drop down to the village before this stretch. Continue up the valley past the houses, following any handy alpaca tracks you may find. There is (or was) no trail. The pass at 4,900m is on the right-hand side of the valley head. It's a hard slog and will take a discouraging two hours from the village. But an incredible view will greet you when you finally reach the top: Ausangate and the whole Vilcanota range stretches along the horizon. If you are finishing your trek at Pitumarca your climbing is over: it is downhill virtually all the way. Just descend to the **Río Pitumarca**, make a left turn (west) and follow the river until its junction with **Quebrada Chillcamayo** – about two hours – then continue to Pitumarca.

To continue your trek north to Tinqui, from the river junction (Pitumarca and Chillcamayu) continue west on the south side of the rivers until you reach the **Uchulucllo bridge**, where you cross. From here follow the directions for the Pitumarca to Tinqui trek (page 332).

THE AUSANGATE LODGE TREK

This organised trek run by Andean Lodges (www.andeanlodges.com) takes you on a seldom-used route, hiking from lodge to lodge through stunning scenery: snow-capped mountains, valleys with herds of alpaca and llama, small local settlements and tremendous views. For most people the highlight comes on the fourth day, when hiking along the multi-coloured mountain ridge of the Yauricunca pass, quite unlike anything you are likely to have seen before.

Walking from lodge to lodge means that you spend the evenings in simple accommodation in front of the fire, rather than shivering in a tent. A big plus at these altitudes! The staff working at the lodges come exclusively from the surrounding communities, and the income provided from the passing trekkers is a vital addition to their otherwise meagre income from alpaca herding and small-scale agriculture. Staff accompany trekkers from lodge to lodge, giving an insight into their lifestyle and culture. To add to the feeling of being in 'The Real Peru', your luggage is carried by llamas.

Distance	About 50km
Altitude	3,886–5,150m
Rating	Moderate–difficult
Timing	5 days
In reverse	Organised trek (not done in reverse)
Start of trail	Pick up in Cusco
Transport at the end	Transfer back to Cusco

WE'VE LANDED ON MARS!   *George Bradt*

In many ways this was the most fascinating hike we did all summer 1978, when we spent three months in Peru. Basically it differed from all the others because we had no map covering our entire projected route, and the scenery was constantly changing in the most surprising ways. Without a map these changes came so unpredictably as to be breathtaking. And no map could have conveyed the many aspects of this remarkable scenery.

Our mission was to walk north from Raqchi until we found a river at the bottom of a canyon running from east to west. These physical features ran along the edge of the map we did have, and we expected to be there in one day at the most. What we didn't know was how far off the map we were in terms of time; not one day, not two days, but three. And, surprise, surprise, the rivers we found didn't come with convenient labels on them. Compounding our problems was the fact that the locals don't speak much Spanish, and we can't speak much Quechua.

We climbed up over a ridge from Raqchi, and saw a river down in the valley. By the time we reached it, we'd convinced ourselves that it was just the river we were looking for. The terrain on the other side could be shaped to fit our 1:100,000 map, but there were discrepancies: there was no bridge, and the locals called the river by another name. A child showed us the fording point, and we watched two locals carefully make their way to the other side. It was much too wide, deep and dangerous for us, so we struck upriver hoping to find a narrower ford.

As we went upstream, the valley closed in on us and at one point the trail went dramatically over a solid rock knob. Black rocks, stubbly tan straw covering the hills, and deep-blue sky contrasted beautifully, and there was always the chalky blue river below us. So beguiled were we by the scenery, we almost abandoned north in favour of west, up this wonderful valley. But the trail petered out and eventually we found a fording point, crossed, and walked back along the other side. A detour of perhaps 15km and by now we accepted the fact that this wasn't the river.

As dusk approached we hurried through a village, after saying goodbye to a boy who had shown us the trail over the ridge and into the next valley. Minutes later he was back, waving his hands, shouting and running all at the same time. 'Please come and eat supper with us,' he begged, 'then you can walk with strength and sleep deeply.' Without giving us a chance to think about it, he herded us through a gate in an adobe wall, and we found ourselves in the small courtyard of a typical Andean house. The cooking hut was tiny and too humble for such exalted visitors, so we were motioned toward two stones covered with a blanket in the courtyard. The boy's parents came out and shyly greeted us. Father kept apologising for nothing in particular, as a counterpoint to our praising nothing in particular.

Soon two earthenware bowls of food arrived, along with more apologies; they needn't have worried, as it was the most delicious meal we'd eaten since leaving Cusco. Would you complain about small tasty potatoes fried in pork fat with cheese? While we ate they whispered about us and we whispered about them. How could we repay them, we wondered? We decided on presents of a box of matches for father, a picture postcard of San Francisco for the son, and decorative hair grips for the mother and little daughter. That gave us an excuse to enter the kitchen and distribute the gifts.

The small stone and adobe hut had a cooking area where a fire continuously burned, a crude table with a maize grinder and an adobe seat covered with sheep skins. The base of the seat was honeycombed with holes through which scuffled and squeaked a large number of guinea pigs.

The family seemed thrilled with their gifts, although they only recognised the matches. The postcard fascinated them; after we'd turned it right way up and pointed out the high buildings and the huge bridge they gasped in amazement, but they couldn't understand the scale of it all. And how could they when their little world was made up of adobe houses, llamas, streams and footpaths? Nor did they understand us when we said how lucky they were.

We continued the next day up another valley through some of the best scenery and most interesting country life we've seen in Peru. Fantastic dark limestone formations spiked into the blue sky, little *molinos* or waterwheels crouched over the valley's stream, and we saw our first herd of pure white alpacas. As we got higher, passing small villages with grass-thatched roofs, we could see the hills had had a sprinkling of snow, the slopes were bare from overgrazing, and the purple-red earth glowed in the afternoon sun. Our path snaked up a series of hills, and we always thought the pass would be just over the next one. Not until we reached an enormous valley tumbling down on our left did we realise the pass was still a long, long way off.

It was getting late. We'd gained 1,300m that day, and I was all for camping below the pass, but Hilary wanted to push on up into the gloaming. She hoped to see our river and the Ausangate range from the top, and sleep soundly with the knowledge she was 'found' on the map at last.

continued overleaf

11

Hilary slogged up to the pass. I watched her stand motionless at the top, fling her backpack off and scamper down toward me. 'George,' she shrieked, 'guess what you see from the top!' I waited until she reached me. 'Cusco?' was all I could think of that would explain such extreme behaviour. 'No, you simply won't believe it.' 'Lima?' 'No', said Hilary, 'we've landed on Mars!'

When I got to the top I had to agree with her. Off to our left, at the very crest of a mountain, was a ribbon of defiant rock weathered into fantastic shapes and spikes, some as much as 30m high. Straight ahead every hill and mountain seemed to be wearing a multi-coloured striped poncho. And the colours were amazing: lilac, green, dark-yellow and deep rich reds. There was not a living thing as far as the eye could see. As clouds swept in front of the sun, a burst of snow and hail startled us out of our bewilderment. We found a trickle of water, set up our tent and scrambled inside. Hilary indulged herself in one of her 'Oh George, we're lost' fits and felt better for it. I was puzzled by this unexpected scene but since we'd been hiking 'blind' for three days, one more could make no difference. I could only suggest we continue north in the morning.

We did, but it wasn't quite as straightforward as I had hoped. There was a village, and friendly people offering chichi, but no trail in the direction they pointed to. We slogged on, and up, toward yet another pass, but with no comforting path to follow. Finally we got to the top and, to our relief and considerable surprise saw Ausangate. We could even see 'our' river.

Three hours later we were walking along the river, marvelling at elegant torrent ducks as they bobbed in the swift currents and eddies. Now and again one would plunge 30m downstream and bounce confidently out on to a boulder. The river had eroded the valley's limestone into shapes resembling Swiss cheese, all shot through with holes. Cachas grazed on the green grasses, taking fright and hopping back into their rocky warrens as we approached. Crops had just been harvested, and field mice were busy scurrying about picking up stray grains.

The following morning we met several smartly dressed people coming up the valley with heavily laden animals: we assumed they were returning from market, but by our estimate it would take another day of walking before we reached Pitumarca. Naturally we were sceptical when we asked a local how far it was, and received the usual 'cerquita' (very near) in reply, but he was right. We could hardly believe it, after all those days trying to get 'on the map'.

Route description The first day is spent travelling by minibus to the valley above Pitumarca, which is one of the most traditional areas of the Andes and where some of the best weavers in Peru live. The first lodge, Chillca Tambo, is just outside the village of Chillca (4,250m), only recently accessible by dirt road which has opened up the area. There is a school in the village, but many of the local people here are semi-nomadic, following their herds as they graze the highland grasses.

On the second day, after a hearty breakfast, you trek up the **Phinaya Valley** passing the many large herds of alpacas and llamas. Majestic Mount Ausangate appears after 90 minutes of walking. Almost as soon as Ausangate comes into view the route takes a turn to the north and the trail starts to climb steadily to 4,700m for a couple of hours. Here you are on part of the Ausangate Circuit. The trail passes the **Pjachaj waterfalls**. Then, surrounded by moraines, glaciers and lagoons you continue walking northwards to the second lodge, Machuracay Tambo, after a day of six to seven hours (15km) of hard trekking.

On the following day you walk north–northwest, heading steeply uphill for an hour, descend a little then continue upwards to the highest point of the trek, the pass at 5,150m, getting there after 1½ hours. Ausangate towers beside you and it's easy to understand why it is so sacred to the people of this area. The views ahead are amazing, too. Multi-coloured landscapes of red, blue-grey, yellow, and glistening snow patches. Descend around 600m to **Ausangatecocha** and continue descending gently then skirting the hills to the right to enter the next valley. The red sandstone sediment formations are extraordinary. Look out for vicuñas and soaring condors. After five to six hours, 12km, you'll arrive at the third lodge, Anantapata Tambo.

On the fourth day another climb awaits, you then drop down to hike alongside **Lake Kayrawiri**, surrounded by rugged mountain peaks and a great valley below. Ahead lies the extraordinary 'stripy mountain' of the **Yauricunca pass**. Continue trekking to **Cerro Laya Grande**, passing the massive glaciers of Nevado del Inca, and onwards towards **Yauricunca**. This is a perfect place for a lunch break. Look out for flocks of Andean geese as you continue to the next lodge, Huampococha Tambo, 12km. On the final day there is one last pass, but it's a big one – 5,000m – before you head southeast down the far side, and on to the end of the trail in **Trapiche** (*6–7hrs; 12km*), where a vehicle will be waiting to take you back to Cusco.

> **Updates website:** For the latest updates go to www.bradtupdates.com/perutrekking. You can also post your feedback here – corrections, changes or even new hikes. Your information will be put on our website for the benefit of other travellers.

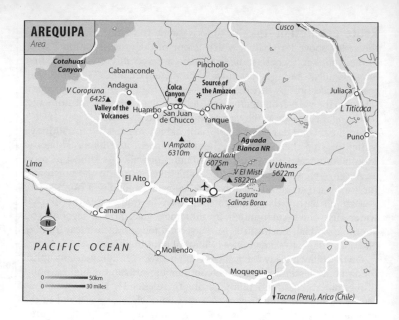

 LIST OF HIKES AND TREKS IN THIS CHAPTER

12

The Arequipa Area

The valley around Arequipa, 1,000km southeast of Lima and 320km from the Chilean border, is a sunny, fertile pocket tucked between the coastal desert and the high Andes. It has a lot to interest the hiker: snow-capped volcanoes, remote Quechua villages, the Colca Canyon, archaeological sites and the dazzling white colonial city of Arequipa. Given the dry climate of the area, trekking is possible all year round.

AREQUIPA *Telephone code: 054*

Peru's second-largest city lies at 2,380m and enjoys an almost idyllic climate: sunny and mostly dry, with a mild rainy season between December and April. Often called 'the White City' after the volcanic *sillar* from which its older buildings are built, it is overlooked by the sometimes snow-capped, perfectly shaped, Volcano El Misti (5,822m).

Arequipeños have never been able to agree on how their city got its name. Does it come from the Aymara 'Ariquipa', meaning 'the place behind the peak'? Or did it originate with the Inca Mayta Kapac who was so gripped by the beauty of this valley that he ordered his retinue to stop, calling out '*Ari quipay*' ('Yes, stay')?

Although an important settlement since pre-Inca times, Arequipa was re-founded by the Spanish in 1545 and this gives *Arequipeños* an excuse to celebrate on and around 15 August every year. Unfortunately, the valley is prone to earthquakes and volcanic eruptions. The city was totally destroyed in 1600, and in 1991–92 the volcano Sabancaya erupted again, covering a huge area in volcanic lava and almost engulfing the village of Maca. Then in 2001, Arequipa had the misfortune of being near the epicentre of a large earthquake, which did a fair amount of damage to many of its buildings. Luckily several of Arequipa's 17th- and 18th-century buildings, including the Santa Catalina Convent, have escaped destruction and are now tourist attractions. The centre of Arequipa is a UNESCO World Heritage Site.

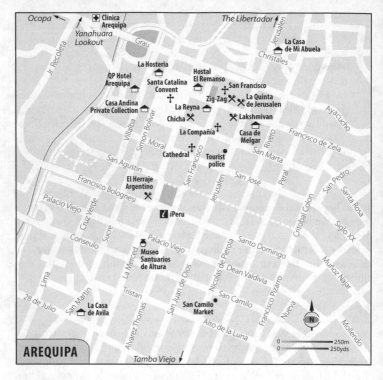

Ocopa ⬅ ↑ ⊞ Clínica
Arequipa
Yanahuara
Lookout Grau The Libertador ↑

La Casa
de Mi Abuela

Christales

La Hosteria ⛪
QP Hotel Hostal
Arequipa ⛪ Santa Catalina El Remanso
Convent ✝ San Francisco
Zig-Zag ✕✕ La Quinta
Casa Andina La Reyna ⛪ ✝ de Jerusalen
Private Collection Chicha ✕ ✕ Lakshmivan
 La Compañía ✝ Casa de
 Melgar
 San Marta
Cathedral ⛪ ✝ Tourist
police
El Herraje San José
Argentino
✕

ℹ iPeru

⛪ Palacio Viejo
Museo
Santuarios
de Altura

Santo Domingo

La Casa
de Avila ⛪ San Camilo ●
Market
Alto de la Luna

AREQUIPA

Tambo Viejo ↓

0 ▭▭▭▭ 250m
0 ▭▭▭▭ 250yds

GETTING THERE AND AWAY

By air Travel between **Lima** and Arequipa by air takes 70 minutes and all domestic airlines serve this route daily.

Check **LAN** (*www.lan.com*), **Star Peru** (*www.starperu.com*), **Peruvian Airlines** (*www.peruvianairlines.pe*), **TACA** (*www.taca.com*) and **Sky Airlines** (*www.skyairline.cl*). Fares from US$143.

Flights between Cusco and Arequipa take 50 minutes and many travellers choose this option as an alternative to the Arequipa to Cusco bus. There are daily flights; most travellers prefer LAN since they fly via Juliaca (beautiful views!) rather than via Lima. The fares are around US$130–160. It takes just half an hour **to fly from Juliaca** and **Puno**; there are daily flights.

By bus Travelling by road from **Lima** via **Nazca** takes 15 hours. Several bus companies operate on this route; **Oltursa** (*www.oltursa.pe*), **TEPSA** (*www.tepsa.com.pe*) and **Cruz del Sur's** (*www.cruzdelsur.com.pe*) First-Class service are recommended (*US$70*). Most companies operate from the *terminal terrestre* a little way out of town (there are two terminals next to each other). Be warned that the bus station area has a bad reputation for theft so it's best to use taxis to get there and away, and keep an eye on your luggage.

Travelling between **Cusco** and Arequipa by bus takes around ten hours. Cruz del Sur buses run daily for US$40–60.

Chivay (for the Colca Canyon) can be reached by daily bus (several companies do the route, but Reyna is recommended) in three to four hours.

Depending on the weather and the state of the roads, it takes six hours to travel by bus to/from **Juliaca** and **Puno** (*US$27*). Cruz del Sur buses and colectivos operate daily, stopping first at Juliaca before going on to Puno.

GETTING AROUND The central part of the city extends five blocks or so from the plaza, so exploring on foot is probably the easiest way to get a feel for the place.

WHERE TO STAY Arequipa has scores of hotels to suit all tastes and budgets. Beware taxi drivers at bus stations and the airport who may tell you your chosen hotel is full, dirty, a rip-off or many other things – often they will take you to a hotel of random standard to earn a commission. Here are some recommended ones:

> **Note:** The Peruvian Mining Convention and Expo (EXTEMIN) takes place in Arequipa in mid-September each year. Often Arequipa's hotels are full during this time.

Expect to pay 22 soles per person (*US$8pp*) upwards for budget accommodation while for mid-range options prices start from US$30 per person upwards for a twin or double room.

Budget

🏠 **La Reyna** Zela 209; 📞 286578. Right in the centre, with a lovely terrace. Also offers tours. About 40 soles.

🏠 **Hostal El Remanso** Calle San Bolívar 403; 📞 227421; www.hostalelremansoperu.com. A 360° view from terrace; features large but basic dorms/rooms at a low price as well as more expensive rooms with en suite. Prices from 42 soles for a dbl.

🏠 **Tambo Viejo** Avda Malecon Socabaya 107; 📞 288195; e room@tamboviejo.com; www.tamboviejo.com. Bright, clean & spacious with dorms & private rooms. Lovely garden, attentive staff. From 42 soles for a dbl.

Mid-range

🏠 **La Casa de Avila** San Martin 116; 📞 213177; www.casadeavila.com. Situated close to the centre, this hotel has a big garden & Wi-Fi. Can also organise cooking tours, foodie tours, Colca tours. Rooms from US$30/48 sgl/dbl.

🏠 **La Casa de Mi Abuela** Jeruslaén 606; 📞 241206; e reservas@ lacasademiabuela.com; www. lacasademiabuela.com. Sprawling complex with nice rooms, lovely gardens & a small pool. From US$60.

🏠 **La Hosteria** Calle Bolívar 405; 📞 289269; e reservas@lahosteriaqp.com.

pe; www.lahosteriaqp.com.pe. Traditional house turned hotel with 11 rooms centred around a courtyard with fountain. Character & quality. US$60/70 sgl/dbl.

🏠 **Casa de Melgar** Calle Melgar 108; ☎ 222459; e lacasademelgar@terra.com. pe; www.lacasademelgar.com. Converted traditional house, blending modern needs with a charming rustic style. No credit cards. From US$75 dbl.

As a treat

🏠 **Casa Andina Private Collection** Calle Ugarte 403; ☎ 226907; e capc-arequipa@casa-andina.com; www. casa-andina.com. Fantastic building, the

---

👁 TEN THINGS TO DO IN AREQUIPA

Arequipa is the second-most popular city for tourists after Cusco. There are several impressive colonial buildings built of *sillar* (a white volcanic stone that is earthquake-resistant), the most well known being the fascinating Santa Catalina Convent; see number 1 below.

1 Explore the city's religious architecture The cathedral, La Compañía, the Baroque San Agustín and the San Fransisco complex of church, convent and cloisters showcase Arequipa's religious architecture. **Santa Catalina convent** (☎ 221213; e informes@santacatalina.org.pe; www.santacatalina.org.pe; ⊕ high season open 08.00–17.00 daily, until 20.00 Tue & Thu when there are candle-lit night tours; entry fee 35 soles) is an exceptionally beautiful and somewhat haunting building – well worth half a day of your time. It's extremely photogenic.

2 Pay a visit to Juanita, the Ice-Maiden Drop by the well-run and informative **Museo Santuarios de Altura de la Universidad Católica de Santa María** (*Museum of Andean Sanctuaries; Santa Catalina 210;* ☎ 252554; e santury@ucsm.edu.pe; www.ucsm.edu.pe/santury; ⊕ 09.00–17.30 Mon–Sat. Auditorium, audiovisuals, translators, guides in English, French & German, souvenir shop) to see Juanita and a collection of other mummies thought to be Inca sacrifices to their gods. As well as the mummies, there are many beautiful gold objects found on the frozen tops of 6,000m volcanoes, accompanying the sacrificed maidens. For more on Juanita, see page 353.

3 Go rafting on the Chili River At only half an hour from the city centre, these Class 2 to 4 rapids give fun for all ages and levels of experience.

4 Watch condors soar at Colca Canyon Take a tour to the impressively deep Colca Canyon. Splash out and stay at the Colca Lodge (page 357), trek to the bottom of the canyon or, even better,

standard rooms are in the new part & the more expensive suites in the older part of the building. Good spa treatments. Rooms from US$120 dbl.

🏠 **QP Hotel Arequipa** Calle Villalba 305; 🔧01 3192900 (Lima for reservations); www. qphotels.com. Brand-new, 4-star boutique hotel with emphasis on clean & modern design within a converted traditional house. From US$120 dbl.

🏠 **The Libertador** Plaza Bolívar s/n; 🔧215110; www.libertador.com.pe. The most luxurious hotel in the city, although a 10min walk from the central plaza, with pool, jacuzzi, gym & all the trimmings. Rooms from US$150 dbl.

take a week and trek really off the beaten track from Cabanaconde to Andagua. See page 357.

5 Climb a volcano For spectacular views of the city and surrounding area. Only for the fit, very well acclimatised and those equipped with suitable high mountain gear. Take plenty of snacks and make sure the agency you go with has given you a written contract with a list of everything included. See page 350.

6 Take in the city from the Plaza de Armas Sit in a bar or café overlooking the Plaza de Armas and watch the world go by.

7 Learn to cook, Peruvian style! Take a cooking lesson with Peruvian Cooking Experience (*www.peruviancookingexperience.com; US$18*) and learn to make cerviche along with other Peruvian delicacies.

8 Walk to the Yanahuara Lookout Some 2km from the centre of Arequipa, this lookout was built in the 19th century. There are a number of sillar (volcanic pumice stone) arches, and a beautiful view of the city and El Misti.

9 Shop for alpaca sweaters Just off the Plaza de Armas, in the cloisters of the La Compañía church, you will find some of the city's better handicraft shops and some good cafés too. It's also worth a look inside the beautiful church interior.

10 Taste the local speciality Eat the very spicy *rocotto relleno* (stuffed peppers) in the market or at one of Arequipa's famous *picanterias*. The neighbourhood of Arancota has several large locally popular picanterias, open only at lunchtimes. Set menus are just 10 soles or so. *Camarones*, freshwater shrimps, are also delicious, when in season and available.

✕ WHERE TO EAT AND DRINK There are many good places to eat in Arequipa. Excellent stuffed potatoes (*papa rellena*) and peppers (*rocotto relleno*) are for sale outside the market. There are plenty of good, cheap local and generally tiny restaurants on Calle Puente Bolognesi, where lunch will set you back just a few soles.

Restaurants

✕ Chicha Santa Catalina 210; ✆287360; www.chicha.com.pe/. Gaston Acurio's restaurant in Arequipa, with a modern take on Peruvian classics, & Arequipa typical dishes: stuffed peppers, meat kebabs, freshwater shrimps.

✕ El Herraje Argentino Puente Bolognesi 127 & Santa Catalina 111; ✆212059. Recommended for the Argentinean-style steaks, BBQ chicken & salad bar.

✕ Lakshmivan Jerusalen 408; ⏰ 12.30–21.00. Vegetarian & vegan food.

✕ La Quinta de Jerusalen Jerusalen 522, Cercado; ✆237149. Known for the high quality of service & the good-quality local food, gardens & outdoor terraces.

✕ Ocopa Miguel Grau 506, Yanahuara; ✆259626. A bit off the beaten track (*2km away from the main square of Arequipa*), but this more upmarket option offers good-quality typical food from Arequipa. Stuffed peppers, guinea pig, pork, corn, beans, salads.

✕ Zig-Zag Zela 210-210; ✆206020. Swiss Peruvian restaurant, the specialities are fish & meat (alpaca inc) cooked on stone. Also has a good wine menu.

USEFUL ADDRESSES
Banks and foreign exchange

Most of the banks & shops are in the few streets immediately around or near to the Plaza de Armas, which is very much the centre of town.

Emergencies

Tourist police Calle Jerusalen 315; ✆201258

Handicrafts

Arequipa is known for very high-quality alpaca & silver products. There are several boutiques such as Alpaca 21 & Alpaca 2000 offering top-of-the-range handicrafts near the Plaza de Armas (in the cloisters of La Compañía) & on Calle Santa Catalina.

Health

✚ Clínica Arequipa Cnr Puente Grau & Avda Bolognesi; ✆253416. Medical emergencies, private hospital.

Shopping for provisions

Campamento Base (Colca Trek) Jerusalen 401-B; ✆206217. Rents & sells camping equipment & IGN maps.

El Super On the Plaza de Armas. Best supermarket for trekking supplies.

Tourist information

🛈 iPerú Portal de la Municipalidad 110, Plaza de Armas; ✆223265; ⏰ 09.00–18.00 Mon–Sat, 09.00–13.00 Sun. Information on Arequipa & the rest of Peru – there's a 2nd office at the airport.

🛈 Tourist information office Portal de la Municipalidad 104, Plaza de Armas, opposite the cathedral; ⏰ 08.00–19.00 daily. Helpful & friendly regional experts, with a good city map.

Tour operators

Carlos Zarate Aventuras EIRL Calle Santa Catalina 204, Office 3; ✆202461, 263107;

e czarate@planet.com; www. zarateadventures.com. Information on trekking, & maps & photos. Carlos Zarate is the recognised expert on the region, & a UIAGM-qualified guide. Offers equipment to rent & buy. Organises treks & climbs for individuals or groups, with professional guides.

Colca Trek Jerusalen 401-B; 206217; e info@colcatrek.com.pe; www. colcatrekperu.com. Vlado Soto & staff offer great advice & trips. Also rent equipment, sell good maps, etc.

Giardino Tours Jerusalen 604-A; 241206; e giardino@terra.com.pe; www. giardinotours.com. Offer good-quality tours & treks, especially Colca.

La Asociacion de Guías de Montaña Pasaje Desaguadero 126, San Lazaro; 043 721811; e agmp@terra.com.pe; ⊕ Jun–Sep, but may soon open year round. Can provide you not only with a guide but also with information & equipment to rent. Regular group treks & climbs.

FESTIVALS IN AND AROUND AREQUIPA

6 January	Anniversary of Mollendo as well as King's Day in Tiabaya, Arequipa. A day of eating and music in the city.
2 February	Virgen de la Candelaria. Celebration in some parts of Arequipa, with a mass then processions through the main streets.
Late February	Carnival. Like in most of South America there is plenty of traditional dancing, and processions when the carnival queen of Arequipa is chosen, and friendly water fights occur.
1 May	Fiesta de la Virgen de Chapi. Catholic pilgrimages to the Santuario de la Virgen de Chapi, 40km to the south of Arequipa. There is plenty of local food such as fried pork (*chicharron*).
Mid-May	Festival of the Holy Trinity. The day starts with mass, followed by street entertainment, dancing, the burning of paper sculptures (*quema de castillos*) and fireworks.

24 June	Día de Characato. A festival to celebrate farmers and farming. Local festivals in farming communities with bull fights, dancing and eating.
14–17 July	Cabanaconde. Fiesta de la Virgen del Carmen. Celebrated with traditional dances. Look out for the dance of 'Los turcos', which represents the battles between the colonising Spaniards and the indigenous people of Peru.
15 August	Semana de Arequipa. A week or so of celebrations to commemorate the founding of Arequipa in 1540. Dances, music, bull fights, cockfights throughout the city. There is also a craft market and trade exhibition. Fireworks on the night of 14 August and a mass ascent of Misti on 15 August.
Early October	La Virgen del Rosario. Arequipa's Yanahuara, Yarabamba and Yura neighbourhoods are central to the various events that take place – mass, eating and dancing.
1 November	All Saints' Day. A national festival throughout Peru. Many people visit cemeteries.

CLIMBING THE VOLCANOES

The dominant geographical feature of the area is the volcanoes, so these are the focus for most trekkers. This is a very dry area and little natural water is available: it must all be carried with you. You climb more for a sense of achievement than for the ever-changing views.

CLIMATE Although enviably sunny for much of the year, the Arequipa area can be subject to heavy downpours between December and April, making trails muddy and dangerous.

CONDITIONS AND WHAT TO TAKE Make sure you carry enough warm clothing and good camping equipment for those freezing nights! For much of the time you'll be hiking above 4,000m, so give yourself time to acclimatise. Wear a hat and protect yourself from the sun. Take plenty of water – several litres per person.

Maps The topographical maps of this area from the IGN are especially useful, as few others are available. You can get these in Lima (page 128) and locally at Colca Trek on Jerusalen 401-B.

Equipment Basic gear can be rented at some tour operators, the Asociacion de Guías, from Campamento Base (Colca Trek), or bought from shops on Jerusalen. It's best to bring your own, especially if taking on the larger peaks. Trekking poles are needed for crossing the scree.

GUIDES AND PACK ANIMALS You don't normally need a guide to hike in this area. Most trails are obvious, and there's usually someone to ask in case of doubt. On the volcanoes, however, routes can be confusing and weather conditions can change quickly and dangerously. For these a guide is recommended, or at least someone who's done it before. Choose your guide with care (see *Tour operators* on page 348) although note that most experienced mountain guides speak only a little English, if any. Younger guides learning the ropes have better English, but less time spent in the peaks. A trekking guide will charge 195 soles per day upwards; a climbing guide 280 soles.

You can arrange for burros or mules if necessary at one of the villages near the starting points of the hikes. Burros cost about 70 soles per day; arrieros 85 soles, depending on where you are.

 VOLCÁN EL MISTI (*5,822m*) This volcano, which provides Arequipa with its splendid backdrop, is a popular climb, best done late in the season when there's less snow. Although not a difficult ascent, El Misti shouldn't be taken lightly. The weather can change without notice from extreme heat to snow, making it easy to get lost, cold and dispirited – a perfect recipe for disaster. If no-one in your party has done the climb before, you should consider taking a guide. Allow at least two days for the trip. You need to carry a lot of water (there's none along the way other than at the reservoir of Aguada Blanca), together with cold-weather clothing and camping equipment. The ascent doesn't, however, involve any technical climbing, but you must be well acclimatised before starting the trek. The northern route offers the better chance of summit success.

Distance	25km
Altitude	2,950–5,822m
Rating	Moderate
Timing	2–3 days
Start of trail	Aguada Blanca (hydro-electric station)
Transport at the end	Organise a 4x4 to take you back to Arequipa from Aguada Blanca
Maps	IGN sheet *Characato* (33-t), 1:100,000

Getting to the trailhead To get to the trailhead you need to organise a 4x4 vehicle in Arequipa. Ask to be let off at Aguada Blanca, a hydro-electric station, where the Chivay and El Fraile roads meet.

Route description Follow the **El Fraile road** to the far side of the first dam. (You may have some difficulty getting through the hydro-electric station's security system.) Then continue for 5½ hours to **Monte Blanco**, a flat area with corrals where you should camp. From Monte Blanco a zigzag path will take you in four hours (rather more if there's a lot of snow) to the summit, which is marked by a 10m iron cross. Trekking poles are invaluable here as the path often crosses bad scree. On fine days the view is magnificent. From here you can continue to the edge of the inner crater where fumaroles can occasionally be seen.

 VOLCÁN CHACHANI (*6,075m*) An impressive volcano about 20km north of Arequipa, which looms over the city. The summit is the central tower of the three snow-capped peaks to the north of the city. Chachani is one of the most accessible 6,000m peaks in the world. A mere three-hour drive from Arequipa, it can, nearly year round, be conquered by trekkers with no technical equipment on this new route outlined below. It is, however, a big mountain and easy to get lost on, so do not climb alone and take plenty of water. After a number of accidents, the formerly popular southern route is no longer recommended. Note that you will camp at the trailhead and make the first part of the ascent before sunrise.

Distance	20km
Altitude	4,700–6,075m
Rating	Moderate
Timing	2–3 days
Start of trail	The easiest way to and from the trailhead is to organise private transport from Arequipa. There is no public transport to the 5,100m starting point; you will have to walk from where the bus drops you.
Transport at the end	Follow the walking route outlined below and wait for a passing bus back to Arequipa, or arrange to be picked up at the end of the climb
Maps	IGN sheets *Arequipa* (33-s) and *Characato* (33-t)

Getting to the trailhead It's a three- to four-hour drive from Arequipa to the start of the walk. The first hour is on tarmac, and then on a dirt road, some of which has been especially constructed for this trek.

If you choose to use **public transport**, you have to add on six to eight hours of trekking. Catch a bus heading to Cusco and Colca which will take you to the north side of Chachani volcano. Ask the driver to drop you off at the road leading to the Chachani col (it marks the starting point). From here, follow the obvious dirt road northwards, always keeping to the east side of the main summit of Chachani. The road makes for easy trekking although there are lots of large stones which may twist an ankle, so take care. There are several deviations in the road as cars take different routes to the col (depending if they are big 4x4s or not and also depending on conditions) but you can see the general line of the road all the way. You need to pack around six to eight

THE ICE-MAIDEN 'JUANITA'

In 1995 Johan Reinhard, anthropologist and Senior Research Fellow of the Mountain Institute, and Miguel Zarate, his Peruvian climbing partner, climbed the volcano of Ampato (6,310m) on a scientific expedition to search for Inca remains. Since the nearby volcano of Sabancaya had erupted in 1990, spewing hot black ash over Ampato, there had been a melting of a considerable amount of snow from the top of this mountain.

They made an amazing discovery: a small frozen body, tightly wrapped in textiles sitting in the foetal position surrounded by scattered pieces of pottery, llama bones, corn kernels, cloth pieces and a spondylus shell figurine.

The team photographed the site, collected the various treasures, wrapped up the mummy to keep her frozen and tied her to Reinhard's backpack. They set off on their long return journey to Arequipa, where the body was put in a freezer at the Catholic University. Fortunately, the precautionary wrapping of the body had protected it from damage.

This was the first intact female mummy to be found anywhere in the Andes, and she was in remarkably good condition, with her skin and even her nails complete. The objects found alongside her had also survived well over the centuries. The fact that the body had been frozen as opposed to freeze-dried or desiccated meant that biological tests could be run on internal organs, which gave scientists an insight into the body's health and nutrition. Work later carried out on the 'ice-maiden' showed her to have been a healthy young girl, between 12 and 14 years old. It's probable that Inca priests sacrificed her to the mountain gods.

Reinhard later returned to Mount Ampato on a National Geographic Society expedition. His party discovered more ritual platforms, the body of an eight- to ten-year-old girl, and the less well-preserved skeleton of a third person. All objects are on display in the Museo Santuarios de Altura in Arequipa (page 346).

litres of water minimum, as there is nowhere to refill once you leave the bus and you will most likely be under a strong Andean sun for most of the day. When returning to Arequipa, take the same route down, and wait for a passing bus to board back to Arequipa. Note that bus times are infrequent and they will not always stop.

If you opt for a private transfer the drive can be bumpy, but the views over nearby Misti and the chance to spot vicuñas, are compensation for what may be a rough trip. There's also the opportunity to stop for photos of Chachani and over Arequipa.

Route description If you have taken private transport, it will drop you at the col (5,000m) at the end of the road. From here, follow a path northwest on an obvious route, albeit with an easy 20-minute scramble through some boulders, to the base camp, **Campo Inca** (Inca Camp) at 5,250m. There are great views to Huacullani and Nevada Calcha mountains as you hike along. The campsite is hidden from the main path by a lump of rocks, and you clamber over them to reach it. If you have started to descend the north side of Chachani, you have walked too far and must retrace your steps and look westwards for the campsite – the pit latrines are the most obvious sign as they have been built recently.

The ascent to the summit is started at 01.00 or 02.00, depending on weather conditions. There are a few boulders to navigate, some very easy scrambling, made easier by the lovely views to Ampato, Coropuna and other snow-capped peaks that litter this volcanic area.

On a clear night the stars are fantastic, and will help light the way up the north side of the mountain, following a **faint trail**, zigzagging up the sometimes slippery gravel to the summit. There is nothing technical about the walk, although some sections are steep and it can be easy to get disorientated in the dark, especially if you are cold and tired.

Towards the top of Chachani, cross a small **field of _penitentes_** – strange ice and snow formations caused by high winds – to make the final westwards path to the top, marked by a cross.

From the summit, at 6,075m and marked by several crosses, there are splendid views of Misti, Ampato, Coropuna and Arequipa.

A second night can be spent at base camp, or if you have transport arranged, you can make it back to Arequipa that day.

THE COLCA CANYON

A hundred kilometres long, this incredible gorge is said to reach a maximum depth of 3,400m – twice that of the Grand Canyon. It was formed through a fault in the earth's crust being eroded during thousands of years by the largest river of the Peruvian coast, the River Colca.

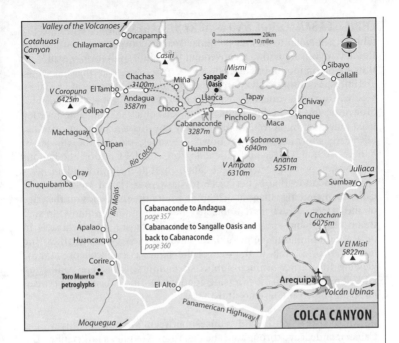

COLCA CANYON

Although a mere 160km north of Arequipa, its full extent was recognised only as recently as 1954; the first major explorations took place in 1978 and the first descent by raft and canoe in 1981. The Colca is a wild and dangerous river – not for the faint-hearted!

On both sides of the canyon you'll find picturesque villages whose inhabitants will help you with directions. Cave paintings suggest that people have lived here since the first humans arrived in the Andes.

> ! **The Boleto Turistico:** The authorities have introduced this '**tourist ticket**' for 70 soles to cover entry to the canyon. It can be bought in Arequipa on Puente Grau 116 or on arrival at Chivay or Cabanaconde. If you're travelling by bus, the bus will stop and you will be asked to buy a ticket on board.

The characteristic terraces of the Colca Valley rival those of the Incas and are still widely used today. They were carved out of the land 1,400 years ago by the Collaguas, who originated from Tiahuanaco (Bolivia) and the Cabanas, who were of Quechua origin. Many locals still wear distinctive and colourful traditional costumes, and the valley boasts an extraordinary genetic variety of potatoes, corn, quinoa, maca, oca, and *isaño*. The most famous inhabitants of this canyon, however, are the Andean condors.

Chivay is a small town and is the centre for conventional tours of the Colca Canyon and makes a convenient first night's stop before exploring the canyon on foot. It has an ATM.

Half an hour's walk away are the very pleasant **hot pools** at La Calera where you can swim, or cross the canyon to the attractive village of **Sibayo** on one of the few bridges built for vehicles. This 35km journey takes an hour by colectivo. If you stay the night in Chivay you can take early morning transport down the valley, passing the villages of Yanque, Achona, Maca and Pinchollo, to **Cruz del Cóndor**, the famous observation point for views of the canyon and its majestic condors.

Cabanaconde is a better place to base yourself for treks into the Colca Canyon; this village at 3,287m is where the road ends on the edge of the canyon. You'll find Cabanaconde's friendly inhabitants dressed in beautiful hand-embroidered clothing. There are several hostels in or around the plaza (see below), restaurants, even a small market. The hill ten minutes' walk to the west of the village is an excellent place for viewing the canyon's much-publicised condors. There are conflicting views on the best time for viewing condors, but most locals say between 06.00 and 09.00 and also around 18.00.

Getting there and away **Buses** between Arequipa, Chivay and Cabanaconde leave throughout the day from Arequipa's bus station. The journey to Chivay and on to Cabanaconde is a rough, dusty trip but with good views and takes four to five hours (*14 soles upwards*).

To the **Cotahuasi Canyon** and the **Valle de los Volcanes**, buses leave Arequipa early afternoon.

There is a regular bus from **Puno** to Chivay run by 4M (*www.4m-express.com*). The stunningly scenic journey takes about six hours, costs 140 soles (price includes water and a snack) and makes a few stops.

Where to stay, eat and drink
Chivay

⌂ **Hostal Anita** Plaza de Armas 607; ☏ 521114. Good value. 42–56 soles per room.

⌂ **La Pascana** Plaza de Armas. A basic but clean, practical hostal with a small garden. 42 to 56 soles per room.

⌂ **Posada del Colca** Avda Salaverry 325; m 959784940. A modern, clean 4-storey hotel with a restaurant. From 70 soles per room.

✕ **Casa Blanca** Plaza de Armas. Popular restaurant which does a lunchtime buffet.

Yanque

⌂ **Colca Lodge** ☏ 531191; e administrador@colca-lodge.com; www.colca-lodge.com. The place for a splurge. Has a great spa. US$175/room.

Cabanaconde

⌂ **Valle del Fuego** ☏ 203737; www.valledelfuego.com. Advertise themselves as a backpacker hostel with advice & accommodation booking for trekkers. It is possible to book accommodation in advance in their Arequipa office, as well as pick up a trekking map & get information on tours, etc. Their office is on Jerusalen Street.

🏠 **Pachamama** ✆767277; www. pachamamahome.com. A recommended guesthouse which can give advice on trek routes into the canyon. From 20 soles pp in a dorm with b/fast. Dbls 40 soles/room.

🏠 **La Posada del Conde & Lodge Hotel** ✆631749; www.posadadelconde.com. Run by the same people as Colca Trek Lodge, below, these are clean & comfortable hotels with hot water & private bathrooms & are both highly recommended. US$30+.

🏠 **Colca Trek Lodge** Avda san Sebastián s/n M-12, Pinchollo; ✆206217; www.colcatreklodge.com. A highly praised upmarket hotel in a glorious location.

At the bottom of the canyon there are dedicated **camping areas** in the oasis of Sangalle, several of which also have rustic rooms. **Paraíso** is recommended – it is clean and peaceful, with a swimming pool (*14 soles pp for a shared room; 8 soles for camping*). A useful website is: www. cabanacondeperu.com/us/sangalle.html.

Camping at Cruz del Cóndor is not allowed.

TREKKING IN THE COLCA CANYON

There is a wide range of possible treks in the Colca Canyon. Those described below are just two of them. For up-to-date information on other possibilities, ask at the Pachamama or Valle del Fuego hotels (see above).

CABANACONDE TO ANDAGUA This is one of the longer Colca Canyon hikes, taking you to the bottom of the canyon, up the other side, over a 5,000m pass and down to the village of Chachas before going on to

Distance	60km
Altitude	1,800–5,000m
Rating	Moderate–difficult
Timing	5–7 days, depending on if you walk on roads or take buses on some sections
Start of trail	Leaving Cabanaconde for the canyon is confusing; ask locals to point the way
In reverse	Possible
Transport at the end	Bus to Arequipa from Andagua
Maps	IGN sheets *Chivay* (32-s), *Huambo* (32-r) and *Orcopampa* (31-r). Also a small picture book, *Arequipa and the Colca Canyon*, can be bought in Arequipa. It includes a map of the canyon.

finish at Andagua (also spelled Andahua), gateway to the 'Valley of the Volcanoes'. It is a very strenuous trek because of the altitude gain and loss: 3,200m. However, veteran trekker Michael Woodman claims that 'the scenery was among the best we have ever seen, with a strong sense of isolation as there is no doubt that few people go out of Colca Canyon this way.' Be sure to carry plenty of water (three to four litres per person). If you want to shorten the trip, there are colectivos from Cabanaconde to Choco, enabling you to reach Choco from Arequipa in one day.

Route description Leaving Cabanaconde for the canyon is rather confusing, as there are many paths. Ask locals for the way to Choco and they'll point you in the right direction (northwest). A road has been built down this way. Apart from a short stretch you don't need to follow the road exactly; you can take the **footpath** instead. After passing the hill just behind the village, the well-used stone path drops gradually into the canyon, keeping to the right, until it crosses a dry river at the bottom of a pampa. From here climb the hill to your left, passing a small house, and keeping left until you see the road. Now make a sharp right turn on a faint short cut to meet the road about two hours from Cabanaconde.

> **Note:** Landslides and rockfalls are quite frequent in the canyon. Other than the obvious danger of rocks falling on your head, these can also obscure paths, and make for very loose, sometimes treacherously slippery, ground underfoot. Ask locals, whenever possible, about conditions of paths and any recent route changes.

The road winds its way into the canyon. Follow it for half an hour until you see a gap in the stone wall and a well-marked trail climbing the hill to your left. This is your path to Choco. It drops gradually westward, with spectacular views of the canyon, to a footbridge over the **Colca River** five to six hours from Cabanaconde. The first water of the day is found in a stream just before here. This bridge, **Puente Colgado de Choco**, lies at a mere 1,800m and until recently was one of Peru's last remaining Inca *manguey* fibre bridges. It became dangerous and has now been reconstructed, but the remains of the fibre bridge have been put on top of the new one. On the other side you'll find some small camping places between the rocks.

From Puente Colgado the path climbs steeply up the other side of the canyon, then turns up a side canyon and climbs more gradually to the village of **Choco** (2,473m), taking about four to five hours. It gets hot in this valley so it's important to make an early start from the bridge.

Choco is one of those increasingly rare Andean villages – beautiful, friendly and so far unspoiled. Resting in the plaza, you'll soon attract an audience: the residents see few visitors and display great curiosity – and friendliness.

Two valleys merge at Choco. Follow the Cusco River valley, staying close to its river, heading northwest most of the way. After 1½ hours, head upwards on a steep, good path to the **Achacota Valley**. At times this is confined to a narrow defile between soaring vertical walls; at others it opens out and progress becomes easier. After about four hours there are cultivated terraces a short way below the path between Paso Cerani and the village of **Miña**. There is a good camping place about 100m higher up. There is water after about four hours from Choco. Continuing up Achacota Valley brings you to the path from Miña to the pass; the two routes meet at 4,400m. ⊛ Up the Chalza Valley out of Choco, below.

Continue climbing towards the pass (from Miña to the pass is about 1,500m of ascent and takes a good four to five hours), banishing feelings of despair (it seems to get no nearer) and filling your water bottles wherever possible, as the valley is dry higher up. There are good campsites before the pass, but it will be freezing cold and there is no water. From Choco to the pass will take ten to 13 hours. There are views from the first pass down to Miña and towards the main Colca Canyon, then, on the way up to the main pass, the landscape becomes ever more extensive and includes rocks and scree with intense mineral colours which contrast with the bright-green clumps of *Llareta* plants.

As it approaches the summit the path becomes very faint, but always picks up again. At last you reach a moraine, and a final steep climb will bring you to the top of the pass. Incredible views! Go over the pass on loose gravel, taking care, and begin the descent (about an hour) to a flat area, with corrals and water, about 400m lower down, where you can camp. From here it's all downhill to the village of Chachas: a steep descent at first, but then easing off into meadows. Stay on the left side of the valley.

From here follow the path to the right (north) over a small hill, across a further pampa, and then drop steeply to cross a river. Head for the settlement of **Umapallca** way below you. From the village ask for the path to Chachas, five to six hours from camp.

Alternative route: There is also a path **up the Chalza Valley out of Choco**, that initially follows the west side (left bank as you look up) of the valley but then crosses the river several times. This path goes to the village of Miña (3,600m; *4–5hrs from Choco*), where there are some possible camping spots, but if there are signs of cultivation be sure to ask permission first. Try the football pitch. From the village ask locals for the path to Chachas. From Miña to the Paso Cerani (5,100m) is around six to seven hours. Follow the river on its left bank, climbing switchbacks tending left (southwest), then following a ridge to the first pass (*3hrs*). From the pass descend for 20 to 30 minutes to meet the **Achacota Valley** and its trail (described above). Cross the river and follow the path on the left bank, heading southwest, gradually climbing.

Overlooking a huge lake and surrounded by rich farming land, **Chachas** (3,100m) is another beauty of the Andes. As in Choco, its people aren't used to strangers and you may find yourself the centre of attention, but the stares are friendly. The village has a basic shop and if you ask around you may be able to get a meal and even accommodation. It might be better, however, to camp across the river. Ask the villagers where.

Daily buses and colectivos make the journey from Chachas to Andagua (*2hrs*), but really the walk is too good to be missed (*6hrs*), so don't forget to fill your water bottles. Begin by climbing to the pass on your right, almost at the end of the mountain range, taking a footpath which short cuts the road. The summit is about an hour from the village, giving breathtaking views of the 'Valley of the Volcanoes' on the other side.

Follow the road from the pass down to the **Challahuire River** (fill your bottles), taking short cuts when they appear, then, leaving the lake on your right, take the footpath up the hill directly opposite for the final climb to Andagua. From the pass to Andagua is four to five hours.

Andagua is a small mountain village at 3,587m, where the road from Chachas joins the Arequipa–Orcapampa road. Basic food and meals can be found in the plaza, and there is also a basic hostel. Or you can camp outside the village. The villagers here are very friendly, well acquainted with gringos, and happy to chat. ◉ Coropuna and Solimana volcanoes, above.

CABANACONDE TO SANGALLE OASIS AND BACK TO CABANACONDE

Trekking in the Colca Canyon is dramatic. However, conditions are tough as you tend to be going either steeply down or steeply up. There is very little water on any of the walks, and temperatures can be high, so go prepared. On organised treks you'll often set off climbing out of the canyon before sunrise to beat the heat. In the rainy season there is a high risk of falling stones, so it is advisable to check conditions locally before setting off. As there are several paths from Cabanaconde down into the canyon, and up the other side, connecting the many hamlets and villages, there are plenty of variations, depending on how much time you have.

Route description Leave Cabanaconde, taking the path that leads to your right from the main square with its beautiful church. Follow the road

Distance	About 20km (round trip)
Altitude	Cabanaconde at 3,290m down to Sangalle at 2,100m and back up
Rating	Moderate
Timing	2 days
In reverse	Several routes possible
Start of trail	Cabanaconde
Transport at the end	Not necessary as you walk back to Cabanaconde
Map	IGN sheet *Chivay* (32-s)

along until you reach a signpost for 'San Galle'. Follow the path beyond the sign and after ten to 15 minutes, you come to the canyon edge. From here the path descends steeply in a zigzag. The two- to three-hour descent is hard on the knees, but at the bottom you will find the lovely **Sangalle tropical gardens** where you may camp or stay at various basic lodgings. You can bathe here in the refreshingly tepid pools. Reservations are not generally necessary and basic meals can be prepared for you on arrival, although choices are limited so take some snacks as backup. If you are unsure about availability (especially when hiking in July or August), ask in Cabanaconde before setting off.

You can return to Cabanaconde by the same route, a climb of three to four hours. ✹ Three-day trek, below.

 Alternative route: You can extend this trek to **three days**: it is possible to cross the river on the Puente Colgado de Sangalle and climb up to Tapay (2,800m) on the other side in two hours. From Tapay there's a path down to the small village of San Juan de Chucco (2,300m), with basic accommodation on offer, and from there the following day you can return to Cabanaconde via the Puente Colgado de Chucco on another path. Ask the locals for details.

Appendix 1

LANGUAGE

SPANISH Below is a basic vocabulary to help hikers with only a smattering of Spanish to communicate with campesinos. For general travel purposes a good phrasebook is indespensible.

On the trail Observing the courtesies of greetings is an essential part of hiking in the Andes. If you observe the local people they will always exchange a few words with a stranger on the trail, however brief the encounter.

Buenas días	Good morning
Buenas tardes	Good afternoon
Como está?	How are you?
Vaya bien	Go well
Adios	Good bye

Most frequently asked questions (theirs)

De donde es (son)?	Where are you (sing or plur) from?
De donde viene?	Where are you coming from?

Most frequent unwelcome question

Dame, regálame	Give me

Most frequent questions (yours)

How much is it?	*Cuanto vale?*
Is it permitted to … ?	*Se puede …?*
What is this place called?	*Como se llama este lugar?*
Where does this trail go?	*A donde va este camino?*
May we camp here?	*Podemos acampar aquí?*

Most frequent answers

Muy cerquita	Very near
Lejos	Far

No puede perdirse
Izquierda/derecha/a derecho

You can't get lost
Left/right/straight on

Backpackers' vocabulary

equipaje	baggage	*puente*	bridge
mochila	backpack	*derrumbe*; *huayco*	landslide
pueblito; *poblado*	settlement or small village	*carro*	truck or bus
carpa	tent	*trámite*	red tape; transaction
río	river	*tienda*	shop

QUECHUA

English	Quechua		
Hello	*Maynalla*	water	*yaku*
Where is…?	*Maypi … ?*	house	*huasi*
Yes	*Ari*	river	*mayu*
No	*Mana*	bridge	*chaka*
good	*walej-pacha*	lake	*cocha*
bad	*mana-walej janiwa*	footpath	*chakinan*
food	*mikuna*	help	*yanapaway*

Appendix 2

LIST OF MAJOR HIKES AND TREKS

CHAPTER 7: CAJAMARCA AND CHACHAPOYAS

Name	Distance	Altitude	Rating	Time	Page
Cumbe Mayo to San Pablo	About 85km	2,750–3,900m descending to 2,365m	Easy–moderate	3–4 days	133–5
From Leymebamba to Laguna de los Condores	About 40km	2,800–3,700m	Difficult	8–10hrs	145–6
Gocta Falls	6km	2,850m	Moderate	2hrs	147
The Waterfall Circuit	15–20km	2,000–2,900m	Moderate	1 or 2 days	147–8

CHAPTER 8: CORDILLERAS BLANCA AND HUAYHUASH

Name	Distance	Altitude	Rating	Time	Page
A day hike outside Huaraz	6km	3,150–3,650m	Easy	3–4hrs	172
The Alpamayo Circuit (or semi-circuit)	About 83km	2,800–4,850m	Difficult	6–10 days	173–80
The Santa Cruz Trek	45km	2,900–4,750m	Moderate	3–4 days	181–3
Lagunas Llanganuco & Laguna 69	About 12km (round trip)	3,840–4,450m	Easy	5–6hrs	183–6
Climbing Pisco	About 40km (round trip)	3,900–5,752m	Difficult	2–4 days	185
Quebrada Ulta to Chacas, Yanama or Colcabamba	About 42km	3,050–4,900m	Easy–moderate	4 days	186–8
Quebrada Ishinca	38km (round trip)	3,200–4,950m	Easy–moderate	1–2 days	188–9
Pitec to Collon via quebradas Quilcayhuanca, Cojup & Ishinca	19–67km	3,850–5,350m	Moderate–difficult	4–8 days	189–90
To Laguna Churup via the quebrada	7km (round trip)	3,850–4,600m	Difficult	4–6hrs	191–2
To Laguna Shallap via the quebrada	16km (round trip)	3,800–4,300m	Easy–moderate	7hrs	192

Name	Distance	Altitude	Rating	Time	Page
To Laguna Rajucolta via the quebrada	38km (round trip)	3,800–4,250m	Easy–moderate	16hrs (portada to lake)	192
Up the Quebrada Quilcayhuanca, to the lagunas Tullpacocha, Cuchillacocha and Paqsacocha	39km (round trip)	3,850–4,650m	Easy–moderate	4 days	194–5
Olleros to Chavín	37km	3,200–4,700m	Moderate	2–3 days	195–8
The Huayhuash Circuit	120–186km	2,750–5,000m	Difficult	6–12 days	198–210

CHAPTER 9: CENTRAL ANDES

Name	Distance	Altitude	Rating	Time	Page
The Ticlla Circuit	About 80km	3,650–5,050m	Moderate–difficult	5–6 days	217–20
The Inca Royal Road: Castillo via Huánuco Viejo to Yanahuanca	About 160km	3,200–4,470m	Moderate	10 days	224–30

CHAPTER 10: CUSCO AND AROUND

Name	Distance	Altitude	Rating	Time	Page
Inca ruins around Cusco	7.5km	3,300–3,755m	Easy	4hrs	255–8
Sacsayhuamán to Chacan and the Devil's Balcony	7.6km (round trip)	3,590–3,765m	Easy	3hrs	258–60
Tambomachay to Pisac	25km	2,930–3,900m	Easy	1–2 days	260–3
Cusco to Lamay via Huchuy Qosqo	31km	2,930–4,350m	Moderate	2 days	263–5
Patabamba to Huchuy Qosqo and Lamay	21km	3,000–4,200m	Easy	1 day	265–6
San Jerónimo to Huanca	15km	2,950–4,250m	Easy	7–8hrs	266–8
Chinchero to Urquillos and Huayllabamba	8km to Huayllabamba, 5km to Urquillos	2,760–3,500m	Easy	3–4hrs to Huayllabamba, 2hrs to Urquillos	269–70
Chinchero to Maras, Salinas and the Urubamba River	27km	2,865–4,057m	Easy	8–9hrs	270–1
Huaran to Lares and Paucarpata	About 60km	2,838–4,400m	Moderate	3–6 days	272–6
Maucau to Yanahuara via Quishuarani and Huacahuasi	54km	3,215–4,607m	Moderate	3–4 days	276–8
Ollantaytambo to Pumamarca	12km (round trip)	2,800–3,400m	Easy	4–6hrs	280
Ollantaytambo to Pumamarca and Lares	About 40km	2,800–4,800m	Moderate	3–4 days	281–2

CHAPTER 11: CORDILLERAS VILCABAMBA AND VILCANOTA

Name	Distance	Altitude	Rating	Time	Page
From Km82 to Machu Picchu (The Inca Trail)	45km	2,400– 4,215m	Moderate	4 days	294–8
From Km104 to Machu Picchu via Huiñay Huayna	13km	2,400–4,215m	Moderate	5–6hrs	297
Chilca to Huayllabamba via Paucarcancha	30km	2,800–4,600m	Moderate– difficult	2–3 days	298–300
Mollepata to Soraypampa	About 16km	2,800–3,500m	Moderate	7–8hrs	301–2
The Salkantay Glacier Trek: Soraypampa to Chilca	About 60km	2,800–4,880m	Difficult	4–5 days	302–4
The Salkantay Trek: Soraypampa to La Playa (or Santa Teresa) or Machu Picchu	About 50km	1,500–4,750m	Moderate– difficult	3–4 days	304–6
La Playa to the hydro-electric plant and Machu Picchu via Llactapata	About 12km	1,870–2,800m	Moderate	1 day	306–10
The Moyoc Circuit	70km	2,790–4,750m	Difficult	5–6 days	310–13
Cachora to Huancacalle via Choquequirao	100km	2,400–4,600m	Moderate	8 days	313–20
The Ausangate Circuit	About 80km	3,800–5,100m	Difficult	5–6 days	321–30
Pitumarca to Laguna Sibinacocha (circuit hike) or Tinqui	145–160km	3,440–5,300m	Difficult	7–10 days	330–2
Pitumarca to Tinqui via Chillca	About 70km	3,440–5,000m	Moderate– difficult	5–6 days	332–3
Raqchi to Pitumarca or Tinqui via Chillca	50–110km	3,440–5,000m	Moderate– difficult	4–9 days	333–7
The Ausangate Lodge Trek	About 50km	3,886– 5,150m	Moderate– difficult	5 days	337–41

CHAPTER 12: AREQUIPA AREA

Name	Distance	Altitude	Rating	Time	Page
Volcán El Misti	25km	2,950–5,822m	Moderate	2–3 days	351–2
Volcán Chachani	20km	4,700–6,075m	Moderate	2–3 days	352–4
Cabanaconde to Andagua	60km	1,800–5,000m	Moderate– difficult	5–7 days	357–60
Cabanaconde to Sangalle Oasis and back	20km (round trip)	2,100–3,290m	Moderate	2 days	360–1

Index

Page numbers in **bold** indicate main entries; those in *italics* indicate maps

INDEX OF ADVERTISERS

PHOTOGRAPHS AND ILLUSTRATIONS

Photographs Alamy: age footstock/Alamy (AF/A); Ana Raquel S Hernandes (AH); Axel Fassio (AF); Corbis: Christian Kober/Corbis (CK/C); Dreamstime: Hotshotsworldwide/Dreamstime (H/DT), Yeolka/Dreamstime (Y/DT); FLPA: Grant Dixon/Minden Pictures/FLPA (GD/MP/FLPA), J-M Labat & F/Biosphoto/ FLPA (JLB/FLPA), Tui De Roy/Minden Pictures/FLPA (TR/MP/FLPA); Gerard Prins (GP); Harleyca (H); Hilary Bradt (HB); Howie Garber/Wanderlustimages. com (HG/W); John Pilkington (JP); Juan Carlos Flores (JF); Kat Dougal (KD); Kathy Jarvis (KJ); Lmuellerleile (L); Matt McClements (MM); Mark Smith (MS); Michael Woodman (MW); Mountain Madness (MOM); PromPeru: Alfonso Zavala (AZ/PP), Gihan Tubbeh (GT/PP), Luis Gamero (LG/PP), Walter Hipiu (WH/PP); Rodolfo Oropeza (RO); Shutterstock: Alexander Ryabintsev (S/AR), Edyta Pawlowska (S/EP), Galyna Andrushko (S/GA), Gleb Aitov (S/GA), Jarno Gonzalez Zarraonandia (S/JGZ), jaroslava V (S/JV), Jarous (S/J), Mikadun (S/M), Pyty (S/P), Rafael Martin-Gaitero (S/RMG), Zachary Aronowitz (S/ZA); SuperStock (SS); Tom Shearman (TS)

Front cover Trekking in the Cordillera Blanca (HG/W)
Back cover Yauricunca Pass, Ausangate Circuit (AF)
Title page Laguna Carhuacocha (S/M); traditional Peruvian dress (S/J); Inca ruin on the Mayoc Circuit (M/S)/

Illustrations Carole Vincer